Formal Approaches to Computing and Information Technology

Springer
London
Berlin
Heidelberg
New York
Barcelona
Budapest
Hong Kong
Milan
Paris
Santa Clara
Singapore
Tokyo

Also in this series:

Proof in VDM: a Practitioner's Guide
J.C. Bicarregui, J.S. Fitzgerald, P.A. Lindsay, R. Moore
and B. Ritchie
ISBN 3-540-19813-X

Systems, Models and Measures
A. Kaposi and M. Myers
ISBN 3-540-19753-2

Notations for Software Design
L.M.G. Feijs, H.B.M. Jonkers and C.A. Middelburg
ISBN 3-540-19902-0

Formal Object-Oriented Development
K. Lano
ISBN 3-540-19978-0

The B Language and Method
K. Lano
ISBN 3-540-76033-4

Formal Methods and Object Technology
S.J. Goldsack and S.J.H. Kent
ISBN 3-540-19977-2

Derek Andrews

A Theory and Practice of Program Development

 Springer

Derek Andrews, BSc, MSc
Department of Mathematics and Computer Science,
Leicester University, University Road, Leicester LE1 7RH, UK

Series Editor
S.A. Schuman, BSc, DEA, CEng
Department of Mathematical and Computing Sciences
University of Surrey, Guildford, Surrey GU2 5XH, UK

ISBN 3-540-76162-4 Springer-Verlag Berlin Heidelberg New York

British Library Cataloguing in Publication Data
Andrews, Derek
  A theory and practice of program development. - (Formal
  approaches to computing and information technology)
  1.Computer software - Development
  I.Title
  005.1
ISBN 3540761624

Library of Congress Cataloging-in-Publication Data
A catalog record for this book is available from the Library of Congress

Apart from any fair dealing for the purposes of research or private study, or criticism or review, as permitted under the Copyright, Designs and Patents Act 1988, this publication may only be reproduced, stored or transmitted, in any form or by any means, with the prior permission in writing of the publishers, or in the case of reprographic reproduction in accordance with the terms of licences issued by the Copyright Licensing Agency. Enquiries concerning reproduction outside those terms should be sent to the publishers.

© Springer-Verlag London Limited 1997
Printed in Great Britain

The use of registered names, trademarks etc. in this publication does not imply, even in the absence of a specific statement, that such names are exempt from the relevant laws and regulations and therefore free for general use.

The publisher makes no representation, express or implied, with regard to the accuracy of the information contained in this book and cannot accept any legal responsibility or liability for any errors or omissions that may be made.

Typesetting: Camera ready by editors
Printed and bound at the Athenæum Press Ltd., Gateshead, Tyne and Wear
34/3830-543210 Printed on acid-free paper

Preface

All software development methods are based on the same basic idea: to provide a way of producing good software from a set of system requirements. A good software development method should provide a notation that can be used during the analysis of the system requirements to produce an abstract model (a specification) that captures the essence of the system and that can be used as the basis of the development. A good development method should try to encourage the specification of what the system does at the early stages of design and provides a series of strategies and transformations (usually described informally) on how to turn the specification into executable code. What is frequently missing from many development methods is a formal (in the mathematical sense) background and justification to both the notation and the transformations. A formal approach can provide an insight into the analysis, specification, design and development of computer systems.

An approach to software development is to focus on the separation of the abstract and concrete views of a system. A good development method should emphasize:

- abstract vs concrete;
- logical vs physical; and
- 'what' vs 'how'.

The abstract view should be easily understood by the system architect and should concentrate on describing what the system does. The concrete view of the system is a program that describes how the system works at a level of detail can be efficiently executed by a computer. Design can be seen as the bridge between these two views of a system. This bridge should have mathematical foundations.

The book provides a weakest pre-condition semantics for almost all of VDM-SL and uses the semantics to derive a software development method and to give the method a rigorous justification. The strategies and transformations that are used are both justified and explained mathematically.

The language described in the book is based on VDM-SL (perhaps it is closer to Meta-IV on which VDM-SL is based). It has been updated with a more modern syntax: it is a subset of VDM-SL with the following restrictions:

- no loose functions;

- restrictions on patterns (including no loose patterns); and
- parameters to functions and procedures must be read only.

Other changes are to the statement part of the language. The main change is the introduction of Dijkstra's guarded commands for the executable part of the language. This has been one for the following reasons:

1. guarded commands are used as one of the basic constructs of the language;
2. they are elegant; and
3. an excellent idea should be republicized!

Simple input and output statements have been introduced so that the executable language could be implemented and used. Some other minor changes to the syntax have been made to make programs more readable. The most important change is the introduction of a specification command for refinement purposes. The author should apologize for these changes, but the advantages of Dijkstra's guarded commands outweigh the need to conform to the ISO Standard for VDM-SL.

The semantics are used to derive appropriate program and data refinement rules. It is easier for a developer attempting a refinement, or proving properties of a specification or a program to derive new, useful, rules using weakest pre-conditions. In particular it has been found that proofs of properties of language constructs can be more easily discharged with this approach.

The book shows that it is now possible to derive both a specification language and development method based on a few simple concepts, and to give a formal explanation of all of the development steps used in producing code from a specification. The book introduces the idea that the purpose of analysis is to provide a specification that can easily be understood by the human mind before the expensive process of developing a program starts. Specifications are 'programs' that should be biased towards a style that allows efficient execution by an intellectual computer, and that programs are 'specifications' that can be executed efficiently by an electronic computer. Design is the process of transforming a specification into efficient code.

The approach provides the formal semantics of a simple, but powerful, wide-spectrum programming language (VDM-WSL) and gives a formal definition of both algorithmic and data refinement. The following topics are covered in detail using a formal approach:

- formal specification;
- proving properties of a specification;
- properties of programs;
- algorithmic refinement;
- data refinement; and
- the correctness of code.

The theory of algorithm and data refinement also provides insight into the design process and development strategies that can be used to produce efficient code. Issues such as why reusable code is difficult to achieve have also been addressed. A mathematical foundation and background to most, if not all, of the ideas of software specification, design and development are given.

A course developed at Leicester over a ten-year period now uses the approach put forward in this book. The course was initially based on the refinement style of C. B. Jones from [23]; it slowly evolved to the current style. In a third-year course at Leicester that uses the ideas in the book, students have carried out the specification and refinement of some small systems, for example a system to manage a book library and a car-hire system. Other examples that have been developed were an analysis of sorting algorithms and the correct implementation of both AVL and 2–3 trees. With teaching in mind, many of the easier lemmas, theorems, and corollaries have been left for the reader to complete; these are terminated with a hollow box.

The book would is suitable for a third- or fourth-year undergraduate or a post-graduate course in formal methods – with this in mind, a complete set of teaching material is available. The material consists of:

1. a complete set of over-head projector slides together with a set of teaching notes;
2. a student study guide consisting of weekly reading suggestions and exercises;
3. a set of worked examples together with model answers, these would be suitable to add to the study guide or for use as examination questions; and
4. a technical report that describes the kernel language, the full language and an executable subset.

This material is available in machine readable form (in LaTeX source) on the World-Wide-Web – contact the author at derek@mcs.le.ac.uk.

Acknowledgements

Weakest pre-conditions were used by Hehner and others to give the semantics of a (subset) of Pascal and by Dijkstra to give the semantics of his guarded command language [20]. The idea of giving the semantics of VDM-SL with relations and a termination condition was used by Cliff Jones in his Ph.D. thesis [24]. This approach extends naturally when using the weakest preconditions to give the semantics of the kernel language used in this book. In a paper by Nelson [30] that gave a slightly different semantics to Dijkstra's guarded command language: undefined ($\perp$) was added as a possible outcome of a command. In [3] Abrial defined the semantics of B in terms of a set of basic commands. The formal semantics of VDM-SL have been given using relations ([18]) and based on this work, proof rules for VDM-SL have been given by Peter Gorm Larsen in his Ph.D. thesis [25]. Work at Oxford ([27, 26]) and work by Morris [28, 29] introduced the ideas of a programming calculus that dealt with both program and data refinement. Based on the Oxford work, in a series of examples, Andrews and Ince mixed program and data refinement to develop executable code from a specification [11, 10, 9]. This book pulls these ideas together to give a weakest pre-condition semantics for a close relative of VDM-SL, and uses these semantics to derive a set of refinement rules.

The author would also like to thank Professors Dr. H Klaeren and S. Schuman and an anonymous referee for their comments on an earlier draft and Rosie Kemp and the staff at Springer-Verlag for their patience and support.

Chapter Summaries

Chapter 1 – Writing Correct Programs Why refinement, the same simple example treated two different ways: starting with a specification, writing the code and then showing it to be correct and secondly deriving the correct code from the specification by a series of transformations – software development as a strategy game.

Chapter 2 – A Small Programming Language A small language for writing both specifications and programs. The semantics of the language are given using both relations and the weakest pre-condition approach. The concept of testing is discussed, leading to a meaning of program correctness.

Chapter 3 – Concepts and Properties The basic properties of the kernel language: simple program transformations. Setting and testing variables. The basic properties of a theory of refinement. A normal form and a framework for proving properties.

Chapter 4 – Building New Commands from Old Extending the language, principles and theory. Recursive definitions. (This is seen as a chapter for the advanced reader, the remainder of the book does not depend on it.)

Chapter 5 – Program Refinement Stepwise refinement. The concept of refinement. Replacing specifications: the meaning of program correctness and program refinement. Three different ways of looking at correctness and their equivalence. What is testing. Other refinement models.

Chapter 6 – The Basic Commands Refining the basic statements. Implementation issues; the language and the compiler writer.

Chapter 7 – Declarations and Blocks Introducing local variables, the idea of scope. Blocks and the refinement rules.

Chapter 8 – Command Sequences Introducing semicolon into a program. Concepts and properties. Refinement rules for semicolon.

Chapter 9 – The Alternative Command The if command and its properties. Using the command in refinement. Refinement rules for alternatives.

Chapter 10 – The Iterative Command The do command and its properties. Using the command in refinement. Refinement rules for iteration. The problem of termination and its proof. Loop parameters: initialization, guards, invariants and termination. Establishing the invariant. Refining loop bodies.

Chapter 11 – Functions and Procedures The definition of procedures. Introducing function procedures and proper procedures. Refinement rules for introducing and removing procedures and their calls. Refinement rules for using recursion.

Chapter 12 – Examples of Refinement at Work From a simple specification to executable code, the emphasis is on showing the ideas at work.

Chapter 13 – On Refinement and Loops How to refine a specification to use iteration. Hints on finding the guard, invariant and variant terms.

Chapter 14 – Functions and Procedures in Refinement Refining to procedures – introducing procedure declarations and procedure calls. Using recursion.

Chapter 15 – Refinement and Performance Using refinement to improve the performance of a program – a fast multiply and a fast integer divide algorithm.

Chapter 16 – Searching and Sorting Refining a search specification to executable code (linear and binary search). Refining a sort specification to executable code.

Chapter 17 – Data Refinement Replacing abstract data models with data that can be implemented by an executable programming language. The idea of data refinement. An informal explanation of the theory. A simple data refinement.

Chapter 18 – A Theory of Data Refinement The theory behind the rules and methods introduced in Chapter 17. Other approaches to data refinement. Dealing with assignment. This chapter is optional, but it does completes the theory of refinement and shows how everything fits together.

Chapter 19 – An Alternative Refinement of the security system Alternative ways of solving the specification used in Chapter 17.

Chapter 20 – Stacks and Queues Refining stacks and queues to executable code to illustrate data refinement in action. Different approaches to the same problem.

Chapter 21 – Dynamic Data Structures How to deal with pointers. Proving the correctness of a data representation that uses pointers.

Chapter 22 – Binary Trees A formal derivation of the standard algorithms for working with ordered binary trees.

Chapter 23 – Epilogue What next.

This book was produced using the software package 'Textures' (Blue Sky Research) and the LaTeX2$_\varepsilon$ and NPL VDM-SL macro packages on an Apple Macintosh computer.

Contents

1. **Writing Correct Programs** 1
   1.1 Satisfying Specifications 1
   1.2 An Alternative Approach 4
   1.3 Summary 6
2. **A Small Programming Language** 7
   2.1 Satisfying Specifications 7
   2.2 Specifications and Programs 11
   2.3 The Semantics of Commands 12
       2.3.1 Some Primitive Commands 15
       2.3.2 A Basic Command 16
       2.3.3 New Commands from Old – Operators 17
   2.4 Non-determinism and Partial Commands 21
   2.5 The Concepts of Predicate Transformers 24
   2.6 Substitution 26
       2.6.1 Rules for Substitution 28
   2.7 The Formal Semantics of the Kernel Language 28
       2.7.1 The Bounded Commands 28
       2.7.2 The Unbounded Commands 31
   2.8 The Weakest Liberal Pre-conditions, Termination, and Relations 32
   2.9 Executable Programs 36
   2.10 Summary 36
3. **Concepts and Properties** 37
   3.1 More Commands 37
   3.2 The Domain of a Command 40
   3.3 Some Properties of Commands 45
       3.3.1 Sequence 45
       3.3.2 Bounded Non-deterministic Choice 46
       3.3.3 Guarded Commands 47
       3.3.4 Unbounded Non-deterministic Choice 49

		3.3.5 Assertions	50
	3.4	A Normal Form	50
	3.5	Some Further Properties...............................	54
		3.5.1 Setting and Testing Variables	56
	3.6	The Primitive Commands Revisited	61
	3.7	Initial Values...	63
	3.8	A Compiler for the Small Language	65
	3.9	Summary	65
4.	**Building New Commands from Old**	66
	4.1	Defining Commands	66
	4.2	An Approach to Recursion	68
	4.3	Sequences of Predicates and their Limit	70
		4.3.1 A Skeptical Result	72
		4.3.2 A Credulous Result	74
	4.4	Limits of Predicate Transformers	75
		4.4.1 The Two Approaches	77
	4.5	Limits of Commands	78
	4.6	Tidying the Loose Ends	81
	4.7	Epilogue..	82
5.	**Program Refinement**	84
	5.1	Stepwise Refinement	84
	5.2	Replacing Specifications	85
	5.3	Conventions..	96
	5.4	Refinement Classes	96
	5.5	Alternative Views of Refinement	99
	5.6	Other Refinement Relations	101
		5.6.1 Weak Refinement	101
		5.6.2 Partial Refinement..............................	102
		5.6.3 Full Refinement	102
		5.6.4 Strong Refinement	102
		5.6.5 Refinement by Simulation	103
	5.7	Summary	104
6.	**The Basic Commands**	105
	6.1	The Constant Commands..............................	105
	6.2	Assertions	109
	6.3	Assignment	112
		6.3.1 Implementation Issues...........................	115
	6.4	Summary	116

7. Declarations and Blocks 117
- 7.1 The Declaration Command 117
- 7.2 Some Interactions Between Commands 118
- 7.3 The Definitional Commands 121
  - 7.3.1 Declarations 122
  - 7.3.2 The Let Command 122
  - 7.3.3 The Def Command 123
  - 7.3.4 The Def and Let Commands Compared 123
- 7.4 Refining Definitional Commands 125
- 7.5 Defining Constant Values 127
  - 7.5.1 Refining Functions and Constants 128
- 7.6 Logical Constants 129
- 7.7 Summary 134

8. Command Sequences 135
- 8.1 Solve a Part and then the Whole 135
  - 8.1.1 Choosing the First Step 137
  - 8.1.2 Choosing the Second Step 140
  - 8.1.3 Choosing Both Steps 142
- 8.2 Summary 144

9. The Alternative Command 145
- 9.1 Divide and Conquer 145
- 9.2 The Partition 147
- 9.3 Reassembly 150
- 9.4 Alternatives – The If Command 152
- 9.5 Refining Specifications 157
- 9.6 Summary 158

10. The Iterative Command 159
- 10.1 Another Approach 164
- 10.2 The Generalized Loop and Refinement 166
- 10.3 The General Variant Theorem 168
- 10.4 An Application 170
- 10.5 Loops 172
- 10.6 Iteration – The Do Command 176
- 10.7 Practical Do Commands 179
- 10.8 The Refinement of Loop Bodies 180
  - 10.8.1 Decreasing Variants 180
  - 10.8.2 Increasing Variants 182
- 10.9 Summary 183

11. Functions and Procedures 184
11.1 Proper Procedures and their Calls 184
11.2 Function Procedures and their Calls 190
11.3 Function Calls in Expressions 193
11.4 An Alternative Approach to Parameters and Arguments 195
11.5 Postscript 195
11.6 Summary 196

12. An Example of Refinement at Work 197
12.1 The Problem – Integer Multiplication 197
    12.1.1 Getting Started 197
    12.1.2 The Refinement Strategy Continued 198
    12.1.3 The Next Step 199
12.2 Logical Constants Revisited 203
12.3 Summary 204

13. On Refinement and Loops 205
13.1 The Factorial Problem 205
    13.1.1 The First Solution 205
    13.1.2 A Second Solution 207
13.2 Finding Guards and Invariants 210
13.3 Identifying the Loop Type Incorrectly 215

14. Functions and Procedures in Refinement 216
14.1 Factorial 216
14.2 Multiply 218
14.3 Summary 221

15. Refinement and Performance 222
15.1 A Second Approach to Multiplication 222
15.2 Fast Division 224
15.3 Summary 229

16. Searching and Sorting 230
16.1 A Diversion – the Array Data Type 230
16.2 Linear Search 231
16.3 Binary Search 234
16.4 A Simple Sort Algorithm 239
    16.4.1 The First Attempt 240
    16.4.2 The Other Approach 243
16.5 Summary 246

17. Data refinement ... 247
- 17.1 The Refinement Strategy ... 247
  - 17.1.1 The Problem ... 248
- 17.2 The Refinement to Executable Code ... 251
- 17.3 The Next Step ... 255
- 17.4 The Refinement of the Operations ... 260
- 17.5 The First Refinement Step ... 266
- 17.6 The Next Refinement Step ... 268
  - 17.6.1 The *check* Operation ... 277
  - 17.6.2 Putting it all Together ... 277
  - 17.6.3 Further Development ... 278
  - 17.6.4 The Final Step ... 278
- 17.7 A Summary of the Approach ... 278
- 17.8 Summary ... 281

18. A Theory of Data Refinement ... 282
- 18.1 An Approach to Data Refinement ... 282
  - 18.1.1 The Data Refinement of Declarations ... 296
  - 18.1.2 Refinement and Specifications ... 296
- 18.2 Data Refinement in Practice ... 299
- 18.3 Another View of Data Refinement ... 300
- 18.4 Functional Refinement ... 303
- 18.5 An Alternative Data Refinement of Assignments ... 304
- 18.6 Summary ... 307

19. An Alternative Refinement of the Security System ... 308
- 19.1 A Data Refinement ... 308
- 19.2 Another Approach to the Refinement ... 313
- 19.3 Summary ... 317

20. Stacks and Queues ... 318
- 20.1 A Finite Stack ... 318
  - 20.1.1 The Refinement ... 319
  - 20.1.2 Reorganizing the Operations ... 321
- 20.2 A stack of Boolean Values ... 327
  - 20.2.1 Some Lemmas about the Representation ... 329
  - 20.2.2 The *empty-stack* Operation ... 330
  - 20.2.3 The *push* Operation ... 330
  - 20.2.4 The *pop* Operation ... 330
  - 20.2.5 The *read* Operation ... 331
  - 20.2.6 The *is-empty* Operation ... 331
  - 20.2.7 The *is-full* Operation ... 332
  - 20.2.8 The Code ... 333
  - 20.2.9 Some Lessons ... 333
- 20.3 A Finite Queue ... 333

	20.3.1 A Refinement of the Queue 336
	20.3.2 Some Theorems 338
	20.3.3 The Operations Transformed 339
	20.3.4 An Extension to the System 343
20.4	An Efficient Queue 345
	20.4.1 Some Properties 347
	20.4.2 Lessons 351

21. Dynamic Data Structures 352
- 21.1 Simulating a Linked List 352
  - 21.1.1 Some Theorems 353
  - 21.1.2 The Operations Transformed 354
- 21.2 Explicit Pointers 355
- 21.3 The Stack Using Explicit Pointers 358
  - 21.3.1 Standard Stack Specification to Pointers 360
- 21.4 Summary 368

22. Binary Trees 370
- 22.1 The Specification 370
- 22.2 The Refinement 370
- 22.3 The Refinement of the *in* Operation 371
- 22.4 The Refinement of the *insert* Operation 374
- 22.5 The Refinement of the *delete* Operation 377
- 22.6 An In-order Traversal 382
- 22.7 Summary 387

23. Epilogue 388
- 23.1 An Approach to Loose Patterns and Functions 389

A. Program Refinement Rules 393
- A.1 Replace Specification 393
- A.2 Assume Pre-condition in Post-condition 393
- A.3 Introduce Assignment 393
- A.4 Introduce Command-semicolon 394
- A.5 Introduce Semicolon-command 394
- A.6 Introduce Leading Assignment 394
- A.7 Introduce Following Assignment 395
- A.8 Introduce Alternatives 395
- A.9 Introduce Iteration 395
- A.10 Introduce Proper Procedure Body 396
- A.11 Introduce Proper Procedure Call 396
- A.12 Introduce Function Procedure Body 397
- A.13 Introduce Function Procedure Call 397
- A.14 Add Variable 397
- A.15 Realize Quantifier 398

A.16	Remove Scope	398
A.17	Expand Frame	398
A.18	Contract Frame	398
A.19	Introduce Logical Constant	398
A.20	Remove Logical Constant	399
A.21	Refine Block	399
A.22	Introduce Skip	399

Bibliography 401

Index 403

1. Writing Correct Programs

When the specification for a computer system is written down, a good style for the author to adopt is to concentrate on describing 'what' the system does and to try to avoid, wherever possible, saying 'how' it does it. This can be achieved by using abstract data structures to describe the data and implicit specifications using pre- and post-conditions to describe the various operations that form the system. However, when the specification has been completed we are faced with the problem of implementing it. So what is the next step? Eventually a computer program has to be produced which will satisfy the specification. We are faced with two tasks: implementing the abstract data structures of the specification in terms of data structures available in a favourite programming language and turning the (implicit) specifications of operations into executable code. A formal specification describes what a computer system should do – this book considers the problem of converting the 'what' into 'how' – the theory and practice of the process of developing executable code that satisfies a specification.

1.1 Satisfying Specifications

There is now an interesting question: what is meant by 'satisfying a specification'? If a program is written to satisfy a specification, the program should produce answers that are defined by the specification. An insight into this can be obtained from the normal course of events that should occur after a program has been written. One way of checking the correctness of the program, that the program matches its specification, is to run some test-cases. The specification defines the outputs that could be obtained from an input, and thus can be used to generate test-cases. To test a program, a valid input value is chosen, the program is run, and the output is checked to see if it is as described by the specification. This can be done for a variety of inputs chosen by some sort of criteria. The more test-cases that are run and that work, the more we should be convinced that the program is correct. However, it is impossible to guarantee the correctness of the program with respect to its specification by running test-cases – there may be an infinite number.

Is there an alternative to testing that would demonstrate a program satisfied its specification? The answer to this question is 'yes' – take, for example, the following specification of division and a program that claims to satisfy the specification. How can we be sure that the program is correct, that it matches the specification? The state (program variable declarations) for this problem is given by:

    state *Example* of
        $a : \mathbb{Z}$
        $b : \mathbb{Z}$
        $q : \mathbb{Z}$
    end

and the specification for a program fragment that does integer division is:

    div
    chg $q : \mathbb{Z}$
    pre $0 \leq a \wedge 0 < b$
    post $\exists r : \mathbb{N} \cdot b \times q + r = a \wedge r < b$

There is frame information which requires that only the value of the variable q can be changed. The pre-condition states that the value in location a must be non-negative, and the value in location b must be positive. The post-condition states that q contains the result of dividing b into a. A program to achieve this is:

    $q := 0;$
    $r := a;$
    do $\neg (r < b) \rightarrow r := r - b;$
                          $q := q + 1$
    od

A temporary variable r has been introduced. The program can be annotated with comments that are derived from the specification, and using these it is possible to sketch a proof of correctness. The proof that this program meets its specification can proceed as follows:

    -- $0 \leq a \wedge 0 < b$
    $q := 0;$
    $r := a;$
    -- *inv*
    do $\neg (r < b) \rightarrow$ -- *inv* $\wedge \neg (r < b)$
                      $r := r - b;$
                      $q := q + 1$
                    -- *inv*
    od
    -- *inv* $\wedge r < b$
    where *inv* $\triangleq b \times q + r = a$

It is fairly easy to see that if *inv* is true just before the do command is entered, it will be true just before the body of the iteration is executed for the first time – the execution of the test, or loop guard, does not change any variables. It is easy to see that *inv* is preserved across the do command body: all that happens is a value equal to the contents of location *b* is moved from one part of the term *inv* to another, leaving the value of the expression unchanged. Thus, if *inv* is true before the body of the iteration is executed, then it is true on completion. Also, if it is true on completion of the body of the do command, it will be true just before the body is executed again. Thus the body of the do command preserves the value of *inv*. The initialization that occurs before the do command establishes *inv*. Thus the following is true:

1. the term *inv* is initially true;
2. it is preserved across the do command body; and
3. on exit from the do command it is true.

In addition, completing the do command makes the value of the Boolean expression $(r < b)$ true and therefore the program can be said to satisfy its specification. We should also show that if the input is valid, the program terminates. Notice that r is initialized to a positive value and decremented by a positive value, so at some point it must be true that the value of r is less than b and the do command must terminate. Notice that this assumes that the pre-condition is satisfied; if it is not, anything can happen and the program could even loop forever.

The above is a long, but fairly straightforward, 'proof of correctness'. Several 'reasonable' steps were taken without explanation: the introduction of a new variable, linking the contents of storage locations with the values denoted by identifiers and the proof of termination. These steps need to be justified. For the doubters, this fairly informal proof can be made formal in the mathematical sense and machine checked. What has been done above is a symbolic execution of the program together with an inductive proof, and by this means all possible test cases have been run simultaneously. This proof strategy will work for any program, although it should be noted that the proofs become complicated for large programs. The lesson that can be gained from the above proof of correctness is that they are possible – that an argument of correctness can be recorded.

If a formal specification exists, what is required is a development method that allows the production of correct code which satisfies the specification. Ideally the proofs should be carried out alongside the code development; the proofs should be used to drive the development of code rather than developing the code and then proving it correct. It can be seen that developing code and then proving it correct is, even for the small example above, tedious. By developing the code and proof together, the final code will be correct by construction. If a development method is to be useful, it must encourage small development steps which are easily understood, and any development decisions documented. It is also necessary to justify such ideas as a correct program and a program satisfying a specification.

1.2 An Alternative Approach

Rather than develop the program and then prove it correct, a better approach might be to develop the proof and program hand-in-hand. Starting with the specification we will transform it into executable code using some of the transformation rules given in Appendix A. These rules allow a specification to be transformed and for the intent (meaning) of the specification to be retained. For the moment, the reader is asked to take the transformation rules on trust – the remainder of the book is concerned with deriving and justifying the rules, defining what is meant by retaining the intent of a specification and showing how the rules can be applied. For those readers familiar with calculus and integration, the style and application of the rules are similar. The specification is repeated for convenience:

div
chg $q : \mathbb{Z}$
pre $0 \leq a \wedge 0 < b$
post $\exists r : \mathbb{N} \cdot b \times q + r = a \wedge r < b$

The first step is to introduce a temporary variable using the *realize quantifier* rule given on page 398 of the appendix. The new version is:

$div \sqsubseteq [\![\, \text{dcl } r : \mathbb{N} \text{ in}$
 $div\text{-}body$
 chg $q : \mathbb{Z}$
 pre $0 \leq a \wedge 0 < b$
 post $b \times q + r = a \wedge r < b \,]\!]$

The $\sqsubseteq$ symbol means that the program fragment denoted by the name on the left of this symbol can be replaced by the program fragment on the right without the customer of the specification noticing – the intent of the specification is preserved.

The specification in the body of the block can be refined by an iterative command, and so the transformation rule that introduces an iterative command can be used (see page 395 in the appendix). The rule requires that we find a predicate that defines the initialization code for the iterative command, a predicate that is the loop guard, and an invariant and a variant term. The Boolean value of the invariant term remains true for any number of executions of the iteration body, The variant term involves a value that is either strictly increased or (as in this example) decreased. The value of the variant term will also have either an upper bound or lower bound that it can obtain – with these constraints termination can be proved. The first step is to find the invariant, an examination of the post-condition (and the proof above) suggests the following candidate:

$$b \times q + r = a$$

The initialization should be simple code that establishes the invariant – setting q to zero and r to the value of a will do this. The negation of the guard together with the invariant should establish the post-condition of the original specification and the variant should decrease the value of r; the invariant also requires that r is never negative. Thus our loop parameters are:

 init $q = 0 \wedge r = a$
 guard $b \leq r$
 inv $b \times q + r = a \wedge 0 \leq r$
 var $r < \overleftarrow{r}$

The additional term in the invariant is to make certain that r is always a natural number, it is never made negative. The loop domain proof obligation is:

$$b \leq r \wedge b \times q + r = a \wedge 0 \leq r \;\Rightarrow\; r : \mathbb{N}$$

which can be seen to be trivially satisfied.

The code for the iteration is easily derived from the loop parameters given above; for the body of the iteration, the pre-condition is given by the guard and the invariant relation and the post-condition by the invariant and variant relations. The *introduce iteration* rule then gives:

 div-body $\sqsubseteq$ $q, r := 0, a$
    do $b \leq r \rightarrow$ *loop-body*
      chg $q, r : \mathbb{Z}$
      pre $b \leq r \wedge b \times q + r = a \wedge 0 \leq r$
      post $b \times q + r = a \wedge 0 \leq r \wedge r < \overleftarrow{r}$
    od

Inspection of the variant term suggests decreasing r by b, and an application of the *leading assignment* rule (see page 394) gives:

 loop-body $\sqsubseteq$ $r := r - b$;
     re-establish-inv
     chg $q, r : \mathbb{Z}$
     pre $b \leq r - b \wedge b \times q + r - b = a \wedge 0 \leq r - b$
     post $b \times q + r = a \wedge 0 \leq r$

and for the invariant to be re-established it will also be necessary to increase q, thus:

$$\textit{re-establish-inv} \sqsubseteq q := q + 1$$

This step, justified by the *introduce assignment* rule (see page 393), is correct providing the following proof obligation is discharged:

$$b \leq r - b \land b \times \overleftarrow{q} + r - b = a \land r - b \land q = \overleftarrow{q} + 1 \Rightarrow$$
$$b \times q + r = a \land 0 \leq r$$

The term $0 \leq r - b$ together with the fact that $0 < b$ and b is unchanged guarantee that $0 \leq r$; and the terms $b \times \overleftarrow{q} + r - b = a$ and $q = \overleftarrow{q} + 1$ guarantee that $b \times q + r = a$. The proof obligation is thus discharged and this allows the assignment rule to be applied to give the refinement given above.

Pulling everything together, the final program is:

$$[\![\text{dcl } r : \mathbb{N} \text{ in}$$
$$q, r := 0, a \ ;$$
$$\text{do } b \leq r \rightarrow r := r - b \ ; \ q := q + 1 \text{ od }]\!]$$

This little example shows how transforming a specification to executable code can be done in a series of steps, some of which may require a proof to be done. If one of these proofs fails, then the step that generated it is wrong. Thus any errors can be found while developing the program, and not after development – it is much easier to derive the program and the proof of correctness together. In fact programming in the normal sense has been replaced by a goal-oriented activity where we look at the post-condition and try to establish parts of it. Traditional programming is replaced by a more systematic approach to developing a program that satisfies a specification.

1.3 Summary

This chapter has introduced the concept of a specification and how to transform that specification into a program using some transformation rules. These rules, in some sense, preserve the correctness of the program (if we think of a specification as a correct program). These concepts and ideas need to be formalized – the topics of subsequent chapters.

2. A Small Programming Language

This chapter will introduce the idea of a specification, the realization of a specification – a program; and what is meant by a program satisfying its specification. All three of these concepts will be defined formally using mathematics so that properties can be investigated and proved and, more important, a better understanding of the ideas can be obtained.

2.1 Satisfying Specifications

The normal process of software development involves three main steps:

1. analysis – understanding the problem;
2. design – designing a solution; and
3. implementation – producing the solution.

The analysis step should produce some sort of description (sometimes called a specification) of the problem and then the design and implementation steps are involved in the development of a computer program that is supposed to solve the problem (satisfy the specification). There are three ideas introduced in this brief (and over simplified) description of the software development process:

1. a specification;
2. the design and development of a program; and
3. the concept of the program satisfying the specification.

The specification should be an abstract description of the problem, abstract in the sense that any details of the solution should be avoided – though the architecture (form) of the solution might be included. The design and development of the final program is about forming or enhancing the architecture of the system and adding sufficient detail so that the resulting description of how to solve the problem can be executed on a computer. To understand the software development process we need to at least understand these three ideas in detail – this will be done using mathematics; however a mathematical approach to the understanding of these concepts must fit in with the informal meanings that we usually work with.

2. A Small Programming Language

The idea behind a formal specification is to provide a mathematical description of the system – this is done by defining all possible input/output pairs. If a formal specification exists we at least have a criteria for judging test cases – the input output pair defined by the test case must be one of the input/output pairs described by the specification. However, this still leaves two problems, how do we describe all possible input/output pairs mathematically and abstractly and how does the developer produce a correct program that satisfies the specification.

First, formalize the concept of a specification and a program satisfying a specification:

– denote the specification for a code fragment by op;

> op
> chg $x : X$
> pre $pre(x)$
> post $post(\overleftarrow{x}, x)$

the informal meaning of this is that the pre-condition defines the acceptable input and the post-condition defines input/output pairs – those that satisfy the post-condition.
– denote a program fragment which satisfies the specification by A; and
– denote input, i.e. values of variables just before executing the code fragment, by i (i could stand for a vector (list) of values).

The program A satisfies this specification if, for input i that satisfies the precondition, execution of the program produces an outcome o and that outcome together with the input satisfies the post-condition. Mathematically, for the test-case pair (i, o):

$$pre(i) \Rightarrow post(i, o)$$

We might need to execute the program with all possible inputs to confirm that the program correctly satisfied the specification – this is not possible for any reasonable program, the number of test cases is too large. An alternative approach is required. A program associates an output with a given input and this can be modelled abstractly by a function. Suppose that we are given a program A, then develop a mathematical function f that accurately models the program; thus if the program produced the outcome o for input i then the function f would guarantee that $f(i) = o$. This is how we can formalize the concept of a program. The correctness criteria could now be written as:

$$\forall i \in X \cdot pre(i) \Rightarrow post(i, f(i))$$

which can now be proved mathematically. However the correctness of the program is now dependent on the need to show that the function f and the program A are, in some sense, equivalent – the function f is a model of the program A. One approach to this is to use the program A to construct the function f. This can be done mechanically by providing a function M that would take a program and 'translate' it into the appropriate function. Before we can continue, a more precise definition of M is required. M is a function from the set of all possible programs (or fragments of programs) and from the set of all possible values of variables – the *State* – into the set of all possible values of variables – the result of executing the program.

$$M : Program \rightarrow (State \rightarrow State)$$
$$f = M[\![A]\!]$$

the concept of a program A satisfying a specification can now be expressed as:

$$A \text{ sat } op \text{ if } \forall i \in State \cdot pre(i) \Rightarrow post(i, M[\![A]\!](i))$$

In words: A satisfies the specification op, if, for any input that satisfies the pre-condition, then the execution of the program A with that input terminates and produces a result which, together with the corresponding input value(s), satisfies the post-condition. The above equation, or proof rule as it is called, is a mathematical definition of the idea that an implementation of a specification, a program, satisfies its specification. Again it is worth emphasizing that this is exactly the criteria used for evaluating a test case when testing a program.

The function M[1] is a mathematical model of program execution. The function M is called the meaning function of the programming language in which A is written: $M[\![A]\!]$ denotes the transformation between the input and the output of the program A – it is the mathematical equivalent of executing A. M must be total over the set of valid programs. Can the M function be realized? It is just the semantics of the programming language in which the program is written and would need to be specified formally; in fact, this function has been defined for many languages including PL/I [22], Pascal [8], Modula-2 [7] and Ada [17]. The translation function M will also provide a bridge between the programming language in which A is written and the specification language. We will leave the definition of M for a particular language, which is beyond the scope of this book, and initially rely on our intuitive understanding of the semantics of programming languages.

The meaning function M, if written carefully, will provide insight and understanding of the semantics of a programming language. If a function M is defined for a programming language, it can be used to develop a correct implementation of that programming language, it can be used to develop a correct compiler – thus we can prove mathematically that a program satisfies a specification by using M to produce the equivalent function, and we can

---

[1] The M function is really a specification of the programming language, and a compiler or interpreter for the language is a realization (implementation) of the specification.

use the compiler to produce executable code which matches the function. However writing a program and proving that it satisfies a specification is difficult (the Modula-2 translation function is about 500 pages long, and after we have translated the program we still need to prove correctness – the reader is asked to imagine the difficulties, especially if the program has an error in it).

Rather than restricting these ideas to deterministic programming languages – an input value to a program can only result in one possible outcome; the ideas can be extended to non-deterministic languages. In these an input value to a program could result in various possible outcomes. Non-deterministic languages are managed by changing the definition of M slightly:

$$M : Program \rightarrow (State \rightarrow \mathcal{P}(State))$$

where we return a set of values, each one representing a possible outcome from an input to the program A. An alternative approach is to allow the alternative outcomes to be represented as a relation:

$$R : Program \rightarrow \mathcal{P}(State \times State)$$

thus $_i R[\![A]\!]_o$ denotes the relation that represents the set of possible outcomes from an input value i. With this approach a program is translated into a relation, where the outcomes for any particular input are related by the relation to that input. Again the translation function R provides the bridge between the programming language and the specification language.

Now with this style of definition the correctness of a program can be expressed as:

$$\forall i \in State \cdot pre(i) \Rightarrow (\exists o \in State \cdot (i,o) \in R[\![A]\!]) \wedge$$
$$(\forall o \in State \cdot (i,o) \in R[\![A]\!] \Rightarrow post(i,o))$$

The first term in the result of the implication states that the meaning relation R must define a possible output for any input that satisfies the pre-condition. It is equivalent to the requirement that M must be total.

The problems identified so far are:

- producing the translation function R (or M) for a given programming language;
- bridging the differences between the semantics of the programming language and the specification language (these could be addressed as the meaning function M is constructed);
- proving the correctness of the (translated) program;
- errors introduced while writing a program to satisfy a given specification; and
- developing a correct compiler for the programming language.

We will deal with the first four issues together, the last problem is beyond the scope of this book.

2.2 Specifications and Programs

The difficulties described above can be avoided by considering an alternative approach to programming. The first step is to change our view of what is a program and what is a specification. Programs can be executed by some sort of mechanical (or more accurately electrical) mechanism – usually called a computer. The execution is very economical in the sense that the mechanism is relatively simple and normally needs no human intervention. Specifications can be executed by some sort of intellectual mechanism – usually a human brain. For a well-written specification, the 'execution' is usually very economical in the sense that little effort is needed to understand very complex systems (because of the abstractions used in the specification – remember it is supposed to be well-written). If we try and execute a specification on a computer it tends to be very uneconomical – sometimes much computer resource is needed to try to execute the specification, this could involve searching a very large state space (set) for an answer. If we try and execute a program in our head, again it tends to be uneconomical – much intellectual effort can be spent trying to understand the detail of what is happening. As the specification is supposed to be a version of the program (or the program a version of the specification) the main difference between the two is the intended vehicle to be used for their execution.

The first step we shall take is to not distinguish between specifications and programs, since the only difference between them is the mechanism that is to be used for their execution. The process of program development will be to transform a specification (an intellectual program) into a form that can be economically executed on a computer (a computer program). The second step is not to write the program independently of the specification, but rather to transform the specification into a program[2]. The transformation process must preserve correctness: if the specification is correct then the corresponding program must also be correct – the program must do the same thing as the specification, it must satisfy the specification. The third step is to combine the specification language and the programming language into one language – usually called a wide-spectrum language. This will avoid the problem of bridging two different semantics (done by the M function in the first approach described earlier).

The transformation of specifications into programs will still generate proofs and the need to prove them. Ideally the proofs should be carried out alongside the code development; and we shall find that the proofs can be used to drive the development of code. By developing the code and proof together, the final code will be correct by construction. If a development method is to be useful, it must encourage small development steps which are easily understood, and any development decisions documented. We shall also find that

---

[2] intellectual programs will be translated into executable specifications.

most of the proofs are simple and some are re-usable (in the sense that a theory can be built which is usable in another development).

With this change of view, the terms program and specification should really be used interchangeably, however we will try to reserve the word specification for a program that can be economically executed by a human brain and to reserve the word program for a specification that can be economically executed by a computer.

With these three steps plus one other, all of the first four issues can be dealt with at a stroke. A further bonus is that by transforming our specifications we will (should) avoid the introduction of bugs – a specification will be transformed in a way that preserves correctness into a form that can be executed economically on a computer. Additionally, we will also discover a criteria for executable. Lastly, we will have an indication of how to develop a correct compiler for our executable specification (programming) language. This will be difficult, but only needs to be done once.

We need to formalize these ideas so that as a specification is translated into a program correctness is preserved – the program satisfies its specification.

2.3 The Semantics of Commands

The first step in providing a theory of program specification and development is to introduce a small programming language that can be used for both specifications and programming. Some mathematical ideas can then be developed based on this language to aid the intellectual execution of both programs and specification. This will be done in several steps:

– identify the basic building blocks (commands) of the language, this will take the form of defining a small, kernel, programming language;
– provide the syntax and semantics of the basic commands; and
– provide ways to assemble new commands from existing ones.

With such a construction kit we can then build a usable wide-spectrum language from the basic commands – the kernel language. Then program development becomes:

– write down a specification using a set of commands; and
– transform the commands by replacing some components by new ones that do the same task, but are executable on a computer.

As has been already stated, defining R (or M) can provide much insight into the semantics of a programming language, so though the following definitions will not be used directly, they will be given to provide this insight. First, let us expand the idea of using a relation to explain the semantics of a programming language.

2.3 The Semantics of Commands

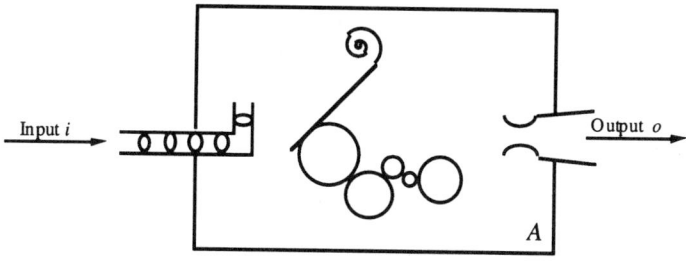

A

Consider a command together with the mechanism on which it is to be executed – the machine could be electronic (a real computer) or biological (a human mind). For a specific input to the command, one of three things can occur:

1. an output is produce;
2. the mechanism whirrs into action, but produces no output; or
3. nothing happens.

In the first case there is no problem, the input i produces the proper outcome (as we shall call it) o. The second and third cases need some thought. In the second case we can (in some sense) hold the mechanism up to our ear and hear that it is working, but however long we wait, there is no output. In this case we denote this lack of output by the symbol $\bot$ and call it the improper outcome. In the third case the mechanism doesn't even start working – the input is not recognized by the command, it is not in its domain. These possibilities can be described using a relation [30]:

> The command A relates an input i to an outcome o, written $_iA_o$, means that o is a possible outcome of executing A with the initial input value i.

For an input i a command A may not produce any outcome, or it can produce a proper outcome, or it can produce the the improper outcome $\bot$ which represents both infinite looping and run-time errors. Partial relations will be allowed: an input value that is not in the domain of the relation that models the command A is one that is not recognized by (the 'execution' of) A – the command will deadlock with its environment if an input value is not in its domain. In a relational style, the semantics of the commands of a language would be given by a set of relations over $State \times State_\bot$.

It must be realized that these are choices that can be made when defining a suitable mathematical model – these are not the only ones. For example we could choose not to model the improper outcome directly and only allow total relations, or allow partial relations but not the improper outcome, etc.

Consider the command loop (which is while true do skip). If we choose not to directly model the improper outcome, this can be done by letting loop be defined as:

$$\text{loop} \triangleq \{(i, o) \mid i, o : State\}$$

Reflecting the discussion above, this should really be written:

$$R[\![\text{loop}]\!] \triangleq \{(i, o) \mid i, o : State\}$$

however the translation function R can be left out without any loss of understanding.

We need to define the set over which the relation is defined. Identifiers declared in a program are bound to values[3] and this can be modelled by a state – a state binds identifiers to their (current) values:

$$Id = \ldots \quad \text{-- a set of identifiers}$$

$$VALUE = \ldots \quad \text{-- a set of values}$$

$$State = Id \xrightarrow{m} VALUE$$

The semantics of a command are defined as a relation over $State$:

$$R : Command \rightarrow \mathcal{P}(State \times State_\bot)$$

as hinted above we can drop explicit use of R and define the semantics of a command A as:

$$A \in \mathcal{P}(State \times State_\bot)$$

or equivalently

$$A \subseteq (State \times State_\bot)$$

where $State_\bot$ denotes the set $State$ with the distinguished element $\bot$ added. Functions will be strict: any function that has $\bot$ as an argument will give $\bot$ as its answer. The intent behind this is to model the idea that once a program is looping, it continues to loop forever (unless some outside interference changes things; we shall not model this possibility).

---

[3] More accurately identifiers are bound to storage locations that contain variables; this can be modelled by

$$Environment = Id \xrightarrow{m} LOC$$
$$Store = LOC \xrightarrow{m} VALUE$$

however this picture is more complicated than we need.

The next step is to provide means by which commands can be combined together to form new commands in such a way that the new, bigger, hopefully more powerful, commands can also be described by relations.

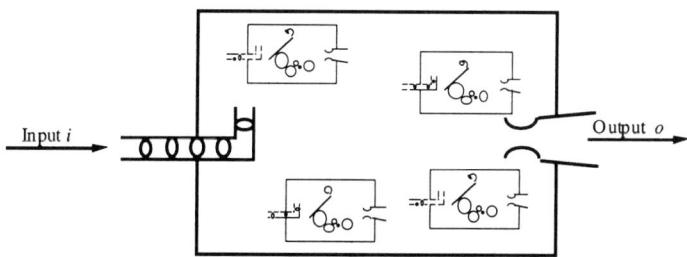

A Convention and the Undefined Element. The relations used to define the language are over $State \times State_\perp$ to emphasis that we do not give meaning to a relation element of the form $(\perp, x)$, which would model a looping outcome suddenly producing the result denoted by x. The denotation $\perp$ is used to write down the concept of undefined and looping (which can be modelled by the same concept). The semantics of the language will be given by hiding $\perp$; it will only appear in a discussion of what is going on behind the scenes in the model, we shall not be concerned with it when writing specifications and deriving programs, which is why it will be hidden. With this in mind, consider the following convention. Types are domains (sets) of values that include $\perp$ that denotes the undefined value. Thus we will write X rather than $X_\perp$ from now on. That $\perp$ is a possible value for a variable of type X will be taken as understood. We shall use $State$ to denote all the types of a program (and therefore values of this type can include the undefined value $\perp$). For binds that occur in, for example, quantifiers we shall write $x : X$ to mean that x ranges over all the values of type X not including the undefined value $\perp$. Occasionally we shall write $x \in X_\perp$ when discussing the model (this will never be written in a specification, in a program or in a proof about a program) in this case x ranges over all the values of the type X including $\perp$. This convention allows $\perp$ to occur in the model, but we need not be concerned with it directly when carrying out a development. For sets, which by their construction can never contain the undefined element, we shall still use the standard notation $x \in S$ for binds in quantifiers, etc.

2.3.1 Some Primitive Commands

The worse (or perhaps the best) command is the one we shall call miracle. This command will accept no input – it always jams – and can be described abstractly by the empty relation:

miracle $\triangleq \{\,\}$

It is obviously the worst command because it does nothing; it could also be called the best command because it satisfies all specifications – since it produces no outcomes, it can never be proved that it doesn't satisfy a given specification! Thus a program consisting of just this command is correct with respect to all specifications. Luckily for the profession of software engineer, as this particular command does not produce any output, it is of no use to the customer – if it was of use, software engineers would all be out of work.

The choice of miracle as the name for this command can be explained: it could have been called halt, but this name might confuse miracle with the *halt* statement found in some programming languages that just cease execution of the program and return control to the operating system (which is not the meaning, semantics, of miracle). Another possibility is abort, but this infers an error return to the operating system (again not the meaning that is intended). The name is derived from Dijkstra's law of the excluded miracle, it is this command and its relatives that are being excluded.

The second command to be considered is skip; it is not interesting as it performs no useful function – for any input it just produces the same value as output; skip is the identity command and can be described by the identity relation:

$$\text{skip} \triangleq \{(s,s) \mid s : State\}$$

The third command is loop – for any input this command just loops: it just whirrs for ever, never producing any (proper) outcome.

$$\text{loop} \triangleq \{(s, \bot) \mid s : State\}$$

The command loop can be activated in any state, but its only outcome is the improper outcome, $\bot$, modelling the fact that the command loops forever.

The most general command that always produces a proper outcome is havoc – this command used in a program would make life exciting: for any given input it could produce any proper outcome. Its relational definition is:

$$\text{havoc} \triangleq \{(s, o) \mid s, o : State\}$$

2.3.2 A Basic Command

The only basic command is assignment; it is also the first useful command. It allows the value denoted by a variable (identifier) to be changed. Its relational definition is complicated, but roughly speaking, it can be defined as:

$$x := E \triangleq \{(s, s \dagger \{x \mapsto M[\![E]\!]s\}) \mid s : State\}$$

where $M[\![E]\!]s$ means evaluate the expression E in the state s. It should be noted that in this language, the evaluation of an expression can have no side-effects. This means that the evaluation of an expression cannot change the values of any variables, its evaluation cannot assign to a variable.

2.3 The Semantics of Commands

The † operator is defined as:

$$s \dagger \{x \mapsto a\}(n) = \begin{cases} s(n), & \text{if } n \neq x \\ y, & \text{if } n = x \end{cases}$$

For example, if the state was given by:

$$s = \{\text{x} \mapsto 4, \text{y} \mapsto -2, \text{z} \mapsto 8\}$$

then

$$M[\![x + y]\!]s = 4 + (-2) = 2$$

and for this s with the corresponding outcome s' then

$$_s(z := x + y)_{s'}$$
$$s' = \{\text{x} \mapsto 4, \text{y} \mapsto -2, \text{z} \mapsto 2\}$$

2.3.3 New Commands from Old – Operators

The basic building blocks have now been defined, we now require a way of assembling new commands from existing ones.

Sequencing. We now turn to the first means of constructing new commands from old, taking the output from one command and providing it as the input of another. If A and B denote two commands, we can denote their composition by $A\,;\,B$.

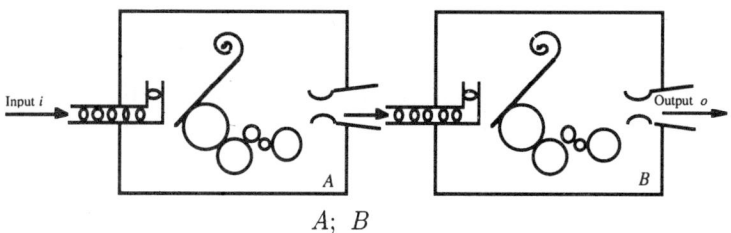

$A;\ B$

The relational definition of this composition is given by:

$$A\,;\,B \triangleq \{(s, o) \mid s : State, o \in State_\bot \cdot \exists t : State \cdot \\ (s, t) \in A \land (t, o) \in B \lor (s, \bot) \in A \land o = \bot\}$$

notice that if the command A loops, then there is no further progress – the composite command $A\,;\,B$ loops.

There are some consequences of this definition. Supposing the *State* for a command is the following (we will assume only one variable is allowed and thus its name can be ignored[4]).

---

[4] If the state variable was n, then n could denote values from the set $State = \{\text{v}, \text{w}, \text{x}, \text{y}, \text{z}\}$ and a possible state value would be $\{n \mapsto \text{v}\}$. The definition for the command A would be:

$$State = \{V, W, X, Y, Z\}$$

A command over this state can be described abstractly by the following relation:

$$A = \{V \mapsto V, W \mapsto \bot, X \mapsto W, X \mapsto \bot, X \mapsto V, Z \mapsto V, Z \mapsto Y\}$$

notice that the command will not accept an input value of Y and will whirr forever (loop) when presented with the input value W. It may or may not loop forever for the input value X.

Supposing we have another command B which is described as follows:

$$B = \{V \mapsto V, W \mapsto Z, W \mapsto \bot, X \mapsto W, X \mapsto \bot, Z \mapsto X\}$$

what happens if we combine these two commands?

$$A \mathbin{;} B$$

What is the result? There are three possibilities, each providing a different computational model. The first possibility is that command A always tries to produce a proper outcome that is acceptable to command B. This would mean that

$$A \mathbin{;} B = \{V \mapsto V, W \mapsto \bot, X \mapsto Z, X \mapsto V, X \mapsto Z, X \mapsto \bot, Z \mapsto V\}$$

Notice that given a helpful or a non-helpful choice, A must try and be helpful to any following command – this means that it the input value Z must alway produce the outcome V since B is not willing to accept Y. This approach is called angelic non-determinism – one can imagine an angel guiding the computation of each command so that it is always possible for it to produce a useful outcome to be passed on to any subsequent command involved in the computation.

The second possibility is that the command A tries to be as awkward as possible – given a choice it always tries to be non-helpful, for the input value Z the command will always produce Y so that B will jam. This approach is called demonic non-determinism – in this case we can imagine having a demon making decisions that guarantee that the total command will always jam if possible (the demon is probably called Murphy). The combination of our two commands is:

$$A = \{(n \mapsto V, n \mapsto V),$$
$$(n \mapsto W, n \mapsto \bot),$$
$$(n \mapsto X, n \mapsto W),$$
$$(n \mapsto X, n \mapsto \bot),$$
$$(n \mapsto X, n \mapsto V),$$
$$(n \mapsto Z, n \mapsto V),$$
$$(n \mapsto Z, n \mapsto Y)\}$$

This level of detail can be left out.

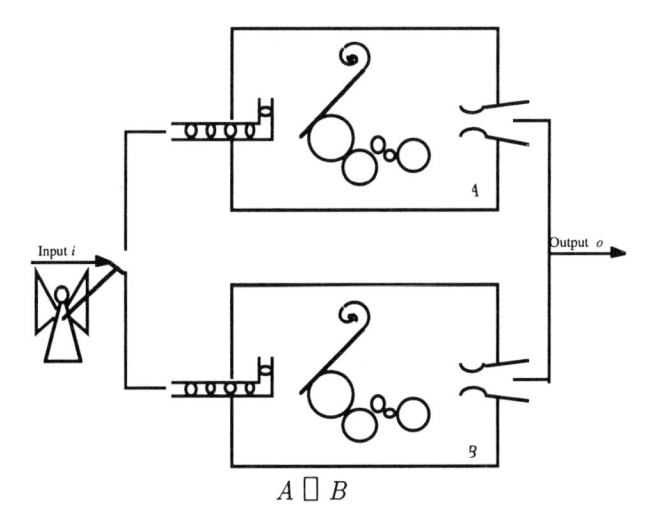

$A\,;\,B$

$A\,;\,B = \{v \mapsto v, w \mapsto \bot, x \mapsto v, x \mapsto z, x \mapsto \bot\}$

The third possibility in neutral non-determinism, neither an angel nor a demon oversees our computation, the result for this is

$A\,;\,B = \{v \mapsto v, w \mapsto \bot, x \mapsto v, x \mapsto z, x \mapsto \bot, z \mapsto v, z \mapsto \cdot\}$

where we have written $z \mapsto \cdot$ to denote the fact that $A\,;\,B$ may jam with an input of z.

For this language angelic non-determinism will be assumed – if commands are joined together with semicolon and if there is a computational path through the combination, then such a path will (must) be found. It must be noted that angelic non-determinism is, in general, not executable – we can only imagine our mechanisms and realize them mathematically (intellectually), we cannot actually build a computer to execute them. To implement angelic non-determinism involves arbitrary look-ahead, or equivalently the ability to back-track. At any point in a computation, the current command must be able to look ahead to see what the effect of any non-deterministic choice is – it must choose a result that allows the whole computation to complete if this is possible. An alternative, but equivalent view is that at any time a command produces an outcome that is not in the domain of the next command it will be necessary to back-track (which will involve undoing the work of commands) and try another outcome of this or any previously executed command until either the situation is resolved and we can continue, or after all outcomes of all commands have been investigated, declare the result miracle.

Non-deterministic Choice. The second technique for assembling new commands from old is non-deterministic choice.

Given two commands denoted by A and B they can be combined to form a new command $A \square B$. For any given input, either A or B will be chosen for execution (but not both). Our angel will make the choice for us, he must not make a choice that could cause problems later on – the choice must be made so that, if possible, the overall mechanism does not jam. If either choice works he will non-deterministically choose one of the commands. If both choices fail, then there is nothing he can do and the result is equivalent to miracle. The relational definition encapsulates this:

$$A \square B \triangleq A \cup B$$

This concept can be generalized (since we are concerned with mathematical, intellectual, execution) to non-deterministic choice between a possibly infinite number of command. Typically a set of commands could be indexed by a (possibly infinite) set I, then the non-deterministic choice between these commands is given by:

$$@i \in I \bullet A_i \triangleq \bigcup \{A_i \mid i \in I\}$$

A type can be used as the index set, and (based on VDM-SL) the following can also be defined:

$$@i : T \bullet A_i \triangleq \bigcup \{A_i \mid i : T\}$$

In VDM-SL types include the value $\bot$, the $i : T$ notation is a reminder that i ranges over all the values of the type T, but *not* including $\bot$.

We can now illustrate that look-ahead or back-tracking is potentially infinite; consider the command A^* defined as follows:

$$A^* \triangleq \text{skip} \square A \square A^2 \square A^3 \square \ldots$$

where

$$A^n \triangleq \underbrace{A\,;\,A\,;\,\ldots\,;\,A}_{n \text{ times}}$$

we can use unbounded choice to write this as

$$A^* \triangleq @n : \mathbb{N} \bullet A^n$$

i.e. we can repeat a command A zero or more times. Angelic non-determinism means that the following program must produce an outcome if possible:

$$A^*\,;\,B$$

and we would need to allow for any number of iterations!

As a final point, we could define bounded choice in terms of unbounded choice. It is only necessary to take the indexing set as $\{A, B\}$ and write

$$C_A \square C_B \triangleq @i \in \{A, B\} \bullet C_i$$

Guarding. The last construction technique is guarding, the execution of a command is guarded by a Boolean expression.

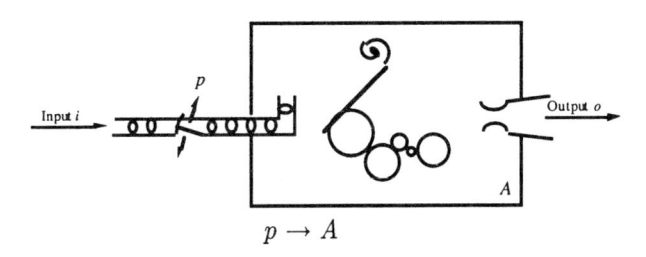

$p \to A$

If the expression is denoted by p and the command denoted by A then the guarded command is denoted by $p \to A$. If the result of evaluating the expression is true then we may execute the command A; if the result is false then the whole command jams.

$$p \to A \triangleq \{(s,o) \mid s : State \cdot M[\![p]\!]s \land (s,o) \in A\}$$

It must be emphasized again that evaluation of an expression must have no side-effects: the state must not change. If an execution model is being used, then if s denotes the value of the state before evaluating the expression E then the value of the state is still denoted by s after E has been evaluated (after we have calculated $M[\![p]\!]s$). An expression denotes a value which is dependent on the state – hence the appearance of the current state value in $M[\![p]\!]s$. Notice that with the language defined so far, the only commands that have a side-effect (change the state) are assignment and havoc; other commands only have a side-effects if they are built from these basic commands.

As we shall see the primitive and basic commands and the operators, together with expressions, are the only tools that are needed to write both our specifications and programs. In fact there are too many commands – we do not really need miracle as this could be defined as

miracle $\triangleq$ false $\to$ skip

2.4 Non-determinism and Partial Commands

Angelic non-determinism and partial commands make certain programs non-executable, so perhaps they should be disallowed. However their ban would remove the ability to specify a system by describing what we want rather than how we obtain it. Not only will we allow non-determinism, we will allow unbounded non-determinism as this will allow us to specify our system. Consider the problem of finding the position i of a value v in an array $a(0, \ldots, N-1)$ – it is guaranteed that v can be found in the array. A program to do this is given by:

@$n \in \{0, \ldots, N-1\} \bullet i := n$;
$a(i) = v \to$ skip

Angelic non-determinism guarantees that the unbounded choice command must choose the right value for n and assign it to i. A compiler would need help to generate efficient code for this, and the efficiency of the code could also depend on what is known about the contents of the array – for example if it was known that the array was sorted, a binary search algorithm could be used. The help the compiler gets in writing code is a program constructed from commands that can be trivially translated into executable code, and it is the responsibility of the programmer to express the algorithm using these easily compiled commands.

This program does assume that the value is in the array – if it not the program is miracle in disguise. It can easily be changed so that it would deal with case were it was not – in this case the program has been designed to do anything:

(@$n \in \{0, \ldots, N-1\} \bullet a(i) = v \to i := n$) $\square$
($\forall k \in \{0, \ldots, N-1\} \cdot a(k) \neq v \to$ (havoc $\square$ loop))

For another example we could (informally) write a program to assign the square root of a natural number $t : \mathbb{N}$ to $r : \mathbb{N}$ as follows:

@$i : \mathbb{N} \bullet (t = i^2) \to r := i$ $\square$ $\neg \exists n : \mathbb{N} \cdot n^2 = t \to$ (havoc $\square$ loop)

If t does not have a square-root that is a natural number, then the result is unspecified, it could be anything including the looping outcome; this is dealing with the problem that it is impossible to find the integer square-root of a natural number that is not a square of a natural number.

The first command of the little program is the one that does the work, it is roughly equivalent to:

$(t = 0) \to r := 0$ $\square$
$(t = 1) \to r := 1$ $\square$
$(t = 4) \to r := 2$ $\square$
$(t = 9) \to r := 3$ $\square$
$\ldots$

For any input value denoted the variable t that is not the square of a natural number, the output from this program is not specified; but this program will assign the square-root of a value that is perfect square to r. By introducing some syntactic sugar, this program (or specification) can be written in a more familiar form:

nat-square-root
chg $r : \mathbb{N}$
pre $\exists n : \mathbb{N} \cdot n^2 = t$

post $r^2 = t$

The first example can also be written in this style:

search
chg $i : \mathbb{N}$
pre $\exists k \in \{0, \ldots, N-1\} \cdot a(k) = v$
post $a(i) = v$

More generally we can consider the following style of command (note that x could stand for a list of variables):

$@x' : X \bullet post(x, x') \rightarrow x := x' \,\square\, \neg pre(x) \rightarrow$ chaos

where chaos has been introduced as an abbreviation for havoc $\square$ loop. Consider what this command does. If the input state value satisfies *pre* then a value x' is chosen to satisfy *post* and then assigned to x. Angelic non-determinism insists that we only assign to x a value such that *post* is satisfied. The following is a syntactic abbreviation for the above combination of commands:

chg $x : X$
pre $pre(x)$
post $post(\overleftarrow{x}, x)$

This is our first piece of 'syntactic sugar' to define the specification command. Informally, under the assumption of *pre*, changing only the variable(s) listed, establish *post*. This is a specification: the *pre* is the contractual obligation for the user of the implementation of this specification. The restriction on the variable(s) x that can be changed and the condition *post* that is to be established is the contractual obligation on the developer. This is a precise mathematical description of a specification which has been defined in terms of our basic language. This command has another abbreviated form that can be written on one line as follows:

$x : [\ pre, \quad post\ ]$

This form is more convenient if we do not need to show the type of the variable x and if the pre- and post-conditions are not very complicated.

It will be seen later that specifications must be total, so perhaps partial commands should be banned. However, partial commands have uses during the process of transforming a specification into a program, and are indispensable, if used in the right way, for writing programs; so we shall keep them. Unbounded non-determinism is useful for writing specifications. Programming can be seen as the process of removing both unbounded commands and angelic non-determinism.

How can we deal with the problems introduced by angelic non-determinism? The problem is caused by partial commands, commands whose domain is not all possible input values. Thus there is an easy solution, the basic commands of the executable part of our language must be total. This means that there is no need to look-ahead (or backtrack) as any outcome of a command in a sequence is acceptable to the next command. Thus we will allow angelic non-determinism in our specifications since these are (in general) not executable, but will have to remove it in order to produce an executable specification – a program. We can define a program as a total specification with bounded look-ahead.

2.5 The Concepts of Predicate Transformers

The relational definitions for our language can be used to define correctness, or the idea of a program satisfying a specification. A program written using the above language can be shown correct using the proof obligation given above. However this involves several steps:

1. writing a specification;
2. constructing a program;
3. using a formal version of the rules sketched above to translate the program into a relation; and
4. showing that the relation (program) satisfies the specification.

There is an alternative approach based on the following idea. Suppose we are given a specification op and we construct a program A that satisfies the specification. Let op be defined as:

op
chg $x : X$
pre $pre(x)$
post $post(\overleftarrow{x}, x)$

where, under the assumption of pre, code that satisfies this specification must establish $post$, changing only the variables in the list $x : X$. The decorated variable $\overleftarrow{x}$ denotes the value of the variable x before the 'execution' of op.

Let $[A]post$ denote a pre-condition that, for an input i that satisfies it, will guarantee the program A will terminate in a state (i.e produce a proper outcome o) that satisfies the post-condition $post$. The term $[A]post$ denotes a transformation of the predicate $post$, which is about outcomes, into a predicate about inputs that will produce an output that satisfies $post$.

The correctness of A can be shown by calculating $[A]post$ and proving that $pre \wedge x = \overleftarrow{x} \Rightarrow [A]post$. The task of calculating $[A]post$ for a program A will be done by providing a mechanism for calculating this predicate for a kernel (core) language, and defining the full language in terms of this kernel.

2.5 The Concepts of Predicate Transformers

To show that this, together with the totality of A, is equivalent to our original definition of correctness is relatively easy. If an input i is in the domain of A and satisfies $[A]post$, then we know that there is a proper outcome t such that $_iA_t$ and $post(i,t)$, i.e. that (roughly speaking):

$$([A]post)(i) \Rightarrow (\forall t \in State \cdot {}_iA_t \Rightarrow post(i,t))$$

since A satisfies the specification op then $pre \Rightarrow [A]post$. For the specification to be useful, it is necessary to guarantee an outcome for a valid input.

$$\forall i: State \cdot pre(i) \Rightarrow \exists o: State \cdot post(i,o)$$

Remembering that

$$(i,t) \in R[\![A]\!] = {}_iA_t$$

all this can be put together to give:

$$\forall i \in State \cdot pre(i) \Rightarrow$$
$$(\exists t \in State \cdot (i,t) \in R[\![A]\!]) \wedge (\forall t \in A \cdot (i,t) \in R[\![A]\!] \Rightarrow post(i,t))$$

which is the original correctness criteria. This sketch motivates our definition of satisfaction:

Definition 2.1
A program A satisfies a specification op given by

op
chg $x : X$
pre $pre(x)$
post $post(\overleftarrow{x}, x)$

if $pre(x) \wedge \overleftarrow{x} = x \Rightarrow [A]post(\overleftarrow{x}, x)$

The additional term involving the decorated identifier x allows the quotation of the input value of x in the post-condition.

Now all we need is a way of calculating $[A]post$. We will do this by providing a way of calculating $[A]post$ for each (basic) command A and for each of the operators. One of the requirements on this transformation of a post-condition to a pre-condition is that an input that satisfies the predicate *must* terminate – we are left in the dark about those inputs that may or may not terminate because of non-determinism: those inputs that may produce either a proper or the improper outcome. The solution is to treat termination and satisfaction of a post-condition separately [24]. For each post-condition Q and command A, two predicates are defined:

$[A]$**true** The termination condition, for an input value that satisfies this predicate, A will terminate and thus produce a proper outcome.

$\langle A \rangle Q$ The weakest liberal pre-condition, for an input value that satisfies this predicate, if A terminates, then the proper outcome will satisfy Q.

Now if an input value terminates and the proper outcome satisfies a predicate Q then we know that it satisfies $[A]\text{true} \wedge \langle A \rangle Q$ so the notation for termination can be extended and we can define:

Definition 2.2
$$[A]Q \triangleq [A]\text{true} \wedge \langle A \rangle Q$$

This property is called the pairing condition and relies on $\langle A \rangle \text{true} = \text{true}$.

It should be noted that $[\ldots]\text{true}$ and $\langle \ldots \rangle R$ are necessary and (more than) sufficient to construct the relation that would also define a command, thus semantics of a programming language can be given in terms of the weakest liberal pre-condition and the termination condition.

2.6 Substitution

Before embarking on the definition of the kernel of the language, it is necessary to define substitution, and this needs an understanding of the concept of bound and free identifiers.

> If the occurrence of an identifier in an expression is bound by a quantifier or unbounded choice operator, then that occurrence is said to be a bound occurrence. An identifier is bound by a quantifier if it occurs in the quantifier's (pattern) bind list (see the full syntax for 'binds' in [6]). The scope of a bound identifier can be deduced (or rather is defined by) from the context of the use of a (pattern) bind in the syntax.
> If the occurrence of an identifier in an expression is not bound by any quantifier, then that occurrence is said to be free occurrence, or the variable is said to be free.

We first define simple substitution: we write $e[x \backslash y]$ for an expression e and two lists of identifiers x and y to mean that all free occurrences of identifiers in the list x that appear in the expression e are replaced by the corresponding identifier in the list y, avoiding – by means of renaming bound variables – free variables becoming bound in e. Note that this is just a syntactic replacement. The notation can be extended by replacing the second list of identifiers by a list of expressions. Thus $e[x \backslash E]$ for a list of identifiers x and a list of expressions E is defined to mean that all free occurrences of identifiers in the list x in the expression e are replaced by the corresponding expression in the list E. There is a problem with this syntactic replacement strategy if there is a possibility of one or more of the expressions in the replacement list being undefined (for certain binding of values to the identifiers of the expression). For example:

$$(x + y)[x\backslash(1/x)]$$

leads from an expression that was defined for all real values of x and y to an expression $((1/x) + y)$ that is not defined for all real values of x and y.

In the standard semantics of VDM-SL, the ranges of expressions are extended to include $\bot$, expressions (and therefore functions) are interpreted as being strict and three valued logic is used. Thus $e[x\backslash E]$ can be given a meaning even when E is undefined. If E is undefined, then for a strict interpretation of the value of an expression e, the result of the substitution must be undefined; for Boolean expressions the result will depend on the predicate in the obvious way. The $e[x\backslash E]$ notation will be extended to work with undefined ($\bot$) such that strictness is preserved.

Definition 2.3
For an expression E of result type T and an expression e then $e[x\backslash E]$ is defined to mean replace all free occurrences of the variable(s) x by the expression(s) E.

Strictness deals with the problem of undefined expressions occurring in the substitution list. Because undefined is a possible result of evaluating an expression, it is useful to have a function to test if a value is defined:

Definition 2.4
If E is an expression of result type T then the predicate $\delta(E:T)$ is defined to mean $\exists u : T \cdot u = E$

Here we follow VDM-SL with the bind expression – since the type T includes the undefined value $\bot$ the symbol ':' is used in place of $\in$ as a reminder that $\bot$ should not be included as a possible binding value.

Two new substitutions can now be introduced for predicates to handle the cases where the value of E could be undefined for certain values of its free variables:

Definition 2.5
For a predicate P and an expression E of type T, define $[x := E]P$ and $\langle x := E \rangle P$ to be

$$[x := E]P \triangleq \delta(E:T) \wedge P[x\backslash E]$$
$$\langle x := E \rangle P \triangleq \delta(E:T) \Rightarrow P[x\backslash E]$$

We will extend these definitions to work with lists of variables and expressions in the obvious way. For example $e[x, y\backslash f, g]$ means simultaneously syntactically replace all instances of x by f and y by g. Note that both f and g can contain x's and y's, but they are not substituted a second time:

$$(x+y+4)[x,y\backslash x+y, a+5] = (x+y)+(a+5)+4$$

the other substitutions can be extended in a similar way:

$$[x, y := F, G](x \wedge y \wedge \neg z) = \delta(F : \mathbb{B}) \wedge \delta(G : \mathbb{B}) \wedge F \wedge G \wedge \neg z$$

It is also useful to define a predicate $\mathsf{trp}(Q(x))$ which is true only if Q is true, otherwise it is false. It is defined as follows:

Definition 2.6
$$\mathsf{trp}(Q(x)) = \forall\, x : X \cdot Q(x)$$

2.6.1 Rules for Substitution

Some basic rules about substitutions. If a function f is defined as follows:

$$f : D \to R$$
$$f(d) \triangleq e$$

then

$$f(a) \text{ is equivalent to } e[d\backslash a]$$

It is also possible to show that

$$[y := g][x := f]R \Leftrightarrow [x, y := f[y\backslash g], g]R$$
$$[x := g][x := f]R \Leftrightarrow [x := f[x\backslash g]]R$$

2.7 The Formal Semantics of the Kernel Language

The semantics will be given in terms of a termination set and the weakest liberal pre-condition with respect to an arbitrary post-condition Q. First, a definition of two programs being semantically equivalent is given:

Definition 2.7
Two programs A and B will be said to be semantically equivalent if, for any given post-condition Q:

$$[A]\mathsf{true} \Leftrightarrow [B]\mathsf{true} \text{ and}$$
$$\langle A \rangle Q \Leftrightarrow \langle B \rangle Q$$

Two programs are identical if they terminate for identical inputs and when they terminate they establish identical post-conditions.

2.7.1 The Bounded Commands

First the bounded, finite, commands and operators are defined.

2.7 The Formal Semantics of the Kernel Language

Two primitive commands. The semantics of the primitive command skip are:

$\langle \mathsf{skip} \rangle Q \triangleq Q$
$[\mathsf{skip}]\mathsf{true} \triangleq \mathsf{true}$

Informally, the skip command does nothing and it can be activated in any state. Since it does nothing, the only way that the post-condition Q can be established is if it is already satisfied. The semantics of the primitive command loop are:

$\langle \mathsf{loop} \rangle Q \triangleq \mathsf{true}$
$[\mathsf{loop}]\mathsf{true} \triangleq \mathsf{false}$

Informally, the loop command only produces the improper outcome $\bot$; it can be activated in any state. If it terminates it will establish true; however, it never terminates.

The assignment command. The semantics of the assignment command of the form $x := E$, where the expression E has the result type T and the variable x is also of type T, are defined by:

$\langle x := E \rangle Q \triangleq \delta(E:X) \Rightarrow Q[x \backslash E]$
$[x := E]\mathsf{true} \triangleq \delta(E:X)$

Informally, the current value denoted by x is changed to denote the value denoted by the expression E. If Q is to be satisfied after executing the assignment, Q with x replaced by E must be true before execution. The assignment command will only terminate if the evaluation of the expression is defined.

The semicolon operator. The semantics of the composite command $A; B$ are defined by:

$\langle A; B \rangle Q \triangleq \langle A \rangle \langle B \rangle Q$
$[A; B]\mathsf{true} \triangleq [A]\mathsf{true} \wedge \langle A \rangle [B]\mathsf{true}$

Informally, activate A, then activate B providing A completes.

For B to deliver an outcome that satisfies Q, the corresponding input value must satisfy $\langle B \rangle Q$. Thus the outcome from A must satisfy this predicate which means the input to A must satisfy $\langle A \rangle \langle B \rangle Q$. If B is to terminate, then A must deliver a value that satisfies the termination pre-condition of B which is denoted by $[B]\mathsf{true}$. The pre-condition for this must be $[A]\mathsf{true} \wedge \langle A \rangle [B]\mathsf{true}$.

Bounded choice. The semantics of bounded choice operator $A \; \square \; B$ are defined by

$\langle A \; \square \; B \rangle Q \triangleq \langle A \rangle Q \wedge \langle B \rangle Q$
$[A \; \square \; B]\mathsf{true} \triangleq [A]\mathsf{true} \wedge [B]\mathsf{true}$

Non-deterministic choice means, operationally, execute either A or B. If the input value is not in the domain of A, B must be executed. If the input value is not in the domain of B, A must be executed. If the input value is in the domain of both A and B, make a non-deterministic choice between the two commands. It could be that the input is not in the domain of either command, in this case $A \,\square\, B$ is partial, and the mechanism jams.

Now $\langle A \rangle Q$ defines those states that, if A terminates, will terminate in state satisfying Q; $\langle B \rangle Q$ defines those states that, if B terminates, will terminate in a state that satisfies Q. Since either A or B could be chosen non-deterministically, then the only way we can guarantee that a result of $A \,\square\, B$ could terminate in a state that satisfies Q is to take the conjunction of the two pre-conditions. A similar explanation can be given for the termination condition.

The definition of the bounded choice operator is strange at first, the temptation might be to define $\langle A \,\square\, B \rangle Q$ as $\langle A \rangle Q \lor \langle B \rangle Q$ (and a similar form for termination) since the semantics are to either execute A or B. However this is wrong; the angel that is aiding the execution of our programs can choose a path that guarantees an outcome occurs if this is possible, it cannot read our minds! If we write $x := +1 \,\square\, x := -1$, this is specifying that x is to be set either to $+1$ or to -1. Thus (using the correct definition):

$$\langle x := +1 \,\square\, x := -1 \rangle x = +1$$
$$\Longleftrightarrow$$
$$\langle x := +1 \rangle x = +1 \land \langle x := -1 \rangle x = +1$$
$$\Longleftrightarrow$$
$$+1 = +1 \land -1 = +1$$
$$\Longleftrightarrow$$
false

We cannot complain if our angel chooses one answer, when we intended the other.

Guarding. The semantics of the guarded command $p \to A$ are defined by

$$\langle p \to A \rangle Q \triangleq p \Rightarrow \langle A \rangle Q$$
$$[p \to A]\text{true} \triangleq p \Rightarrow [A]\text{true}$$

Activate A in a state in which p is true. If the command cannot be activated it is then in a deadlocked situation with its environment. The weakest liberal pre-condition just states that if p is true then the guarded command will establish Q provided A does. If p is false, as there is no output then Q is vacuously established. The termination condition states that the guarded command will terminate if p is true and A terminates. If p is false, there are no outcomes and therefore A 'terminates' – it does not even produce the looping outcome. This at first sight seems strange, but the semantics are explicitly modelling looping outcomes.

The priority of operators from low to high is:

'☐', '→', ';', and ':='.

Brackets can be used to turn a group of commands into the syntactic equivalent of a single command.

2.7.2 The Unbounded Commands

The commands defined so far only allow finite programs to be written; there is no construct that allows an arbitrary number of commands to be strung together – some unbounded commands are necessary. The next command and operator provide building blocks for constructing unbounded programs.

Another primitive command. The semantics of the primitive command havoc are:

$\langle \text{havoc} \rangle Q \triangleq \text{trp}(Q)$
$[\text{havoc}]\text{true} \triangleq \text{true}$

where $\text{trp}(\text{true}) = \text{true}$ and $\text{trp}(P) = \text{false}$ for all other predicates P.

Informally, the havoc command can establish anything and it decides what it will establish. For any input we cannot guarantee that the corresponding outcome will satisfy a given post-condition, thus in general the calculated pre-condition is false, but it is also necessary for $\langle \text{havoc} \rangle \text{true} = \text{true}$ – thus the form of its definition. The havoc command will always produce a proper outcome; its main use will be in the definition of an assert command – note that the havoc cannot be implemented, for it would be a truly random number generator.

Unbounded choice. The semantics of bounded choice operator can be extended to a potentially infinite number of choices and can be defined by:

$\langle @i \in I \bullet A_i \rangle Q \triangleq \forall i \in I \cdot \langle A_i \rangle Q$
$[@i \in I \bullet A_i]\text{true} \triangleq \forall i \in I \cdot [A_i]\text{true}$

where I is some (possibly infinite) index set. Informally, activate one of the A_i's. A type can be used as the index, and (based on standard VDM-SL) the following can also be defined:

$\langle @i : T \bullet A_i \rangle Q \triangleq \forall i : T \cdot \langle A_i \rangle Q$
$[@i : T \bullet A_i]\text{true} \triangleq \forall i : T \cdot [A_i]\text{true}$

In standard VDM-SL types include the value $\bot$, remember that the $i : T$ notation is a reminder that i ranges over all the values of the type T, but *not* including $\bot$.

This completes the definition of a core, or kernel language. This language can be used to write both specifications and programs. If a program is to be executable, then some syntactic restrictions are needed to limit the look-ahead (or equivalently backtracking) that is required and to provide hints to the compiler. Thus it will be useful for readers of programs and necessary for compiler writers to introduce some syntactic sugar into the language.

2.8 The Weakest Liberal Pre-conditions, Termination, and Relations

This chapter started by giving a relational semantics for the basic commands and operators of the language. We can relate the predicate transformer approach given above to the relational approach in the following way: if we have a relational definition for a command A, we can define the predicate transformers for that command as follows (cheating slightly with the use of $\bot$):

$$\langle A \rangle R \triangleq \forall o' \in State_\bot \cdot {}_iA_{o'} \Rightarrow R(o') \vee o' = \bot$$
$$[A]\text{true} \triangleq \forall o' \in State_\bot \cdot {}_iA_{o'} \Rightarrow o' \neq \bot$$

This is just a formalization of the definitions given earlier. For the above to work it is necessary to treat $\bot$ as a value in the style of [18], hence the use of '$\in$' rather than ':' in the binding expression. Because of the presence of $\bot$, these are informal 'formal' definitions, making them formal will require $\bot$ to be hidden; this is another reason the predicate transformer approach has been taken – $\bot$ need not be mentioned directly.

With these definitions, we can show that:

$$[A]R = [A]\text{true} \wedge \langle A \rangle R$$

and that

$$[A]R \triangleq \forall o' \in State_\bot \cdot {}_iA_{o'} \Rightarrow R(o') \wedge o' \neq \bot$$

Let us now try doing things the other way around. Given a predicate transformer definition of a command A, if we want to produce a relational definition we can proceed as follows. A first try would be to consider an output value Y (for the moment we will write an output value in upper-case to remind ourself that it is arbitrary, but fixed). Then the input values for which A terminates and produce Y as the output value are given by:

$$[A](x = Y)$$

This predicate defines those input values that terminate and give Y as the output value, this would indicate that we should write:

$$_xA_Y = [A](x = Y)$$

2.8 The Weakest Liberal Pre-conditions, Termination, and Relations

with suitable restrictions on the use of Y in A. However, this doesn't quite do the job – there would be problems with an A that had a relational definition as follows:

$$\{\ldots, \text{I} \mapsto \bot, \text{I} \mapsto Y, \ldots\}$$

since I can non-deterministically produce either Y or $\bot$ it would not appear in the relation derived from its weakest pre-condition definition. Another approach needs to be tried: since the problem is with inputs that produce improper outcomes another possibility is to use the weakest liberal pre-condition and define:

$$_xA_Y = \langle A \rangle (x = Y)$$

Though this picks up the $\text{I} \mapsto Y$ term, a little thought shows that any input value that only gives the improper outcome $\bot$ as output will also be associated with Y. A slightly twisted approach will solve the problem. Now $x \neq Y$ defines those (output) values that are not equal to Y and $\langle A \rangle (x \neq Y)$ defines those input values that either do not terminate or do not produce Y as the corresponding output value. Thus those values that do not satisfy this predicate, if they terminate, must produce Y – hence the following definition:

$$_xA_Y = \neg \langle A \rangle (x \neq Y)$$

Now $[A]$true is all those input values that either terminate with a proper outcome or are not acceptable to A – they are not in the domain of A. Thus any value in $\neg [A]$true will have at least one outcome that is $\bot$. Thus

$$_sA_\bot \Rightarrow \neg [A]\text{true}(s)$$

This fact allows us to characterize those values that must be mapped to bottom in the relational definition.

If a command has been defined by giving the weakest liberal pre-condition, $\langle A \rangle R$, and the termination set, $[A]$true, we have sufficient information to build the full definition of A as a relation. Now to formalize how this can be done – we start by defining two operators, one that defines a predicate and one that defines a relation:

Definition 2.8
    pr $A = [A]$true
    $_i(\text{in } A)_o \triangleq \neg \langle A \rangle (i \neq o)$

The command A is defined as

$$A = (@x' \in State \bullet {_x}(\text{in } A)_{x'} \to x := x') \,\square\, \neg \text{pr } A \to \text{loop}$$

Those inputs that only produce the improper outcome are covered by the second term of the choice operator, the proper outcomes are covered by the first term, and those inputs which could either produce a proper or improper outcome are covered by the non-determinism of the choice operator. From this definition we can calculate $\langle A \rangle R$:

$$\langle @x' \in State \bullet {}_x(\text{in } A)_{x'} \to x := x' \,\square\, \neg \text{pr } A \to \text{loop} \rangle R$$

$\Longleftrightarrow$

$$(\forall x' \in State \cdot {}_x(\text{in } A)_{x'} \Rightarrow \langle x := x' \rangle R) \land (\neg \text{pr } A \Rightarrow \langle \text{loop} \rangle R)$$

$\Longleftrightarrow$

$$(\forall x' \in State \cdot {}_x(\text{in } A)_{x'} \Rightarrow \langle x := x' \rangle R) \land (\neg \text{pr } A \Rightarrow \text{true})$$

$\Longleftrightarrow$

$$\forall x' \in State \cdot {}_x(\text{in } A)_{x'} \Rightarrow \langle x := x' \rangle R$$

$\Longleftrightarrow$

$$\forall x' \in State_\bot \cdot {}_x(\text{in } A)_{x'} \Rightarrow (\text{def}(x') \Rightarrow R(x'))$$

$\Longleftrightarrow$

$$\langle A \rangle R$$

and $[A]$true:

$$[@x' \in State \bullet {}_x(\text{in } A)_{x'} \to x := x' \,\square\, \neg \text{pr } A \to \text{loop}]\text{true}$$

$\Longleftrightarrow$

$$(\forall x' \in State \cdot {}_x(\text{in } A)_{x'} \Rightarrow [x := x']\text{true}) \land (\neg \text{pr } A \Rightarrow [\text{loop}]\text{true})$$

$\Longleftrightarrow$

$$(\forall x' \in State \cdot {}_x(\text{in } A)_{x'} \Rightarrow \text{def}(x')) \land \text{pr } A$$

$\Longleftrightarrow$

$$[A]\text{true}$$

It is worth investigating the antepenultimate term in the derivation of $\langle A \rangle R$ given above, we have:

$$\langle A \rangle R \equiv \forall x' \in State \cdot {}_x(\text{in } A)_{x'} \Rightarrow \langle x := x' \rangle R$$

which can be rewritten as

$$\langle A \rangle R \equiv \forall x' \in State \cdot \neg \langle A \rangle x \neq x' \lor R(x')$$

An informal description of this property is that for each x', either A never produces x', or if it does then x' satisfy R. The property also shows that to define the weakest liberal pre-condition of a command A, there is no need to define $\langle A \rangle R$ for all R, it is only necessary to define $\langle A \rangle i \neq o$. This result should not be too surprising, as it is this predicate that defines the proper outcomes of A.

The above derivation also justifies the definition of two programs being semantically equivalent given in Definition 2.7: if two programs are semantically equivalent, by this definition they will have the same relational description.

skip	Do nothing. This command can be activated in any state.
loop	Loop. This command can be activated in any state and always produces the improper outcome.
$x := E$	Assignment; change the value denoted by x to the value of the expression E.
$A \mathbin{;} B$	Sequencing; A and B are commands. Activate A, then activate B.
$A \mathbin{[\!]} B$	Bounded choice; A and B are commands. Activate either A or B.
$p \to A$	Guarding; p is a predicate and A is a command. Activate A in a state in which p is true.
havoc	Do anything. This command can be activated in any state. and could produce any proper outcome.
$@i \in I \bullet A_i$	Unbounded choice; A_i are commands indexed by I. Activate any A_i.

Priority of operators from low to high:

'$[\!]$', '$\to$', '$;$', and '$:=$'.

Brackets can be used to turn a group of commands into the syntactic equivalent of a single command.

Fig. 2.1. The kernel language

2.9 Executable Programs

To be able to execute a program written in this language, it is necessary to remove all the unbounded commands and to remove the need for unbounded look-ahead, or equivalently remove the need to back-track, by the removal of partial commands. Rather than just writing a specification and then checking for and removing such problems, it is easier to introduce some syntactic restrictions that disallow any unbounded commands and remove the need for any look-ahead. Unbounded commands can be removed by disallowing infinite index sets in the unbounded choice command. Unbounded look-ahead can be removed by restricting the use of partial commands and completing the domain of those that remain so they are no longer partial. The development strategy we shall adopt is to start with a program written for ease of intellectual execution, a specification, and then provide some transformation rules that allow the specification to be massaged into a syntactic form for ease of execution on a computer.

2.10 Summary

The basic programming language is given in Fig. 2.1. The semantics of the language have been defined mathematically. A way of writing very abstract programs has been described (these we call specifications). A definition of an executable specification has been given (these we call programs), together with the concept of a program satisfying a specification. If commands to do input and output are provided, we would have sufficient tools to write any program. As a programmer needs some hints on how to structure their programs to guarantee the programs are executable (and perhaps even readable), some syntactic sugar for frequently used combinations of commands of the kernel language will need to be introduced. In future chapters these concepts will be extended to provide a full specification and programming language together with a development method to produce executable programs that satisfy their specifications.

A final point: it has been found that showing programmers that it is possible to prove programs correct can have a radical effect on the way they approach programming. Bugs can no longer be 'blamed' on some outside interference – it is possible to develop correct programs. By carrying out a proof of correctness, by showing that a program satisfies its specification, the level of confidence in the correctness of a program has been increased. The use of formal methods in computing should be seen as doing just that. We are probably more confident in those buildings put together by skilled engineers who have checked their designs mathematically than those buildings designed on the back of an envelope by amateurs. This philosophy should be carried over to the builders of computer programs.

3. Concepts and Properties

Before the problem of transforming specifications into executable programs is tackled, the properties of the core language introduced in the previous chapter need to be investigated. The properties of the core language will also provide some insight into the semantics of the language. Many of these properties will be useful when defining additional commands or carrying out a refinement. The theorems will provide an understanding of how the commands of the language interact and provide a way for programs to be manipulated and simplified. The proofs of many of the theorems are straightforward and many are left for the reader.

It is also necessary to extend the core programming language so that it is easier to identify an executable form. Certain sequences of commands occur frequently enough or denote useful ideas that it is worth introducing abbreviations (or syntactic sugar) for them. The syntactic sugar will be used to make constructs such as declarations, alternation (the 'if' command) and iteration (the 'do' command) more obvious.

3.1 More Commands

The extensions to the core language that were introduced informally in the previous chapter need to be defined.

Iteration. The first step is to introduce the syntax and semantics for finite iteration, a simple iterative command can be defined:

Definition 3.1
$$A^0 \triangleq \mathsf{skip}$$
$$A^n \triangleq A \,;\, A^{n-1}$$

An unbounded form of iteration can be defined using unbounded choice:

Definition 3.2
$$A^* \triangleq @n : \mathbb{N} \bullet A^n$$
$$A^+ \triangleq @n : \mathbb{N}_1 \bullet A^n$$

3. Concepts and Properties

This infinite iteration looks a likely candidate on which to base the definition of a looping construct, however it is too well-behaved to be used as the basis for defining a while-loop, for it is not quite unbounded enough and thus does not encompass all possibilities for looping – more of this problem in a later chapter.

More primitive statements. Two more primitive commands that introduce useful concepts can be defined, these are miracle and chaos.

Definition 3.3
$$\text{miracle} \triangleq \text{false} \rightarrow \text{skip}$$
$$\text{chaos} \triangleq \text{havoc} \;\square\; \text{loop}$$

Informally, the miracle command can establish anything – anything the user requires; however it cannot be activated in any state and does not produce any outcomes. The command chaos can produce any outcome – it can produce any proper outcome or loop forever; remember havoc must produce a proper outcome, it cannot loop. A third primitive command, slip, is introduced just for completeness:

Definition 3.4
$$\text{slip} \triangleq \text{skip} \;\square\; \text{loop}$$

Many of the theorems concerning properties of commands involve showing that two command expressions are equivalent – the two forms have the same semantics. This is normally done by showing that the termination conditions are equivalent and the weakest liberal pre-conditions are equivalent. An example will show how this style of proof can be done:

Theorem 3.1
For any command A:

$$\text{miracle} = \text{false} \rightarrow A$$

Proof
Now for the termination condition:

$\quad$ [false $\rightarrow A$]true
$\iff$ semantics
$\quad$ false $\Rightarrow [A]$true
$\iff$ predicate calculus
$\quad$ true
$\iff$ predicate calculus
$\quad$ false $\Rightarrow$ true
$\iff$ semantics
$\quad$ [false $\rightarrow$ skip]true

$\iff$ definition of miracle

   [miracle]true

and for the weakest liberal pre-condition:

   $\langle \text{false} \to A \rangle R$

$\iff$ semantics

   false $\Rightarrow$ $\langle A \rangle R$

$\iff$ predicate calculus

   true

$\iff$ predicate calculus

   false $\Rightarrow$ $\langle \text{skip} \rangle R$

$\iff$ semantics

   $\langle \text{false} \to \text{skip} \rangle R$

$\iff$ definition of miracle

   $\langle \text{miracle} \rangle R$

and by Definition 2.7 the two constructions are semantically equivalent. ∎

The proof of many of the other theorems of this and subsequent chapters follow a similar pattern, and are left for the reader. A convention that will be used in many of the proofs that are presented is that the justifications for a step of 'semantics' or 'predicate calculus' will be left for the reader to supply.

Assertion. The semantics of the assert command are defined by:

Definition 3.5

$$\{p\} \triangleq p \to \text{skip} \;\square\; \neg p \to \text{chaos}$$

Informally if $\{p\}$ is activated in a state in which p is true then it is equivalent to skip, otherwise the command is equivalent to chaos. This command is used to make assertions about the state at a particular point in the program. We will write $\{p\}\, A$ as an abbreviation for $\{p\}\,;\, A$. The semantics can easily be derived from the definition:

$$\langle \{p\} \rangle Q \iff p \wedge Q \vee \text{trp}(Q) \qquad\qquad [\{p\}]\text{true} \iff p$$

The purpose of the assert command is to provide a mechanism for checking the progress of the execution of a program – checking that it is proceeding along the right lines. The result of chaos rather than loop for those inputs that do not satisfy the assertion allows a compiler to ignore the statement when generating executable code. If the outcome had to be loop, code to check the predicate would need to be produced. The result of a false assertion is chosen to be unpredictable, it is equivalent to chaos. Because of the semantics for this command, it is not necessary for a compiler to generate any code.

Unbounded specification. This command has already been discussed in the previous chapter, for a variable x of type X, the specification command can be defined as:

Definition 3.6
$$x : [\ pre,\quad post\ ]\ \triangleq\ @x' : X \bullet post(x, x') \to x := x'\ \square\ \neg pre \to chaos$$

If the input state value satisfies *pre* then a value x' is chosen to satisfy *post* and then assigned to x. Angelic non-determinism insists that we only assign to x a value such that *post* is satisfied. The following alternative syntax will also be used if the type of the variable x needs to be recorded, or if either of the pre- or post-conditions are particularly complicated:

Definition 3.7
chg $x : X$
pre $pre(x)$ $\quad\triangleq\quad @x' : X \bullet post(x, x') \to x := x'\ \square\ \neg pre \to chaos$
post $post(\overleftarrow{x}, x)$

This completes the first part of the definition of some extensions to the small language. So far we have a programming language that can really only be used for writing abstract programs that can be executed on an abstract machine rather than on a proper computer. There is still a problem with unbounded commands and unbounded look-ahead caused by angelic non-determinism that makes writing a compiler for this language impossible. The next step will be to introduce more syntactic sugar for constructs that restrict any look-ahead. We need some restrictions on exactly what can be written – for this we need the concept of the domain of a command and feasibility.

3.2 The Domain of a Command

The expression $[A]$true characterizes those states from which proper outcomes (error free termination) is guaranteed; then what does $[A]$false characterize? It defines those inputs that have outcomes that satisfy false, but no value satisfies false, thus this predicate characterizes those input values that have no outcomes. The negation of this predicate defines those inputs that do produce an outcome. We thus define the feasibility set or guards of a command as follows:

$$\mathcal{G}(A) = \neg [A]\text{false}$$

Informally we have:

$\mathcal{G}(A)$
$\Longleftrightarrow$
$\neg [A]\text{false}$

3.2 The Domain of a Command

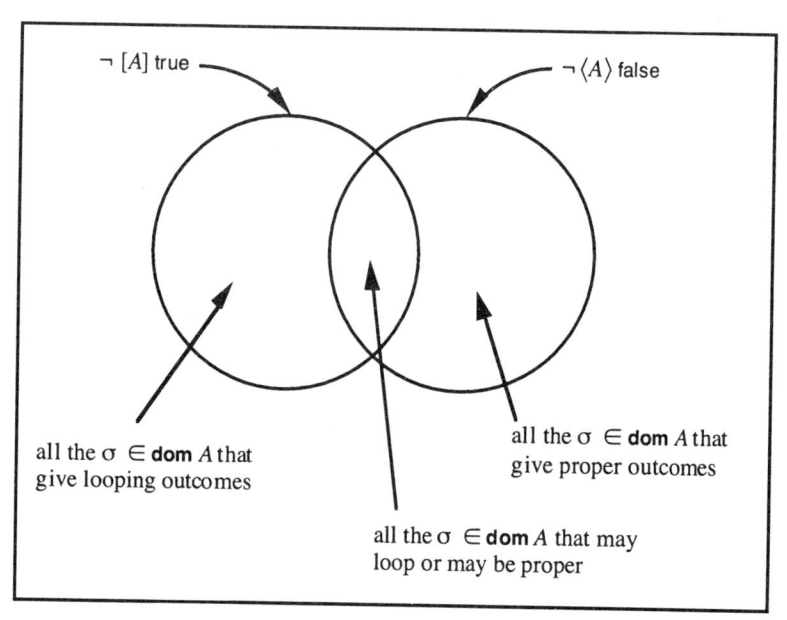

Fig. 3.1. The domain of a command.

(Figure shows two overlapping circles. Left circle labeled "¬[A] true" with arrow pointing to "all the σ ∈ **dom** A that give looping outcomes". Right circle labeled "¬⟨A⟩ false" with arrow pointing to "all the σ ∈ **dom** A that give proper outcomes". The intersection is labeled "all the σ ∈ **dom** A that may loop or may be proper".)

$$\iff$$
$$\neg \forall o' \in State_\bot \cdot {}_i A_{o'} \Rightarrow \text{false} \land o' \neq \bot$$
$$\iff$$
$$\neg \forall o' \in State_\bot \cdot \neg {}_i A_{o'}$$
$$\iff$$
$$\exists o' \in State_\bot \cdot {}_i A_{o'}$$
$$\iff$$
$$\text{dom } A \qquad \text{(interpreting } A \text{ as a relation)}$$

which provides the motivation behind the definition: $\mathcal{G}(A)$ defines the domain of the command A; this includes those input values whose outcome is improper – those inputs that cause the command to loop. It should be realized that even if an input value i satisfies the predicate $[A]$true this does not guarantee an outcome; only that if i has an outcome, it is a *proper* outcome. An input value that is not in the domain of A will satisfy this predicate, but will not have an outcome. For an input value i to be guaranteed a proper outcome in must both satisfy the termination predicate and also be in the domain of A. Now the pairing condition gives $[A]$false $= [A]$true$\land \langle A \rangle$false thus:

$$\mathcal{G}(A) = \neg [A]\text{false} = \neg [A]\text{true} \lor \neg \langle A \rangle \text{false}$$

We can look at each of the terms that make up this expression.

¬[A]false   The domain of the command A; there are outcomes from an input σ that satisfies this predicate.

¬[A]true   This predicate defines the set of inputs σ such that not all outcomes of σ are proper.

¬⟨A⟩false   This predicate defines the set of inputs such that not all outcomes of σ are improper (loop), thus there is at least one proper outcome from A.

Thus the set defined by [A]true ∩ ¬⟨A⟩false contains all those inputs that are in the domain of A and produce proper outcomes; the set ¬[A]true ∩ ⟨A⟩false contains all those inputs that are in the domain of A and produce an improper outcome – in execution terms, the input causes the command to loop forever. Finally ¬[A]true ∩ ¬⟨A⟩false defines those inputs that are in the domain of A and have outcomes – the inputs that may cause a loop or may produce a result. These results are illustrated in Fig. 3.1. It can be seen that [A]true defines both the input values that have proper outcomes (that must terminate) and if A is not total, those state values that are not in the domain of A:

Theorem 3.2
$\neg \mathcal{G}(A) \Rightarrow [A]\text{true}$

Proof
Now false $\Rightarrow$ true, so as A is monotonic[1]:

   [A]false $\Rightarrow$ [A]true

$\iff$

   $\neg \mathcal{G}(A) \Rightarrow [A]\text{true}$

■

A feasible program is implementable, it can be transformed into a form that can be executed on a computer. The main restriction is that all commands must be total – the law of the excluded miracle holds:

$\mathcal{G}(A) = \neg[A]\text{false} = \text{true}$

Feasibility can be defined as follows:

Definition 3.8
A program A is feasible iff [A]false = false. Otherwise it is infeasible, or miraculous.

This is equivalent to the property that A is total – not partial. Notice that $\mathcal{G}(\text{miracle}) = \text{false}$ and that for partial commands, any input value not in the domain of the command will alway produce correct output (since the

---
[1] See Theorem 3.31 on page 54.

command does not produce any output, it is impossible to show that the 'output' is wrong).

It is also interesting to check the domains of each of the fundamental commands, the following theorem does this.

Theorem 3.3

$\mathcal{G}(\text{skip})$
$\mathcal{G}(\text{loop})$
$\mathcal{G}(x := E)$
$\mathcal{G}(A \,;\, B) = \neg[A]\neg\mathcal{G}(B)$
$\mathcal{G}(A \,\square\, B) = \mathcal{G}(A) \vee \mathcal{G}(B)$
$\mathcal{G}(p \rightarrow A) = p \wedge \mathcal{G}(A)$
$\mathcal{G}(\text{havoc})$
$\mathcal{G}(@i \in I \bullet A_i) = \exists i \in I \cdot \mathcal{G}(A_i)$

The basic commands are all total, the domains of constructed commands depend on the domains of their components and any guards that are used.

Proof
We will prove two of these, the others follow in a similar style. For the ; operator:

$\mathcal{G}(A \,;\, B)$
$\Longleftrightarrow$ definition of the domain operator
$\neg[A \,;\, B]\text{false}$
$\Longleftrightarrow$ semantics
$\neg[A][B]\text{false}$
$\Longleftrightarrow$ semantics
$\neg[A]\neg\mathcal{G}(B)$

For unbounded choice:

$\mathcal{G}(@i \in I \bullet A_i)$
$\Longleftrightarrow$ definition of the domain operator
$\neg[@i \in I \bullet A_i]\text{false}$
$\Longleftrightarrow$ semantics
$\neg\forall i \in I \cdot [A_i]\text{false}$
$\Longleftrightarrow$
$\exists i \in I \cdot \neg[A_i]\text{false}$
$\Longleftrightarrow$
$\exists i \in I \cdot \mathcal{G}(A_i)$

■

Angelic non-determinism requires that the domain of $A \,\square\, B$ is the union of the domains of A and B. The domain of a guarded command must be the intersection of the set of valid inputs as defined by the guard and the domain of the command itself. Finally non-determinism demands that the domain of an unbounded choice must be the union of domains of the individual commands available in the choice.

For a sequence, if B is total, then the domain of $A\ ;\ B$ depends on the domain of A:

Corollary 3.1
If B is total then
$$\mathcal{G}(A\ ;\ B) = \mathcal{G}(A)$$

Proof
$$\mathcal{G}(A\ ;\ B)$$
$$\iff$$
$$\neg[A]\neg\mathcal{G}(B)$$
$$\iff$$
$$\neg[A]\neg\text{true}$$
$$\iff$$
$$\neg[A]\text{false}$$
$$\iff$$
$$\mathcal{G}(A)$$

∎

By Theorem 3.3, all the basic commands are total; and all of the constructors, except guarding, will result in a total command if their components are total. The only way of introducing a partial command is with guarding: even if A is total, in general $p \to A$ is partial. We could ban this construct, but then programming would become difficult (if not impossible). How can we deal with guarded command? One way to do this is to make certain a guarded command is in a context where angelic non-determinism means that they can always be executed. We can guarantee this if a command is in a context where it is feasible. Consider

$$\{p\}\ A$$

Providing $p \Rightarrow \mathcal{G}(A)$ then the partial command A (other than miracle) can always be executed: for an input value, if the assertion p is true, the assert command is equivalent to skip and A will execute. If p is false then $\{p\}$ can produce any outcome – angelic non-determinism demands that it either produces an outcome in the domain of A so that A can execute or if this is not possible, $\bot$. Thus if A is total then

$$\{p\}\ q \to A$$

is total provided $p \Rightarrow q$. Certainly if A is total, then $\{p\}p \to A$ is total. Also

$p \to A \,[\!]\, \neg p \to B$

is total; in fact it is equivalent to our familiar friend

if p then A else B

However we will not be using this version of selection in the extended language, there is a more general, symmetric, construct that can be built; this will be introduced in Chapter 9.

As the two examples above suggest, the easiest way of ensuring feasibility is to enforce certain sequences of commands by syntax such that only total commands are allowed. Subsequent chapters will show ways of doing this.

Now a command A is implementable if $\mathcal{G}(A)$ is true – it is interesting to apply this to a specification, for a list of variables of types X:

$\neg [x : [\; pre, \quad post \;]]\mathsf{false}$

$\iff$

$\neg [@x' : X \bullet post(x, x') \to x := x' \,[\!]\, \neg pre(x) \to \mathsf{chaos}]\mathsf{false}$

$\iff$

$\neg (\forall x' : X \cdot post(x, x') \Rightarrow [x := x']\mathsf{false} \land pre(x))$

$\iff$

$\neg (pre(x) \land \forall x' : X \cdot \neg post(x, x') \lor \mathsf{false})$

$\iff$

$\neg pre(x) \lor \exists x' : X \cdot post(x, x')$

$\iff$

$pre(x) \Rightarrow \exists x' : X \cdot post(x, x')$

This is the usual definition for an implementable specification.

3.3 Some Properties of Commands

In the following A, B, and C denote any command; p and q denote predicates that are defined everywhere on the state.

3.3.1 Sequence

Writing $A \,;\, B$ means execute the command A followed by the command B, taking care to make non-deterministic choices so that the result of executing A will, if possible, allow B to be executed. Because, in general, substitution is not commutative, the semicolon operator is not commutative:

$A \,;\, B \neq B \,;\, A$

However, the semicolon operator is associative:

Theorem 3.4
   $A\,;\,(B\,;\,C) = (A\,;\,B)\,;\,C$
□

It is not necessary to write any brackets when writing down a sequence of commands. An important thing to notice that semicolon is an dyadic *operator* and is written *between* commands, it is not a terminator that is written after a command, writing

   $A;\ B;$

is both meaningless and wrong! It is rather like writing $4 + 2 +\,$.
   We expect skip to really mean do nothing:

Theorem 3.5
   $A\,;\,\text{skip} = \text{skip}\,;\,A = A$
□

and once we have either a miracle or a loop, we cannot get rid of it:

Theorem 3.6
   $\text{loop}\,;\,A = \text{loop}$
   $\text{miracle}\,;\,A = \text{miracle}$
□

The order of combining these primitive commands with others is significant:

Theorem 3.7
   $A\,;\,\text{loop} = \mathcal{G}(A) \rightarrow \text{loop}$
   $A\,;\,\text{miracle} = \neg[A]\text{true} \rightarrow \text{loop}$
□

In the first case, only those input values in the domain of A will get through to the execution of the loop command, and angelic nondeterminism demands that if A can loop, it must – an abstract program must try to avoid jamming.

3.3.2 Bounded Non-deterministic Choice

Some properties of the choice operator, it is associative:

Theorem 3.8
   $A \sqcap (B \sqcap C) = (A \sqcap B) \sqcap C$
□

Because of this, brackets can be left out from sequences of this operator.
   It should not matter in which order we non-deterministically choose to do either A or B, the choice operator is commutative:

Theorem 3.9
$$A \sqcap B = B \sqcap A$$
□

Choosing between a command and itself provides no new function:

Theorem 3.10
$$A \sqcap A = A$$
□

Angelic non-determinism means that if we combine a command with miracle, then we must execute the command:

Theorem 3.11
$$A \sqcap \text{miracle} = A$$

□

Combining chaos with a command is just chaos:

Theorem 3.12
$$A \sqcap \text{chaos} = \text{chaos}$$
□

We can show how bounded choice and sequence interact, the semicolon operator distributes over the choice operator in both directions:

Theorem 3.13
$$(A \sqcap B); C = A; C \sqcap B; C$$
$$C; (A \sqcap B) = C; A \sqcap C; B$$
□

3.3.3 Guarded Commands

Guarded commands could also be be known as minor miracles; a guarded command is of the form:

$$p \rightarrow A$$

where p is a Boolean expression and is called the guard. The command A will only be executed if the guard is (evaluates to) true and will not be executed at all if the guard is false:

Theorem 3.14
$$\text{true} \rightarrow A = A$$
$$\text{false} \rightarrow A = \text{miracle}$$
□

3. Concepts and Properties

If the guard of a command is false, execution deadlocks – in this case the command is equivalent to miracle:

Corollary 3.2
$$p \to A = p \to A \,[\!]\, \neg p \to \text{miracle}$$
□

Guarding a command with its domain has no effect:

Theorem 3.15
$$\mathcal{G}(A) \to A = A$$
□

Corollary 3.3
$$A = \mathcal{G}(A) \to A \,[\!]\, \neg \mathcal{G}(A) \to \text{miracle}$$
□

Two guards in succession are equivalent to guarding with their conjunction:

Theorem 3.16
$$p \to q \to A = p \land q \to A$$
□

Any subsequent commands following a guarded command can be absorbed under the guard, since these commands will only be executed if the guard is satisfied:

Theorem 3.17
$$(p \to A)\,;\, B = (p \to A; B)$$
□

An assignment command can be moved through a guard, providing the guard is suitably modified:

Theorem 3.18
$$x := E\,;\, p \to B \;=\; \neg\, [x := E] \neg p \to x := E\,;\, B$$
□

A guard can be distributed through a choice operator:

Theorem 3.19
$$p \to (A \,[\!]\, B) = p \to A \,[\!]\, p \to B$$
□

Finally, a disjunction of predicates that form a guard can be split:

3.3 Some Properties of Commands

Theorem 3.20
$$p \vee q \to A = p \to A \,\square\, q \to A$$
□

Note that, in general, a guarded command is partial and is therefore not feasible, we will therefore need a way of combining guarded commands into a form that are total, more of this in a later chapter.

3.3.4 Unbounded Non-deterministic Choice

The properties of bounded choice can be generalized to unbounded choice. First the unbounded version of Theorem 3.13, we can show that the semicolon operator distributes over the unbounded choice operator in both directions:

Theorem 3.21
If x is not free in C then

$$(@x : X \bullet A); C = @x : X \bullet A \,;\, C$$
$$C \,;\, (@x : X \bullet A) = @x : X \bullet C \,;\, A$$
□

The unbounded version of Theorem 3.19:

Theorem 3.22
If x is not free in p then

$$@x : X \bullet p \to A = p \to @x : X \bullet A$$
□

The unbounded version of Theorem 3.20 is:

Theorem 3.23
If x is not free in A then

$$@x : X \bullet p \to A = (\exists x : X \cdot p) \to A$$
□

Unbounded and bounded choice interact in the obvious way:

Theorem 3.24
$$@x \bullet (A \,\square\, B) = (@x : X \bullet A) \,\square\, (@x : X \bullet B)$$
□

The order in which unbounded choices are applied can be changed:

Theorem 3.25
$$@x : X \bullet @y : Y \bullet A = @y : Y \bullet @x : X \bullet A$$
□

We can write $@x, y : X \bullet A$ for $@x : X \bullet @y : X \bullet A$

3.3.5 Assertions

The assert command is total:

Theorem 3.26
$$\mathcal{G}(\{p\})$$
□

A true assertion means no state values are wrong, so it should have no effect and thus an assertion that is equivalent to true can be removed:

Theorem 3.27
$$\{\text{true}\} = \text{skip}$$
□

Corollary 3.4
$$\{\text{true}\}A = A$$
□

If we have two assertions adjacent to each other, we would expect both to hold; if either evaluates to false, then chaos should be the result. Thus two adjacent assertions can be interchanged or combined:

Theorem 3.28
$$\{p\}\{q\} = \{p \wedge q\} = \{q\}\{p\}$$
□

Inside a guard, the guard can be asserted to hold:

Theorem 3.29
$$p \to A = p \to \{p\} A$$
□

3.4 A Normal Form

The idea of a specification has been introduced in an earlier chapter, as has the concept of a program satisfying a specification. An interesting question is can this idea be turned around – given a program is there a specification that is satisfied by it? It turns out that any program (command) can be written in a normal form, and the following theorem defines the normal form and demonstrates the necessary transformations that can be used to transform a program into that normal form. Any program is build from commands that are either fundamental commands or defined in terms of the fundamental commands, it is only necessary to show that the fundamental commands can be written in the normal form. Later it will be shown that there exists a specification that is equivalent to the normal form.

3.4 A Normal Form

Theorem 3.30
Every command C working with a (collection) of variables x of type X can be put in the following form:

$$@x' : X \bullet q(x, x') \rightarrow x := x' \,\square\, \neg p(x) \rightarrow \mathsf{loop}$$

Proof
The proof is by structural induction. We first prove the theorem for the basic commands. For an assignment statement $x := E$, if the type of the expression E and the variable x is X, then the proof is:

$\qquad x := E$
$=\quad$ property of assignment
$\qquad x := E \,\square\, \neg \delta(E : X) \rightarrow \mathsf{loop}$
$=\quad$ semantics
$\qquad @x' : X \bullet (x' = E \rightarrow x := x') \,\square\, \neg \delta(E : X) \rightarrow \mathsf{loop}$

The proof for skip is:

$\qquad \mathsf{skip}$
$=$
$\qquad x := x$
$=$
$\qquad @x' : X \bullet (x' = x \rightarrow x := x') \,\square\, \neg \mathsf{true} \rightarrow \mathsf{loop}$

Note that x is the set of all variables currently in scope at this point in the program.

The proof for loop is:

$\qquad \mathsf{loop}$
$=$
$\qquad @x' : X \bullet (\mathsf{false} \rightarrow x := x') \,\square\, \neg \mathsf{false} \rightarrow \mathsf{loop}$

Again, x is the set of all variables currently in scope.

The proof for havoc is:

$\qquad \mathsf{havoc}$
$=$
$\qquad @x' : X \bullet (\mathsf{true} \rightarrow x := x') \,\square\, \neg \mathsf{true} \rightarrow \mathsf{loop}$

Again note that x is the set of all variables that are either local (i.e. nonestate variables in scope at this point in the program) or are components of the state.

We can now prove it for the other commands using structural induction. The proof for bounded choice is:

3. Concepts and Properties

$$(@x' : X \bullet A(x,x') \to x := x' \;\square\; \neg p(x) \to \text{loop})\; \square$$
$$(@x' : X \bullet B(x,x') \to x := x' \;\square\; \neg q(x) \to \text{loop})$$

= $\square$ is commutative

$$@x' : X \bullet A(x,x') \to x := x' \;\square\; @x' : X \bullet B(x,x') \to x := x' \;\square$$
$$\neg p(x) \to \text{loop} \;\square\; \neg q(x) \to \text{loop}$$

= property of guards

$$@x' : X \bullet A(x,x') \vee B(x,x') \to x := x' \;\square\; \neg p(x) \vee \neg q(x) \to \text{loop}$$

=

$$@x' : X \bullet A(x,x') \vee B(x,x') \to x := x' \;\square\; \neg(p(x) \wedge q(x)) \to \text{loop}$$

The proof for guarding is:

$$p \to (@x' : X \bullet (A(x,x') \to x := x') \;\square\; \neg q \to \text{loop})$$

= Theorem 3.19

$$p \to @x' : X \bullet (A(x,x') \to x := x') \;\square\; p \to \neg q \to \text{loop}$$

= Theorem 3.16

$$p \wedge @x' : X \bullet (A(x,x') \to x := x') \;\square\; p \wedge \neg q \to \text{loop}$$

=

$$@x' : X \bullet (p \wedge A(x,x') \to x := x') \;\square\; \neg(p \Rightarrow q) \to \text{loop}$$

Before writing down the proof for semicolon, the following rule for the semicolon combinator is required:

$$@x' : X \bullet (A(x,x') \to x := x')\; ;\; @x' : X \bullet (B(x,x') \to x := x')$$

=

$$@x' : X \bullet (A(x,x') \to x := x'\; ;\; @x'' : X \bullet (B(x,x'') \to x := x''))$$

=

$$@x' : X \bullet (A(x,x') \to @x'' : X \bullet (x := x'\; ;\; B(x,x'') \to x := x''))$$

=

$$@x':X \bullet (A(x,x') \to @x'':X \bullet (\neg[x := x'] \neg B(x,x'') \to x := x'\;;\; x := x''))$$

=

$$@x' : X \bullet (A(x,x') \to @x'' : X \bullet (\neg\neg B(x',x'') \to x := x'\; ;\; x := x''))$$

=

$$@x' : X \bullet (A(x,x') \to @x'' : X \bullet (B(x',x'') \to x := x''))$$

=

$$@x', x'' : X \bullet (A(x,x') \wedge B(x',x'') \to x := x'')$$

=

$$@x'' : X \bullet \exists x' : X \cdot (A(x,x') \wedge B(x',x'') \to x := x'')$$

Now the proof for semicolon can now be written down:

3.4 A Normal Form 53

$$@x':X\bullet(A(x,x')\to x:=x')\,\square\,\neg\,p\to\mathsf{loop}\,;$$
$$@x':X\bullet(B(x,x')\to x:=x')\,\square\,\neg\,q\to\mathsf{loop}$$

= Theorem 3.13

$$@x':X\bullet(A(x,x')\to x:=x')\,;$$
$$(@x':X\bullet(B(x,x')\to x:=x')\,\square\,\neg\,q\to\mathsf{loop})\,\square$$
$$\neg\,p\to\mathsf{loop}\,;$$
$$(@x':X\bullet(B(x,x')\to x:=x')\,\square\,\neg\,q\to\mathsf{loop})$$

= Theorem 3.6

$$@x':X\bullet(A(x,x')\to x:=x')\,;$$
$$(@x':X\bullet(B(x,x')\to x:=x')\,\square\,\neg\,q\to\mathsf{loop})\,\square$$
$$\neg\,p\to\mathsf{loop}$$

=

$$@x':X\bullet(A(x,x')\to x:=x')\,;\,(@x':X\bullet(B(x,x')\to x:=x')\,\square$$
$$@x':X\bullet(A(x,x')\to x:=x')\,;\,\neg\,q\to\mathsf{loop}\,\square$$
$$\neg\,p\to\mathsf{loop}$$

=

$$@x':X\bullet(A(x,x')\to x:=x')\,;\,(@x':X\bullet(B(x,x')\to x:=x')\,\square$$
$$@x':X\bullet A(x,x')\to x:=x'\,;\,\neg\,q\to\mathsf{loop}\,\square$$
$$\neg\,p\to\mathsf{loop}$$

=

$$@x':X\bullet(A(x,x')\to x:=x')\,;\,(@x':X\bullet(B(x,x')\to x:=x')\,\square$$
$$@x':X\bullet A(x,x')\to\neg\,[x:=x']q\to x:=x'\,;\,\mathsf{loop}\,\square$$
$$\neg\,p\to\mathsf{loop}$$

=

$$@x':X\bullet(A(x,x')\to x:=x')\,;\,(@x':X\bullet(B(x,x')\to x:=x')\,\square$$
$$@x':X\bullet A(x,x')\land\neg\,q(x')\to\mathsf{loop}\,\square$$
$$\neg\,p\to\mathsf{loop}$$

=

$$@x':X\bullet(A(x,x')\to x:=x')\,;\,(@x':X\bullet(B(x,x')\to x:=x')\,\square$$
$$\neg\,p\lor @x'\bullet A(x,x')\land\neg\,q(x')\to\mathsf{loop}$$

=

$$@x':X\bullet(A(x,x')\to x:=x')\,;\,(@x':X\bullet(B(x,x')\to x:=x')\,\square$$
$$\neg\,p\lor\exists\,x'\cdot A(x,x')\land\neg\,q(x')\to\mathsf{loop}$$

=

$$@x'':X\bullet(\exists\,x':X\cdot A(x,x')\land B(x',x'')\to x:=x'')\,\square$$
$$\neg\,(p\land\forall x':X\cdot A(x,x')\,\Rightarrow\,q(x'))\to\mathsf{loop}$$

The proof for unbounded choice is:

$$@z:Z\bullet(@x':X\bullet A(x,x')\to x:=x'\,\square\,\neg\,p\to\mathsf{loop})$$

=

$$@z:Z\bullet(@x':X\bullet A(x,x')\to x:=x')\,\square\,@z:Z\bullet(\neg\,p\to\mathsf{loop})$$

$$= @x':X\bullet(@z:Z\bullet A(x,x'))\to x:=x')\,\square\,\exists z:Z\cdot\neg p\to \mathsf{loop}$$
$$= @x':X\bullet(\exists z:Z\cdot A(x,x'))\to x:=x'\,\square\,\neg(\forall z:Z\cdot p)\to \mathsf{loop}$$
∎

This theorem means that each block of a program can be translated into a normal form. Later we will show that the normal form is equivalent to a specification statement, thus we have the theoretical possibility of reverse engineering any program to produce its specification.

A useful corollary for combining specification statements can be derived:

Corollary 3.5
$$x:[\ pre_A,\ post_A\ ]\ ;\ x:[\ pre_B,\ post_B\ ]\ =$$
$$x:[\ pre_a \wedge \forall x':X\cdot post_A(x,x') \Rightarrow pre_B(x'),$$
$$(\exists x':X\cdot post_A(x,x') \wedge post_B(x',x''))\ ]$$

Proof
Similar to the proof for semicolon in the normal form theorem (Theorem 3.30).
∎

3.5 Some Further Properties

Some important properties of the commands, but first a lemma:

Lemma 3.1
$$[@x':X\bullet q(x,x')\to x:=x'\,\square\,\neg p(x)\to \mathsf{loop}]R \Leftrightarrow$$
$$p \wedge (\forall x':X\cdot q(x,x') \Rightarrow R(x'))$$

Proof
$$[@x':X\bullet q(x,x')\to x:=x'\,\square\,\neg p(x)\to \mathsf{loop}]R$$
$\Longleftrightarrow$ semantics
$$(\forall x':X\cdot q(x,x') \Rightarrow [x:=x']R(x)) \wedge p(x)$$
$\Longleftrightarrow$ substitution semantics
$$p(x) \wedge (\forall x':X\cdot q(x,x') \Rightarrow R(x'))$$
∎

Theorem 3.31
A command A is monotonic:

$$(P \Rightarrow Q) \Rightarrow (\langle A\rangle P \Rightarrow \langle A\rangle Q)$$
$$(P \Rightarrow Q) \Rightarrow ([A]P \Rightarrow [A]Q)$$

A command A is $\wedge$-distributive:

$$\langle A\rangle P \wedge \langle A\rangle Q \Leftrightarrow \langle A\rangle (P \wedge Q)$$
$$[A]P \wedge [A]Q \Leftrightarrow [A](P \wedge Q)$$

A command A is almost $\vee$-distributive

$$\langle A\rangle P \vee \langle A\rangle Q \Rightarrow \langle A\rangle (P \vee Q)$$
$$[A]P \vee [A]Q \Rightarrow [A](P \vee Q)$$

A command A satisfies the pairing condition:

$$[A]P = [A]\text{true} \wedge \langle A\rangle P$$

Proof
We shall prove the $\wedge$-distribution property for the weakest pre-condition transformer, the others are proved in a similar style.

$\quad [A](P \wedge Q)$
$\Longleftrightarrow$ Theorem 3.30
$\quad [@x' \bullet q(x, x') \to x := x' \,\square\, \neg p \to \text{loop}](P \wedge Q)$
$\Longleftrightarrow$ Lemma 3.1
$\quad p \wedge (\forall x' \cdot q(x, x')) \Rightarrow [x := x']P \wedge [x := x']Q$
$\Longleftrightarrow$ predicate calculus
$\quad p \wedge (\forall x' \cdot q(x, x')) \Rightarrow [x := x']P \wedge p \wedge (\forall x' \cdot q(x, x')) \Rightarrow [x := x']Q$
$\Longleftrightarrow$ Lemma 3.1
$\quad [@x' \bullet q(x, x') \to x := x' \,\square\, \neg p \to \text{loop}]P \,\wedge$
$\quad [@x' \bullet q(x, x') \to x := x' \,\square\, \neg p \to \text{loop}]Q$
$\Longleftrightarrow$ Theorem 3.30
$\quad [A]P \wedge [A]Q$

■

Finally, we can provide another link between the weakest pre-condition semantics of a command, and relational semantics. We have already seen that the relational definition of a command A depend only on $[A]$true and $\neg \langle A\rangle i \neq o$; we have always defined a command using pre-conditions by giving $[A]$true and $\langle A\rangle R$ which appears to give too much information. The next property provides the explanation, if A is a command that only changes the variables in the list x, then for any predicated R:

$$\langle A\rangle R = (\forall x' : X \cdot \langle A\rangle x \neq x') \vee R[x\backslash x']$$

The left-hand side of this property states that the proper outcomes from A satisfy R; the right-hand side states that for any state value x', either A never produces x' (there is no proper outcome) or there is an outcome x' that satisfies R.

3.5.1 Setting and Testing Variables

Given a program, if we remove all uses of skip with other commands using Theorem 3.5, but introduce skip (briefly) to match the bounded variables when translating a bounded choice expression as follows:

$$@x : X, y : Y \bullet A \;\square\; @y : Y, z : Z \bullet B$$
$$\iff$$
$$@x : X, y : Y \bullet A;\; \text{skip} \;\square\; @y : Y, z : Z \bullet B;\; \text{skip}$$
$$\iff$$
$$@x : X, y : Y, z : Z \bullet A \;\square\; @x : X, y : Y, z : Z \bullet B$$
$$\iff$$
$$@x : X, y : Y, z : Z \bullet (A \;\square\; B)$$

then it is easy to see that we only introduce a bound variable when an assignment statement is introduce, we have a means of defining when a command sets a variable and when it tests a variable.

An intuitive definition of a command testing a variable is that the value of the variable will effect the execution of the command, but will not be changed by that execution. An alternative definition is that the variable only appears in guards and in expressions on the right-hand side of assignment statements. An intuitive definition of a command setting a variable is that the value of the variable will not affect the execution of the command, and its value will be changed by the execution of the command. The alternative definition in this case is that the variable only occurs on the left-hand side of assignment statements. A variable that is both tested and set by a command will effect execution and its value be changed.

Consider a command A that does not test x, then for termination we have:

$$[A]\text{true}$$
$$\iff$$
$$[@x', y' \bullet q(y, x', y') \to x, y := x', y' \;\square\; \neg p(y) \to \text{loop}]\text{true}$$
$$\iff$$
$$\forall x', y' \cdot q(y, x', y') \;\Rightarrow\; [x, y := x', y']\text{true} \wedge p(y)$$
$$\iff$$
$$\forall x', y' \cdot q(y, x', y') \;\Rightarrow\; \text{true} \wedge p(y)$$
$$\iff$$
$$p(y)$$

Thus $[A]$true is independent of x. For the weakest liberal pre-condition:

$\langle A \rangle R$
$\iff$
$\langle @x', y' \bullet q(y, x', y') \to x, y := x', y' \,\square\, \neg p(x) \;\Rightarrow\; \mathsf{loop} \rangle R(x, y)$
$\iff$
$\forall\, x', y' \cdot q(y, x', y') \;\Rightarrow\; \langle x, y := x', y' \rangle R(x, y)$
$\iff$
$\forall\, x', y' \cdot q(y, x', y') \;\Rightarrow\; R(x', y')$

and for any predicate R, $\langle A \rangle R$ is independent of x. The analysis suggests the following definition:

Definition 3.9
A command A does not test a variable x, if for any predicate R, both $[A]\mathsf{true}$ and $\langle A \rangle R$ are independent of x.

For a command A that does not set x, then for any predicate R that is only dependent on x:

$\langle A \rangle R$
$\iff$
$\langle @y \bullet q(x, y, y') \to y := y' \,\square\, \neg p(x) \;\Rightarrow\; \mathsf{loop} \rangle R(x)$
$\iff$
$\forall\, y' \cdot q(x, y, y') \;\Rightarrow\; \langle y := y' \rangle R(x)$
$\iff$
$\forall\, y' \cdot q(x, y, y') \;\Rightarrow\; R(x)$
$\iff$
$\forall\, y' \cdot \neg q(x, y, y') \lor R(x)$
$\iff$
$(\forall\, y' \cdot q(x, y, y') \;\Rightarrow\; \langle y := y' \rangle \mathsf{false}) \lor R(x)$
$\iff$
$\langle A \rangle \mathsf{false} \lor R$

If we examine this, it states that, for any input, either that input does not terminate (it satisfies $\langle A \rangle \mathsf{false}$) or it satisfies R, and since A does not set x, the only way an outcome from executing A can still satisfy R is if it did as input. This analysis suggests the following:

Definition 3.10
A command A does not set a variable x if for any x-predicate R, $\langle A \rangle R = \langle A \rangle \mathsf{false} \lor R$

We can define the independence of a command from a variable:

Definition 3.11
A command A is said to be independent of x if it neither tests nor sets x.

and the dependence of a command on a variable:

Definition 3.12
A command A independent of all variables except x is called an x-command.

In both of the above definitions, x could denote a single variable or a set of variables.

The next two sketch proofs show that the definitions of testing and setting given above are consistent with our intuition. Consider a command $A(x, y)$ that does not test a variable x, then we would expect its execution to be independent of the value of x. This means that for any values x_1, x_2, and y and any outcome o from an input i, then:

$$_i A(x_1, y)_o = {}_i A(x_2, y)_o$$

Now:

$$_i A(x_1, y) \bot$$
$$\iff$$
$$\neg [A(x_1, y)] \text{true}$$
$$\iff \text{weakest pre-condition independent of } x$$
$$\neg [A(x_2, y)] \text{true}$$
$$\iff$$
$$_i A(x_2, y) \bot$$

$$_i A(x_1, y)_o$$
$$\iff$$
$$\neg \langle A(x_1, y) \rangle i \neq o$$
$$\iff \text{weakest pre-condition independent of } x$$
$$\neg \langle A(x_2, y) \rangle i \neq o$$
$$\iff$$
$$_i A(x_2, y)_o$$

For a command A that does not set x, for any input value, we would expect x to be unchanged:

$$c = x \Rightarrow \langle A \rangle (c = x)$$
$$\iff c = x \text{ is an } x\text{-predicate}$$
$$c = x \Rightarrow \langle A \rangle \text{false} \vee (c = x)$$
$$\iff$$
$$\text{true}$$

3.5 Some Further Properties

If we denote the input by (x, y), an alternative view is given by the following theorem:

Theorem 3.32
For a command A that does not set x then

$$_{(x,y)}A_{(x',y')} \Rightarrow x = x'$$

Proof
Now

$$x \neq x' \Rightarrow x \neq x' \vee y \neq y'$$
$$\Longrightarrow \text{ wlp monotonic}$$
$$\langle A \rangle x \neq x' \Rightarrow \langle A \rangle (x \neq x' \vee y \neq y')$$
$$\Longleftrightarrow$$
$$\neg \langle A \rangle (x \neq x' \vee y \neq y') \Rightarrow \neg \langle A \rangle x \neq x'$$

thus

$$_{(x,y)}A_{(x',y')}$$
$$\Longleftrightarrow$$
$$\neg \langle A \rangle (x, y) \neq (x', y')$$
$$\Longleftrightarrow$$
$$\neg \langle A \rangle (x \neq x' \vee y \neq y')$$
$$\Longrightarrow$$
$$\neg \langle A \rangle x \neq x'$$
$$\Longrightarrow x \neq x' \text{ is dependent on } x$$
$$\neg (\langle A \rangle \text{false} \vee x \neq x')$$
$$\Longrightarrow$$
$$\neg \langle A \rangle \text{false} \wedge x = x'$$
$$\Longrightarrow$$
$$x = x'$$

∎

Lemma 3.2
If the command A and the predicate p are independent, then for any predicate R defined over the state:

$$\langle A \rangle (p \vee R) = p \vee \langle A \rangle R$$

Proof
For the predicate R:

true
$$\Longleftrightarrow \text{ predicate calculus}$$
$$\langle A \rangle \text{false} \vee p \vee \langle A \rangle \text{false} \vee \neg p$$

$\iff$ hypothesis

$$\langle A \rangle p \vee \langle A \rangle \neg p$$

$\implies$ wlp is monotonic

$$\langle A \rangle p \vee \langle A \rangle (\neg p \vee R)$$

Then we have:

$$\langle A \rangle (p \vee R)$$

$\iff$ proved above

$$\langle A \rangle (p \vee R) \wedge (\langle A \rangle p \vee \langle A \rangle (\neg p \vee R))$$

$\iff$ predicate calculus

$$\langle A \rangle (p \vee R) \wedge \langle A \rangle p \vee \langle A \rangle (p \vee R) \wedge \langle A \rangle (\neg p \vee R)$$

$\iff$ $\wedge$-distributivity of wlp and predicate calculus

$$\langle A \rangle p \vee \langle A \rangle R$$

$\iff$ hypothesis

$$\langle A \rangle \mathsf{false} \vee p \vee \langle A \rangle R$$

$\iff$ wlp is monotonic

$$p \vee \langle A \rangle R$$

∎

Corollary 3.6

If the predicate p is not dependent on any state variable then:

$$\langle A \rangle (p \vee R) \Leftrightarrow p \vee \langle A \rangle R$$

□

The last theorem of the section will provide another link between the precondition semantics of a command, and relational semantics. We have already seen in Chapter 2 that the relational definition of a command A depend only on $[A]\mathsf{true}$ and $\neg \langle A \rangle i \neq o$; however we have always defined the semantics of a command using predicate transformers by giving $[A]\mathsf{true}$ and $\langle A \rangle R$ which appears to give too much information. The theorem provides another view interaction between these two approaches.

Theorem 3.33

If A is an x-command, then for any predicated R,

$$\langle A \rangle R = \forall x' : X \cdot \langle A \rangle (x \neq x') \vee R[x \backslash x']$$

Before going into the proof, it is worth considering exactly what the theorem is saying: the left-hand side says that the proper outcomes from A satisfy R; the right-hand side says that for any state value x', either A never produces x' – it is not a proper outcome, or x' is a proper outcome and satisfies R.

Proof
$$\langle A \rangle R$$
$\iff$
$$\langle A \rangle (\forall\, x' : X \cdot x = x' \Rightarrow R[x \backslash x'])$$
$\iff$
$$\langle A \rangle (\forall\, x' : X \cdot x \neq x' \lor R[x \backslash x'])$$
$\iff$ $\land$-distributivity
$$\forall\, x' : X \cdot \langle A \rangle (x \neq x' \lor R[x \backslash x'])$$
$\iff$ Lemma 3.2
$$\forall\, x' : X \cdot \langle A \rangle (x \neq x') \lor R[x \backslash x']$$
∎

3.6 The Primitive Commands Revisited

A summary of the semantics of the primitive commands is given in Fig. 3.2. To provide more understanding of these commands a series of theorems can be proved, some properties of miracle:

Theorem 3.34
For any predicate R defined over the state, $[A]R =$ true iff $A =$ miracle

Proof
Suppose $[A]R =$ true for any R, then in particular $[A]$true $=$ true. From the pairing condition we have $[A]R = [A]$true $\land \langle A \rangle R$. Thus $\langle A \rangle R =$ true which is the definition of miracle. The proof of the other direction is trivial from the definition of miracle.
∎

A	$\langle A \rangle R$	$[A]$true	$[A]R$	$\mathcal{G}(A)$
miracle	true	true	true	false
loop	true	false	false	true
havoc	trp(R)	true	trp(R)	true
skip	R	true	R	true
slip	R	false	false	true
chaos	trp(R)	false	false	true

Fig. 3.2. The semantics of the primitive commands.

3. Concepts and Properties

Corollary 3.7
If $[A]\mathsf{false} = \mathsf{true}$ then $A = \mathsf{miracle}$

Proof
Now for all predicates R we have $\mathsf{false} \Rightarrow R$. By monotonicity we have $[A]\mathsf{false} \Rightarrow [A]R$. Thus $[A]R = \mathsf{true}$.
∎

Any command preceded by chaos is total, since by angelic non-determinism chaos must produce an outcome so that the command following can execute:

Theorem 3.35
$\mathcal{G}(\mathsf{chaos}\,;\ A)$

Proof
Now

$\qquad \mathcal{G}(\mathsf{chaos}\,;\ A)$
$\Longleftrightarrow$
$\qquad \neg\,[\mathsf{chaos}\,;\ A]\mathsf{false}$
$\Longleftrightarrow$
$\qquad \neg\,[\mathsf{chaos}][A]\mathsf{false}$
$\Longleftrightarrow$
$\qquad \neg\,\mathsf{false}$
$\Longleftrightarrow$
$\qquad \mathsf{true}$

∎

There is no restriction on the command A in the above theorem, it can even be miracle, for if we are trying to execute chaos ; miracle, the outcome from chaos must be $\bot$ to prevent miracle from 'executing' and thus the output of this sequence of commands is $\bot$. However, if we replace chaos by havoc things are slightly different:

Theorem 3.36
If A is not miracle then $\mathcal{G}(\mathsf{havoc}\,;\ A)$

Proof
Now

$\qquad \mathcal{G}(\mathsf{havoc}\,;\ A)$
$\Longleftrightarrow$
$\qquad \neg\,[\mathsf{havoc}\,;\ A]\mathsf{false}$
$\Longleftrightarrow$
$\qquad \neg\,[\mathsf{havoc}][A]\mathsf{false}$
$\Longleftrightarrow$ A is not miracle
$\qquad \neg\,\mathsf{false}$

$$\iff$$
   true

∎

In the above proof, we can only proceed if $[A]$false is not always true – if A is not miracle. By angelic non-determinism, execution of havoc must, if at all possible, produce an outcome that is acceptable to the following command; but no outcome from havoc is acceptable to miracle, nor can we prevent miracle from 'executing' (or rather trying to execute and jamming) by producing the improper outcome, since this is not a possible outcome of havoc.

To conclude, there are two other possible combinations for termination and the weakest liberal pre-condition missing from the table in Fig. 3.2, but they are meaningless as they do not satisfy either the pairing or the $\wedge$-distribution conditions, the two combinations are

A	$[A]$true	$\langle A \rangle R$	
?	true	false	(fails the pairing condition)
??	false	false	(fails $\wedge$-distribution)

3.7 Initial Values

There is a problem with transformations of predicates that contain decorated (hooked) variables that denote initial values (we will call decorated variables initial values). As far as the transformation rules are concerned they are treated as constants and thus do not take part, but there are problems – consider:

$$[x := x + y]x = \overleftarrow{x} + y$$

where x and y are Integers. The transformation of the post-condition is easily calculated:

$$[x := x + y]x = \overleftarrow{x} + y$$
$$\iff$$
$$\delta((x + y) : \mathbb{Z}) \wedge x + y = \overleftarrow{x} + y$$

After the transformation the variable x denotes the value of x before execution of the assignment, but this is (probably) what $\overleftarrow{x}$ also denotes. The last steps of this transformation are:

$$(x + y = x + y)$$
$$\iff$$
   true

3. Concepts and Properties

But was the assumption identifying x and $\overleftarrow{x}$ valid? The meaning of an initial value occurring in a specification is well-defined, so for a specification statement A the final value of applying A to a predicate R is given by:

$$([A]R)[\overleftarrow{x}\backslash x]$$

Since $\overleftarrow{x}$ is the initial value of x. There is no (real) problem if A denoted any single statement, so the derivation above is valid; but there is a problem with the following:

$$[A;\ B]R(\overleftarrow{x},x)$$

This could be interpreted either as

$$[A](([B]R)[\overleftarrow{x}\backslash x])$$

where $\overleftarrow{x}$ denotes the initial value of x just before the execution of B, or as:

$$([A][B]R)[\overleftarrow{x}\backslash x]$$

where $\overleftarrow{x}$ denotes the value of x just before A is executed.

To remove all doubt, some sort of convention or scope rule is necessary for initial variables. When they occur in a specification there is no problem, but if they occur in a predicate on the state it is necessary to indicate what initial values the hooked variables are referring to. There are several ways of doing this, we shall use a rigorous rather than formal approach. A vertical line decorated with the variable name will be used to indicate it is at this point that the initial value should be taken from. The semantics are easily defined: after a transformation has been calculated, the hooks can be dropped between the definition point and the predicate that contained the initial variables. Thus the first example would be written:

$$[\vert_{\underline{x}}\ x := x+y]x = \overleftarrow{x}+y$$
$$\Longleftrightarrow$$
$$(x+y = \overleftarrow{x}+y)[\overleftarrow{x}\backslash x]$$
$$\Longleftrightarrow$$
$$(x+y = x+y)$$
$$\Longleftrightarrow$$
true

The ambiguity of two or more commands can also be resolved:

$$[A;\ \vert_{\underline{x}}\ B]R(\overleftarrow{x},x) = [A](([B]R)[\overleftarrow{x}\backslash x])$$
$$[\vert_{\underline{x}}\ A;\ B]R(\overleftarrow{x},x) = ([A][B]R)[\overleftarrow{x}\backslash x]$$

In fact, this convention will not be needed; in Chapter 7 another way of dealing with initial values will be developed, this will generalize the concept and deal with the problem of the scope of an initial variable in a more familiar way.

3.8 A Compiler for the Small Language

Now is the time to return to the problem of producing a correct compiler for the language. For the executable constructs in our wide-spectrum language we can recover their relational definition; based on these a compiler can be developed. The ideas developed in this book indicate how this might be done and is left as an exercise for the reader.

A further point – we are used to thinking that it is the compiler that dictates the properties of our programming language; this is wrong, it is the properties of the language that dictate what the compiler does! If this seems strange, then ask the question 'what if the compiler has bugs in it?' and then it is necessary to define what is meant by a bug in the compiler. All of these ideas lead to the concept that we define the semantics of our programming language by mathematics and show that it has the right sort of properties, properties that we require or expect, and then develop a compiler for the language that produces code that, when executed, has these properties.

3.9 Summary

The properties developed in this chapter allows a programmer to transform their program without changing its meaning. Such transformations are usually taken for granted, and/or learnt by experience and/or just accepted as part of the programming mythology. This chapter illustrates that such properties come from the semantics of the commands that make up the language and it is necessary to both understand and prove the correctness of such properties.

Many of the properties listed and proved in this chapter have been to check and improve our understanding of the programming language. To show that it behaves in the way that we expect, and if it doesn't, why it doesn't. It may be that some of the properties are ones we don't want, in this case will need to change definitions and rework all the theorems in the light of the changes. The result should be a language with properties that we require.

4. Building New Commands from Old

New commands have already defined in terms of, as syntactic sugar for, existing commands. These definitions did not use, or even allow, for recursion; there is a need to extend this approach to allow for commands to be defined in terms of themselves, a need to allow recursion.

4.1 Defining Commands

It will be useful to be able to give recursive definitions of new commands – definitions of the form $X \triangleq f(X)$. Such a definition needs to be meaningful and that it has a 'proper' or 'distinguished' solution. The meaning given to such a definition is that it defines the command C if and only if $C = f(C)$. For example consider the following definition:

$X \triangleq$ skip $\Box$ X

This could be viewed as a defining equation for skip since:

skip $=$ skip $\Box$ skip

by Theorem 3.6, so this style of definition is, in some sense, meaningful.

Recursive definitions provide an alternative way of introducing certain unbounded commands, for example it might be possible to define A^* as the solution to the following defining equation:

$X \triangleq$ skip $\Box$ $A \mathbin{;} X$

Operationally X is defined to be a choice between executing skip or executing A followed by X, which is either skip or A followed by X .... A little thought provides the following guess for the command defined by this equation:

skip $\Box$ A $\Box$ A^2 $\Box$ A^3 $\Box$ ...

To progress further, the definition could be unwound by substituting X into its own definition to get the following sequence of definitions for X:

$X \triangleq$ skip $\square\ A$; X
$X \triangleq$ skip $\square\ A$; (skip $\square\ A$; X)
$X \triangleq$ skip $\square\ A$; (skip $\square\ A$; (skip $\square\ A$; X))
...

each of these equations could be thought of as a better solution – the unknown value for X becomes less and less significant. Each equation can be simplified and used to define the following sequence of commands that can be thought of as a series of approximations to a solution of the recursive definition:

$C_1 \triangleq$ skip $\square\ A$; X
$C_2 \triangleq$ skip $\square\ A\ \square\ A^2$; X
$C_3 \triangleq$ skip $\square\ A\ \square\ A^2\ \square\ A^3$; X
...
$C_i \triangleq @n \in \{0,\ldots,i-1\} \bullet A^n\ \square\ A^i$; X
...

Leading (informally) to the idea that the solution to the recursive definition is, in some sense, the limit of repeating this substitution n times as n becomes arbitrarily large, as n tends to ∞:

$$C = \lim_{i \to \infty} C_i = \lim_{i \to \infty} @n \in \{0,\ldots,i-1\} \bullet A^n\ \square\ A^i\ ;\ X$$

This definition looks suspiciously like the previous definition given for A^* and we would thus expect $@n : \mathbb{N} \bullet A^n$ to be a 'solution' to the definition:

$\quad$ skip $\square\ A$; A^*
$=$
$\quad$ skip $\square\ A$; $(@n : \mathbb{N} \bullet A^n)$
$=$
$\quad$ skip $\square\ @n : \mathbb{N} \bullet A$; A^n
$=$
$\quad$ skip $\square\ @n : \mathbb{N} \bullet A^{n+1}$
$=$
$\quad @n : \mathbb{N} \bullet A^n$
$=$
$\quad A^*$

So A^* is a solution. This suggests that it might be possible to formalize the idea of repeated substitution and taking limits. However there are problems with this approach to defining a new command, consider

$X \triangleq X$

Every command satisfies this equation – so what is the 'distinguished' solution? If we consider an execution model of this definition, executing X means we execute X, we execute X etc. – this seems suspiciously like loop, so is loop the 'distinguished' solution?

4.2 An Approach to Recursion

These definitions are of the form:

$$X \triangleq f(X)$$

where the new command X is defined in terms of some function of itself. We seek a single, 'distinguished', solution to recursive definitions of this form. This is done by considering the above definition as an equation in X that needs to be solved.

The recursion can be removed by a generalization of the idea given above – we take the limit of repeated substitution to define a (hopefully) distinguished solution to the definition. Let C denote a possible solution to the definition; it is given by:

$$C = \lim_{i \to \infty} f^i(X)$$

To give this approach formality, it is necessary to define exactly what is meant by a limit and to provide an initial value for the X. We proceed as follows: we will find a sequence of commands, called the defining sequence, that can be thought of as approximations to the definition: $C_0, C_1, C_2, \ldots$. A starting value C_0 is given and each command in the sequence is defined in terms of its predecessor:

$$C_0 = \ldots$$
$$C_{i+1} = f(C_i)$$

and it is easy to see (avoiding the issue of the initial approximation for the moment, which is equivalent to the problem of what value X should have in the limit equation above) that:

$$C = \lim_{i \to \infty} C_i = \lim_{i \to \infty} f^i(C_0)$$

Under what conditions is the above a solution to the recursive definition? Now we have:

$$C$$
$$\Longleftrightarrow$$
$$\lim_{i \to \infty} C_i$$
$$\Longleftrightarrow$$
$$\lim_{i \to \infty} C_{i+1}$$

$$\iff \lim_{i \to \infty} f(C_i)$$
$$\iff f(\lim_{i \to \infty} C_i)$$
$$\iff f(C)$$

So provided we can justify the step from $\lim_{i \to \infty} f(C_i)$ to $f(\lim_{i \to \infty} C_i)$, then this approach does produce a solution. We will first introduce the following definition:

Definition 4.1
A function over commands is continuous in a variable X at C if and only if for every sequence C_i that has a limit C, the sequence $f(C_i)$ has as its limit $f(C)$

$$\lim_{i \to \infty} f(C_i) = f(\lim_{i \to \infty} C_i)$$

Thus if f is continuous at the limit C of the sequence C_i, then this limit is a solution. Although this can be shown to work, it is rather complicated and involves discussing the equality of commands. Now, we know that two commands are equal:

$$A = B$$

iff for all predicates R defined over the state we have:

$$[A]\text{true} = [B]\text{true} \text{ and } \langle A \rangle R = \langle B \rangle R$$

This suggests the following approach. To define $\lim_{i \to \infty} C_i$ it is only necessary to define $[\lim_{i \to \infty} C_i]\text{true}$ and $\langle \lim_{i \to \infty} C_i \rangle R$. With the right sort of 'continuity' this suggest that we define these as:

Definition 4.2
A sequence of commands, C_i, has a limit, denoted by $\lim_{i \to \infty} C_i$, if and only if for every predicate R, the sequences of predicates $[C_i]\text{true}$ and $\langle C_i \rangle R$ have limits. When such limits exist then

$$[\lim_{i \to \infty} C_i]\text{true} \triangleq \lim_{i \to \infty}([C_i]\text{true})$$
$$\langle \lim_{i \to \infty} C_i \rangle R \triangleq \lim_{i \to \infty}(\langle C_i \rangle R)$$

However, now it is necessary to think about limits of predicates as the two sets of equations given above to define a command are limits of Boolean expressions.

We could also switch to using recursive predicate definitions for the commands. Termination for a command that is defined recursively by $X \triangleq f(X)$ is given by the solution to the equation:

$$[X]\text{true} = [f(X)]\text{true}$$

and the weakest liberal pre-condition is the solution to

$$\langle X \rangle R = \langle f(X) \rangle R$$

Suppose we can find a function g such that

$$[f(X)]\text{true} = g([X]\text{true})$$

The function g can be found by expanding the left-hand term. The first of the above two equations can then be written as

$$[X]\text{true} = g([X]\text{true})$$

and if we write $p = [X]\text{true}$, then p is a solution to

$$p = g(p)$$

Similarly, if we can find an h (by expanding the left-hand term below) such that

$$\langle f(X) \rangle R = h(\langle X \rangle R)$$

then $q = \langle X \rangle R$ is a solution to

$$q = h(q)$$

Later it will shown that these two ways of finding a solution to a recursive defining equation are equivalent, but first it is necessary to study recursive definitions of predicates (and their solutions) and limits of sequences of predicates.

4.3 Sequences of Predicates and their Limit

Given a (recursive) equation that defines a predicate

$$P \triangleq g(P)$$

by using the repeated substitution approach, it can be shown that, under the right circumstances, $\lim_{i \to \infty} g^i(p_0)$ is the distinguished solution. We progress as before; firstly introduce the concept of a defining sequence:

$$p_0 = \ldots$$
$$p_{i+1} = g(p_i)$$

where again the issue of initial value has been ignored. Then a solution p to $P \triangleq g(P)$ is given by:

$$p = \lim_{i \to \infty} g^i(p_0) = \lim_{i \to \infty} p_i$$

and formalize the idea of a limit – the sequence settling down to a value – as follows: a sequence of predicates p_i dependent on the identifier x has a limit if:

$$\exists n : \mathbb{N} \cdot \forall x : X \cdot \forall i, j : \mathbb{N} \cdot n \leq i \wedge n \leq j \Rightarrow p_i(x) = p_j(x)$$

this states that if we choose any value for x then at some point in the sequence of predicates past which there is no change in the value of the predicate. The limit is given by:

$$\lim_{i \to \infty} p_i \triangleq \exists n \cdot \forall i \cdot n \leq i \Rightarrow p_i$$

It is also necessary to guarantee that things work properly at the limit, that things really do settle down. This introduces the concept of continuity: a function g is continuous in x at p if for every sequence $p_0, p_1, p_2, \ldots$ that has p as its limit, the sequence $g(p_0), g(p_1), g(p_2), \ldots$ has the limit $g(p)$.

Definition 4.3
A predicate expression $g(x)$ is continuous in the predicate variable x at p iff, for each sequence p_i that has as its limit p, the sequence $g(p_i)$ has the limit $g(p)$.

$$\lim_{i \to \infty} g(p_i) = g(\lim_{i \to \infty} p_i)$$

Finally we can also define by what we mean by a distinguished solution, we can characterize the unique solution to a recursive definition:

Definition 4.4
The (recursive) definition $P \triangleq g(P)$ is called proper iff the limit of its defining sequence exists, and g is continuous in P at the limit. The limit is called the proper solution to $P \triangleq g(P)$.

Theorem 4.1
If p is the proper solution to $P \triangleq g(P)$, then $p = g(p)$.

Proof
Continuity gives us:

$$p$$
$$=$$
$$\lim_{i \to \infty} p_i$$

$$= \lim_{i \to \infty} p_{i+1}$$
$$= \lim_{i \to \infty} g(p_i)$$
$$= g(\lim_{i \to \infty} p_i)$$
$$= g(p)$$

∎

The only thing left to do is choose an initial value for the defining sequence, there are two obvious possibilities false and true. The first gives us a skeptics (doubters) theory:

$p_0 = \text{false}$
$p_{i+1} = g(p_i)$

The second choice gives a credulous (believers) theory:

$p_0 = \text{true}$
$p_{i+1} = g(p_i)$

We can characterize a proper solution provided by either of these theories.

4.3.1 A Skeptical Result

Firstly, we can now define the defining sequence for a recursive definition

Definition 4.5
The skeptical defining sequence for a (recursive) predicate definition of the form $P = g(P)$ is $p_0, p_1, p_2, \ldots$ for some initial value p_0 and is given by:

$p_0 = \text{false}$
$p_{i+1} = g(p_i)$

We already have the notion of continuity so that we can go straight to the definition of a skeptical proper solution:

Definition 4.6
The definition $P = g(P)$ is called skeptically proper iff the limit of its defining sequence exists, and g is continuous in P at the limit.

We will introduce an order relation on predicates as follows:

Definition 4.7
$p \sqsubseteq_{\text{SKEPTIC}} q$ iff $p \Rightarrow q$

4.3 Sequences of Predicates and their Limit

It is easy to show that $\sqsubseteq_{\text{SKEPTIC}}$ is an order relation. The next step is to introduce a definition of monotonic:

Definition 4.8
An function is skeptically monotonic in a variable x iff for all values

$$x \sqsubseteq_{\text{SKEPTIC}} y \Rightarrow g(x) \sqsubseteq_{\text{SKEPTIC}} g(y)$$

a sequence p_i is skeptically monotonic iff $\forall i : \mathbb{N} \cdot p_i \sqsubseteq_{\text{SKEPTIC}} p_{i+1}$

It is easy to show that with this we have:

Theorem 4.2
If p_i is a skeptically monotonic sequence of predicates, then

$$\lim_{i \to \infty} p_i = \exists i : \mathbb{N} \cdot p_i$$

□

Theorem 4.3
The defining sequence of a recursive definition of that uses a skeptically monotonic function is skeptically monotonic:

$$\forall i : \mathbb{N} \cdot p_i \sqsubseteq_{\text{SKEPTIC}} p_{i+1}$$

□

Now the proper solution to a recursive definition can be characterized:

Theorem 4.4
If p is the proper solution to the defining equation $P = g(P)$, and if q is another solution, then $p \sqsubseteq_{\text{SKEPTIC}} q$.

Proof
By induction

$$\text{false} \Rightarrow q$$

$$=$$

$$p_0 \Rightarrow q$$

$$p_i \Rightarrow q$$

$$=$$

$$g(p_i) \Rightarrow g(q)$$

$$=$$

$$p_{i+1} \Rightarrow q$$

Thus for $i : \mathbb{N}$ we have $p_i \Rightarrow q$ and therefore $\lim_{i \to \infty} p_i \Rightarrow q$ and $p \sqsubseteq_{\text{SKEPTIC}} q$.

■

4.3.2 A Credulous Result

Again, we can define the defining sequence for a recursive definition

Definition 4.9
The credulous defining sequence for a (recursive) predicate definition of the form $P = g(P)$ is $p_0, p_1, p_2, \ldots$ for some initial value p_0 and is given by:

$$p_0 = \text{true}$$
$$p_{i+1} = g(p_i)$$

Again we can go straight to the definition of a proper solution:

Definition 4.10
The definition $P = g(P)$ is called credulously proper iff the limit of its defining sequence exists, and g is continuous in X at the limit.

For the credulous theory we introduce an order relation $\sqsubseteq_{\text{CREDULOUS}}$:

Definition 4.11
$p \sqsubseteq_{\text{CREDULOUS}} q$ iff $q \Rightarrow p$

A definition of monotonicity can be given in terms of this order relation:

Definition 4.12
An function is credulously monotonic in a variable x iff for all values

$$x \sqsubseteq_{\text{CREDULOUS}} y \Rightarrow g(x) \sqsubseteq_{\text{CREDULOUS}} g(y)$$

A sequence p_i is credulously monotonic iff $\forall i : \mathbb{N} \cdot p_{i+1} \Rightarrow p_i$

and in this case we have

Theorem 4.5
If p_i is a credulously monotonic sequence of predicates, then

$$\lim_{i \to \infty} p_i = \forall i : \mathbb{N} \cdot p_i$$

☐

Theorem 4.6
The defining sequence of a recursive definition that uses a credulously monotonic function is credulously monotonic:

$$\forall i : \mathbb{N} \cdot p_i \sqsubseteq_{\text{CREDULOUS}} p_{i+1}$$

☐

Again a characterization of the proper solution can be given:

Theorem 4.7
If p is the proper solution to the defining equation $P = g(P)$, and if q is another solution, then $p \sqsubseteq_{\text{CREDULOUS}} q$.
☐

4.4 Limits of Predicate Transformers

As all the mechanisms that are necessary to solve recursive predicate equations are available, it is possible to proceed – we must also decide on a starting value for our iterations, it must be the value true for $\langle X_0 \rangle R$, since we must have $\langle X_0 \rangle \text{true} = \text{true}$. For termination, the choice is not so simple, returning to the first example

$$X \triangleq \text{skip} \, \square \, X$$

If the solution to this equation is denoted by C, then an intuitive operational view of the solution to this is that at some point either C does nothing (choose the skip alternative at some point) or loops (choose the X alternative). If we use the credulous theory, then

$[C_0]\text{true} \triangleq \text{true}$
$[C_{n+1}]\text{true} \triangleq [\text{skip} \, \square \, C_n]\text{true}$

which means

$$\begin{aligned}[C_{n+1}]\text{true} &= [\text{skip} \, \square \, C_n]\text{true} \\ &= [\text{skip}]\text{true} \wedge [C_n]\text{true} \\ &= [C_n]\text{true}\end{aligned}$$

thus

$$[\lim_{i \to \infty} C_i]\text{true} = \text{true}$$

But the value of $[C]$true cannot be true since this would mean that the command C is guaranteed to terminate – but we could keep choosing X and thus not terminate, this definition does not agree with our intuition. However, under the skeptical theory we have:

$[C_0]\text{true} \triangleq \text{false}$
$[C_{n+1}]\text{true} \triangleq [\text{skip} \, \square \, C_n]\text{true}$

giving

$$[\lim_{i \to \infty} C_i]\text{true} = \text{false}$$

which means that C is not guaranteed to terminate and this does agree with our intuitive execution model. Thus we define the defining sequences for both termination and the weakest pre-condition as:

$[C_0]\text{true} \triangleq \text{false}$
$[C_{n+1}]\text{true} \triangleq [f(C_n)]\text{true}$

and

$\langle C_0 \rangle R \triangleq \text{true}$
$\langle C_{n+1} \rangle R \triangleq \langle f(C_n) \rangle R$

Returning to $X \triangleq \text{skip} \,\square\, X$, with this definition we have

$\langle C \rangle R = R$
$[C]\text{true} = \text{false}$

which is slip and this solution seems to agree with our intuitive solution based on considering an execution model.

Theorem 4.8
If $X \triangleq f(X)$ then the defining sequence $[C_i]\text{true}$ is skeptically monotonic:

$[C_i]\text{true} \sqsubseteq_{\text{SKEPTIC}} [C_{i+1}]\text{true}$

In terms of implication:

$[C_0]\text{true} \Rightarrow [C_1]\text{true} \Rightarrow [C_2]\text{true} \Rightarrow \ldots [C_i]\text{true} \Rightarrow [C_{i+1}]\text{true} \Rightarrow \ldots$

□

Theorem 4.9
If $X \triangleq f(X)$ then the defining sequence $\langle C_i \rangle R$ is credulously monotonic:

$\langle C_i \rangle R \sqsubseteq_{\text{CREDULOUS}} \langle C_{i+1} \rangle R$

In terms of implication:

$\ldots \Rightarrow \langle C_{i+1} \rangle R \Rightarrow \langle C_i \rangle R \Rightarrow \ldots \Rightarrow \langle C_2 \rangle R \Rightarrow \langle C_1 \rangle R \Rightarrow \langle C_0 \rangle R$

□

Theorem 4.10
If C is the skeptical limit of the defining sequence of

$X = f(X)$

then it is the least fixed point solution to the equation, in the sense that if Q is any other fixed point then

$[C]\text{true} \Rightarrow [Q]\text{true}$

Proof
This follows from Theorems 4.7 and 4.8, and the definition of $\sqsubseteq_{\text{CREDULOUS}}$.
■

Theorem 4.11
If C is the credulous limit of the defining sequence of

$X = f(X)$

4.4 Limits of Predicate Transformers

then it is the greatest fixed point solution to the equation, in the sense that if Q is any other fixed point then

$$\langle Q \rangle R \Rightarrow \langle C \rangle R$$

□

4.4.1 The Two Approaches

The study of sequence of predicates and their limits was motivated by considering two approaches to finding a solution to $X \triangleq f(X)$. The first of these approaches was to define a sequence of approximations

$$[C_0]\text{true} = \text{false} \qquad \langle C_0 \rangle R = \text{true}$$
$$[C_{i+1}]\text{true} = [f(C_i)]\text{true} \qquad \langle C_{i+1} \rangle R = \langle f(C_i) \rangle R$$

and defining the solution we are looking for, C, as the limit of the sequence of predicates by:

$$[C]\text{true} \triangleq \lim_{i \to \infty} ([C_i]\text{true})$$
$$\langle C \rangle R \triangleq \lim_{i \to \infty} (\langle C_i \rangle R)$$

The second approach was to find two functions g and h such that

$$[f(X)]\text{true} = g([X]\text{true})$$
$$\langle f(X) \rangle R = h(\langle X \rangle R)$$

and if p is the skeptically proper solution of $x = g(x)$ and q is the credulously proper solution to $x = h(x)$, then

$$[C]\text{true} \triangleq p$$
$$\langle C \rangle R \triangleq q$$

We can easily show that the two approaches are equivalent by a simple inductive proof. If p_i is the defining sequence for p, then for termination we have:

$$p_0 = \text{false} = [C_0]\text{true}$$

For the inductive step, assume $p_i = [C_i]\text{true}$ then

$$\begin{aligned}
& p_{i+1} \\
= \; & g(p_i) \\
= \; & \text{by induction hypothesis} \\
& g([C_i]\text{true}) \\
= \; & \text{definition of } g \\
& [f(C_i)]\text{true}
\end{aligned}$$

$$= [C_{i+1}]\text{true}$$

For the weakest liberal pre-condition, if q_i is the defining sequence for q then

$$\langle C_0 \rangle R = \text{true} = q_0$$

For the inductive step, assume $q_i = \langle C_i \rangle R$ then

$$\begin{aligned}
& q_{i+1} \\
=\ & h(q_i) \\
& \text{by induction hypothesis} \\
=\ & h(\langle C_i \rangle R) \\
& \text{definition of } h \\
=\ & \langle f(C_i) \rangle R \\
=\ & \langle C_{i+1} \rangle R
\end{aligned}$$

Thus the two approaches are identical.

Theorem 4.12
If $X \triangleq f(X)$ is a command definition and f is monotonic in X, the limit to the defining sequence exists and is given by

$$[(\lim_{i \to \infty} C_i)]\text{true} = \exists\, i : \mathbb{N} \cdot [C_i]\text{true}$$
$$\langle (\lim_{i \to \infty} C_i) \rangle R = \forall\, i : \mathbb{N} \cdot \langle C_i \rangle R$$

□

4.5 Limits of Commands

Can commands be defined directly? Is it really necessary to go from a recursive definition of a command X to definitions of the weakest liberal pre-condition and termination by taking limits of predicates – is it possible to go straight to the limit of a command? The problem of 'distinguishedness' is also still left to be tackled. If we can introduce a concept of order on commands then the distinguished solution we require could be identified as the least solution to $X \triangleq F(X)$. If we look at the starting value for the iteration we find that

$$[C_0]\text{true} = \text{false}$$
$$\langle C_0 \rangle R = \text{true}$$

4.5 Limits of Commands

and this is just the definition of loop. This suggests that the defining sequence for a command definition $X \triangleq f(X)$ is given by:

$$C_0 = \text{loop}$$
$$C_{i+1} = f(C_i)$$

and the proper solution C to $X = f(X)$ is defined to be

$$C = \lim_{i \to \infty} C_i$$

for the appropriate ordering (see below).

Definition 4.13
The command definition $X \triangleq f(X)$ is proper if and only if the limit of its defining sequence exists, and f is continuous in X at the limit.

It is only left to prove that

Theorem 4.13
If C_i is the defining sequence for the proper solution to $X \triangleq f(X)$ then

$$[\lim_{i \to \infty} C_i]\text{true} = \lim_{i \to \infty} [C_i]\text{true}$$
$$\langle \lim_{i \to \infty} C_i \rangle R = \lim_{i \to \infty} \langle C_i \rangle R$$

Proof
Straight forward from the definitions.
■

Definition 4.14
$A \sqsubseteq_{\text{FULL}} B$ iff $\langle A \rangle R \Rightarrow \langle B \rangle R$ for all R and $[B]\text{true} \Rightarrow [A]\text{true}$.

Definition 4.15
A function f over commands is monotonic in the command variable X iff and only if for all commands A and B

$$A \sqsubseteq_{\text{FULL}} B \Rightarrow f(A) \sqsubseteq_{\text{FULL}} f(B)$$

The following theorems sheds some light on the matter of multiple solutions to a recursive definition.

Theorem 4.14
The defining sequence to a proper definition $X \triangleq f(X)$ is monotonic.
□

Theorem 4.15
If A is a proper solution to the definition $X \triangleq f(X)$ and f is monotonic in X then if B is also a solution, then

$$B \sqsubseteq_{\text{FULL}} A$$

□

At this point it is worth reviewing what has been done. We wish to give a recursive definition of a command in the form

$$X \triangleq f(X)$$

The definition gives rise to the concept of a defining sequence given by:

$$C_0 = \text{loop}$$
$$C_{i+1} = f(C_i)$$

We can now define the solution to the recursive definition, denoted by the command C, as

$$C = \lim_{i \to \infty} C_i$$

for the appropriate ordering. We have shown that:

$$C = f(C)$$

and if A is any other solution, i.e. $A = f(A)$ then

$$A \sqsubseteq_{\text{FULL}} C$$

We can now return to the question posed earlier: what does $X \triangleq X$ define? The work done above suggests that if C denotes the solution to this definition then it is defined by the limit of the sequence C_i where

$$[C_0]\text{true} = \text{false}$$
$$[C_{i+1}]\text{true} = [C_i]\text{true}$$

and

$$\langle C_0 \rangle R = \text{true}$$
$$\langle C_{i+1} \rangle R = \langle C_i \rangle R$$

which gives

$$[C]\text{true} = \text{false}$$
$$\langle C \rangle R = \text{true}$$

and this is the definition of loop, which fits with the intuitive meaning of $X \triangleq X$ – we keep doing X forever.

Finally returning to the second example:

$$X \triangleq \text{skip} \ \square \ A; X$$

The defining sequence for this definition is:

$$C_0 = \mathsf{loop}$$
$$C_n = @n \in \{0,\ldots,i-1\} \bullet A^n \mathbin{\square} A^i \mathbin{;} \mathsf{loop}$$

and thus the unique solution is given by

$$\lim_{i\to\infty} C_i = \lim_{i\to\infty} @n \in \{0,\ldots,i-1\} \bullet A^n \mathbin{\square} A^i \mathbin{;} \mathsf{loop}$$

which is not A^*, so what has gone wrong? The clue is in the analysis of $X \triangleq X$ which obviously has any command as a solution, but has loop as the proper solution since $C \sqsubseteq_{\mathsf{FULL}} \mathsf{loop}$ for all commands C. Some recursive definitions that can be calculated are

loop is the proper solution to $X \triangleq X$
slip is the proper solution to $X \triangleq \mathsf{skip} \mathbin{\square} X$

We will return to this matter in a later chapter.

4.6 Tidying the Loose Ends

Let C denote the proper solution to

$$X = f(X)$$

Since C is the proper solution we know that the defining sequences are given by

$$T_0 = \mathsf{false} \qquad\qquad W_0(R) = \mathsf{true}$$
$$T_{i+1} = g(T_i) \qquad\qquad W_{i+1}(R) = h(W_i(R))$$

and since C is the proper solution, then its semantics are given by:

$$[C]\mathsf{true} \triangleq \exists i : \mathbb{N} \cdot T_i$$
$$\langle C \rangle R \triangleq \forall i : \mathbb{N} \cdot W_i(R)$$

For refinement we need to consider $[C]R$, the value of which is given by

$$[C]R = [C]\mathsf{true} \wedge \langle C \rangle R$$
$$= \exists i : \mathbb{N} \cdot T_i \wedge \forall i : \mathbb{N} \cdot W_i(R)$$

which is not in a very useful form; however with the following lemmas we can attempt to reorganize this equation, and to provide some insight into the definition.

Lemma 4.1
For $m < n$ then $T_m \wedge W_n(R) = T_m$.

Proof
Now when $m < n$ we have by credulity

$[f^m(\text{loop})]\text{false} \Rightarrow [f^n(\text{loop})]\text{false}$

and by monotonicity

$\langle f^n(\text{loop})\rangle\text{false} \Rightarrow \langle f^n(\text{loop})\rangle R$

thus

$[f^n(\text{loop})]\text{true} \wedge \langle f^n(\text{loop})\rangle\text{false} \Rightarrow \langle f^n(\text{loop})\rangle\text{false}$
$\iff$
$[f^n(\text{loop})]\text{false} \Rightarrow \langle f^n(\text{loop})\rangle\text{false}$
$\Longrightarrow$
$[f^m(\text{loop})]\text{false} \Rightarrow \langle f^n(\text{loop})\rangle\text{false}$
$\Longrightarrow$
$[f^m(\text{loop})]\text{false} \Rightarrow \langle f^n(\text{loop})\rangle R$
$\iff$
$T_m \Rightarrow W_n(R)$

∎

Returning to the definition of $[C]R$ we have

$[C]R$
$\iff$
$\exists\, m : \mathbb{N} \cdot T_m \wedge \forall\, n : \mathbb{N} \cdot W_n(R)$
$\iff$
$\exists\, m : \mathbb{N} \cdot (T_m \wedge \forall\, n : \mathbb{N} \cdot W_n(R))$
$\iff$
$\exists\, m : \mathbb{N} \cdot (T_m \wedge \forall\, n \in \{0, \ldots, m\} \cdot W_n(R))$
$\iff$
$\exists\, m : \mathbb{N} \cdot (T_m \wedge W_m(R))$

We can now proceed as follows: define $H_m(R)$ as

$H_m(R) = T_m \wedge W_m(R)$

then we have

$[C]R = \exists\, m : \mathbb{N} \cdot H_m(R)$

4.7 Epilogue

The similarity between the three processes of solving recursive definitions in different domains cannot be ignored. In fact the strategy that was used need only be done once. We define an order relation on a set S and then just go through the mechanism of defining sequence, limit, monotonicity and proper solution. All we need do then is show that our set has an order relation on it and then all the properties hold.

There are four classes of command that can be defined, these are:

- undefined;
- miraculous (not feasible);
- implementable (feasible); and
- executable.

The first class occurs if a poor recursive definition is given, either there are no reasonable solutions to the definition, or far too many of which the 'best' is loop. The second occurs when a command is defined that is not total, these commands cannot ever be implemented. The third class are those commands that could be implementable, but are sufficiently unbounded that it would be difficult, if not impossible, for a compiler to generate code. The last class are those commands that are both feasible and bounded enough that a compiler can generate code that has the desired effect.

5. Program Refinement

In this and the following chapters we will consider the problem of converting a specification of an operation expressed as pre- and post-conditions into executable code. This chapter will consider a more general idea, the problem of converting any program into an equivalent one that would still be of use to the user or customer. The concept of a program satisfying a specification will be addressed formally.

5.1 Stepwise Refinement

A well-known method of solving a large problem is to break it into smaller sub-problems, solve these sub-problems and then assemble their solutions to provide the required answer. This approach will be used to transform a specification into executable code. To develop executable code from a specification, it will be broken down into smaller sub-specifications, each defining an easier problem. These easier problems are solved: code is produced that satisfies each of the sub-specifications and is assembled to produce a program that satisfies the original specification. The sub-specifications can be tackled in a similar way: each in turn can be broken down into even smaller specifications until a point is eventually reached where the the code that satisfies a specification and the corresponding proofs of correctness are trivial. A further bonus will be that the techniques used to split a specification will provide the glue to assemble the code fragments that will satisfy the specification (see Fig. 5.1).

What is the 'glue' that will be used to join everything together? The 'glue' will be the programming constructs described in the previous chapters; these are semicolon, guard and choice. We will stop the decomposition of larger specifications into smaller ones when a situation is reached where the specification can be easily satisfied by an assignment command. At each step of this process a proof of correctness may need to be carried out to show that any new decomposition, or 'refinement', of a specification does not effectively change anything. Also, adjustments will be made to pre- and post-conditions without fundamentally changing a specification. The form of the final program should be such that there are no unbounded commands, all choices

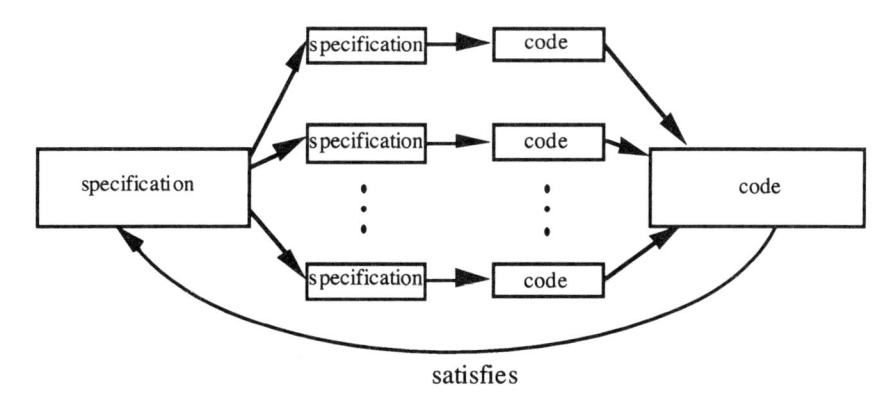

Fig. 5.1. From specification to code.

should be finite, and no back-tracking is necessary as any look-ahead can be statically determined.

5.2 Replacing Specifications

How can a specification be replaced without changing its intent? If a program is written to satisfy the new specification, it must satisfy the original one. What, then, are the restrictions on the replacement specification, what sort of adjustments can be made to pre- and post-conditions without really changing anything? We will take as our starting point the following specification:

> *op*
> chg $w : W$
> pre *pre*
> post *post*

and consider replacing it with another specification that has the same intent:

> *op'*
> chg $w : W$
> pre *pre'*
> post *post'*

This new specification is a replacement for *op* if any program that satisfies *op'* also satisfies *op*. What we need to do is to remove the 'any program' part of this informal definition, and also to make it more formal.

Now if the pre-condition for *op* was non-trivial and we replaced it by true to get a replacement specification:

op'
chg $w : W$
pre true
post $post$

Then, assuming that op' is implementable[1], any program developed to satisfy op' would also satisfy op. In some sense such a program could be considered to do a better job in that it would deliver answers from input that did not satisfy the pre-condition of the original specification op. The new specification op' is equally acceptable as the old specification op.

We can extend this idea: any input that satisfies the pre-condition of op must also satisfy the pre-condition of op', since any program that satisfies op' must also satisfy op and therefore deliver correct answers under the assumption of the original pre-condition. Therefore it must certainly work under those conditions where the pre-condition of op is true. This means that a pre-condition can be replaced providing:

$$\forall\, i \in State \cdot pre(i) \;\Rightarrow\; pre'(i)$$

With this proof obligation notice that if the original pre-condition is false for an input value, then the new pre-condition can also be false (the new specification does not say what should happen) or it could be true (the post-condition of the new specification will then describe what should happen). In this later case the new specification would be more prescriptive, it describes what should happen with some invalid inputs. The domain of acceptable inputs can be widened – made more general.

Also for any input value that satisfies the pre-condition for op, the two specifications must agree on an answer for such input. Remembering that the post-condition for a particular piece of input can specify a range of possible answers, any one of which would do. This means that the pairs of input/output values defined by op', where the input value satisfies the pre-condition of OP, must be acceptable to the post-condition of op. This can be written:

$$\forall\, i, o \in State \cdot pre(i) \land post'(i, o) \;\Rightarrow\; post(i, o)$$

In execution terms non-determinism can be removed. If the original specification allowed a choice of results for a particular input value, the new specification can remove some of that choice. It should not remove all of the choices for a valid input.

These two rules together give one definition of a replacement specification – however this definition does not take implementability into account. The informal reasoning has been in terms of a specification 'executing' – for any input that satisfies the pre-condition, by some 'magic', produce an output

---

[1] The issue of implementability will be addressed later.

that satisfies the post-condition. It is the idea of a specification in some sense 'terminating' that needs to be added to the idea of a replacement specification discussed above. We already have a way of stating that a program A satisfies a specification op:

$\forall\, i \in State \cdot pre(i)\ \Rightarrow$
$\qquad (\exists\, o \in State \cdot {}_iA_o) \wedge (\forall\, o \in State \cdot {}_iA_o\ \Rightarrow\ post(i,o))$

This means that the program p satisfies the specification defined by the pre-condition and the post-condition. We also showed informally in Chapter 2 that this was equivalent to

$pre\ \Rightarrow\ [A]post$

These characterizations of satisfaction assumes that the program *terminates* with an output value that, together with a valid input value, satisfies the post-condition. The equivalent idea to termination for a specification is that it is implementable, and it is this concept that will be used:

op' sat op if
$\forall\, i \in State \cdot pre(i)\ \Rightarrow\ pre'(i)$
$\forall\, i, o \in State \cdot pre(i) \wedge post'(i,o)\ \Rightarrow\ post(i,o)$
$\forall\, i \in State \cdot pre'(i)\ \Rightarrow\ \exists\, o \in State \cdot post'(i,o)$

The third equation is the specification version of the statement 'the program must terminate ...'. With this definition a program can be thought of as an executable specification, and, equivalently, a specification is a non-executable program. This equation prevents the possibility of replacing any specification by the following command (remember programs are specifications and specifications are programs):

    miracle
    pre true
    post false

The miracle program is willing to accept any input and produce no output – and a program that just loops would not do; such a program 'produces' an output of $\perp$, which is output. It can be shown that the implementability test prevents miracle being proposed as a solution to a specification.

We will not be too worried about proving that specifications are satisfiable – the production of a working program that satisfies the specification will be evidence that a specification is satisfiable. There is a problem, however – the miracle program can occur in disguise as an innocent specification, and there is the danger of introducing a disguised miracle while carrying out program refinement. If at some point miracle is introduced, it is impossible to remove and to return to an implementable specification. So if we do make a decision which accidentally introduces a miracle, it is impossible to remove. Thus the only danger with miracle is for it to be introduced in a disguised form and for the refinement to be continued. The only result will be wasted effort as a disguised miracle is slowly refined to the undisguised version. Experience will help in avoiding such development steps.

We will use a weaker form of satisfaction that allows the miracle program, calling this 'refinement', and denote it by the symbol $\sqsubseteq$ which is read as 'is refined by'. We can easily show the following:

A sat $B \nrightarrow B \sqsubseteq A$
and
$B \sqsubseteq A \land$ 'A is implementable' $\Rightarrow A$ sat B

In a previous chapter it was indicated that A was implementable if and only if it was total:

A is implementable $\Leftrightarrow \mathcal{G}(A)$

the following theorem finishes the task

Theorem 5.1
If

$A \sqsubseteq B$
$\mathcal{G}(B)$

then

$\mathcal{G}(A)$

$\square$

the proof will be left until later.

With the concept of refinement, we will have a specification S and a series of refinements $R_1, R_2, \ldots, R_n$, and finally p where the final step is to produce an *executable* program p. The following will be true:

$S \sqsubseteq R_1 \sqsubseteq R_2 \sqsubseteq \ldots \sqsubseteq R_n \sqsubseteq p \land \mathcal{G}(p) \Rightarrow p$ sat S

Since the final step produces an executable program, the development is valid. If any of the steps produce either miracle or miracle in disguise, we are in trouble and we will not be able to produce an executable program. It turns out that this is not usually a problem.

We can abbreviate the first two rules by leaving out the quantification which is over the state (restricted to the frame – the ext identifiers), and knowing that the pre-condition is a function of the undecorated frame variables, and the post-condition a function of both decorated and undecorated frame variables. With these conventions the first two rules of the above definition become:

if $\left\{ \begin{array}{c} pre \Rightarrow pre' \\ pre[w\backslash \overleftarrow{w}] \wedge post' \Rightarrow post \end{array} \right\}$ then

$$
\begin{array}{ccc}
op & & op' \\
\text{chg } w & & \text{chg } w \\
\text{pre } pre & \sqsubseteq & \text{pre } pre' \\
\text{post } post & & \text{post } post'
\end{array}
$$

Remembering that the idea behind refinement is to replace a command by an equivalent one that does less. Equivalent in the sense that, given any input, a user cannot tell the difference between the new command and the one it refines; does less in the sense that some non-determinism may be removed. The motivation for the definition of refinement is just this: we could define a refinement of A by B as follows.

For input s, if t is a proper outcome of B then t is a proper outcome of A, this means that for all predicates R,

$$[A]\text{true} \wedge \langle A\rangle R \;\Rightarrow\; \langle B\rangle R \tag{a}$$

This is saying for those values that will terminate, whatever A can establish, B can too. For improper outcomes from the input s, if B could loop, then A could also. This is equivalent to

$$\neg [B]\text{true} \;\Rightarrow\; \neg [A]\text{true} \tag{b}$$

An operational description of simulation refinement is to replace a command by one that does less. For executable commands both A and an 'executable' replacement B will be total, thus we shall be mainly looking at executable approximations. Now from (b) we have

$$[A]\text{true} \;\Rightarrow\; [B]\text{true} \tag{c}$$

and by (a) and (c) we have

$$[A]\text{true} \wedge \langle A\rangle R \;\Rightarrow\; [B]\text{true} \wedge \langle B\rangle R$$

$\iff$

$$[A]R \;\Rightarrow\; [B]R$$

Thus our definition of simulation is as follows:

Definition 5.1

B is a refinement of A, written $A \sqsubseteq B$ if, for all predicates R over the state:

$$[A]R \;\Rightarrow\; [B]R$$

The definition states that whatever A will establish, B will. Note that B may establish a predicate when A does not – it may work in circumstances where A doesn't. However B does work and delivers the same outcome whenever A does.

The refinement relation has some expected properties. A specification satisfies itself, or equivalently a program refines itself:

Theorem 5.2
The relation $\sqsubseteq$ is reflexive:

$$A \sqsubseteq A$$

Proof
For any R we have $[A]R \Rightarrow [A]R$.
∎

Refinement is transitive:

Theorem 5.3
The relation $\sqsubseteq$ is transitive:

$$A \sqsubseteq B \text{ and } B \sqsubseteq C \text{ then } A \sqsubseteq C$$

Proof
For any R we have that $A \sqsubseteq B$ means $[A]R \Rightarrow [B]R$ and $B \sqsubseteq C$ means we have $[B]R \Rightarrow [C]R$. Thus $[A]R \Rightarrow [C]R$. As R was arbitrary we can deduce $A \sqsubseteq C$.
∎

The equivalence of two commands can be defined:

Definition 5.2
A is equivalent to B, written $A \equiv B$ if:

$$A \sqsubseteq B \text{ and } B \sqsubseteq A$$

Two commands are equivalent if they refine each other.

Now this definition was derived informally in a similar way to the version just using implicit specifications – an immediate question is are they equivalent? In Chapter 2 we used the following idea for refinement: an implicit specification op is refined by a program A if

$$pre \wedge \overleftarrow{w} = w \Rightarrow [A]post$$

or if there are no hooked variables in the post-condition

$$pre \Rightarrow [A]post$$

so we have two versions of refinement and a rule for refining specifications, and it can be shown that they are all equivalent, in fact they are all just slight variations of the same statement of a correctness. First a lemma that allows the manipulation of predicates.

Lemma 5.1
If A does not assign to any variables that occur free in an assertion R then
$$[A]R \Leftrightarrow \mathcal{G}(A) \Rightarrow R \wedge [A]\text{true}$$

Proof
Now by Theorem 3.34, A can be expressed as
$$@x' \bullet q(x, x') \rightarrow x := x' \,\square\, \neg p(x) \rightarrow \text{loop}$$

for some p and q and by the assumption, R does not depend on x, thus:

$[@x' \bullet q(x, x') \rightarrow x := x' \,\square\, \neg p(x) \rightarrow \text{loop}]R$
$\Longleftrightarrow$
$p(x) \wedge (\forall x' \cdot q(x, x') \Rightarrow [x := x']R)$
$\Longleftrightarrow$
$p(x) \wedge (\forall x' \cdot q(x, x') \Rightarrow R)$
$\Longleftrightarrow$
$p(x) \wedge (\neg \exists x' \cdot q(x, x') \vee R)$
$\Longleftrightarrow$
$p(x) \wedge \neg \exists x' \cdot q(x, x') \vee p(x) \wedge R$
$\Longleftrightarrow$
$\neg \mathcal{G}(A) \vee p(x) \wedge R$
$\Longleftrightarrow$
$\mathcal{G}(A) \Rightarrow p(x) \wedge R$
$\Longleftrightarrow$
$\mathcal{G}(A) \Rightarrow R \wedge [A]\text{true}$

∎

This lemma proves an obvious property: for those values in the domain of a command that satisfy a predicate R independent of A, if A terminates, then R will still be true.

Theorem 5.4
If $pre \wedge \overleftarrow{w} = w \Rightarrow [A]post$ and $A \sqsubseteq B$ then $pre \wedge \overleftarrow{w} = w \Rightarrow [B]post$.

Proof
Since $A \sqsubseteq B$ then $[A]post \Rightarrow [B]post$ and the result follows immediately.
∎

As a specification can be considered to be a program, does a specification command satisfy itself; the following lemma addresses this issue:

5. Program Refinement

Lemma 5.2
If x and y partition the vector of program variables w then

$$pre \land \overleftarrow{w} = w \Rightarrow [y:[\ pre,\ post\ ]](post \land \overleftarrow{x} = x)$$

Proof

$$pre \land \overleftarrow{w} = w \Rightarrow [y:[\ pre,\ post\ ]](post \land \overleftarrow{x} = x)$$

$\iff$

$$pre \land \overleftarrow{w} = w \Rightarrow pre \land (\forall y' \cdot post(w, y') \Rightarrow post(w, y') \land \overleftarrow{x} = x)$$

$\iff$

$$\overleftarrow{w} = w \Rightarrow (\forall y' \cdot post(w, y') \Rightarrow post(w, y') \land \overleftarrow{x} = x)$$

$\iff$

$$\overleftarrow{w} = w \Rightarrow \overleftarrow{x} = x$$

$\iff$

true

∎

The next lemma takes things a step further, if a command, under the assumption of the pre-condition, establishes the post-condition, then the command is a refinement of the specification.

Lemma 5.3
If

x and y partition the vector of program variables w
$pre \land \overleftarrow{w} = w \Rightarrow [A](post \land \overleftarrow{x} = x)$

then

$$y:[\ pre,\ post\ ] \sqsubseteq A$$

Proof
If $y:[\ pre,\ post\ ] \sqsubseteq A$ then for any predicate R:

$[y:[\ pre,\ post\ ]]R \Rightarrow [A]R$

$\iff$ semantics

$pre \land \overleftarrow{w} = w \land (\forall y \cdot post \Rightarrow R) \Rightarrow [A]R$

$\Longleftarrow$ hypothesis

$[A](post \land \overleftarrow{x} = x) \land (\forall y \cdot post \Rightarrow R) \Rightarrow [A]R$

$\Longleftarrow$ Lemma 5.1

$[A](post \land \overleftarrow{x} = x) \land [A](\forall y \cdot post \Rightarrow R) \Rightarrow [A]R$

$\iff$ ∧-distribution

$[A](post \land \overleftarrow{x} = x \land (\forall y \cdot post \Rightarrow R)) \Rightarrow [A]R$

$\Leftarrow$ A is monotonic
$$post \land (\forall y \cdot post \Rightarrow R) \Rightarrow R$$
$=$ predicate calculus
$$(\forall y \cdot post \Rightarrow R) \Rightarrow (post \Rightarrow R)$$
$=$ predicate calculus
   true

∎

Theorem 5.5
If x and y partition the program variables w then

$$pre \land \overleftarrow{w} = w \Rightarrow [A](post \land \overleftarrow{x} = x)$$
iff
$$y : [\ pre,\ \ post\ ] \sqsubseteq A$$

Proof
Now for any predicate R over the state:

$$y : [\ pre,\ \ post\ ] \sqsubseteq A$$
$$\Longleftrightarrow$$
$$[y : [\ pre,\ \ post\ ]] R \Rightarrow [A] R$$

thus

$$[y : [\ pre,\ \ post\ ]](post \land \overleftarrow{x} = x) \Rightarrow [A](post \land \overleftarrow{x} = x)$$
$\Longrightarrow$ Lemma 5.2
$$pre \land \overleftarrow{y} = w \Rightarrow [A](post \land \overleftarrow{x} = x)$$

The other direction is just Lemma 5.3.

∎

We return to the first motivation of refinement in Section 5.2 on page 85 and prove the rule formally:

Theorem 5.6 (replace specification rule)

if $\left\{ \begin{array}{c} pre \Rightarrow pre' \\ pre[w \backslash \overleftarrow{w}] \land post' \Rightarrow post \end{array} \right\}$ then

op   op'
chg w chg w
pre pre $\sqsubseteq$ pre pre'
post $post$ post $post'$

Proof
By Theorem 5.4 we should show that under the assumption of the pre-condition, the command will establish the post-condition:

$pre(w) \wedge \overleftarrow{w} = w \Rightarrow$
$\quad [@w' \bullet post'(w, w') \rightarrow w := w' \ \square \ \neg pre'(w) \rightarrow \textsf{chaos}] post(\overleftarrow{w}, w)$
$\iff$ semantics
$pre(w) \wedge \overleftarrow{w} = w \Rightarrow$
$\quad pre'(w) \wedge (\forall w' \cdot post'(w, w') \Rightarrow [w := w'] post(\overleftarrow{w}, w))$
$\iff$ substitution
$pre(w) \wedge \overleftarrow{w} = w \Rightarrow pre'(w) \wedge (\forall w' \cdot post'(w, w') \Rightarrow post(\overleftarrow{w}, w'))$
$\iff$ predicate calculus
$pre(\overleftarrow{w}) \Rightarrow pre'(\overleftarrow{w}) \wedge \forall w \cdot post'(\overleftarrow{w}, w) \Rightarrow post(\overleftarrow{w}, w)$
$\iff$ predicate calculus and hypothesis
$\quad$ true

∎

Corollary 5.1
For any predicate q

$$x : [\ pre,\ post\ ] \sqsubseteq x : [\ pre,\ post \wedge q\ ]$$

□

This corollary may seem strange, but it follows immediately from the theorem, so what has gone wrong? If q is the predicate false then the replacement specification is miracle, and this is the explanation. If we add a term that is too restrictive, then the new specification may not be implementable – it may well be miracle in disguise. If the additional term does not make the new specification unimplementable, then all is well, a program written to satisfy it will still satisfy the old specification. If both the original and new specification are implementable, both are total, then for all valid inputs – inputs that satisfy the pre-condition – they will establish both the original post-condition $post$ and the additional predicate q. In this case the additional predicate q will be removing non-determinism.

We are now in a position to prove Theorem 5.1 stated above:

Theorem 5.1
If

$\quad A \sqsubseteq B$
$\quad \mathcal{G}(B)$

then

$\quad \mathcal{G}(A)$

Proof
For any predicate R defined over the state:

$A \sqsubseteq B$

$\iff$

$[A]R \Rightarrow [B]R$

$\Longrightarrow$

$[A]\text{false} \Rightarrow [B]\text{false}$

$\iff$

$\neg[B]\text{false} \Rightarrow \neg[A]\text{false}$

$\iff$

$\mathcal{G}(B) \Rightarrow \mathcal{G}(A)$

∎

A way to produce a replacement specification is to add the pre-condition to the post-condition. We are just reminding ourselves that the pre-condition must hold:

op
chg $w : W$
pre *pre*
post *post*

is identical to the new specification:

op'
chg $w : W$
pre *pre*
post $pre[w\backslash\overleftarrow{w}] \land post$

or equivalently, writing it as a theorem/rule:

Theorem 5.7 (assume pre-condition in post-condition rule)

chg w		chg w
pre *pre*	$\equiv$	pre *pre*
post *post*		post $pre[w\backslash\overleftarrow{w}] \land post$

Proof
It is easily proved using Theorem 5.6 and Corollary 5.1.
∎

The main use of this rule is to simplify a post-condition; the rules explained above each change the pre-condition with the intent of making the post-condition easier to establish. This rule will enable the modified pre-condition to be assumed in the post-condition as part of the simplification process.

5.3 Conventions

When refining operations there is much duplication of information, particularly if the frame is rewritten each time that a refinement step is made. This just leads to verbosity if the refinements are machine aided – if a computer is used to manage most, if not all the transformations. However, if refinements are written out by hand, some sort of convention is needed to reduce the amount of writing. The convention that we shall use is as follows: if a frame is left out of any specifications on the right-hand-side of the $\sqsubseteq$ symbol, then the missing frame is identical to the frame of the operation being refined – the operation on the left-hand-side of the $\sqsubseteq$ symbol. It may be necessary to trace back through several levels; if there is any ambiguity – if in doubt – write the frame information.

A similar convention for the types of identifiers in a frame will be used: if the type of an identifier is not stated, then its type is the same as it was in the frame of the operation (usually denoted by an identifier) on the left-hand-side of the $\sqsubseteq$ symbol.

The following notation will be used to write down the refinement rules. The proof obligations must be satisfied in order for the refinement step to be valid.

if { proof obligations } then

refinement rule

This style of expressing the statement of a theorem will be the way of flagging a refinement rule.

5.4 Refinement Classes

We saw earlier that the relation $\sqsubseteq$ is reflexive and transitive, however it is not antisymmetric, so that it is not partial order.

The relation $\sqsubseteq$ is not antisymmetric since $A \sqsubseteq B$ and $B \sqsubseteq A$ does not imply $A = B$, however it does imply $[A]R = [B]R$ for all R. This is because for refinement we do not care what happens outside of the pre-condition, thus for a command A, and for any command B we have

$A \sqsubseteq [A]\text{true} \rightarrow A \,[\!]\, \neg [A]\text{true} \rightarrow B$

is a refinement of A, since for any R:

$$[A]R \Rightarrow [A]\text{true}$$

Thus for any command B we have:

$$[A]R$$
$$\Longrightarrow$$
$$(\neg[A]\text{true} \vee [A]R) \wedge ([A]\text{true} \vee [B]R)$$
$$\Longrightarrow$$
$$([A]\text{true} \Rightarrow [A]R) \wedge (\neg[A]\text{true} \Rightarrow [B]R)$$
$$\Longleftrightarrow$$
$$[[A]\text{true} \rightarrow A \,\square\, \neg[A]\text{true} \rightarrow B]R$$

The 'best' and 'worst' cases for B could be considered to be loop and chaos.

This problem is the motivation for the introduction early of the idea of an equivalent specification. A specification OP is equivalent to OP' (written $OP \equiv OP'$) when OP can be replaced by OP' and OP' can be replaced by OP. Thus

$$OP \sqsubseteq OP' \wedge OP' \sqsubseteq OP \text{ iff } OP \equiv OP'$$

The $\equiv$ operator is an equivalence relation:

Theorem 5.8
$\equiv$ is reflexive: $A \equiv A$
$\equiv$ is symmetric: $A \equiv B \Rightarrow B \equiv A$
$\equiv$ is transitive: $A \equiv B \wedge B \equiv C \Rightarrow A \equiv C$

Proof
Straight from the definition of $\equiv$.
■

Thus $\equiv$ can be used to partition the set of all commands (programs) P in the usual way to give the set of equivalence classes:

$$P/\equiv$$

The relation $\sqsubseteq$ can be extended to $P/\equiv$:

$$[A] \sqsubseteq_\equiv [B] \text{ iff } A \sqsubseteq B$$

and $\sqsubseteq_\equiv$ is a partial order over $P/\equiv$. Thus we shall treat $\sqsubseteq$ as if it is a partial order over P, where really we mean a partial order $\sqsubseteq_\equiv$ over $P/\equiv$. If we require the program A that satisfies the relation $A \sqsubseteq B$ for all programs B we mean any member of $[A]$ that satisfies $[A] \sqsubseteq_\equiv [B]$ for all $[B]$. In other words we shall ignore the fact that $\sqsubseteq$ is not a partial order relation – we can always move to $P/\equiv$ if it is really necessary. This is one of the prices we pay for distinguishing loop as a special command that is different from chaos.

To give some understanding of this, to characterize an equivalence relation we could choose either $[A]$true $\to A \mathbin{\square} \neg [A]$true $\to$ loop or $[A]$true $\to A \mathbin{\square} \neg [A]$true $\to$ chaos. We could even choose $[A]$true $\to A$, but this command is not total! It should also be recorded that loop $\equiv$ chaos and this means that loop $\sqsubseteq$ chaos and chaos $\sqsubseteq$ loop. A little thought shows that this is what we should expect. We do not need for $\sqsubseteq$ to be a partial order relation; we do need refinement to be piecewise, that if $A \sqsubseteq A'$ then $F(A) \sqsubseteq F(A')$ where F is made up from our basic operators and is thus piecewise monotonic. We shall address this problem in the next chapters.

We can finish off by showing that ignoring those values that do not satisfy the pre-condition of a command, those values that are not guaranteed to terminate, if two commands are equivalent, then within their pre-conditions they are equal. We can ignore what happens outside the pre-condition by either using an assertion or guarding.

Theorem 5.9
If $A \equiv B$ then $\{[A]\text{true}\}A = \{[B]\text{true}\}B$.

Proof
From the definition of command equivalence we have

$$[A]R = [B]R$$

thus

$$[A]\text{true} = [B]\text{true}$$
$$\iff$$
$$[A]\text{true} \land [A]\text{true} = [B]\text{true} \land [B]\text{true}$$
$$\iff$$
$$[\{[A]\text{true}\}A]\text{true} = [\{[B]\text{true}\}B]\text{true}$$

and

$$[A]R = [B]R$$
$$\iff$$
$$[A]\text{true} \land \langle A \rangle R = [B]\text{true} \land \langle B \rangle R$$
$$\iff$$
$$\langle \{[A]\text{true}\}A \rangle R = \langle \{[B]\text{true}\}B \rangle R$$

therefore $\{[A]\text{true}\}A = \{[B]\text{true}\}B$.
∎

Theorem 5.10
If $A \equiv B$ then $[A]\text{true} \to A = [B]\text{true} \to B$.

Proof
From the definition of command equivalence we have

$$[A]R = [B]R$$

thus

$$[A]\text{true} = [B]\text{true}$$

and thus

$$([A]\text{true} \Rightarrow [A]\text{true}) = ([B]\text{true} \Rightarrow [B]\text{true})$$
$$\Longleftrightarrow$$
$$[[A]\text{true} \rightarrow A]\text{true} = [[B]\text{true} \rightarrow B]\text{true}$$

and

$$[A]\text{true} \Rightarrow [A]R = [B]\text{true} \Rightarrow [B]R$$
$$\Longleftrightarrow$$
$$[A]\text{true} \Rightarrow [A]\text{true} \wedge \langle A \rangle R = [B]\text{true} \Rightarrow [B]\text{true} \wedge \langle B \rangle R$$
$$\Longleftrightarrow$$
$$\neg [A]\text{true} \vee [A]\text{true} \wedge \langle A \rangle R = \neg [B]\text{true} \vee [B]\text{true} \wedge \langle B \rangle R$$
$$\Longleftrightarrow$$
$$\neg [A]\text{true} \vee \langle A \rangle R = \neg [B]\text{true} \vee \langle B \rangle R$$
$$\Longleftrightarrow$$
$$[A]\text{true} \Rightarrow \langle A \rangle R = [B]\text{true} \Rightarrow \langle B \rangle R$$
$$\Longleftrightarrow$$
$$\langle [A]\text{true} \rightarrow A \rangle R = \langle [B]\text{true} \rightarrow B \rangle R$$

therefore $[A]\text{true} \rightarrow A = [B]\text{true} \rightarrow B$.
∎

Finally a theorem on the equivalence of the normal form of a command and a specification:

Theorem 5.11
$$@x' : X \bullet q(x, x') \rightarrow x := x' \,[\!]\, \neg p \rightarrow \text{loop}$$
$$\equiv$$
$$@x' : X \bullet q(x, x') \rightarrow x := x' \,[\!]\, \neg p \rightarrow \text{chaos}$$
□

5.5 Alternative Views of Refinement

To get more insight into the process of algorithmic or program refinement, the weakest pre-condition approach can be translated into an equivalent re-

5. Program Refinement

lational version of refinement. Now if A is refined by B then the following informal derivation can be carried out, for any predicate R:

$[A]R \Rightarrow [B]R$
$\Longleftrightarrow$
$[A]\text{true} \Rightarrow [B]\text{true} \wedge (\langle A \rangle R \Rightarrow \langle B \rangle R)$
$\Longleftrightarrow$
$\forall s \cdot \neg {}_sA_\perp \Rightarrow (\neg {}_sB_\perp \wedge (\forall t \cdot {}_sB_t \Rightarrow {}_sA_t))$
$\Longleftrightarrow$
$\forall s \cdot \neg {}_sA_\perp \Rightarrow (\forall o \cdot {}_sB_o \Rightarrow {}_sA_o)$
$\Longleftrightarrow$
$\forall s, o \cdot {}_sB_o \Rightarrow ({}_aA_o \vee {}_sA_\perp)$

Thus every outcome of the refinement is either an outcome of the specification or was the improper outcome – the improper outcome can be replaced either by a proper outcome or left alone.

If A terminates, then B does; this is equivalent to $\neg {}_sA_\perp \Rightarrow \neg {}_sB_\perp$ which is the same as ${}_sB_\perp \Rightarrow {}_sA_\perp$. It is also necessary that B be implementable – i.e. that B is total.

Writing $\mathcal{T}(A)$ for the set defined by the predicate $[A]\text{true}$, the refinement $A \sqsubseteq B$ could be defined intuitively using relations:

$\mathcal{T}(A) \triangleleft B \subseteq \mathcal{T}(A) \triangleleft A$
$\mathcal{T}(A) \subseteq \mathcal{T}(B)$

This means that if we just consider the refinement B restricted to only those input values to A that are guaranteed to produce proper outcomes, the input/outputs pairs produced by B should be a subset of the input/output pairs produced by A under the same restriction.
Now

$\forall s, o \cdot \neg {}_sA_\perp \wedge {}_sB_o \Rightarrow \neg {}_sA_\perp \wedge {}_sA_o$
= definition of $\Rightarrow$
$\forall s, o \cdot {}_sA_\perp \vee \neg {}_sB_o \vee (\neg {}_sA_\perp \wedge {}_sA_o)$
= distribute $\wedge$ over $\vee$
$\forall s, o \cdot {}_sA_\perp \vee \neg {}_sB_o \vee \neg {}_sA_\perp \wedge {}_sA_\perp \vee \neg {}_sB_\perp \vee {}_sA_o$
= simplify
$\forall s, o \cdot {}_sA_\perp \vee \neg {}_sB_o \vee {}_sA_o$
= definition of $\Rightarrow$
$\forall s, o \cdot {}_sB_o \Rightarrow {}_sA_\perp \vee {}_sA_o$

which is equivalent to the original definition.

The relational definition might also be written

$$T(A) \triangleleft B \subseteq A$$
$$T(A) \subseteq T(B)$$

The proof is now

$$\forall s, o \cdot \neg {}_sA_\bot \wedge {}_sB_o \Rightarrow {}_sA_o$$
$$= \text{ definition of } \Rightarrow$$
$$\forall s, o \cdot {}_sA_\bot \vee \neg {}_sB_o \vee {}_sA_o$$
$$= \text{ definition of } \Rightarrow$$
$$\forall s, o \cdot {}_sB_o \Rightarrow {}_sA_\bot \vee {}_sA_o$$

Refinement can be seen to be widening pre-conditions, narrowing post-conditions by removing choice and perhaps replacing the improper outcome by a proper one. In Chapter 2 it was mentioned that loop could also be considered as abort. With this approach one of the things that can be done during refinement is to replace loop by a more useful error message!

5.6 Other Refinement Relations

The above refinement rule is just one possibility amongst many. In this section we shall briefly consider other possibilities and discuss their use. The idea behind a refinement is that the customer cannot tell the difference between the original program and its refinement.

5.6.1 Weak Refinement
Definition 5.3
B is a weak refinement of A, written $A \sqsubseteq_{\text{WEAK}} B$ if

$$[A]\text{true} \wedge [B]\text{true} \wedge \langle A \rangle R \Rightarrow \langle B \rangle R$$

What this rule says is that for those input values where both A and its refinement B are guaranteed to terminate, then B does the same as A. Notice that with this refinement rule:

$A \sqsubseteq_{\text{WEAK}}$ loop
$A \sqsubseteq_{\text{WEAK}}$ miracle
$A \sqsubseteq_{\text{WEAK}}$ chaos

All this refinement rule guarantees is that if, for a given input value, both A and B produce a proper result, then the result produced by B is one that A could produce.

This is really the minimum requirement on a refinement; it could be argued that if a refinement relation does not satisfy this, then it is not refinement – it is something else. A problem with this refinement relation is that it is not transitive, there is too much freedom to replace proper outcomes by the improper outcome and vice-versa.

5.6.2 Partial Refinement

The restrictions on the input values could be removed to give another possible definition for refinement:

Definition 5.4
B is a partial refinement of A, written $A \sqsubseteq_{PARTIAL} B$ if

$$\langle A \rangle R \Rightarrow \langle B \rangle R$$

This is a slightly stronger refinement relation, but it allows a proper outcome from A to be replaced by an improper outcome. With this rule, if we get an outcome from B, either A would loop with the input, or could produce the same result. With this refinement rule:

$A \sqsubseteq_{PARTIAL}$ loop
$A \sqsubseteq_{PARTIAL}$ miracle

5.6.3 Full Refinement

It is because the previous two rules did not impose any restrictions on how the input values that satisfy $[A]$true should be dealt with that caused the problem. There are two possibilities here. The first is full refinement, this was used in Chapter 4 when defining the limit of commands; the definition is repeated for completeness:

Definition 5.5
B is a full refinement of A, written $A \sqsubseteq_{FULL} B$ if

$[B]$true $\Rightarrow [A]$true
$\langle A \rangle R \Rightarrow \langle B \rangle R$

This rule demands that whenever B would terminate, A does too, and the outcomes of B could all be produced by A. This refinement class has the following property:

Theorem 5.12
If $A \sqsubseteq_{FULL} B$ and $B \sqsubseteq_{FULL} A$ then $A = B$.

Proof
The proof is trivial and follows from the definition.
∎

5.6.4 Strong Refinement

The second stronger version of refinement is called strong refinement, it is defined as follows:

5.6 Other Refinement Relations

Definition 5.6
B is a strong refinement of A, written $A \sqsubseteq_{\text{STRONG}} B$ if

$[A]\text{true} \Rightarrow [B]\text{true}$

$\langle A \rangle R \Rightarrow \langle B \rangle R$

This refinement class has the following property:

Theorem 5.13
If $A \sqsubseteq_{\text{STRONG}} B$ and $B \sqsubseteq_{\text{STRONG}} A$ then $A = B$.

Proof
The proof is trivial and follows from the definition.
∎

This rule demands that whenever A would terminate, B does too, and the outcomes of B could all be produced by A.

However, this refinement is too strong, it only allows removal of non-determinism. It requires that both A and B do the same thing with those input values that are not guaranteed to terminate, to produce proper outcomes — for specifications this means that the refinement of a specification must concern itself with values that do not satisfy the pre-condition. What is required is a refinement relation which lies somewhere between weak refinement and strong requirement.

5.6.5 Refinement by Simulation

For refinement we are normally interested that B should terminate whenever A would, and in addition, for those input values that A guarantees to produce a proper outcome, that B should produce an outcome for these values that A could. This suggests the following definition:

Definition 5.7
A is simulated by B, written $A \sqsubseteq_{\text{SIM}} B$ if

$[A]\text{true} \Rightarrow [B]\text{true}$

$[A]\text{true} \wedge \langle A \rangle R \Rightarrow \langle B \rangle R$

and we have already shown that this is equivalent to:

$[A]R \Rightarrow [B]R$ iff $A \sqsubseteq_{\text{SIM}} B$

This book uses simulation refinement, we will drop the SIM subscript and define the refinement class we want as:

Definition 5.8
B is a simulation refinement of A, written $A \sqsubseteq B$ if for all R defined over the state:

$[A]R \Rightarrow [B]R$

Note that strong refinement is equivalent to

$A \sqsubseteq_{\text{PARTIAL}} B$
$A \sqsubseteq_{\text{SIM}} B$

5.7 Summary

The initial sections of this chapter gave various definitions for algorithmic or program refinement and showed that they are all equivalent. Each of the definitions was motivated by intuition based on the sort of properties refinement should have – under what circumstances can be change a program and still satisfy the requirements of the user or the customer. We have also discussed other possible refinement rules and tried to explain the differences. These alternative refinements each have their use, they are about different software engineering decisions to that of the refinement relation introduced in the first part of the chapter.

A further point. If a compiler is being written for a non-deterministic language, it should be realized that it is impossible for the compiler to generate code that is truly non-deterministic. Thus for a non-deterministic program, the compiler will remove non-determinism, the compiler must make decisions between non-deterministic choices, and thus perform a 'final' refinement step. The compiler will have refinement rules built-in, so the developer needs to be aware of what refinement rules will be provided by the compiler – they should match those the developer was using for his or her refinement steps.

6. The Basic Commands

In this chapter we shall look at refinements associated with the basic commands. The pattern of presentation followed in this, and in subsequent chapters, will be to introduce theorems about refinement that can be used as refinement rules. The main purpose of many of the theorems is to provide insight into the refinement process, and to confirm understanding of the semantics of a command and its refinement. However, some of the refinement rules are more useful than others when transforming a specification – these rules have be flagged and collected in Appendix A.

6.1 The Constant Commands

It is unlikely that we would wish to refine any of the constant commands, or to use any of them (other than skip) in refinement. Thus most of the theorems in this section provide insight and understanding rather than useful refinement rules, the exception being the skip introduction rule. We will start by refining the loop command; since algorithmic refinement allows the improper outcome to be replaced by anything, we have immediately:

Theorem 6.1
$\quad$ loop $\sqsubseteq A$

Proof
For any predicate R defined over the state:

$\quad$ false $\Rightarrow [A]R$
$\Longleftrightarrow$
$\quad$ [loop]$R \Rightarrow [A]R$

■

Refinement involves the reduction of non-determinism, thus any command can be used to refine chaos:

Theorem 6.2
$\quad$ chaos $\sqsubseteq A$

Proof
For any predicate R defined over the state:

$$\text{false} \Rightarrow [A]R$$
$$\Longleftrightarrow$$
$$[\text{chaos}]R \Rightarrow [A]R$$

∎

Remembering that the havoc command can produce any proper outcome, it can be refined by any command that does not produce the improper outcome:

Theorem 6.3
If $[A]\text{true}$ then

$$\text{havoc} \sqsubseteq A$$

Proof
For any predicate R other than the predicate true we have:

$$\text{false} \Rightarrow [A]R$$
$$\Longleftrightarrow$$
$$[\text{havoc}]R \Rightarrow [A]R$$

For the predicate true we have

$$\text{true} \Rightarrow \text{true}$$
$$\Longleftrightarrow$$
$$[\text{havoc}]\text{true} \Rightarrow [A]\text{true}$$

∎

A miracle command can refine anything:

Theorem 6.4
$$A \sqsubseteq \text{miracle}$$

□

But once we have a miracle, it cannot be removed – the miracle command can only be refined by another miracle:

Theorem 6.5
$$\text{miracle} \sqsubseteq A \text{ iff } A = \text{miracle}$$

Proof
For a command A that refines miracle and any predicate R defined over the state:

$$\text{miracle} \sqsubseteq A$$
$$\Longleftrightarrow$$
$$[\text{miracle}]R \Rightarrow [A]R$$
$$\Longleftrightarrow$$
$$\text{true} \Rightarrow [A]R$$
$$\Longleftrightarrow$$
$$[A]R$$

thus for any R, if A refines miracle, it must be true that $[A]R$ holds:

$$[A]R = \text{true}$$

and

$$\text{true} = [A]R = [A]\text{true} \wedge \langle A \rangle R = \langle A \rangle R$$

thus $A = \text{miracle}$.

The proof of the other direction is trivial.
∎

The following refinements hold:

Theorem 6.6
    chaos ≡ slip ≡ loop
    chaos ⊑ havoc
    slip ⊑ skip

□

The equivalence of chaos, slip and loop can also be seen from a consideration of their relational definition – all three have ⊥ as a possible outcome, and that can be refined by anything. The refinement relationships seen so far are summarized in Fig. 6.1.

The first useful refinement rule is about replacing a specification by skip; if the post-condition is true whenever the pre-condition is, then nothing need be done to implement the specification:

Theorem 6.7 (introduce skip rule)

if $\left\{ pre[w \backslash \overleftarrow{w}] \Rightarrow post \right\}$ then

    chg $w : W$
    pre pre ⊑ skip
    post $post$

Proof
By the definition of refinement, it is just necessary to show that:

108   6. *The Basic Commands*

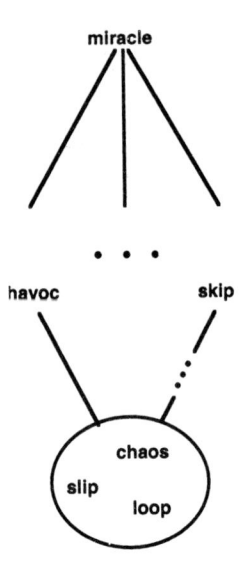

Fig. 6.1. The primitive commands and their refinements.

$$[w : [\ pre,\quad post\ ]]R \;\Rightarrow\; [\mathsf{skip}]R$$

Now

$$[w : [\ pre,\quad post\ ]]R$$
$$\Longleftrightarrow$$
$$pre \wedge \forall\, w' : W \cdot post \;\Rightarrow\; R[w\backslash w']$$
$$\Longleftrightarrow$$
$$\forall\, w' : W \cdot pre \wedge (post \;\Rightarrow\; R[w\backslash w'])$$
$$\Longrightarrow$$
$$R$$

∎

Earlier, the possibility of introducing miracle in disguise was discussed, what is the disguise? Any partial command is miracle in disguise. If A is a partial command and B is a refinement of A, we must have

$$[A]R \;\Rightarrow\; [B]R$$

then it follows that

$$[A]\mathsf{false} \;\Rightarrow\; [B]\mathsf{false}$$
$$\Longleftrightarrow$$
$$\neg[B]\mathsf{false} \;\Rightarrow\; \neg[A]\mathsf{false}$$
$$\Longleftrightarrow$$
$$\mathcal{G}(B) \;\Rightarrow\; \mathcal{G}(A)$$

Thus if A is partial (there are state values that make $\mathcal{G}(A)$ have the value false), then B must be partial – it can even be 'more' partial (have a smaller domain), but it can never be 'less' partial (have a larger domain). So for a partial command, all refinements of it must have the same or a smaller domain, leading eventually to miracle when all other refinement possibilities have been exhausted.

6.2 Assertions

As far as execution is concerned, assertions can be ignored. The following theorem shows that correctness is not affected by removing an assert command:

Theorem 6.8 (remove assertion rule)
$$\{p\} \sqsubseteq \mathsf{skip}$$
□

Corollary 6.1
$$\{p\}A \sqsubseteq A$$
□

Thus by their very nature, an assertion command need not be refined; but as they provide a context (assumptions) that can be used in refinements, it is often useful to be able to transform an assertion during refinement. The following theorems add to the properties discussed in an earlier chapter. Firstly we can widen (weaken) an assertion; this is really a special case of the equivalent specification rule:

Theorem 6.9
$$\text{if } \{ p \Rightarrow q \} \text{ then } \{p\} \sqsubseteq \{q\}$$
□

Corollary 6.2
$$\text{if } \{ p \Rightarrow q \} \text{ then } \{p\}A \sqsubseteq \{q\}A$$
□

The following theorem is used when a component is refined within the context of an assertion; the context need not be explicitly carried along:

Theorem 6.10
$\{p\}A \sqsubseteq B$ iff $\{p\}A \sqsubseteq \{p\}B$
□

Theorem 6.11

$$\text{if} \left\{ \begin{array}{c} q \text{ is independent of initial values} \\ p \Rightarrow [A]q \end{array} \right\} \text{ then } \{p\} A = \{p\} A\{q\}$$

□

Corollary 6.3
If *post* is independent of initial values,

$$w : [\ pre,\quad post\ ] = \{pre\}\ w : [\ pre,\quad post\ ]\{post\}$$

□

It is easy to show that

$$[\{p\}]R = p \wedge R$$

since

$$[\{p\}]R$$
$$\iff$$
$$[p \to \text{skip} \ \square\ \neg p \to \text{chaos}]R$$
$$\iff$$
$$(p \Rightarrow R) \wedge (\neg p \Rightarrow \text{false})$$
$$\iff$$
$$(p \Rightarrow R) \wedge p$$
$$\iff$$
$$p \wedge R$$

During refinement, an assertion can be swapped with a command, but we would expect the command to have some effect on the form of the assertion, especially if the command changes the value of one of the variables that occurs in the assertion. If the predicate $\{p\}$ is to be true after execution of A, then up to refinement, we would expect $[A]p$ to be true before its execution:

Theorem 6.12
$$A\ \{p\} \equiv \{[A]p\}\ A$$

Proof
$$[A\ \{p\}]R$$
$$\iff$$
$$[A][\{p\}]R$$
$$\iff$$
$$[A](p \wedge R)$$
$$\iff$$
$$[A]p \wedge [A]R$$

$$\iff$$
$$[\{[A]p\}\ ][A]R$$
$$\iff$$
$$[\{[A]p\}\ A]R$$
∎

Corollary 6.4
$$x := E\ \{p\} \equiv \{[x := E]p\}\ A$$
□

During refinement, a guard can be added after an assertion:

Theorem 6.13
$$\{p\}\ p \to A \equiv \{p\}\ A$$
□

Because of angelic non-determinism, during refinement an assertion can be absorbed into either or both sides of a non-deterministic choice operator:

Theorem 6.14
$$\{p\}\ (A \sqcap B) \equiv (\{p\}\ A) \sqcap B \equiv A \sqcap (\{p\}\ B) \equiv (\{p\}\ A) \sqcap (\{p\}\ B)$$

Proof
All of the terms are equivalent to $p \wedge [A]R \wedge [B]R$, for example:

$$[\{p\}\ (A \sqcap B)]R$$
$$\iff$$
$$[\{p\}\ ][A \sqcap B]R$$
$$\iff$$
$$p \wedge [A \sqcap B]R$$
$$\iff$$
$$p \wedge [A]R \wedge [B]R$$
∎

During a refinement, we can pull all the assertions out from a choice operation:

Corollary 6.5
$$(\{p\}\ A) \sqcap (\{q\}\ B) \equiv \{p \wedge q\}\ (A \sqcap B)$$
□

During assignment, an assertion can be moved through a guard in either direction:

Theorem 6.15
$$\{p\}\ q \to A \equiv (p \Rightarrow q) \to \{p\}\ A$$
$$p \to \{q\}\ A \equiv \{p \Rightarrow q\}\ p \to A$$
□

There is an unbounded version of Theorem 6.14:

Theorem 6.16
$$@x : X \bullet \{p\}\ A \equiv \{\forall x : X \cdot p\}\ @x \bullet A$$
□

6.3 Assignment

The basic building block of all procedural programming languages is the assignment command; so when can a specification be satisfied by an assignment? Consider the following specification:

op
chg $w : W$
pre pre
post $post$

Under what conditions could this be replaced by an assignment command? Firstly the right-hand side of the assignment command would need to be defined for all input values that satisfied the pre-condition; secondly the assignment must only change w; finally the assignment must establish the post-condition. Thus given a specification op, we need to find an expression E with the right properties such that:

$$op \sqsubseteq w := E$$

Before continuing it is worth considering some real examples, the specification:

op
chg $x : \mathbb{N}$
pre true
post $x = \overleftarrow{x} + y - 1$

can obviously be satisfied by

$$x := x + y - 1$$

This seems to indicate that a specification of the form

6.3 Assignment

op
chg $w : W$
pre true
post $w = D$

where D involves $\overleftarrow{w}$, but does not involve w, can be realized by

$$w := D[\overleftarrow{w}\backslash w]$$

However this is not quite correct: there is a problem if the expression denoted by $D[\overleftarrow{w}\backslash w]$ on the right-hand side of the assignment command evaluates to undefined ($\bot$). To solve this difficulty it is necessary to us the predicate $\delta(D[\overleftarrow{w}\backslash w]:W)$ which has the value true if the value denoted by the expression $D[\overleftarrow{w}\backslash w]$ is of type W (which thus precludes the undefined value), and false if it is not. Using this we can write:

chg $w : W$
pre $\delta(D[\overleftarrow{w}\backslash w] : W)$
post $w = D$
$\sqsubseteq$
$w := D[\overleftarrow{w}\backslash w]$

It can also be shown that an assignment command of the form:

$$w := E$$

can be 'refined' by the specification

chg $w : W$
pre $\delta(E : W)$
post $w = E[w\backslash \overleftarrow{w}]$

For example, if x and y are integers, the assignment command:

$$x := x + y + 1$$

can be refined by the following specification command:

chg $x : \mathbb{Z}$
post $x = \overleftarrow{x} + y + 1$

This refinement illustrates the idea that there is no real difference between a specification and an assignment, but we should have expected this from Theorem 3.30 and Theorem 5.11. This idea can be generalized, a specification of the form:

chg $x : X$
$\ldots$
$y : Y$
pre $\delta(E : X) \wedge \ldots \wedge \delta(F : Y)$
post $x = E[x, \ldots, y\backslash \overleftarrow{x}, \ldots, \overleftarrow{y}] \wedge$
$\ldots \wedge$
$y = F[x, \ldots, y\backslash \overleftarrow{x}, \ldots, \overleftarrow{y}]$

can be refined by the assignment command

$x, \ldots, y := E, \ldots, F$

and vice-versa. This can be encapsulated in a theorem:

Theorem 6.17

$$\begin{array}{l}\text{chg } w : W \\ \text{pre } \delta(E : W) \\ \text{post } w = E[w\backslash \overleftarrow{w}]\end{array} \equiv w := E$$

Note: w could denote a list of variables and E a list of expressions.

Proof
It is necessary to show that for all R defined over the state

$$[w : [\ \delta(E : W),\ w = E[w\backslash \overleftarrow{w}]\ ]]R \Leftrightarrow [w := E]R$$

Now

$$[w : [\ \delta(E : W),\ w = E[w\backslash \overleftarrow{w}]\ ]]R$$
$\Longleftrightarrow$
$$\delta(E : W) \wedge (\forall w' : W \cdot w' = E \Rightarrow R[w\backslash w'])$$
$\Longleftrightarrow$
$$\delta(E : W) \wedge R[w\backslash E]$$
$\Longleftrightarrow$
$$[w := E]R$$

■

These ideas can be developed to give a more general assignment rule. If we use the *replace specification* rule, we can derive the following refinement rule:

6.3 Assignment

Theorem 6.18 (introduce assignment rule)

$$\text{if} \left\{ \begin{array}{c} pre \Rightarrow \delta(E:W) \\ pre[w\backslash\overleftarrow{w}] \wedge w = E[w\backslash\overleftarrow{w}] \Rightarrow post \end{array} \right\} \text{then}$$

chg $w:W$
pre pre $\quad\sqsubseteq\quad w := E$
post $post$

Note 1. Type information may be needed to prove the first proof obligation.
Note 2. w could denote a list of write variables and E a list of expressions.

Proof
By the replace specification refinement rule (Theorem 5.5) and Theorem 6.17.
∎

We can argue informally that this is a valid refinement transformation:

- The first proof obligation requires that, for those inputs that satisfy the pre-condition, the right-hand side of the assignment command must be defined.
- The second proof obligation requires that, for valid input, the result of evaluating the right-hand side of the assignment command together with the input values satisfy the post-condition – which is exactly what is required for satisfaction.

6.3.1 Implementation Issues

The presence of the term $pre \Rightarrow \delta(E:W)$ in proof obligations of the refinement rule is a little puzzling at first sight. To understand its presence, consider the case when the pre-condition is true – if we could not show that $\delta(E:W)$ was satisfied for all input values, this would mean that for one (or more) input values the expression E was undefined and though the original pre-condition required that the refinement should work for all inputs, some input values (those that made E undefined) would exist where the refinement could be chaos. If the proof obligation is not discharged, we may be accidently narrowing a pre-condition and thus not performing a valid refinement.

The expression on the right of an assignment may not be executable, therefore it will need to be replaced by one that is, the following theorem states under what circumstances that this can be done.

Theorem 6.19

$$\text{if } \{ pre \Rightarrow E_0 = E_1 \} \text{ then}$$

chg $w:W$
pre $pre \wedge \delta(E_0:W)$ $\quad\equiv\quad w := E_1$
post $w = E_0[w\backslash\overleftarrow{w}]$

□

There is a (more) useful corollary:

Corollary 6.6
$$\text{if } \{\, p \Rightarrow E_0 = E_1 \,\} \text{ then } \{p\}x := E_0 \sqsubseteq x := E_1$$
□

6.4 Summary

Most of the theorems in this chapter, especially those dealing with the refinement of the constant commands, are really to provide an understanding of the refinement process. It is unlikely that we would wish to refine havoc, chaos or loop, but the rules do re-enforce the concepts, for example that refinement is about removing nondeterminism and that the looping outcome can be replaced by anything.[1]

---

[1] In Chapter 2 it was mentioned in passing that $\bot$ also represented the error outcome, since it can be refined by anything, a useful refinement would be an error message.

7. Declarations and Blocks

A programming language needs a way of introducing new identifiers, VDM-SL has three constructs for this purpose. Though the three constructs are based on the same definition, restrictions are placed on their use to give different semantics that assist with proof obligations, and thus the three constructs provide different facilities.

7.1 The Declaration Command

A simple declaration can been defined using the kernel language:

$$[\![\mathsf{dcl}\ x : X\ \mathsf{in}\ A]\!] \triangleq @x : X \bullet A$$

The purpose of a declaration is to introduce a local identifier that can denote a value – to introduce a new (local) state variable. The new identifier is added to the state at the start of its scope and removed at the end. The normal hiding rules apply (i.e. when a local identifier has the same name as an identifier in the surrounding state, the one in the outer scope is hidden) and these can be derived from the above definition using the conventional scope rules of qualification.

Now, suppose we wish to introduce a local variable x, initialize it to a value defined by a predicate, and then execute the command A; the fragment given below shows one way this can be achieved:

$$[\![\mathsf{dcl}\ x : X\ \mathsf{in}\ x : [\ \mathsf{true},\quad init(x)\ ]\ ;\ A]\!]$$

The fragment can be transformed:

$\quad\quad [\![\mathsf{dcl}\ x : X\ \mathsf{in}\ x : [\ \mathsf{true},\quad init(x)\ ]\ ;\ A]\!]$
$=\quad$ semantics
$\quad\quad @x : X \bullet @x' : X \bullet init(x') \to x := x'\ ;\ A$
$=\quad$ no free x
$\quad\quad @x' : X \bullet init(x') \to x := x'\ ;\ A$
$=\quad$ property of a guarded command
$\quad\quad @x' : X \bullet init(x') \to (x := x'\ ;\ A)$

118   7. Declarations and Blocks

$$= \text{ change bound identifier}$$
$$@x : X \bullet init(x) \to A$$

which suggests the following syntax and definition:

Definition 7.1
$$[\![\text{dcl } x : X \text{ be st } init \text{ in } A]\!] \triangleq @x : X \bullet init \to A$$

The informal semantics of this command can be given as follows: extend the state with variable x, initialize as required by the predicate $init$, execute A and then withdraw the variable x from the state. Angelic non-determinism forces a choice of x, if possible, such that $init$ is satisfied. If such an x cannot be found, the command is equivalent to miracle. Note that it is only this type of declaration that allows the value denoted by the new identifier (variable) to be changed by an assignment command.

The definition can be extended to multiple declarations:

$$[\![\text{dcl } x : X \text{ be st } init_x,$$
$$\qquad y : Y \text{ be st } init_y \text{ in} \quad \triangleq @mk\text{-}(x, y) : X \times Y \bullet init_x \wedge init_y \to A$$
$$A \,]\!]$$

Further properties of this definition depends on how $init$ and the value of x can be based on the (execution of the) command A – there are various possibilities (other combinations are not very interesting or useful):

A both tests and sets (assigns to) x;
A does not affect $init$, tests x, but does not set it; or
A affects $init$, tests x, but does not set it.

The first possibility is dealt with by declarations, it is worth distinguishing the second and third possibilities with syntax, but first some theorems.

7.2 Some Interactions Between Commands

In Chapter 3 the following definitions were shown to hold:

A command A does not test a variable x if for any predicate R, both $[A]$true and $\langle A \rangle R$ are independent of x.
A command A does not set a variable x if for any x-predicate R, $\langle A \rangle R = \langle A \rangle \text{false} \vee R$.

These definitions were extended to an expression E by identifying the identifiers of the expression that it is dependent on, and then demanding that A does not set or test any of them. It should also be remembered that the 'evaluation' of an expression has no side-effects; the value denoted by any state variable occurring in the expression will remain unchanged. The next

7.2 Some Interactions Between Commands

series of theorems expand on these ideas and go some way towards explaining why some combinations discussed above are interesting, and others are not. In the following think of the assignment to x as an initialization; first a useful lemma:

Lemma 7.1
For $\delta(E:X)$:

$$x := E \; ; \; \neg p \to \text{loop} = \neg p[x \backslash E] \to \text{loop}$$

Proof

$\quad x := E \; ; \; \neg p \to \text{loop}$

$=$

$\quad \neg [x := E]p \to x := E \; ; \; \text{loop}$

$=$

$\quad \neg p[x \backslash E] \to \mathcal{G}(x := E) \to \text{loop}$

$=$

$\quad \neg p[x \backslash E] \to \text{loop}$

∎

The next theorem shows that if we initialize x (set it) but do not test it, the initialization need not be done if the next statement sets x.

Theorem 7.1
If $\delta(E:X)$ and A sets but does not test x then

$$(x := E \; ; \; A) = A$$

Proof

$\quad x := E \; ; \; A$

$=$ Theorem 3.30

$\quad x := E \; ;$
$\quad (@x', y' \in X \bullet in_A(y, x', y') \to x, y := x', y' \; \Box \; \neg pre_A(y) \to \text{loop})$

$=$ by Corollary 3.5

$\quad x := E \; ; \; @x', y' \in X \bullet in_A(y, x', y') \to x, y := x', y' \; \Box$
$\quad x := E \; ; \; \neg pre_A(y) \to \text{loop}$

$=$ Lemma 7.1

$\quad @x', y' \in X \bullet x := E \; ; \; in_A(y, x', y') \to x, y := x', y' \; \Box$
$\quad \neg pre_A(y) \to \text{loop}$

$=$

$\quad @x', y' \in X \bullet \neg [x := E] \neg in_A(y, x', y') \to x := E \; ; \; x, y := x', y' \; \Box$
$\quad \neg pre_A(y) \to \text{loop}$

$=$

$\quad @x', y' \in X \bullet in_A(y, x', y') \to x := E \; ; \; x, y := x', y' \; \Box$

120   7. Declarations and Blocks

$$= \quad \neg pre_A(y) \rightarrow \text{loop}$$

$$= \quad @x', y' \in X \bullet in_A(y, x', y') \rightarrow x, y := x', y' \;\square\; \neg pre_A(y) \rightarrow \text{loop}$$

$$= \quad A$$

■

If A does not change the value of any of the variables used in calculating the initial value of x and also if A does not set x, then it is possible to syntactically replace x by the initialization expression and then initialize x after A:

Theorem 7.2
If $\delta(E : X)$ and A does not set x and the value of E is independent of the command A then

$$(x := E \,;\, A) = (A[x\backslash E] \,;\, x := E)$$

Proof
$$x := E \,;\, A$$

$$= \quad x := E \,;\, (@y' \in X \bullet in_A(x, y, y') \rightarrow y := y' \;\square\; \neg pre_A(x, y) \rightarrow \text{loop})$$

$$= \quad x := E \,;\, @y' \in X \bullet in_A(x, y, y') \rightarrow y := y' \;\square$$
$$\quad x := E \,;\, \neg pre_A(x, y) \rightarrow \text{loop}$$

= Lemma 7.1
$$@y' \in X \bullet \neg [x := E]\neg in_A(x, y, y') \rightarrow x := E \,;\, y := y' \;\square$$
$$\neg pre_A(E, y) \rightarrow \text{loop}$$

$$= \quad @y' \in X \bullet in_A(E, y, y') \rightarrow y := y' \,;\, x := E \;\square$$
$$\quad \neg pre_A(E, y) \rightarrow \text{loop} \,;\, x := E$$

$$= \quad A[x\backslash E] \,;\, x := E$$

■

This transformation does not lead to anything silly, since A does not set x, as it does not occur on the left-hand side of an assignment command of A, it will only occur in expressions, thus the syntactic replacement of x is valid as E is independent of A.

If x is local to a scope block, then there is no need to initialize it:

Corollary 7.1
If $\delta(E : X)$ and A does not set x and the value of E is independent of the command A, then

$$[\![\,\mathsf{dcl}\ x:X\ \mathsf{in}\ x:=E\ ;\ A\,]\!] = A[x\backslash E]$$
∎

If A does not change the value of any of the state variables used in calculating the initial value for x and does not either test or set x, then it is possible to initialize x after the execution of A.

Corollary 7.2
If $\delta(E:X)$ and A does not test or set x and the expression E is independent of A then

$$(x:=E\ ;\ A) = (A\ ;\ x:=E)$$

Proof
Immediately from Theorem 7.2 and from the hypothesis that $A = A[x\backslash E]$ (since A neither sets or tests x, it does not appear anywhere in A).
■

It immediately follows that, within a scope block, there would be no need to introduce x:

Corollary 7.3
If $\delta(E:X)$ and A does not set or test x then

$$[\![\,\mathsf{dcl}\ x:X\ \mathsf{in}\ x:=E\ ;\ A\,]\!] = [\![\,\mathsf{dcl}\ x:X\ \mathsf{in}\ A\,]\!] = A$$
∎

Syntactic sugar can be used when introducing a new identifier to distinguish the three cases listed above. The main possibilities are that the body of the command both tests and sets the value of the new identifier, or the body only tests the value of the new identifier. In this later case the initialization may or may not be affected by the body: the expression (predicate) used to define the initial value denoted by the new identifier may be independent of any changes to the state in the body of the command. Rather than needing to prove that an expression E is independent of the execution of a command A – the value of the expression is independent of any changes to the state that A might make; we will use strict rules based on syntax to guarantee this independence. The strict rule does not allow for any state variables to occur in the expression E. In a later section (see below) this choice will be discussed further.

7.3 The Definitional Commands

There are three sorts of definitional commands, corresponding to the three cases discussed in the previous section.

7.3.1 Declarations

The first case is where the command A within the scope of the declaration of a variable x both tests and sets it. This case has already been covered, the definitions are pulled together here for completeness. Note that A may or may not change the value of the *init* expression that defines the initial value, but this is irrelevant since an assignment statement executed in A can set x to a new value. Thus the predicate used for the initial value is irrelevant in these circumstances.

$$[\![\,\text{dcl}\ x : X\ \text{be st}\ \textit{init}\ \text{in}\ A\,]\!] \triangleq @x : X \bullet \textit{init} \rightarrow A$$

If the new variable is not initialized, equivalently the initialization is true, the definition becomes:

$$[\![\,\text{dcl}\ x : X\ \text{in}\ A\,]\!] \triangleq @x : X \bullet A$$

A special version for a simple form of the predicate can be given:

$$[\![\,\text{dcl}\ x : X = E\ \text{in}\ A\,]\!] \triangleq [\![\,\text{dcl}\ x : X\ \text{be st}\ x = E\ \text{in}\ A\,]\!]$$

Note that E does not contain any free x.

7.3.2 The Let Command

The first case is where A does not affect *init*, it tests the value of x, but does not set it. This rule will be enforced by a simple syntax-based requirement: only those identifiers defined as constants, those defined in values definitions and functions definitions can be used in the predicate *init* that defines the initialization (see below). The let command is defined as:

$$\text{let}\ x : X\ \text{be st}\ \textit{init}\ \text{in}\ A \triangleq @x : X \bullet \textit{init} \rightarrow A$$

The initializing predicate *init* must not depend on (refer to) any state or local identifiers. Special versions of this command can be introduced, first a simple let command:

$$\text{let}\ x : X = E\ \text{in}\ A \triangleq \text{let}\ x : X\ \text{be st}\ x = E\ \text{in}\ A$$

if the type of expression is obvious, this can be abbreviated to

$$\text{let}\ x = E\ \text{in}\ A \triangleq \text{let}\ x : \tau(E)\ \text{be st}\ x = E\ \text{in}\ A$$

The operator τ extracts the type of the expression, it would need to use static environment information (and in extreme cases it might need some help with a proof or two). The informal interpretation of this is that x denotes the same value as the expression E – remember E must not depend on any state variables. By Theorem 7.2 it is possible to syntactically replace x by the expression E, so the semantics could be defined as:

7.3 The Definitional Commands

let $x = E$ in $A \triangleq A[x \backslash E]$

A slightly more general version of this form can also be defined using the pattern concept from VDM-SL:

let $pattern = E$ in $A \triangleq$ let $\alpha\tau(pattern)$ be st $pattern = E$ in A

Roughly speaking, a *pattern* is an expression with 'undefined' (unknown) identifiers that are about to be defined. The operator $\alpha\tau$ extracts the undefined identifiers from the pattern and deduces their type to give a list of identifiers together with their type (it might also need some help) as in the first form of the let command – its definition can be deduced from the syntax of a pattern, it would also need to use static environment information. The full syntactic definition of a pattern can be found in [6].

7.3.3 The Def Command

Now consider the next case: (the execution of) A affects the values of any free variables used in the predicate *init*, tests x, but does not set it. The value denoted by the newly introduced identifier can be dependent on the state, but it is not changed by the commands that uses the value. Again special syntax will be used to distinguish this case, though the definition of the def command is identical to the let command.

def $x : X$ be st *init* in $A \triangleq @x : X \bullet init \to A$

The initializing predicate *init* can depend on state variables. This means that x is a local constant whose value depends on the state. It is useful to have special versions that match the other forms of the let command. First two simple versions of the def command were the initial value can be defined by an expression:

def $x : X = E$ in $A \triangleq$ def $x : X$ be st $x = E$ in A
def $x = E$ in $A \triangleq$ def $x : \tau(E)$ be st $x = E$ in A

The informal semantics are as for the let command, except that the initializing expression E can refer to state variables. The def command can also be extended to pattern matching:

def $pattern = E$ in $A \triangleq$ def $\alpha\tau(pattern)$ be st $pattern = E$ in A

with an identical definition to the let command, but again the expression E can contain state variables.

7.3.4 The Def and Let Commands Compared

It is not immediately clear for the need for both the def and let commands, the major difference between

124   7. Declarations and Blocks

let $x = E$ in A

and

def $x = E$ in A

can be summed up as the difference between $[[x := E]A]R$ and $[x := E][A]R$. In the first case, the substitution can be calculated independently of R, in the second it cannot. This means that a let command allows the properties of the newly introduced variable to be made local to a command, the following theorem illustrates this:

Theorem 7.3
let $x : X$ be st $p(x)$ in $(A \ ; \ B) =$
(let $x : X$ be st $p(x)$ in A) ; (let $x : X$ be st $p(x)$ in B)

Proof
For the weakest liberal pre-condition:

$\langle(\text{let } x : X \text{ be st } p(x) \text{ in } A) \ ; \ (\text{let } x : X \text{ be st } p(x) \text{ in } B)\rangle R$

$\iff$

$\langle\text{let } x : X \text{ be st } p(x) \text{ in } A\rangle(\forall x : X \cdot p(x) \Rightarrow \langle B\rangle R)$

$\iff$

$\forall x : X \cdot p(x) \Rightarrow \langle A\rangle(\forall x : X \cdot p(x) \Rightarrow \langle B\rangle R)$

$\iff$

$\forall x : X \cdot p(x) \Rightarrow \forall x : X \cdot \langle A\rangle(p(x) \Rightarrow \langle B\rangle R)$

$\iff$

$\forall x : X \cdot p(x) \Rightarrow \forall x : X \cdot \langle A\rangle(\neg p(x) \vee \langle B\rangle R)$

$\iff$ by Lemma 3.2

$\forall x : X \cdot p(x) \Rightarrow \forall x : X \cdot (\neg p(x) \vee \langle A\rangle\langle B\rangle R)$

$\iff$

$\forall x : X \cdot p(x) \Rightarrow \langle A\rangle\langle B\rangle R$

$\iff$

$\langle\text{let } x : X \text{ be st } p(x) \text{ in } A; B\rangle R$

For termination:

$[(\text{let } x : X \text{ be st } p(x) \text{ in } A) \ ; \ (\text{let } x : X \text{ be st } p(x) \text{ in } B)]\text{true}$

$\iff$

$[\text{let } x : X \text{ be st } p(x) \text{ in } A](\forall x : X \cdot p(x) \Rightarrow [B]\text{true})$

$\iff$

$\forall x : X \cdot p(x) \Rightarrow [A](\forall x : X \cdot p(x) \Rightarrow [B]\text{true})$

$\iff$

$\forall x : X \cdot p(x) \Rightarrow \forall x : X \cdot [A](p(x) \Rightarrow [B]\text{true})$

$$\iff$$
$$\forall x : X \cdot p(x) \;\Rightarrow\; \forall x : X \cdot [A](\neg p(x) \vee [B]\text{true})$$
$$\iff$$
$$\forall x : X \cdot p(x) \;\Rightarrow\; \forall x : X \cdot (\neg p(x) \vee [A][B]\text{true})$$
$$\iff$$
$$\forall x : X \cdot p(x) \;\Rightarrow\; [A][B]\text{true}$$
$$\iff$$
$$[\text{let } x : X \text{ be st } p(x) \text{ in } A; B]\text{true}$$

■

This property allows the value of a newly introduced identifier to be made local to a command. This property is not (generally) true of the def command as the execution of the command A can change the second evaluation of the predicate p as it could contain state variables that are changed by A.

The define command is not so useful as the let command, but a compiler for the language can safely assume x is not changed by the command A. The use of the def command improves the readability of a program, it will also be used in the definition of the semantics of procedures and procedure calls.

7.4 Refining Definitional Commands

The commands with an initialization predicate are, in general, not executable. Therefore this form must be transformed into the form that uses an initializing expression, which is executable (subject to the expression being executable). A useful theorem is:

Theorem 7.4 (refine block rule)
If $init' \;\Rightarrow\; init$ and $A \sqsubseteq A'$ then

$$[\![\text{dcl } x : X \text{ be st } init \text{ in } A]\!] \sqsubseteq [\![\text{dcl } x : \text{ be st } init' \text{ in } A']\!]$$

Proof
$$[\![\text{dcl } x : X \text{ be st } init \text{ in } A]\!]$$
$$=$$
$$@x : X \bullet init \to A$$
$$\sqsubseteq$$
$$@x : X \bullet init' \to A$$
$$\sqsubseteq$$
$$@x : X \bullet init' \to A'$$
$$=$$
$$[\![\text{dcl } x : X \text{ be st } init' \text{ in } A']\!]$$

■

7. Declarations and Blocks

If a specification command is replaced by a block with some local declarations containing that command, we can do whatever we like with the new variables. Of course, the specification command must not contain any free variables that clash with those introduced in the block:

Theorem 7.5 (add variable rule)

if { *pre* and *post* do not contain any free instances of x } then

$$
\begin{array}{l}
\text{chg } w : W \\
\text{pre } \textit{pre} \\
\text{post } \textit{post}
\end{array}
\quad \sqsubseteq \quad
\begin{array}{l}
[\![\text{dcl } x : X \text{ in} \\
\quad \text{chg } w : W \\
\quad\quad x : X \\
\quad \text{pre } \textit{pre} \\
\quad \text{post } \textit{post}]\!]
\end{array}
$$

□

Sometimes it is useful to materialize a bound variable used in a quantified expression:

Theorem 7.6 (realize quantifier rule)

if { *pre* does not contain any free instances of x } then

$$
\begin{array}{l}
\text{chg } w : W \\
\text{pre } \textit{pre} \\
\text{post } \exists x : X \cdot \textit{post}
\end{array}
\quad = \quad
\begin{array}{l}
[\![\text{dcl } x : X \text{ in} \\
\quad \text{chg } w : W \\
\quad\quad x : X \\
\quad \text{pre } \textit{pre} \\
\quad \text{post } \textit{post}]\!]
\end{array}
$$

□

It is also possible to remove a block if the command is independent of the variable – see Corollary 7.1. Scopes can be collapsed, perhaps to make a program more readable; but note that care is needed to avoid variable capture.

Theorem 7.7 (remove scope rule)

if { A and C do not contain any free instances of y } then

$[\![\text{dcl } x : X \text{ in } A; [\![\text{dcl } y : Y \text{ in } B]\!]; C]\!] \quad \sqsubseteq \quad [\![\text{dcl } x : X, y : Y \text{ in } A; B; C]\!]$

□

It is always possible to expand the frame component with a variable that is in scope:

Theorem 7.8 (expand frame rule)

if { x is a local or state variable } then

$$\begin{array}{l}\text{chg } w:W\\ \text{pre } pre\\ \text{post } post\end{array} \sqsubseteq \begin{array}{l}\text{chg } w:W\\ \quad x:X\\ \text{pre } pre\\ \text{post } post \land x = \overleftarrow{x}\end{array}$$

□

It is also possible to contract a frame, but beware – this is a way of introducing miracle.

Theorem 7.9 (contract frame rule)

$$\begin{array}{l}\text{chg } w:W\\ \quad x:X\\ \text{pre } pre\\ \text{post } post\end{array} \sqsubseteq \begin{array}{l}\text{chg } w:W\\ \text{pre } pre\\ \text{post } post[\overleftarrow{x}\setminus x]\end{array}$$

□

A simple example will show the problem with miracle:

$$x,y:\left[\ \text{true},\quad y=\overleftarrow{y}-1 \land x=\overleftarrow{x}+1\ \right] \sqsubseteq$$
$$y:\left[\ \text{true},\quad y=\overleftarrow{y}-1 \land x=x+1\ \right] =$$
$$y:\left[\ \text{true},\quad \text{false}\ \right] =$$
miracle

Another approach to the refinement of all three forms of declaration can be seen from the definition of the commands, they were all defined in terms of expression of the form

$$@x:X \bullet p \to A$$

and we have already seen, or will see, many strategies for refining commands of this form.

7.5 Defining Constant Values

The easiest way of guaranteeing that the value of an expression is independent of a command that can change the state is to make the value of the expression independent of the state. We shall introduce a way of defining constants, definitions for values and functions, with the property that their value cannot be changed – thus they cannot occur on the left-hand side of an assignment command. The simple form introduces an identifier that denotes a constant value define by a predicate p which contains no local or state variables:

$id : X$ be st p

As for declarations, if the predicate is of the form $id = E$ the definition can be written:

$id : X = expression$

or if the type of the expression is obvious, as

$id = expression$

All the identifiers used in the expression must have either have been defined as functions or as values – they must not denote state variables. Functions that do not depend on the state can also be defined:

$id : D \rightarrow R$

$id\,(d) \triangleq expression$

Again, any identifiers used in the expression can only denote other functions or values. Note that it is unnecessary to have both of these forms, since functions could be defined as a value:

$id : D \rightarrow R = \lambda\,d \cdot expression$

and values could be defined as functions:

$id : () \rightarrow X$

$id\,() \triangleq \text{let } x : X \text{ be st } p \text{ in } x$

For reasons of readability (and attempting to enforce the definition of only deterministic functions), we will use both forms according to whether we are defining a constant value or a function. It must be emphasized that in neither of these two definitions can state variables be used. Thus any expressions used in such a definition can be evaluated independently of the state. There is no restriction in the use of recursion or some definitions using values defined in other definitions; such definitions always define values (though the value denoted by some of the identifiers could be $\bot$).

These declarations for constant values are just global let commands that are defined for the complete program.

7.5.1 Refining Functions and Constants

As may be deduced from the way that constant definitions have been introduced, the values definitions can be seen as a means of making specifications more readable as each instance of the identifier can be replaced by its definition (of course scope rules must be obeyed and '...' must been replaced by a value before doing this). However, since constant definitions have been introduced to improve readability it would seem reasonable to leave them in the final program. The definition of constant values can be translated into constant declarations. Functions can be left if the compiler can handle them; alternatively they can be translated into function procedure specifications and refined in the usual style. A function definition of the form:

$f : D \to R$
$f(d) \triangleq expression$
pre *pre*

can be translated into

$f(d : D) \ r : R$
pre *pre*
post $r = expression$

Since functions are not loose, there is no non-determinism – functions are always deterministic, and as refinement does not introduce non-determinism, the result of refinement will be deterministic. Note also that the function has no side-effects, its specification has no external frame since it references no state variables – thus it can be used in expressions, more of this in Chapter 11.

7.6 Logical Constants

We will next introduce a special sort of constant whose value is set by expressions that are dependent on the state – these are a close relative of identifiers introduced by the def command. Given the following specification:

OP
chg $w : W$
pre *pre*
post *post*

we can undertake this refinement:

$OP \sqsubseteq c := E;$
$\quad OPc$
$\quad\quad$chg $w : W$
$\quad\quad$pre *pre* $\land c = E$
$\quad\quad$post *post*

The idea is to refine OPc to executable code such that the identifier c does not occur anywhere. Suppose we denote this refinement by *prog*, we then have:

$OP \sqsubseteq c := E \ ; \ OPc \sqsubseteq c := E \ ; \ prog$

The above assumes that ';' behaves nicely with respect to refinement (as we shall find later that it does). Since *prog* does not contain c then the initial assignment to c can be thrown away to give finally:

$OP \sqsubseteq prog$

The purpose behind the introduction of the new variable c is that OPc should be easier to refine than OP, even with the necessity of removing the extra variable during the refinement process.

A more general rule can be derived. Since the expression $c = E$ in the precondition was obtained by introducing a temporary variable and an assignment command of the form $c := E$ into the code that refines a specification, and since this command is deleted from the final code, it does not matter if it can not actually be executed! In fact we could write something like:

$c :=$ let x be st $p(x)$ in x

The only restriction is that the value 'assigned' to c must exist; this gives a more general rule:

$OP \sqsubseteq c :=$ let x be st $p(x)$ in x;
    OPc
    chg $w : W$
    pre $pre \wedge p(c)$
    post $post$

All that is needed now is a neat way of flagging c and defining its scope. This form of identifier is called a logical constant.

The idea behind logical constants is to save the 'current' value of a variable so that it can be used in a predicate later on, even if the value of the variable has been changed. The $\overleftarrow{x}$ notation does this over the 'scope' of a specification, we have been rigorous, but not formal, in our use of this convention. To give the semantics of a specification command, it was just stated that $\overleftarrow{x}$ is the initial value of x and carry out the appropriate substitutions as necessary. The semantics of a specification command and the use of x could be based on:

$$@\overleftarrow{x} : X \bullet \overleftarrow{x} = x \to x : \left[\ pre(x),\ post(\overleftarrow{x}, x)\ \right]$$

were $\overleftarrow{x}$ is set to the initial value of x. Since

$$[@\overleftarrow{x} : X \bullet \overleftarrow{x} = x \to x : \left[\ pre(x),\ post(\overleftarrow{x}, x)\ \right]] R(\overleftarrow{x}, x)$$
$$\iff$$
$$\forall \overleftarrow{x} : X \cdot \overleftarrow{x} = x \implies pre(x) \wedge \forall x' \cdot post(\overleftarrow{x}, x) \implies [x := x']R(\overleftarrow{x}, x)$$
$$\iff$$
$$\forall \overleftarrow{x} : X \cdot \overleftarrow{x} = x \implies pre(x) \wedge \forall x' \cdot post(x, x') \implies R(\overleftarrow{x}, x')$$

7.6 Logical Constants

$$\iff$$
$$pre(x) \wedge \forall x' \cdot post(x,x') \Rightarrow R(x,x')$$

which agrees with the previous definition given in Chapter 2.

In a more general context, consider:

$$@\overleftarrow{x} : X \bullet \overleftarrow{x} = x \to A$$

where the again guard is used to 'save' the current value of x. If we look at this definition of the more general form, after some simplification we get:

$$\forall \overleftarrow{x} : X \cdot \overleftarrow{x} = x \Rightarrow [A]\text{true}$$
$$\forall \overleftarrow{x} : X \cdot \overleftarrow{x} = x \Rightarrow \langle A \rangle R$$

these equations could just as easily be written:

$$\exists \overleftarrow{x} : X \cdot \overleftarrow{x} = x \wedge [A]\text{true}$$
$$\exists \overleftarrow{x} : X \cdot \overleftarrow{x} = x \wedge \langle A \rangle R$$

which leads to this question: could we define a command that is equivalent to unbounded choice, but is based on the existential quantifier? A new operator © is defined as:

$$[© x : X \bullet A]\text{true} \triangleq \exists x : X \cdot [A]\text{true}$$
$$\langle © x : X \bullet A \rangle R \triangleq \exists x : X \cdot \langle A \rangle R$$

What are the properties of this new operator? Firstly a finite version:

$$A_1 \ddagger A_2 \triangleq © i \in \{1,2\} \bullet A_i$$

and it is easy to show:

$$[A_1 \ddagger A_2]\text{true} = [A_1]\text{true} \vee [A_2]\text{true}$$
$$\langle A_1 \ddagger A_2 \rangle R = \langle A_1 \rangle R \vee \langle A_2 \rangle R$$

This finite version of the operator can be investigated to see how it works, we notice that:

$$A \sqsubseteq A \ddagger B$$
$$B \sqsubseteq A \ddagger B$$

This means that $A \ddagger B$ is a program that refines both A and B; this will be an interesting program if A and B are wildly different! The relational definition of this operator gives some indication of what its execution model might be:

$$A_1 \ddagger A_2 = A_1 \cap A_2$$

In execution terms, the program $A \ddagger B$ means execute A and B to give all possible outcomes and then take the intersection as the result – difficult to implement. The refinement rule and the relational definition of the operator suggests that in some cases (e.g. if A and B are wildly different) it is possible that using the relational model $A \ddagger B = \{\}$ and thus $A \ddagger B =$ miracle. Is this command really useful? Consider the command:

$$ⓒ\, i : \mathbb{N} \bullet x : [\ x = i, \quad x = i + 1\ ]$$

We can show that this is refined by $x := x + 1$. We have already introduced a second version of the unbounded choice command that was based on the concept of declaration, we can do the same for conjunction:

$$[\![\, \text{con}\ x : X\ \text{in}\ A\,]\!] \triangleq ⓒ\, x : X \bullet A$$

this allows us to delimit the scope of the declaration in the usual programming language style. We can now formalize the use of initial values:

$$x : \left[\ pre(x), \quad post(\overleftarrow{x}, x)\ \right]$$

is shorthand for

$$[\![\, \text{con}\ c : X\ \text{in}\ x : [\ pre(x) \wedge x = c, \quad post(c, x)\ ]\,]\!]$$

which is just a formalization of the substitution that we have been doing informally up until now. From this definition, it can be seen that a hooked variable is just a special case of a logical constant, and in fact a hooking convention is not really needed, but it is useful.

The logical constant is a useful artifact and it must be remembered that there is no equivalent in the executable programming language subset: they must be removed during algorithmic refinement.

The introduction of logical constants can now be formalized:

Theorem 7.10 (introduce logical constant rule)

if $\left\{\begin{array}{c} c\ \text{does not occur free in}\ w,\ pre,\ \text{or}\ post \\ pre \Rightarrow \exists c \in C \cdot pre' \end{array}\right\}$ then

chg $w : W$
pre pre
post $post$

$\sqsubseteq$

$[\![\ \text{con}\ c : C\ \text{in}$
chg $w : W$
pre pre'
post $post\,]\!]$

□

The declaration of c as a logical constant is a reminder that it should not occur in the final program. This refinement rule is just a formalized version of the strategy given at the start of this section; and since the 'assignment' of a value to c is to be thrown away anyway, why show it, why not make it implicit, i.e. invisible?

7.6 Logical Constants

Logical constants can be dealt with as part of algorithmic refinement, the refinement steps should be such that the final code does not use them: they have been removed from the body of a block. It is then only necessary to remove their declaration:

Theorem 7.11 (remove logical constant rule)
If A is independent of c then

$$[\![\text{con } c : C \text{ in } A]\!] \equiv A$$

Proof
For any R defined over the state:

$[\![\text{con } c : C \text{ in } A]\!]R$
$\iff$ definition
    $\exists c : C \cdot [A]R$
$\iff$
    $[A]R$

∎

This theorem formalizes the throwing away of the (now invisible) assignment that initialized the logical constant c.

Corollary 7.4
If B is independent of c then:

$$[\![\text{con } c : C \text{ in } A \,;\, B]\!] \equiv [\![\text{con } c : C \text{ in } A]\!] \,;\, B$$

and if A is independent of c then:

$$[\![\text{con } c : C \text{ in } A \,;\, B]\!] \sqsubseteq A \,;\, [\![\text{con } c : C \text{ in } B]\!]$$

Proof
For any R defined over the state:

$[\![\text{con } c : C \text{ in } A \,;\, B]\!]R$
$\iff$
    $\exists c : C \cdot ([A \,;\, B]R)$
$\iff$
    $\exists c : C \cdot [A][B]R$
$\iff$ $[B]R$ is independent of c
    $[\![\text{con } c : C \text{ in } A]\!][B]R$
$\iff$
    $[\![\text{con } c : C \text{ in } A]\!] \,;\, B]R$

Thus

$$[\![\operatorname{con} c : C \text{ in } A\ ;\ B]\!] \equiv [\![\operatorname{con} c : C \text{ in } A]\!]\ ;\ B$$

The proof of the second statement is similar in style.

∎

The use of logical constants should be undertaken with care – the following command sequence cannot be implemented:

$$[\![\operatorname{con} c : C \text{ in } x : [\ c = x,\quad x > c\ ]\ ;\ x : [\ c = x,\quad x > c\ ]]\!]$$

If we try to fix a value of c, it is impossible. The scope of a logical constant should only be the specification it was introduced in, and a good refinement strategy is to remove the logical constant as quickly as possible. The 'variable' c is really a constant within its scope, which is the specification that introduces it, and any refinements of that specification. In order to make the above example work we must write:

$$[\![\operatorname{con} c : C \text{ in } x : [\ c = x,\quad x > c\ ]]\!]\ ;\ [\![\operatorname{con} c : C \text{ in } x : [\ c = x,\quad x > c\ ]]\!]$$

and the two logical constants are distinct.

7.7 Summary

This chapter has been concerned with the various ways of introducing new identifiers, whether they be constant values or temporary state declarations. In most cases their use in this book are kept fairly simple, so that the refinement strategy is straightforward. The difficult issues have been addressed briefly enough for the keen reader to derive a complete set of refinement rules from these commands.

The various different forms of declarations have been introduced to make specifications and programs easier to read and to make proofs easier – if the value of an identifier is not changed by a command (or sequence of commands) or if its value is independent of the state, proving that certain properties hold becomes much easier. A bonus is that a compiler for the executable part of the language can use the different semantics provided by the various forms of declarations to generate efficient code.

8. Command Sequences

One of the glues for assembling components of a program is the semicolon operator, and so one tactic to refining a large specification would be to break it into smaller specifications, these are refined to executable code, and the resulting components are re-assembled using the semicolon operator. It is necessary to prove that this tactic does produce a program that satisfies the original specification.

8.1 Solve a Part and then the Whole

Suppose that we wish to refine a specification op by this approach. The strategy is to try and discover two specifications op_A and op_B such that, if executable code A is developed to satisfy the specification op_A and executable code B is developed to satisfy the op_B then the code $A\,;\,B$ should satisfy the original specification op. The idea is that each of op_A and op_B are easier to refine, or at least no harder, than op. Formally, we are saying that given a specification op, find specifications op_A and op_B that can be worked on separately, such that if:

$op \sqsubseteq op_A; op_B$

and

$op_A \sqsubseteq A$
$op_B \sqsubseteq B$

then

$op \sqsubseteq A\,;\,B$

What sort of conditions should the two subspecifications op_A and op_B satisfy? They should be the most general specifications that, when glued together with a semicolon, are equivalent to the original specification; it should be up to the implementors of the two new specifications to decide on any widening of pre-conditions or narrowing of post-conditions that should be applied.

The refinement step is to produce two sub-specifications that, when put together with a semicolon, are equivalent to the original specification. The following theorem guarantees all is well:

Theorem 8.1
If

$$A \sqsubseteq A'$$
$$B \sqsubseteq B'$$

then

$$A\,;\,B \sqsubseteq A'\,;\,B'$$

Proof
Since $B \sqsubseteq B'$, by definition, for all predicates R defined over the state, we have

$$[B]R \Rightarrow [B']R$$

by monotonicity

$$[A][B]R \Rightarrow [A][B']R$$

since $A \sqsubseteq A'$, we also have

$$[A][B']R \Rightarrow [A'][B']R$$

thus for R

$$[A][B]R \Rightarrow [A'][B']R$$
$$\Longleftrightarrow$$
$$[A\,;\,B]R \Rightarrow [A'\,;\,B']R$$
$$\Longleftrightarrow$$
$$A\,;\,B \sqsubseteq A'\,;\,B'$$

■

Normally it is a specification that is to be refined by two commands A and B:

$$x : [\ pre, \quad post\ ] \sqsubseteq A\,;\,B$$

What are possible candidates for A and B? There are three alternatives, either design A and calculate B, design B and calculate A, or design both A and B and show that their combination with a semicolon satisfies the specification.

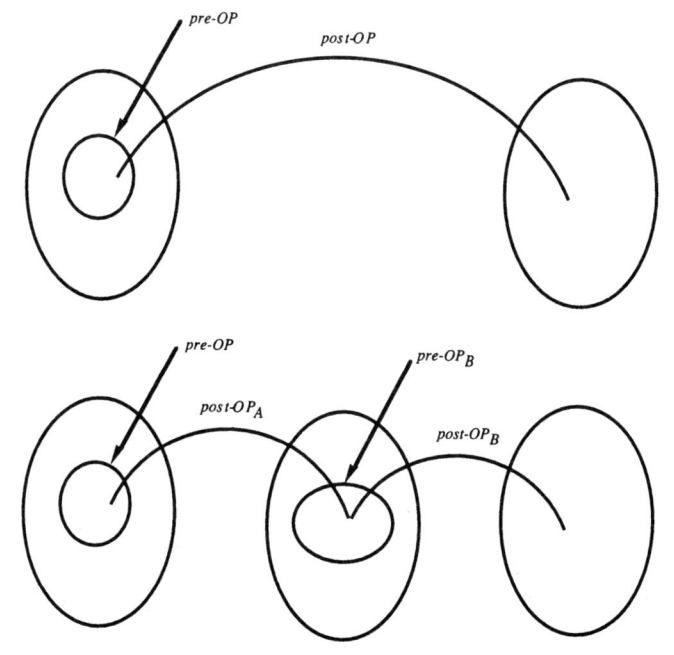

Fig. 8.1. 'Divide and conquer' used to establish a subgoal.

8.1.1 Choosing the First Step

The first alternative involves designing the first component A, in this case we will need to calculate the second step B. The task of the first component is to established a subgoal, and then B can proceed from this subgoal to the final solution (Fig. 8.1). How to choose the subgoal? Given a specification to implement, there are two main approaches:

- If the specification had a different pre-condition, it might be easier to establish the post-condition. With this strategy we now have a subgoal, an intermediate step, to establish the new pre-condition.
- An alternative view is to try and establish only part of the post-condition (or equivalently a weaker post-condition). Again we have a subgoal, to establish the weaker post-condition and then go on to establish the full post-condition from this weaker one.

Both of these give a way of decomposing a large specification into two smaller ones, we first do something to establish part of the solution, then do something else to complete the remainder. It turns out that anything will do for the intermediate sub-goal. We will take a simple case first, if the post-condition *post* is independent of some of the initial values, then for certain predicates M that do not contain any initial values, we have the following:

138   8. Command Sequences

If x and y are a partition of the variables w and $post$ is not dependent on $\overleftarrow{x}$ and M is only dependent on x, then:

$$x : [\ pre(w),\quad M(x)\ ]\ ;\ w : [\ M(x),\quad post(\overleftarrow{y}, w)\ ]$$

= expand frame rule

$$w : [\ pre(w),\quad M(x) \wedge \overleftarrow{y} = y\ ]\ ;\ w : [\ M(x),\quad post(\overleftarrow{y}, w)\ ]$$

= semantics and Corollary 3.5

$$@w'' \bullet (\exists\, x', y' \cdot M(x') \wedge y = y' \wedge post(y', w'')) \to w := w''\ \square$$
$$\neg\,(pre(w) \wedge \forall\, x', y' \cdot M(x') \wedge y = y' \Rightarrow M(x')) \to \mathsf{chaos}$$

=

$$@w' \bullet (\exists\, x' \cdot M(x') \wedge post(y, w')) \to w := w'\ \square\ \neg\, pre(w) \to \mathsf{chaos}$$

= semantics

$$w : [\ pre(w),\quad \exists\, x' \cdot M(x') \wedge post(\overleftarrow{y}, w)\ ]$$

Now by the replace specification rule (Theorem 5.6):

$$w : [\ pre(w),\quad post(\overleftarrow{y}, w)\ ] \sqsubseteq w : [\ pre(w),\quad \exists\, x' \cdot M(x') \wedge post(\overleftarrow{y}, w)\ ]$$

Thus

$$w : [\ pre(w),\quad post(\overleftarrow{y}, w)\ ]$$
$$\sqsubseteq$$
$$x : [\ pre(w),\quad M(x)\ ]\ ;\ w : [\ M(x),\quad post(\overleftarrow{y}, w)\ ]$$

and we have proved the following lemma:

Lemma 8.1

if $\left\{\begin{array}{c} x \text{ is a subset of the variables } w \\ M \text{ is an } x\text{-predicate, independent of initial } x \\ post \text{ is independent of initial } x \end{array}\right\}$ then

$$\begin{array}{l}\mathsf{chg}\ w \\ \mathsf{pre}\ pre \\ \mathsf{post}\ post\end{array} \sqsubseteq \begin{array}{l}\mathsf{chg}\ x \\ \mathsf{pre}\ pre \\ \mathsf{post}\ M \\ ; \\ \mathsf{chg}\ w \\ \mathsf{pre}\ M \\ \mathsf{post}\ post\end{array}$$

□

Are there any restrictions on M other than those described by the proof obligations? There are none, any predicate satisfying the proof obligations will do! Of course, it is a good idea to choose an M that is either suitable for use as a more restrictive pre-condition for the second step, or that goes some way towards establishing the final post-condition *post*. It should be noted that an unwise choice for M could make one of the new specifications miracle in disguise.

What if all of the interesting state variables used in the post-condition *post* are hooked? Can M be more general? For any predicate M over some (not necessarily proper) subset x of the set of variables w:

$$w : [\ pre,\ post\ ]$$
$$=$$
$$[\![\ \text{con } c \text{ in } w : [\ pre \land c = x,\ post[\overleftarrow{x}\backslash c]\ ]\ ]\!]$$
$$\sqsubseteq \quad \text{Lemma 8.1}$$
$$[\![\ \text{con } c \text{ in } x : [\ pre \land c = x,\ M(c,x)\ ];\ w : [\ M(c,x),\ post[\overleftarrow{x}\backslash c]\ ]\ ]\!]$$

Now if we refine the second specification by B that does not contain any instances of the logical constant c, then we have

$$[\![\ \text{con } c \text{ in } x : [\ pre \land c = x,\ M(c,x)\ ];\ w : [\ M(c,x),\ post[\overleftarrow{x}\backslash c]\ ]\ ]\!]$$
$$\sqsubseteq$$
$$[\![\ \text{con } c \text{ in } x : [\ pre \land c = x,\ M(c,x)\ ]\ ]\!]\ ;\ B$$
$$\sqsubseteq$$
$$x : [\ pre,\ M(\overleftarrow{x},x)\ ]\ ;\ B$$

Thus we have the following rule:

Theorem 8.2 (introduce command-semicolon rule)

if $\left\{\begin{array}{c} x \text{ is a subset of the variables } w \\ M \text{ is an } x\text{-predicate} \end{array}\right\}$ then

$$\begin{array}{c} \text{chg } w \\ \text{pre } pre \\ \text{post } post \end{array} \quad \sqsubseteq \quad \begin{array}{l} \text{chg } x \\ \text{pre } pre \\ \text{post } M \\ ; \\ [\![\ \text{con } c \text{ in} \\ \quad \text{chg } w \\ \quad \text{pre } M[\overleftarrow{x}\backslash c] \\ \quad \text{post } post[\overleftarrow{x}\backslash c]\ ]\!] \end{array}$$

$\square$

Remember that the block containing the logical constants and the specification must be refined by code that does not contain any logical constants.

8. Command Sequences

There is a useful extension to this rule: when the first operation is an assignment command – this rule is included since it is particularly useful when refining the body of an iterative command. The extension looks rather complicated as it requires a certain amount of thinking backwards:

Theorem 8.3 (introduce leading assignment rule)

$$\text{if} \left\{ \begin{array}{c} x \text{ is a subset of the variables } w \\ pre[x\backslash E] \Rightarrow \delta(E : X) \end{array} \right\} \text{ then}$$

$$\begin{array}{l} \text{chg } w \\ \text{pre } pre[x\backslash E] \\ \text{post } post[\overleftarrow{x}\backslash \overleftarrow{E}] \end{array} \sqsubseteq \begin{array}{l} x := E \\ ; \\ \text{chg } w \\ \text{pre } pre \\ \text{post } post \end{array}$$

where $\overleftarrow{E}$ equivalent to $E[x\backslash \overleftarrow{x}]$

□

This rule, however, does has a simpler form: if the expression on the right-hand side of the assignment command has an inverse, the rule has the following simple form:

Corollary 8.1 (introduce leading assignment rule)

$$\text{if} \left\{ \begin{array}{c} x \text{ is a subset of the variables } w \\ pre \Rightarrow \delta(f(x) : X) \\ pre \Rightarrow \delta(f^{-1}(x) : X) \end{array} \right\} \text{ then}$$

$$\begin{array}{l} \text{chg } w \\ \text{pre } pre \\ \text{post } post \end{array} \sqsubseteq \begin{array}{l} x := f(x) \\ ; \\ \text{chg } w \\ \text{pre } pre[x\backslash f^{-1}(x)] \\ \text{post } post[\overleftarrow{x}\backslash f^{-1}(\overleftarrow{x})] \end{array}$$

□

The proof obligations for f just state that it must have an inverse everywhere it is defined.

8.1.2 Choosing the Second Step

Consider the second alternative of choosing B and calculating A. The second operation B must establish the post-condition of the specification, and it can

8.1 Solve a Part and then the Whole

only do this if the input to B satisfies $[B]post$. Thus a possible specification for A is $x : [\ pre,\ [B]post\ ]$ as this will establish the appropriate condition for B to establish the post-condition of the specification. Thus we need to prove that:

$$x : [\ pre,\ post\ ] \sqsubseteq x : [\ pre,\ [B]post\ ]\ ;\ B$$

First a lemma:

Lemma 8.2
For $x : X$

$$\text{con } c \text{ in } x : [\ p(x) \land (\forall x' : X \cdot q(x, x') \Rightarrow post(c, x')),\ post(c, x)\ ] \sqsubseteq$$
$$x : [\ p(x),\ q(\overleftarrow{x}, x)\ ]$$

Proof
Apply the replace specification rule, the proof obligations are:

$$p(x) \land (\forall x' : X \cdot q(x, x') \Rightarrow post(c, x'))$$
$$\Longrightarrow$$
$$p(x)$$

$$p(\overleftarrow{x}) \land (\forall x' : X \cdot q(\overleftarrow{x}, x') \Rightarrow post(c, x')) \land q(\overleftarrow{x}, x)$$
$$\Longleftrightarrow$$
$$p(\overleftarrow{x}) \land (\forall x' : X \cdot q(\overleftarrow{x}, x) \land (q(\overleftarrow{x}, x') \Rightarrow post(c, x')))$$
$$\Longleftrightarrow$$
$$p(\overleftarrow{x}) \land q(\overleftarrow{x}, x) \land post(c, x)$$
$$\Longrightarrow$$
$$post(c, x)$$

Since the refinement does not contain the logical constant, its declaration can be removed, thus completing the proof.
∎

Theorem 8.4 (introduce semicolon-command rule)
$$x : [\ pre,\ post\ ] \sqsubseteq x : [\ pre,\ [B]post\ ]\ ;\ B$$

Proof
Using the normal form theorem, B can be written as

$$B = @x' : X \bullet q(x, x') \rightarrow x := x'\ \square\ \neg p(x) \rightarrow \text{loop}$$

Then

$$[B]post(\overleftarrow{x}, x) = p(x) \land (\forall x' : X \cdot q(x, x') \Rightarrow post(\overleftarrow{x}, x'))$$

Now

142   8. *Command Sequences*

$$x : \left[\; pre(x), \quad post(\overleftarrow{x}, x) \; \right]$$

$\sqsubseteq$ Theorem 8.2

$$x : \left[\begin{array}{l} pre(x), \quad p(x) \wedge (\forall x' \cdot q(x, x') \Rightarrow post(\overleftarrow{x}, x')) \\ [\![\text{con } c \text{ in } x : [\; p(x) \wedge (\forall x' \cdot q(x, x') \Rightarrow post(c, x')), \quad post(c, x) \;]]\!] \end{array} \right] ;$$

$\sqsubseteq$ Lemma 8.2

$$x : \left[\begin{array}{l} pre(x), \quad [B]post(\overleftarrow{x}, x) \\ [\![\text{con } c \text{ in } x : [\; p(x), \quad q(\overleftarrow{x}, x) \;]]\!] \end{array} \right] ;$$

$\sqsubseteq$

$$x : \left[\; pre(x), \quad [B]post(\overleftarrow{x}, x) \; \right] ; \; B$$

∎

Again there is a special case of this approach which is useful when refining the body of an iteration. The extension is the following assignment rule, where the second command is by choice an assignment. It is easy to show that:

Theorem 8.5 (introduce following assignment rule)

if $\left\{ \begin{array}{c} x \text{ is a subset of the variables } w \\ \delta(E : X) \end{array} \right\}$ then

```
                        chg w
chg w                   pre pre
pre  pre        ⊑       post post[x\E]
post post               ;
                        x := E
```

□

The safest restriction on E is that it must be defined everywhere – that E is total.

8.1.3 Choosing Both Steps

The final case is to discover both A and B. Now Theorem 3.30 states that both A and B are either specifications or (for refinement) equivalent to specifications, thus we can write:

$$A \equiv @w' : W \bullet post_A \rightarrow w := w' \; [\!] \; pre_A(w) \rightarrow \text{chaos}$$
$$B \equiv @w' : W \bullet post_B \rightarrow w := w' \; [\!] \; pre_B(w) \rightarrow \text{chaos}$$

and the corollary to the same theorem can be used to write $A \; ; \; B$ in the form:

8.1 Solve a Part and then the Whole 143

@w'' : $W \bullet (\exists w' : W \cdot post_A(w, w') \wedge post_B(w', w'') \to w := w'')$ □
$pre_A(w) \wedge (\forall w' : W \cdot post_A(w, w') \Rightarrow pre_B(w')) \to $ chaos

and it is easy to see that, using the equivalent specification rule:

$pre(w) \Rightarrow pre_A(w) \wedge \forall w' \cdot post_A(w, w') \Rightarrow pre_B(w')$
$pre(w) \wedge (\exists w' : W \cdot post_A(w, w') \wedge post_B(w', w'')) \Rightarrow post(w, w'')$

then the following theorem holds:

Theorem 8.6 (introduce semicolon rule)

if $\left\{ \begin{array}{c} pre(w) \Rightarrow pre_A(w) \\ pre(w) \wedge \forall w' \cdot post_A(w, w') \Rightarrow pre_B(w') \\ pre(w) \wedge (\exists w' \cdot post_A(w, w') \wedge post_B(w', w'')) \\ \Rightarrow post(w, w'') \end{array} \right\}$ then

```
                    chg w
                    pre pre_A
chg w               post post_A
pre pre      ⊑  ;
post post           chg w
                    pre pre_B
                    post post_B
```

□

Two useful corollaries hold for post-conditions that are in a certain form:

Corollary 8.2

if $\{$ P is independent of any initial values $\}$ then

```
                    chg w
                    pre pre
chg w               post P
pre pre      ⊑  ;
post P ∧ Q          chg w
                    pre P
                    post P ∧ Q
```

□

Corollary 8.3

if $\left\{ \begin{array}{l} P \text{ does not contain } x \text{ free} \\ Q \text{ does not contain } y \text{ free} \end{array} \right\}$ then

$$\begin{array}{c}\text{chg } x,y\\ \text{post } P\wedge Q\end{array} \quad\sqsubseteq\quad \begin{array}{l}\text{chg } y\\ \text{post } P\\ ;\\ \text{chg } x\\ \text{post } Q\end{array}$$

□

8.2 Summary

Once again, more rules have been introduced than are really necessary; and again the motivation is to provide understanding of both the language and the algorithmic refinement process. The reader is encouraged to try and understand the rules using the view that refinement is about widening preconditions and narrowing post-conditions (removing non-determinism). Each of the rules should be understood using the relational model.

9. The Alternative Command

The next step in developing an executable subset of the specification and programming language is to construct a command that will allow choices to be made, and to show how a specification can be transformed into a program that uses the command.

9.1 Divide and Conquer

Given a specification to refine, if the specification had a more restrictive (stronger) pre-condition, it might be easier to establish the post-condition. For example, given the specification

> *abs*
> chg $a : \mathbb{Z}$
> pre true
> post $(a = \overleftarrow{a} \lor a = -\overleftarrow{a}) \land 0 \leq a$

It is easier to refine either

> *abs*
> chg $a : \mathbb{Z}$
> pre $0 \leq a$
> post $(a = \overleftarrow{a} \lor a = -\overleftarrow{a}) \land 0 \leq a$

or

> *abs*
> chg $a : \mathbb{Z}$
> pre $a \leq 0$
> post $(a = \overleftarrow{a} \lor a = -\overleftarrow{a}) \land 0 \leq a$

In the general case, given a specification:

> *op*
> chg $w : W$

pre *pre*
post *post*

it might be easier to refine

op
chg $w : W$
pre *pre* ∧ *extra*
post *post*

However, this means that some input values are no longer dealt with – those values that satisfy the original pre-condition predicate *pre*, but do not satisfy *extra*. One possible solution to this problem has already been seen, the solution was to introduce an additional command, using ';', whose task was to establish this more restrictive pre-condition.

[Figure: Case analysis diagram showing nested ovals with labels "partition the pre-condition" and "pre-condition"]

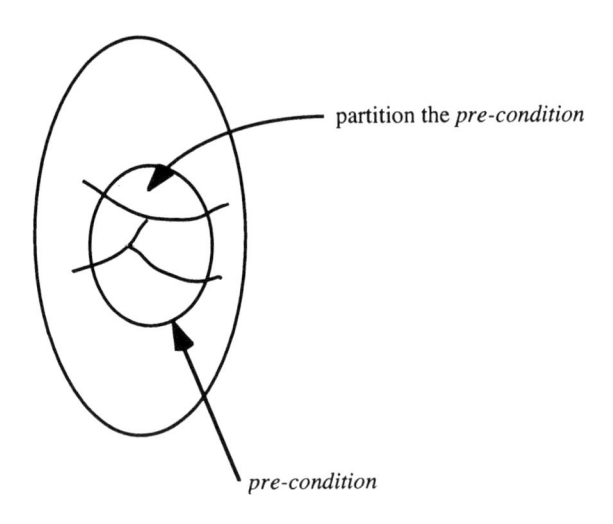

Fig. 9.1. Case analysis.

An alternative approach is to partition the given pre-condition into parts, each of which is more restrictive than the complete pre-condition (Fig. 9.1) and each part making the post-condition easier to establish. Between them, the pre-conditions must cover all possible inputs – otherwise some input values would not be dealt with. The pre-condition can partitioned by conjoining various additional predicates, the disjunction of these additional predicates being implied by the original pre-condition. The problem is solved in each of the sub-domains of input values, and then the solutions are re-assembled to solve the complete problem.

Notice that adding an additional term to the pre-condition is equivalent to adding an assertion just before the specification – a pre-condition can always be transformed into an assertion. Conversely, if we have an assertion followed by a specification, we can move the assertion into the pre-condition.

Theorem 9.1
$$\{assert\}\ x : [\ pre,\quad post\ ] = x : [\ assert \land pre,\quad post\ ]$$

Proof
Straight from the definition of a specification command and Theorem 3.28.
∎

9.2 The Partition

The strategy to be used is to discover a way of partitioning the pre-condition into a set of more restrictive conditions such that under each of these restrictions the problem is easier to solve – the post-condition will be easier to establish. It will be necessary to provide a way of guarding the execution of a sub-solution, a way of guaranteeing that the reduced specification is only executed under the assumption of the new restriction. The following theorems summarizes these ideas, but first a lemma:

Lemma 9.1
$$A \sqsubseteq p \to A$$

Proof
It is necessary to show that, for all predicates R defined over the state:
$$[A]R \Rightarrow \neg p \lor [A]R$$
which is trivial.
∎

It should be remembered that for non-trivial guard, $p \to A$ is not total, and thus is not implementable. Those input values that satisfy an assertion should be refined correctly:

Lemma 9.2
$$\{p\}A \sqsubseteq p \to A$$

Proof
By Corollary 6.1 and Lemma 9.1 we have:
$$\{p\}A \sqsubseteq A \sqsubseteq p \to A$$
∎

Those input values that do not satisfy an assertion can be refined by anything:

Lemma 9.3
$$\{p\}A \sqsubseteq \neg p \to B$$

Proof
For any R defined over the state:

$[\{p\}A]R$
$\iff$
$p \wedge [A]R$
$\implies$
p
$\implies$
$p \vee [B]R$
$\iff$
$\neg p \implies [B]R$
$\iff$
$[\neg p \to B]R$

■

Theorem 9.2
$$A \sqsubseteq (extra \to \{extra\} \; A)$$

Proof
By Lemma 9.1 and Theorem 3.29.

■

If the command A was not total, but was in a context where it could be executed, then we have:

Corollary 9.1
$$\{p\} \; A \sqsubseteq extra \to \{p \wedge extra\} \; A$$

□

If A is a specification, the *extra* assertion can be added to the pre-condition (see Theorem 9.1). Thus we can always carry out this refinement strategy at the expense of introducing miraculous commands; commands that cannot be implemented. The miracles will need to be removed if the code is to be executed.

The ideas seen so far can be gathered together, a specification and its refinement under a more restricted pre-condition can be related:

Theorem 9.3
$$pre \wedge extra \implies [A]post$$

if and only if

    chg $w : W$
    pre pre $\sqsubseteq$ $extra \rightarrow A$
    post $post$

Proof

$$[w : [\ pre,\quad post\ ]]R \;\Rightarrow\; [extra \rightarrow A]R$$
$$\Longleftrightarrow$$
$$[w : [\ pre,\quad post\ ]]R \;\Rightarrow\; (extra \Rightarrow [A]R)$$
$$\Longleftrightarrow$$
$$extra \wedge [w : [\ pre,\quad post\ ]]R \;\Rightarrow\; [A]R$$
$$\Longleftrightarrow$$
$$[extra \wedge w : [\ pre,\quad post\ ]]R \;\Rightarrow\; [A]R$$
$$\Longleftrightarrow$$
$$[w : [\ extra \wedge pre,\quad post\ ]]R \;\Rightarrow\; [A]R$$

Thus

$$pre \wedge extra \;\Rightarrow\; [A]post$$
$$\Longleftrightarrow$$
$$w : [\ extra \wedge pre,\quad post\ ] \sqsubseteq A$$
$$\Longleftrightarrow$$
$$w : [\ pre,\quad post\ ] \sqsubseteq extra \rightarrow A$$

■

There may be a need to change a guard, it can easily be made more restrictive:

Theorem 9.4
If

$$q \;\Rightarrow\; p$$

then

$$p \rightarrow A \sqsubseteq q \rightarrow A$$

□

Notice that this refinement step, in general, requires a proof. It is always true that $false \Rightarrow p$, thus by the above theorem $p \rightarrow A \sqsubseteq false \rightarrow A = $ miracle, as is to be expected. This theorem is really a more general version of Theorem 6.4.

For refinement to work in a stepwise manner, it is necessary to show that refining body of a guarded command is equivalent to refining the guarded command.

Theorem 9.5 (monotonicity)
If

$$A \sqsubseteq B$$

then

$$p \to A \sqsubseteq p \to B$$

□

The following theorem allows guards to be removed. If a guarded command is in a context where the guard is true, it can be removed.

Theorem 9.6

$$\text{if } \{ p \Rightarrow q \} \text{ then } \{p\} (q \to A) \sqsubseteq A$$

□

Returning to the original problem, if A is a total command, and we can partition the domain of the command by two predicates p and q such that $p \lor q$ is true, then

$$A \sqsubseteq p \to A$$
$$A \sqsubseteq q \to A$$

All that is needed is a way of reassembling these miraculous commands to give a non-miraculous command, this can be done by the choice operator.

9.3 Reassembly

It is now time to consider how to re-assemble our miraculous solutions to a problem, the choice operator can be used to put partial solutions together again; but first some properties. A useful property of ⊓ is about removing non-determinism:

Theorem 9.7
$$A \sqcap B \sqsubseteq A$$
$$A \sqcap B \sqsubseteq B$$

□

The command $A \sqcap B$ is the largest common specification that is refined by both A and B – the largest common specification is that specification that has, in some sense, the 'least' number of refinements.

Refining each alternative separately is equivalent to refining the whole:

Theorem 9.8 (monotonicity)

$$\text{if } \left\{ \begin{array}{l} A \sqsubseteq C \\ B \sqsubseteq D \end{array} \right\} \text{ then } A \sqcap B \sqsubseteq C \sqcap D$$

□

A more general version of this for unbounded choice is

Corollary 9.2

$$\text{if } \{ \forall i \in I \cdot A_i \sqsubseteq B_i \} \text{ then } @i \in I \bullet A_i \sqsubseteq @i \in I \bullet B_i$$

□

The choice operator $\sqcap$ can be used to re-assemble solutions:

Theorem 9.9

$$\text{if } \left\{ \begin{array}{l} A \sqsubseteq B \\ A \sqsubseteq C \end{array} \right\} \text{ then } A \sqsubseteq B \sqcap C$$

□

Supposing under some assumption p we know that the command A can be simplified to solve the problem, and under another assumption q the command A can again be simplified to solve the problem. If the two assumptions cover all possibilities, then $p \to A \sqcap q \to A$ will solve the whole problem under either assumption, providing the non-deterministic choice can be made to choose the right command in the right circumstances, and the guards guarantee this for us. We can show this is valid as follows, if

$$A \sqsubseteq p \to A$$
$$A \sqsubseteq q \to A$$

and then we have

$$A \sqsubseteq p \to A \sqcap q \to A$$

If the predicate $p \vee q$ is **true** then the refinement above is total (and thus feasible). Again if A is partial, but in a context where it is executable and where $P \Rightarrow p \vee q$ then:

$\qquad \{P\}\ A$
$\sqsubseteq \quad$ Corollary 6.3
$\qquad \{p \vee q\}\ A$
$= \quad$ Lemma 9.2
$\qquad p \vee q \to A$
$= \quad$ Theorem 3.18
$\qquad p \to A \sqcap q \to A$

and by Theorem 6.13 we have

$$\{P\}\ A \sqsubseteq \{P\}\ (p \rightarrow A \,\square\, q \rightarrow A)$$

In the above it is assumed that the assumptions p and q cover all possibilities or are implied by the context, however there are still problems, especially under those conditions where neither of the guards is true.

9.4 Alternatives – The If Command

The strategies introduced above allow the choice operator to be used to combine guarded commands to produce code that refines a specification. Judicious introduction, manipulation and removal of guards and assertions can produce executable code. What is required is a way to automate this process and a way of guaranteeing totality. We need some way of guaranteeing that a set of guarded commands linked together by non-deterministic choice operators are total or that their execution is guaranteed by the context, otherwise the resulting command will be miraculous and thus not feasible. Consider:

$$p \rightarrow A \,\square\, q \rightarrow B$$

before attempting to generate code, the compiler must know that either $p \vee q$ is true; or that the context guarantees that it is true – these conditions would need to be checked by the compiler. In general this is not decidable – the compiler would need to do some theorem proving. The solution is to, in some sense, finish off the command so that it is total.

A solution to the problem of using guarded commands to provide choices is as follows: given a predicate p, if it is true execute the command A; if it is false execute a command B (which could be skip). Such a construction is obviously total. This give the following possibility:

$$p \rightarrow A \,\square\, \neg p \rightarrow B$$

this is usually given the following syntactic sugar:

if p then A else B

Though it solves the problem, the else clause catch-all is dangerous. During the development of a program we should know what is going on at any point; there should not be an automatically chosen alternative – the programmer should specify all possibilities. However the idea of the if-then-else command can be used, since it has the functionality that is required.

Continuing the non-deterministic philosophy, if A is in a context P then we could find p and q so that $P \Rightarrow p \vee q$, but as has been discussed above: someone or something needs to prove this. The problems occur outside the domain of values in which $p \vee q$ are true, when none of the guards are true.

There are several sensible possibilities of what to do in this case, of which executing either skip and loop are the least troublesome. We will choose the latter as it is safer. The next step in developing an alternative command is to remove the need for any proofs. Notice that Corollary 9.1 and Theorem 9.4 can be used to give:

$$\{P\}\ A \sqsubseteq \neg P \to \mathsf{loop} \sqsubseteq \neg p \land \neg q \to \mathsf{loop}$$

Now the three refinements of a command can be put together to give:

$$\{P\}\ A \sqsubseteq p \to A \mathbin{\square} q \to A \mathbin{\square} \neg p \land \neg q \to \mathsf{loop}$$

with the advantage that this refinement is always total. The command in the refinement will be abbreviated to

if $p \to A \mathbin{\square} q \to B$ fi

The idea can be generalized as follows:

if A fi $\triangleq \mathcal{G}(A) \to A \mathbin{\square} \neg \mathcal{G}(A) \to \mathsf{loop}$

This command is total, and when the command A is made up from a set of alternative guarded commands, easy to implement. Because of Theorem 3.15 this can be written:

Definition 9.1 (the if command)
if A fi $\triangleq A \mathbin{\square} \neg \mathcal{G}(A) \to \mathsf{loop}$

Notice we have added a syntactic boundary to a partial command to limit any look-ahead, as discussed in an earlier chapter.

Theorem 9.10
$\langle \text{if } A \text{ fi} \rangle Q = \langle A \rangle Q$
$[\text{if } A \text{ fi}]\mathsf{true} = \mathcal{G}(A) \land [A]\mathsf{true}$

□

It is easy to show, providing the feasibility of A is defined, that the new command is total:

Theorem 9.11
If $\delta(\mathcal{G}(A) : \mathbb{B})$ then $\mathcal{G}(\text{if } A \text{ fi})$.

Proof
$\quad \mathcal{G}(\text{if } A \text{ fi})$
$\quad \iff$ definition of feasibility and semantics
$\quad\quad \neg([A \mathbin{\square} \neg \mathcal{G}(A) \to \mathsf{loop}]\mathsf{false})$
$\quad \iff$ semantics
$\quad\quad \neg([A]\mathsf{false} \land (\neg \mathcal{G}(A) \Rightarrow [\mathsf{loop}]\mathsf{false}))$

$\iff$ semantics

$\quad \neg ([A]\text{false} \land \mathcal{G}(A))$

$\iff$ definition of feasibility

$\quad \mathcal{G}(A) \lor \neg \mathcal{G}(A)$

$\iff$ hypothesis

$\quad$ true

■

If A is total, we have

Theorem 9.12
If $\mathcal{G}(A)$ (i.e. A is total) then

$\quad$ if A fi $= A$

□

In this case the syntactic boundary can be removed; however it is needed by a compiler as in general it is impossible to compute the domain of a command, so the hint will not be removed in the syntax for the executable subset of the language.

Theorem 9.13
$\quad$ if A fi ; $B =$ if A ; B fi

Proof

$\quad\quad$ if A fi ; B

$=$

$\quad\quad (A \,\square\, \neg \mathcal{G}(A) \to \text{loop}) \,;\, B$

$=\quad$ Theorem 3.13

$\quad\quad A \,;\, B \,\square\, (\neg \mathcal{G}(A) \to \text{loop}) \,;\, B$

$=\quad$ Theorem 3.17

$\quad\quad A \,;\, B \,\square\, \neg \mathcal{G}(A) \to \text{loop} \,;\, B$

$=\quad$ Theorem 3.6

$\quad\quad A \,;\, B \,\square\, \neg \mathcal{G}(A) \to \text{loop}$

$=$

$\quad\quad$ if $A \,;\, B$ fi

■

Another property that provides some more understanding of the if command is:

Theorem 9.14
$\quad$ loop $=$ if miracle fi

□

9.4 Alternatives – The If Command

Now to do refinement, we need a rule of a form that allows the refinement of the body of an if command:

if $A \sqsubseteq B$ then if A fi $\sqsubseteq$ if B fi

This will allow the refinement of an if command by just refining its body. Unfortunately this rule is not true. The proof would go as follows, for any predicate R:

$[$if A fi$]R$
$\iff$ definition of if-command
$\quad \mathcal{G}(A) \wedge [A]R$
$\implies$
$\quad \ldots$
$\implies$
$\quad \mathcal{G}(B) \wedge [B]R$
$\iff$ definition of if-command
$[$if B fi$]R$

The assumption $A \sqsubseteq B$ provides one of the terms needed to fill in the gaps, but it is also necessary to have $\mathcal{G}(A) \Rightarrow \mathcal{G}(B)$. Since $A \sqsubseteq B$ means that $\mathcal{G}(B) \Rightarrow \mathcal{G}(A)$, we have the following theorem:

Theorem 9.15
if $A \sqsubseteq B$ and $\mathcal{G}(A) = \mathcal{G}(B)$ then if A fi $\sqsubseteq$ if B fi
□

We already require that all command constructors are total, and that the if command has been introduced to make a partial command total so that it can be implemented. Since the basic commands are all total, we will need a way of constructing partial commands from total commands, and the easiest way of doing this is by guarding. The body of an if command will normally be be a set of guarded commands combined with the choice operator. It turns out that under the conditions that both A and B are total and if $A \sqsubseteq A'$ and $B \sqsubseteq B'$ then:

if $p \to A \,\square\, q \to B$ fi $\sqsubseteq$ if $p \to A' \,\square\, q \to B'$ fi

and it is this refinement step that we will use. Thus there are two rules that are needed, introducing an if command and refining an if command. The first theorem provides the most general refinement step:

Theorem 9.16

if $\left\{ \begin{array}{l} \forall i \in I \cdot P \Rightarrow \delta(p_i : \mathbb{B}) \\ \{P\}\, A \sqsubseteq p_i \to B_i \\ P \Rightarrow \exists i \in I \cdot p_i \end{array} \right\}$ then

$\{P\}\ A \sqsubseteq$ if $@i \in I \bullet p_i \to B_i$ fi

□

The first proof obligation demands that all the guards are defined, the second demands that each of the guarded commands refine the specification, and the third demands that all possible valid inputs are covered. Under these conditions all of the guarded commands can be reassembled to provide the refinement.

It might be a good strategy to leave the refinement of the bodies of the guarded commands to later, then the above theorem can be simplified:

Corollary 9.3

if $\left\{ \begin{array}{c} \forall i \in I \cdot P \Rightarrow \delta(p_i : \mathbb{B}) \\ P \Rightarrow \exists i \in I \cdot p_i \end{array} \right\}$ then

$\{P\}\ A \sqsubseteq$ if $@i \in I \bullet p_i \to \{p_i \wedge P\}\ A$ fi

□

We also have the property we need for refinement:

Theorem 9.17

if $\{$ for all $i \in I$ the refinements $A_i \sqsubseteq B_i$ hold $\}$ then

if $@i \in I \bullet p_i \to A_i$ fi $\sqsubseteq$ if $@i \in I \bullet p_i \to B_i$ fi

□

It is possible to transform the guards of an if-statement to replace non-executable expressions by executable ones, to improve efficiently, or to expedite data refinement (addressed in later chapters).

Theorem 9.18

if $\{\ \forall i \in I \cdot P \Rightarrow (p_i \Leftrightarrow q_i)\ \}$ then

$\{P\}$ if $@i \in I \bullet p_i \to A_i$ fi $\sqsubseteq$ if $@i \in I \bullet q_i \to A_i$ fi

Proof
By Theorem 9.15.
■

It will be useful to be able to move a command into and out from an if statement:

Theorem 9.19

(if $@i \in I \bullet p_i \to A_i$ fi) ; B = if $@i \in I \bullet (p_i \to A_i\ ;\ B)$ fi

Proof
Use Theorems 3.17 and 9.13.
∎

This transformation will be used when building procedure bodies.

9.5 Refining Specifications

For specifications a refinement rule can be derived. A possible choice for the guards is to choose a set of them so that for the pre-condition pre we have $pre \Rightarrow \exists i \in \{1,\ldots,n\} \cdot p_i$ – in this case it would be easy to transform any pre-condition (since conjoining it with itself does not change it). This suggests the following form of the rule which can easily be derived from the above rules:

Theorem 9.20 (introduce alternatives rule)

$$\text{if } \left\{ \begin{array}{c} \forall i \in \{1,\ldots,n\} \cdot pre \Rightarrow \delta(p_i : \mathbb{B}) \\ pre \Rightarrow \exists i \in \{1,\ldots,n\} \cdot p_i \end{array} \right\} \text{ then}$$

$$\begin{array}{l} op \\ \text{chg } w \\ \text{pre } pre \\ \text{post } post \end{array} \quad \sqsubseteq \quad \begin{array}{l} \text{if } p_1 \to op_1 \\ [\!]\ \ldots \\ [\!]\ p_n \to op_n \\ \text{fi} \end{array}$$

where op_i is given by

op_i
chg w
pre $p_i \wedge pre$
post $post$

□

It can be argued informally that this is a correct refinement step:

- the first proof obligation requires that, for valid input, the guards are all defined;
- the second proof obligation ensures that any valid input satisfies at least one of the guards – thus at least one of the guarded commands can be executed; and

- the post-condition of the body of each of the guarded commands is identical to the post-condition of the specification OP, thus when these specifications are implemented, their refinements all produce outputs that satisfy the original specification.

Each of the bodies of the guarded commands should be easier to implement as their pre-condition is more restrictive.

9.6 Summary

Several refinement rules have been introduced, the two most important ones have been flagged – one give a general refinement step at the probable cost of some difficult proof obligations to be discharged, the other which gives a simple refinement step from a specification with (usually) simple proof obligations to discharge. It is the later one that will be used most often. Note also the rule for changing the guards – this will be needed when carrying out data refinement.

10. The Iterative Command

As mentioned earlier, the closure of A (given by A^*) is too well-behaved to be a candidate for defining a looping construct. It does not have the right properties, its definition does not allow for the possibility of looping forever.

Remember that A^* was defined as:

$$A^* = @i \in \mathbb{N} \bullet A^i$$

which is, roughly speaking:

$$\text{skip} \,\square\, A \,\square\, A^2 \,\square\, A^3 \,\square\, \ldots$$

From this definition it can be seen that, for the execution of the command, non-determinism must choose how many times to iterate before starting execution. Any number of iterations can be chosen, but once this has been done there is no possibility of it changing. We can see the problem this causes by investigating two simple examples, consider the following state:

$$State = \{W, X, Y, Z\}$$

and the command (relation) B^1 defined on $State$ and given by:

$$B = \{W \mapsto X, X \mapsto Y\}$$

The closure of this relation is:

$$B^* = \{W \mapsto W, W \mapsto X, W \mapsto Y, X \mapsto X, X \mapsto Y, Y \mapsto Y, Z \mapsto Z\}$$

which is what we would expect. (For the input value W, the possible outcomes are W, X, or Y; non-determinism chooses which one for any particular execution of B.) However, if we consider the command C given by:

$$C = \{W \mapsto X, X \mapsto Y, Y \mapsto W\}$$

then its closure would be:

$$C^* = \{W \mapsto W, W \mapsto X, W \mapsto Y, X \mapsto X, X \mapsto Y, Y \mapsto Y, Y \mapsto W, Z \mapsto Z\}$$

---

[1] As before, we shall ignore the name of the state component for clarity.

which might not be what we expect (or require) for a general loop; however, missing from the above closure are the infinite cycles that are possible from the definition of C. The infinite cycle:

$$W \to X \to Y \to W \to X \to \ldots$$

is missing (not characterized), as are the other two infinite cycles that start with either X or Y. Writing C^* for the generalized loop based on C, we would expect

$$C^* = \{W \mapsto X, X \mapsto Y, W \mapsto Y, Y \mapsto W, W \mapsto W, X \mapsto X, Y \mapsto Y, Z \mapsto Z\} \cup$$
$$\{W \mapsto \bot, X \mapsto \bot, Y \mapsto \bot\}$$

Each of the values that start an infinite cycle has been mapped onto $\bot$, since this is how the model deals with infinite loops.

A command could also have an infinite chain, for example the command D over a state that just consists of the natural numbers could be defined as

$$D = \{m \mapsto m + 1 \mid m : \mathbb{N}\}$$

which has the following closure:

$$D^* = \{m \mapsto n \mid m, n \in \mathbb{N} \cdot m \leq n\}$$

In the representation (model) of a looping command that is based on D, any element on an infinite chain needs to be mapped to $\bot$. For this example the model should really be:

$$D^* = \{m \mapsto n \mid m, n \in \mathbb{N} \cdot m \leq n\} \cup \{m \mapsto \bot \mid m \in \mathbb{N}\}$$

If we are to repeatedly execute a command A then for the execution to continue the output of A must also be acceptable input to A (be in the domain of A) otherwise the loop will jam. A further problem is that A^* is not the proper solution to the following recursive definition (which looks like a good candidate to define an iterative command):

$$X \triangleq A\, ;\, X \,\square\, \mathsf{skip}$$

As the missing part of a generalized loop are those values that could loop forever, so it is these that we shall initially concentrate on. We also need to remove the explicit reference to $\bot$ as it is part of the underlying model and the philosophy has been to hide this value. To do this we divide the problem of defining the semantics of looping into two parts – defining the outcomes for those input values that the loop terminates, and characterizing those input values that cause non-termination. As the termination part of the general loop can be defined using closure, we need to study the infinite loop problem in more detail.

Given a command A, we wish to define A^*, the generalized loop. As a first step, we shall characterize by a predicate p those input states that could loop forever; what properties does this predicate have? Looking at a single iteration of the command A, if on termination, the proper outcome of an input that satisfied p still satisfies p then this value could cause non-termination; for if the outcome does not satisfy p, on a subsequent iteration it will eventually terminate. So it looks as if we are looking for predicates that satisfy $p \Rightarrow [A]p$. However, those input values that produce the improper outcome should also satisfy p, but they certainly will not satisfy $[A]p$, so we are not quite there yet.

Before continuing, it is necessary to fully understand the implication of this predicate p we are searching for. If inputs to the iteration satisfy p then these inputs could either loop forever through a cycle of values or may have $\bot$ as their outcome. The predicate p defines those input values that may cause looping – thus if $p(x)$ is true, this means that $A^\star$ could loop forever (it may not because of non-determinism). However, if $(i, \bot) \in A^\star$ then certainly i satisfies p.

We need to be crafty: now $[A]\neg p$ defines those input values that have proper outcomes that do not satisfy p. So $\neg[A]\neg p$ defines those inputs that either have $\bot$ as their outcome or the proper outcome satisfies p and could thus potentially causing looping, which is exactly the input values we are interested in. We are interested in the conjunction of all predicates that satisfy

$$p \Rightarrow \neg[A]\neg p$$

and this is given by the credulously proper solution to

$$p = \neg[A]\neg p$$

This solution will be denoted by $\mathrm{circ} A$.

The problem can also be understood from the relational view. We are interested in those cases were the repetitive execution of a command may never terminate – this could occur when the execution of the loop consisting of the command is started with a value that is either in a cycle or on in an infinite chain that can be constructed from pairs of values belonging to the relation. Given a command (relation) A on *State* × *State* and a predicate p over the *State*, we can define when each element of the state that satisfies p is part of a cycle or part of an infinite chain defined by p produced by repeated execution of A. We are looking for those predicates p that contain either a cycle or an infinite chain. The answer is simple, p will define a cycle or an infinite chain when, from each element of the set defined by p you can reach another element of it; formally:

$$\forall x \in \mathit{State} \cdot p(x) \Rightarrow \exists y \in \mathit{State} \cdot {}_xA_y \wedge p(y)$$

Now examine the conclusion of this implication:

$$\exists\, y \in State \cdot {}_xA_y \wedge p(y)$$
$$\iff$$
$$\exists\, y \in State \cdot \exists\, z \in State \cdot {}_xA_z \wedge p(z) \wedge z = y$$
$$\iff$$
$$\exists\, y \in State \cdot \exists\, z \in State \cdot {}_xA_z \wedge p(z) \wedge {}_z\mathsf{skip}_y$$
$$\iff$$
$$\exists\, y \in State \cdot \exists\, z \in State \cdot {}_xA_z \wedge {}_z(p \to \mathsf{skip})_y$$
$$\iff$$
$$\exists\, y \in State \cdot {}_x(A; p \to \mathsf{skip})_y$$
$$\iff$$
$$\mathcal{G}(A; p \to \mathsf{skip})$$

If we define
$$cycle_A(p) \triangleq \mathcal{G}(A; p \to \mathsf{skip})$$
then it is possible to show that $\mathrm{circ}A$ is the credulous proper solution to
$$p = cycle_A(p)$$

Some simple properties of $cycle$ are given by the following lemma:

Lemma 10.1
$$cycle_A(p) = \neg[A]\neg p$$
$$cycle_A(p) \wedge cycle_A(q) \Rightarrow cycle_A(p \wedge q)$$
$$cycle_A(p) \vee cycle_A(q) \Leftrightarrow cycle_A(p \vee q)$$

Proof
All can be shown to be true from the definition.
∎

This means that the recursive equation for defining $\mathrm{circ}A$ is
$$p = \neg[A]\neg p$$
and the credulous proper solution is given by:

$\mathrm{circ}A = \forall\, i : \mathbb{N} \cdot L_i$
where
$L_0 = \mathcal{G}(A)$
$L_{i+1} = \neg[A]\neg L_i$

Every element of an infinite chain or a cycle should have $\bot$ as a possible outcome; the infinite looping part of our generalized loop can be defined as follows:
$$A^\circ = \mathrm{circ}A \to \mathsf{loop}$$

The usual characterization (semantics) of A° can now be defined:

$[A^\circ]\text{true} = \neg\, \text{circ}\, A$
$\langle A^\circ \rangle R = \text{true}$

which is what might be expected.

The candidate for a looping structure is made up of the finite part and the looping part:

$A^* \triangleq A^\star \,\square\, A^\circ$

From the definition of $A^\star$ we have

$[A^*]\text{true} = [A^\star \,\square\, A^\circ]\text{true} = [A^\star]\text{true} \wedge \neg\,\text{circ}\,A$

Consider $\neg[A^*]\text{true}$

$\quad cycle_A(\neg[A^*]\text{true})$
$\iff$ from the definition of the termination set
$\quad cycle_A(\exists\, i \in \mathbb{N} \cdot \neg[A^i]\text{true})$
$\iff$
$\quad \exists\, i \in \mathbb{N} \cdot cycle_A(\neg[A^i]\text{true})$
$\iff$
$\quad \exists\, i \in \mathbb{N} \cdot \neg[A^{i+1}]\text{true}$
$\iff$
$\quad \text{false} \vee \exists\, i \in \mathbb{N}_1 \cdot \neg[A^i]\text{true}$
$\iff$
$\quad \exists\, i \in \mathbb{N} \cdot \neg[A^i]\text{true}$
$\iff$
$\quad \neg[A^*]\text{true}$

Thus $\neg[A^*]\text{true}$ is a fixed point of $cycle_A$ and therefore, since $\text{circ}\,A$ is the proper credulous solution:

$\neg[A^*]\text{true} \Rightarrow \text{circ}\,A$

and it trivially follows that:

$\neg\,\text{circ}\,A \Rightarrow [A^*]\text{true}$

Thus we have

$[A^*]\text{true} = \neg\,\text{circ}\,A$

The other part of the definition of A^* can be obtained thus:

$$\langle A^\star \rangle R$$
$$= \langle A^* \mathbin{\square} A^\circ \rangle R$$
$$= \langle A^* \rangle R \wedge \langle A^\circ \rangle R$$
$$= \langle A^* \rangle R$$

If the possibility of infinite looping is ignored (if we do not worry about termination) then $A^\star$ and A^* behave the same way. The two commands only differ in the characterization of those input values that terminate – $A^\star$ will always terminate for any input that A^* will terminate on, but $A^\star$ may loop for some input values that A^* will terminate on.

10.1 Another Approach

The starting point for the definition of a generalized loop was the following recursive definition:

$$X = A; X \mathbin{\square} \mathsf{skip}$$

This has the intuitive properties we require, it can loop zero or more times – and even, in some cases, loop forever. The termination solution to this recursive equation is:

$[A^\star]\mathsf{true} \triangleq \exists n : \mathbb{N} \cdot T_n$
where
$T_0 \triangleq \neg \mathcal{G}(A)$
$T_n \triangleq [A] T_{n-1}$

This can be explained as follows: suppose x terminates after at most n iterations (executions) of A. Suppose we let T_n denote those states that terminate after at most n iterations. Now if $x \in T_n$ then $x \in [A] T_{n-1}$.

The weakest liberal pre-condition solution to the equation is:

$\langle A^\star \rangle R \triangleq \forall i : \mathbb{N} \cdot W_i(R)$
where
$W_0(R) \triangleq R$
$W_n(R) \triangleq \langle A \rangle W_{n-1}(R) \wedge R$

This can be explained in a similar style to the termination predicate. An input value x will either choose to execute skip and thus will satisfy R; or will execute A and then will be faced with X again. $W_n(R)$ is the weakest liberal pre-condition such that if $A^\star$ terminates, it will terminate after at most n

iterations (executions) of A leaving the system in a state that satisfies R. If we take the above as the definition of A^* then the following theorem holds:

Theorem 10.1
$$A^* = A^\circ \mathbin{\square} A^*$$
□

Thus the two approaches are equivalent. From the recursive definition, it can easily be shown that the following holds:

Theorem 10.2
$$[A^*]R = \exists i : \mathbb{N} \cdot H_n(R)$$
where
$$H_0(R) = R \wedge \neg \mathcal{G}(A)$$
$$H_n(R) = R \wedge [A]H_{n-1}(R)$$
□

The following refinement properties hold for all of the iterative operators that have been defined so far:

Theorem 10.3 (monotonicity)
If $A \sqsubseteq B$ then

$$\mathrm{circ}\, B \Rightarrow \mathrm{circ}\, A$$
$$\forall n : \mathbb{N} \cdot A^n \sqsubseteq B^n$$
$$A^\circ \sqsubseteq B^\circ$$
$$A^* \sqsubseteq B^*$$
$$A^* \sqsubseteq B^*$$
□

Returning to the recursive definition of A^*, we have from the definition (roughly):

$$[X]R$$
$$=$$
$$[A; X \mathbin{\square} \mathsf{skip}]R$$
$$=$$
$$[A; X]R \wedge [\mathsf{skip}]R$$
$$=$$
$$[A][X]R \wedge R$$

thus writing P for $[X]R$ we get

$$P = R \wedge [A]P$$

or

$$P = [\{R\}A]P$$

This can be formalized:

Theorem 10.4
$[A^*]R$ is the greatest fixed point solution to

$$P = [\{R\}A]P$$

in the sense that if Q is any other fixed point then

$$Q \Rightarrow [A^*]R$$
□

Corollary 10.1
$[A^*]$true is the greatest fixed point solution to $[A]P = P$.
□

10.2 The Generalized Loop and Refinement

For refinement and for correctness, we are interested in calculating $[A^*]R$. This can be done using one of its characterizations, but this is not simple enough for practical use in refinement. Typically we are interested in refining a specification command:

$$x : [\ pre, \quad post\ ] \sqsubseteq A^*$$

This can be done by proving:

$$pre \Rightarrow [A^*]post$$

Now we can attack the problem from a slightly different angle, suppose we can find a P such that

$$P \Rightarrow [A^*]P$$

and in addition we can show that

$$pre \Rightarrow P$$
$$P \Rightarrow post$$

then we are done. With this in mind we proceed as follows.

Definition 10.1
P is an invariant of the command A if

$$P \Rightarrow [A]P$$

10.2 The Generalized Loop and Refinement

Using the property that the weakest liberal pre-condition is monotonic, the following lemma can be proved:

Lemma 10.2
If

$$P \Rightarrow \langle A \rangle P$$
$$P \Rightarrow [A^*]\text{true}$$

then

$$P \Rightarrow [A^*]P$$

Proof
By monotonicity of $\langle A \rangle$ we have $P \Rightarrow \langle A^* \rangle P$, and

$$P \Rightarrow \text{true}$$
$$\Longleftrightarrow$$
$$P \Rightarrow \langle \text{circ} A \rightarrow \text{loop} \rangle P$$

thus $P \Rightarrow \langle A^* \rangle P$. This, together with the second hypothesis, gives the conclusion.
∎

Now the first part of a simplified approach can be proved:

Theorem 10.5
If

$$P \Rightarrow [A]P \qquad (0)$$
$$P \Rightarrow [A^*]\text{true} \qquad (1)$$

then

$$P \Rightarrow [A^*]P$$

Proof
Hypothesis (1) is equivalent to $P \Rightarrow [A]\text{true} \wedge \langle A \rangle P$, and then use Lemma 10.2.
∎

Things have improved a little, to prove a refinement step using the generalized loop, a first step would be to find an appropriate command invariant that guarantees termination – but we are still left with the problem of calculating the termination set to prove termination; so the next step is to simplify the termination condition that must be proved.

10.3 The General Variant Theorem

To deal with the problem of termination, the following very general theorem from [21] is useful.

Theorem 10.6
P and Q are predicates defined everywhere over $State$
A is a predicate transformer
$e : State \to T$
$\_ < \_ : T \times T$
$C \subseteq T$
$(C, <)$ is well-founded (0)
$P \wedge e \notin C \Rightarrow Q$ (1)
$P \wedge e = c \Rightarrow [A](P \wedge e < c)$ (2)
$[A]Q \Leftrightarrow Q$ (3)
A is monotonic (4)
$\Longrightarrow$
$P \Rightarrow Q$

The function e can be thought of as an expression that is defined over the state; the result type of the expression e is T. The relation $<$ is an order relation on T with the following properties:

- it is transitive, and

- it is well-founded over the set C.

The transitive property means:

$$a < b \wedge b < c \Rightarrow a < c$$

A set C is well founded if the relation $\_ < \_$ over T is such that every non-empty subset of C has a minimal element: if $X \subseteq C$ and $a \in X$, then a is the minimal element of X if there is no $b \in X$ such that $b < a$ and $b \neq a$. The well-founded property is, roughly speaking, about there being no infinite chains in the relation. Infinite chains can occur in two ways: by having a loop in the relation, $x < x$ for some value x is allowed, and by having an infinite chain, something like $0, -1, -2, \ldots$ for the integers. Note that with a transitive relation, a loop can occur indirectly, it would be possible for the following chain of inequalities

$$a < b < c < d \ldots e < a$$

to be true, which would give a loop because of the transitivity property. If every non-empty set has a minimal element, it is impossible to construct either a finite or an infinite chain.

10.3 The General Variant Theorem

More formally, a set C is partially ordered with respect to an order relation $<$ and is said to be well-founded if, for any non-empty subset X of C

$$\exists k \in X \cdot \forall i \in X \cdot k \leq i$$

where (as usual) $a \leq b$ is an abbreviation for $a < b \lor a = b$. This means that all non-empty subsets of C have a 'smallest' element.

Proof
First a little lemma

$$P \land e < x \Rightarrow Q$$
$\Longrightarrow$ premise 4
$$[A](P \land e < x) \Rightarrow [A]Q$$
$\Longleftrightarrow$ premise 3
$$[A](P \land e < x) \Rightarrow Q$$
$\Longleftrightarrow$ premise 2
$$P \land e = x \Rightarrow Q$$

That $(C, <)$ is well founded is equivalent to

$$\forall x \in C \cdot S(x) \Leftrightarrow \forall x \in C \cdot S(x) \Rightarrow (\forall y \in C \cdot y < x \Rightarrow S(y))$$

Remembering that

$$P \land e \notin C \Rightarrow Q$$
$\Longleftrightarrow$
$$Q \Leftrightarrow (Q \lor P \land e \notin C) \quad (5)$$

we have for any $Z(e)$

$$P \land Z \Rightarrow Q$$
$\Longleftrightarrow$ premise 1 and (5)
$$P \land Z \Rightarrow (Q \lor P \land e \notin C)$$
$\Longleftrightarrow$ reorganize using definition of $\Rightarrow$
$$\neg P \lor \neg Z \lor Q \lor P \land e \notin C$$
$\Longleftrightarrow$ reorganize using definition of $\Rightarrow$ and De Morgan
$$P \land Z \land (\neg P \lor e \in C) \Rightarrow Q$$
$\Longleftrightarrow$ remove brackets, and P and Q are defined everywhere
$$P \land Z \land e \in C \Rightarrow Q$$
$\Longleftrightarrow$ one-point rule
$$\forall x \cdot x = e \Rightarrow P \land [e := x]Z \land x \in C \Rightarrow Q$$
$\Longleftrightarrow$ reorganize
$$\forall x \cdot [e := x]Z \land x \in C \Rightarrow (P \land x = e \Rightarrow Q)$$
$\Longleftarrow$ the lemma
$$\forall x \cdot [e := x]Z \land x \in C \Rightarrow P \land e < x \Rightarrow Q$$

thus

$$P \Rightarrow Q$$
$$\Longleftarrow$$
$$\forall x \cdot x \in C \Rightarrow P \wedge e < x \Rightarrow Q$$
$$\Longleftrightarrow$$
$$\forall x \in C \cdot P \wedge e < x \Rightarrow Q$$
$$\Longleftrightarrow$$
$$\forall y \in C \cdot y < x \Rightarrow P \wedge e < y \Rightarrow Q \Rightarrow \forall x \in C \cdot P \wedge e < x \Rightarrow Q$$
$$\Longleftrightarrow$$
$$\forall x \in C \cdot \text{true}$$
$$\Longleftrightarrow$$
$$\text{true}$$

∎

10.4 An Application

It is not obvious why the general theorem proved above is useful. A slightly different set of assumptions gives some idea of where we are going.

Theorem 10.7
If

$e : State \to T$
$\_ < \_ : T \times T$
$C \subseteq T$
$(C, <)$ is well-founded   (0)
$P \Rightarrow e \in C$ (1)
$P \wedge e = x \Rightarrow [A]e < x$ (2)
$P \Rightarrow [A]P$ (3)

then

$$P \Rightarrow [A^*]\text{true}$$

Proof
From hypothesis (1) we have for any Q

$$P \Rightarrow e \in C$$
$$\Longleftrightarrow$$
$$\neg P \vee e \in C$$
$$\Longrightarrow$$
$$\neg P \vee e \in C \vee Q$$

$$\iff$$
$$P \wedge e \notin C \Rightarrow Q$$

From hypothesis (2) and (3) we have:
$$P \wedge e = x \Rightarrow [A]P \wedge [A]e < x$$
$$\iff$$
$$P \wedge e = x \Rightarrow [A](P \wedge e < x)$$

We also have that $[A^*]$true is a fixed point of $[A]Q = Q$.

Hence by the general variant theorem we have

$$P \Rightarrow [A^*]\text{true}$$

■

The final step is to combine the theorems we have proved so far to give a refinement rule for the generalized loop operator:

Theorem 10.8
If

$e : State \rightarrow T$
$\_ < \_ : T \times T$
$C \subseteq T$
$(C, <)$ is well-founded (0)
$P \Rightarrow e \in C$ (1)
$P \wedge e = x \Rightarrow [A]e < x$ (2)
$P \Rightarrow [A]P$ (3)

then

$$P \Rightarrow [A^*]P$$

Proof
From Theorems 10.5 and 10.7.
■

This removes the need to calculate the termination set, but at the cost of what appears to be a major complication – the introduction of a set of extra conditions involving a well-founded set. A special version of this theorem can be derived, in this case the result type of the expression e is the integers, the well-founded subset is the natural numbers with the normal order relation. With these changes the theorem becomes:

Corollary 10.2
If

$e : State \to \mathbb{Z}$
$P \Rightarrow e : \mathbb{N}$
$P \Rightarrow [A]e < \overleftarrow{e}$
P is an invariant of A

then

$P \Rightarrow [A^\star]P$

□

Theorem 10.2 tells us that we only need to find an invariant and prove termination to prove a refinement. Theorem 10.7 provides an easy way of proving termination.

Two important facts have been illustrated so far. For generalized loops, a loop invariant is strongly related to what the semantics of the loop are; it almost *is* the semantics of the loop! Secondly to refine a specification by a generalized loop, only a loop invariant and a variant expression needs to be found. These ideas carry through to the more specialized and familiar looping construct considered in the next section.

10.5 Loops

The generalized loop constructor defined and investigated above has the right sort of properties that is expected of iteration, but it is still not suitable for use in programs. The problem is that, for a particular loop body many alternatives could occur: the loop might not terminate, could terminate correctly or could loop too many or too few times. The problems can be illustrated with a little example, consider a stack of natural numbers with the operation *pop* defined as follows:

$Stack = \mathbb{N}^\star \mid \text{EMPTY}$

pop
chg $st : Stack$
post $\overleftarrow{st} \neq [\,] \wedge st = \text{tl } \overleftarrow{st}$
$\vee$
$\overleftarrow{st} = [\,] \wedge st = \text{EMPTY}$
$\vee$
$\overleftarrow{st} = \text{EMPTY} \wedge st = \overleftarrow{st}$

notice that this version of *pop* has been made total. Consider the following code, the intent of which is to empty a stack.

pop*

10.5 Loops

If the initial contents of the stack is $[1, 2, 3]$, then after execution of the code fragment there are six possibilities for the result, depending on how many times we execute the body of the loop:

Number of times loop body executed	Result
0	$[1, 2, 3]$
1	$[2, 3]$
2	$[3]$
3	$[\,]$
4 or more	EMPTY
infinite	$\bot$

These results are caused by the non-deterministic properties of loop execution. How can we improve this? The first attempt might be to guard the body of the loop so that execution does not continue once the stack is empty:

$(st \neq [\,] \rightarrow pop)^*$

Now we must stop execution of the body of the loop when the stack is empty. However this does not solve all of the problem – the possible executions are reduced, but the stack may still not be empty on completion:

Number of times loop body executed	Result
0	$[1, 2, 3]$
1	$[2, 3]$
2	$[3]$
3	$[\,]$

Another possibility is to let angelic nondeterministic choice do the work for us, consider

$pop^*; (st = [\,] \rightarrow \mathsf{skip})$

Now the loop cannot terminate until the stack is empty – the possible executions are:

Number of times loop body executed	Result
3	$[\,]$
infinite	$\bot$

but the loop could still loop forever! The obvious solution is to guard both the loop body and the termination, suggesting the following:

$(st \neq [\,] \rightarrow pop)^*; st = [\,] \rightarrow \mathsf{skip}$

The only possible execution is

Number of times loop body executed	Result
3	[]

which is what we want. This suggest the following definition for a program loop:

$$\text{do } p \to A \text{ od} \triangleq (p \to A)^*; \neg p \to \text{skip}$$

Though this solves the problem, the idea can be generalized to give the following constructor (operator) on commands:

Definition 10.2 (the do command)
$$\text{do } A \text{ od} \triangleq A^*; \neg \mathcal{G}(A) \to \text{skip}$$

where the body of the do loop need not be total: as we shall see, if the loop is to terminate A must not be total. It must also be remembered that $A = \mathcal{G}(A) \to A$. First some simple properties to provide some more insight:

Theorem 10.9
loop = do skip od
skip = do miracle od
if $\mathcal{G}(A)$ then do A od = loop

Proof
All follow from the definition.
∎

As with the alternative command, there is still a problem: $A \sqsubseteq B$ does not imply that do A od $\sqsubseteq$ do B od. However we do have a similar theorem to that of iteration:

Theorem 10.10
If $A \sqsubseteq B$ and $\mathcal{G}(A) \Leftrightarrow \mathcal{G}(B)$ then do A od $\sqsubseteq$ do B od.
□

For executable code, the do-command body will be choice of one or more guarded commands, thus if we do not change the guards or more generally the domain of the body, then all is fine.

A recurrence relation that calculate the weakest pre-condition for a do command can be calculated:

Theorem 10.11
$$[\text{do } A \text{ od}]Q \triangleq \exists n \in \mathbb{N} \cdot H_n(Q)$$

where $H_0(Q) = \mathcal{G}(A) \vee Q$
$H_k(Q) = [A]H_{k-1}(Q) \wedge H_0(Q)$

□

The previous sections have been about avoiding the problem of calculations that would be needed using the above properties. This work can be extended to the do command. Now

$$P \wedge \neg \mathcal{G}(A) \Rightarrow R$$
$$\iff$$
$$P \Rightarrow (\neg \mathcal{G}(A) \Rightarrow R)$$
$$\Longrightarrow$$
$$[A^*]P \Rightarrow [A^*](\neg \mathcal{G}(A) \Rightarrow R)$$
$$\iff$$
$$[A^*]P \Rightarrow [A^*][\neg \mathcal{G}(A) \rightarrow \mathsf{skip}]R$$
$$\iff$$
$$[A^*]P \Rightarrow [A^*; \neg \mathcal{G}(A) \rightarrow \mathsf{skip}]R$$
$$\iff$$
$$[A^*]P \Rightarrow [\mathsf{do}\ A\ \mathsf{od}]R$$

Consequently, if

$$P \Rightarrow [A^*]P$$

then

$$P \Rightarrow [\mathsf{do}\ A\ \mathsf{od}]R$$

Combining the above and using Theorem 10.5, we have:

Lemma 10.3
If

$$P \Rightarrow [A]P$$
$$P \Rightarrow [A^*]\mathsf{true}$$
$$P \wedge \neg \mathcal{G}(A) \Rightarrow R$$

then

$$P \Rightarrow [\mathsf{do}\ A\ \mathsf{od}]R$$

□

From this, with a simple choice for R and Theorem 10.8 we can prove the property that is needed for refinement:

176   10. The Iterative Command

Theorem 10.12
$e : State \to T$
$\_ < \_ : T \times T$
$C \subseteq T$
$(C, <)$ is well-founded
$P \wedge \mathcal{G}(A) \Rightarrow var \in C$ (0)
$P \wedge \mathcal{G}(A) \Rightarrow [A]P$ (1)
$P \wedge \mathcal{G}(A) \wedge var = c \Rightarrow [A](var < c)$ (2)

then

$P \Rightarrow [\text{do } A \text{ od}](P \wedge \neg \mathcal{G}(A))$

□

If the command that is to be refined is a specification command in a particular form, then we have the following refinement rule:

Corollary 10.3
$var : State \to T$
$\_ < \_ : T \times T$
$C \subseteq T$
$(C, <)$ is well-founded
$P \wedge \mathcal{G}(A) \Rightarrow [A]P$
$P \wedge \mathcal{G}(A) \Rightarrow e \in C$
$P \wedge \mathcal{G}(A) \wedge e = c \Rightarrow [A](e < c)$

then

$x : [\ P, \ \neg \mathcal{G}(A) \wedge P\ ] \sqsubseteq \text{do } A \text{ od}$

□

10.6 Iteration – The Do Command

If we have a specification that we wish to refine with an iterative command, what is a possible form of the body, and what are the proof obligations? Given a specification in the form:

op
  chg $x : X$
  pre inv
  post $inv \wedge \neg \mathcal{G}(A)$

Now Corollary 10.3 above states that this is refined by do A od provided we can find a variant function var of result type T that is defined over a well-founded subset of C of T and that satisfies hypothesis (0) to (3) of the theorem. By Theorem 10.9, the body of the command must be partial for the command to be useful, and the usual way of introducing a partial command is with one or more guarded commands. We shall start with an easy, and a useful, form for the body:

$$guard \to x : [\ pre,\quad post\ ]$$

With this candidate for A, the specification command that forms the execution part of the guarded command is total provided it is implementable, so it is easy to calculate that $\mathcal{G}(A)$ for this form is just $guard$. The specification command must establish the variant and preserve the invariant, thus a good guess at the post-condition is $inv \wedge var < \overleftarrow{var}$; we will use this as a starting point to calculate the other two terms. It can be seen that, in general, this is the minimum requirement of the post-condition so that the two properties we require are established. The next step will be to calculate what pre-condition will preserve the invariant. Now:

$$[guard \to x : [\ pre,\quad inv \wedge var < \overleftarrow{var}\ ]] inv$$
$$\iff$$
$$guard \Rightarrow pre \wedge (\forall x' : X \cdot inv[x \backslash x'] \wedge var[x \backslash x'] < var \Rightarrow inv[x \backslash x'])$$
$$\iff$$
$$guard \Rightarrow pre$$

thus we must have from condition (1) of the proof obligations that:

$$guard \wedge inv \Rightarrow (guard \Rightarrow pre)$$
$$\iff$$
$$guard \wedge inv \Rightarrow pre$$

To establish the variant, it is simple to calculate that the weakest pre-condition that guarantees that the value of the variant function is decreased by the loop body; this is also found to be:

$$guard \wedge inv \Rightarrow pre$$

and using condition (2) this leads to an identical requirement on the pre-condition. A good candidate for the pre-condition of our specification is thus:

$$pre = guard \wedge inv$$

The specification part of the loop body is therefore:

$$x : [\ guard \wedge inv,\quad inv \wedge var < \overleftarrow{var}\ ]$$

and this has been shown to satisfy all the conditions required of the execution part of the guarded command denoted by A.

The invariant records what the loop body does, and the variant function that it terminates. The specification of the body of the loop derived here is, in some sense, the best: the specification demands the optimum amount of work that needs to be done – not too much and not too little. We should also prove this is implementable, for feasibility we require:

$$guard \land inv \Rightarrow (\exists x' : X \cdot inv[x\backslash x'] \land var[x\backslash x'] < var)$$

The feasibility condition just state that the specification is implementable if we can decrease x and preserve the invariant – as usual, since we cannot ever remove miracle, we will rely on the fact that a successful refinement is implementable.

All of this can now be pulled together and with an application of the mid rule and the equivalent specification rule we can obtain the following refinement rule:

Theorem 10.13 (introduce iteration rule)

if $\left\{ \begin{array}{c} var : State \to T \\ \_<\_ : T \times T \\ (C, <) \text{ is well-founded subset of } T \\ guard \land inv \Rightarrow var \in C \\ pre \land inv \land \neg guard \Rightarrow post \end{array} \right\}$ then

$$\begin{array}{c} chg\ w \\ pre\ pre \\ post\ post \end{array} \sqsubseteq \begin{array}{l} chg\ w \\ pre\ pre \\ post\ inv \\ ; \\ do\ guard \to \begin{array}{l} chg\ w \\ pre\ guard \land inv \\ post\ inv \land var < \overleftarrow{var} \end{array} \\ od \end{array}$$

□

This looks rather complicated, however this problem is better solved if we change it slightly – rather than look for a guard and an invariant, we will sneak-up on the problem. The first step will be to massage the post-condition *post* into the form $inv \land \neg guard$, with a judicious choice for both terms. From the theorems so far it can be seen that any two terms will do, provided their conjunction is implies the *post* predicate. However, a certain approach to the massaging will produce a guard and a specification for the loop body such that it is easy to show:

$$pre \land inv \land \neg guard \Rightarrow post$$

We shall do many examples in later chapters that will illustrate this point. Notice also that with this approach, we have the *guard* term for free. Secondly it is necessary to discover the variant function *var*, again with some judicious choices, this terms out to be fairly simple. Typically it will be an integer expression over the state, and the well-founded subset of the integers is the natural numbers. Having found these three terms, the final step is to calculate the initialization for the loop, what work needs to be done to establish the invariant, again in most cases this is trivial – the predicate *init* should be a version of the invariant *inv* that can be established easily. We will establish a frame-work for this approach:

> init *init*
> guard *guard*
> inv *inv*
> var *var*

After each step in the above strategy, we can fill in one of the four terms and then trivially complete the refinement step.

Finally remember that it is possible to derive an iterative loop whose body is infeasible – only miracle can satisfy it.

10.7 Practical Do Commands

For most purposes, we can avoid finding a well-founded set S, a transitive relation $<$ over S and an expression *var* of type S. Instead we can find an integer expression *var* whose value is based on the frame variables and is either strictly decreasing and bound by 0 below, or strictly increasing and bound by some constant N above. (With this change a useful well-founded set is the natural numbers, $\mathbb{N}$, with the standard order.) These changes give two loop refinement rules, for a decreasing expression:

$$\text{if } \left\{ \begin{array}{c} var : \mathbb{Z} \\ guard \wedge inv \Rightarrow 0 \leq var \\ pre \wedge inv \wedge \neg\, guard \Rightarrow post \end{array} \right\} \text{ then}$$

chg w
pre *pre*   ⊑   chg w
post *post*   pre *pre*
                      post *inv*
                      ;
                      do *guard* → chg w
                          pre *guard* ∧ *inv*
                          post *inv* ∧ *var* < $\overleftarrow{var}$
                      od

and for an increasing expression:

180   10. The Iterative Command

$$\text{if } \left\{ \begin{array}{c} var : \mathbb{Z} \\ guard \wedge inv \Rightarrow var \leq N \\ pre \wedge inv \wedge \neg guard \Rightarrow post \end{array} \right\} \text{ then}$$

$$\begin{array}{l} \text{chg } w \\ \text{pre } pre \\ \text{post } post \end{array} \sqsubseteq \begin{array}{l} \text{chg } w \\ \text{pre } pre \\ \text{post } inv \\ ; \\ \text{do } guard \rightarrow \begin{array}{l} \text{chg } w \\ \text{pre } guard \wedge inv \\ \text{post } inv \wedge \overleftarrow{var} < var \end{array} \\ \text{od} \end{array}$$

The above rule is easily derived from the decreasing rule by considering $0 \leq N - e$ and $N - e \leq N - \overleftarrow{e}$.

If the post-condition of the operation to be refined does contain hooked variables, these can always be removed by introducing logical constants:

$$\begin{array}{l} \text{chg } w \\ \text{pre } pre \\ \text{post } post \end{array} \sqsubseteq \begin{array}{l} [\![\text{ con } c \text{ in} \\ \quad \text{chg } w \\ \quad \text{pre } pre \wedge w = c \\ \quad \text{post } post[\overleftarrow{w} \backslash c]]\!] \end{array}$$

10.8 The Refinement of Loop Bodies

More tactical ideas for refining loop bodies can be based on the approach found in [28].

10.8.1 Decreasing Variants

We again take the approach of separating concerns: the problem of establishing the variant will be considered separately from the necessity of preserving the invariant. The following theorems generalizes the idea. Decreasing variant functions will be dealt with first, to simplify the presentation, a predicate can be defined:

$$A \text{ decs } e \triangleq \forall c : T \cdot c = e \Rightarrow [A]e < c$$

For any specification, the problem of decreasing a variant function can be separated from satisfying a post-condition:

Theorem 10.14
If

$$pre \Rightarrow A \text{ decs } e$$
$$x : [\; pre, \; post \;] \sqsubseteq A$$

then
$$x : [\ pre,\ post \wedge e < \overleftarrow{e}\ ] \sqsubseteq A$$

Proof
$$pre \wedge e = k\ \Rightarrow\ [A](post \wedge e < k)$$
$\Longleftrightarrow$
$$pre \wedge e = k\ \Rightarrow\ [A]post \wedge [A]e < k$$
$\Longleftarrow$
$$(pre\ \Rightarrow\ [A]post) \wedge (pre \wedge e = k\ \Rightarrow\ [A]e < k)$$
$\Longleftrightarrow$
$$x : [\ pre,\ post\ ] \sqsubseteq A \wedge (pre\ \Rightarrow\ (e = k\ \Rightarrow\ [A]e < k))$$
$\Longleftarrow$
$$pre\ \Rightarrow\ A\ \mathsf{decs}\ e$$
$\Longleftrightarrow$
true

$$x : [\ pre,\ post \wedge e < \overleftarrow{e}\ ] \sqsubseteq A$$
$\Longleftrightarrow$
$$pre \wedge k = e \wedge (\forall x : X \cdot post \wedge e < k\ \Rightarrow\ X)\ \Rightarrow\ [A]X$$
$\Longleftarrow$
$$[A](post \wedge e < k) \wedge (\forall x : X \cdot post \wedge e < k\ \Rightarrow\ X)\ \Rightarrow\ [A]X$$
$\Longleftarrow$
$$post \wedge e < k \wedge (\forall x : X \cdot post \wedge e < k\ \Rightarrow\ X)\ \Rightarrow\ X$$
$\Longleftrightarrow$
$$(\forall x : X \cdot post \wedge e < k\ \Rightarrow\ X)\ \Rightarrow\ (post \wedge e < k\ \Rightarrow\ X)$$
$\Longleftrightarrow$
true

∎

In many cases things can be simplified even more, frequently the variant expression is just a single variable, let it be denoted by v. Then there is a particular strategy for refining the body of a loop; the strategy is to first establish the variant by decreasing the value of v and then, as this usually breaks the invariant, to re-establish the invariant. This strategy is used so frequently it is worth deriving the rules that will streamline this approach. If we can find a monotonically decreasing function on v that has an inverse, the variant can be established first using the function, and then the postcondition can be established, using Theorem 10.14 it is possible to show:

Theorem 10.15

if $\left\{ \begin{array}{c} pre \Rightarrow f(v) < v \\ f \text{ has an inverse } f^{-1} \end{array} \right\}$ then

$$x, v : [\; pre, \quad post \wedge v < \overleftarrow{v} \;] \sqsubseteq v := f(v) \,;\, x : [\; pre[v \backslash f^{-1}(v)], \quad post \;]$$

□

Alternatively, we can deal with establishing the post-condition first, and then establish the variant:

Theorem 10.16

if $\{\; pre \Rightarrow f(v) < v \;\}$ then

$$x, v : [\; pre, \quad post \wedge v < \overleftarrow{v} \;] \sqsubseteq x : [\; pre, \quad post[v \backslash f(v)] \;] \,;\, v := f(v)$$

□

10.8.2 Increasing Variants

For increasing variant functions a similar set of theorems can be proved: First, the following predicate can be defined:

$$A \text{ incs } e \;\triangleq\; \forall c : T \cdot c = e \;\Rightarrow\; [A]c < e$$

Theorem 10.17
If

$pre \Rightarrow A \text{ incs } e$
$x : [\; pre, \quad post \;] \sqsubseteq A$

then

$$x : [\; pre, \quad post \wedge \overleftarrow{e} < e \;] \sqsubseteq A$$

□

Then the variant can be increased first, and the post-condition established:

Theorem 10.18

if $\left\{ \begin{array}{c} pre \Rightarrow v < g(v) \\ g \text{ has an inverse } g^{-1} \end{array} \right\}$ then

$$x, v : [\; pre, \quad post \wedge v < \overleftarrow{v} \;] \sqsubseteq v := g(v) \,;\, x : [\; pre[v \backslash g^{-1}(v)], \quad post \;]$$

□

Alternatively, we can deal with establishing the post-condition first, and then increasing the variant:

Theorem 10.19

if $\{\ pre \Rightarrow v < g(v)\ \}$ then

$x, v : \left[\ pre,\quad post \wedge v < \overleftarrow{v}\ \right] \sqsubseteq x : \left[\ pre,\quad post[v \backslash g(v)]\ \right]\ ;\ v := g(v)$

□

10.9 Summary

The refinement of a specification with an iterative command is difficult. Even with certain assumptions and simplifications, the amount of work to be done is still large (and confusing) and also gives rise to more refinement rules than one would like. It turns out that the application of the appropriate rules really depends on how easy it is to find a variant variable; the discovery of the invariant and guard is, after a little practice, relatively straightforward. Sometimes it is not possible to find a variant that is an integer expression, in which case it is necessary to use the general rule described in Theorem 10.13. Applications of the rules in subsequent chapters will show things are, in fact, easier than they look from the derivation of the refinement rules.

11. Functions and Procedures

The last step in the definition of the specification and programming language is to introduce the concept of a procedure. The idea behind a procedure is that the same process occurs in different places in a program; rather than repeating an implementation of this process, an abbreviation convention can be introduced. The definition of the abbreviation is called a procedure, and its use is called a procedure call. Two types of procedures can be identified, proper procedures which are the equivalent of sequence of command, and functional procedures that return a result and can be used in the same context as expressions (however with some restrictions).

11.1 Proper Procedures and their Calls

Proper procedure declarations and calls to them need to be defined. The first step is to define what is meant by a procedure declaration, a proper procedure is declared as follows:

$proc\,(a:A)$
ext rd $d:X$
  wr $w:Y$ ≙
$command$

In the above sketch, the symbol ≙ is part of the syntax, it is in a slightly smaller and bolder font to try and distinguish it from the other use of the symbol $\triangleq$ in definitions. The procedure has (zero or more) parameters a of type A – $a:A$ is used to denote a list of parameters and their corresponding types. The body of a proper procedure is a command. The external clause, marked by the keyword ext, lists the global state components used by the procedure, it has read access to the variables in a list denoted by d and write access to the variables in a list denoted by w. The command that forms the body of the procedure tests the variables in the list d and tests and sets the variables in the list w. The frame contains more information than the frame component of a specification command – this convention allows a procedure declaration to be passed to a developer without the need for the complete state to be available since any free identifier not defined should be either a function or a value and thus can be treated as constants. (For the full syntax, see [6]).

If a procedure is declared as described above, a call to the procedure, a call command, is written as follows:

$proc(E)$

were E is a list of expressions with result types that match the type list A. The definitions behind these ideas are:

Definition 11.1 (Proper procedure definitions and calls)
An explicit procedure definition takes the form:

$proc\,(a:A)$
ext rd $d:X$
    wr $w:Y\;\triangleq$
$command$

A call to this procedure is defined as:

$proc(E) \triangleq$ def $a:A = E$ in $command$

where $a:A$ denotes a list of parameters with their corresponding types, E denotes a list of arguments and $command$ is the body. The result type of an expression in the list denoted by E must be the same as the type of the corresponding parameter in the procedure definition. The evaluation of the expressions in the list E cannot have any side-effects when they are evaluated.

The definition means that the procedure call command on the left can be replaced by the command on the right. The right hand side of this definition is defined in terms of existing concepts.

As the extension of the definition to procedures with more than one parameter works as follows: when a denotes a list of parameters $a_1, \ldots, a_n$ with corresponding types $A_1, \ldots, A_n$ and E the corresponding list of arguments $E_1, \ldots, E_n$ then:

$proc(E_1, \ldots, E_n) \triangleq$
    def $mk\text{-}(a_1, \ldots, a_n): A_1 \times \ldots \times A_n = mk\text{-}(E_1, \ldots, E_n)$ in $command$

As the evaluation of each expression in the argument list has no side-effects, so (in execution terms) the order of evaluation does not matter.

If there is a proper procedure declaration and a procedure call to that procedure, the call can be replaced by the command (text) that forms the procedure body. A command (or a block – which is syntactically equivalent to a command) can be replaced by a procedure call to a procedure with the command as its body. There is now have a way of introducing and removing procedure calls and procedure declarations.

11. Functions and Procedures

The syntax and the semantics of the specification of a proper procedure can be defined in terms of the following expansion, in the sense that the specification on the left of the definition can be replaced by the expansion on the right to obtain its semantics. The command that forms the body of the procedure declaration is a specification command.

Definition 11.2 (Implicit proper procedure definition)
An implicit proper procedure definition takes the form:

$$
\begin{array}{l}
proc(a:A) \\
\text{ext rd } d:X \\
\quad \text{wr } w:Y \\
\text{pre } pre \\
\text{post } post
\end{array}
\triangleq
\begin{array}{l}
proc(a:A) \\
\text{ext rd } d:X \\
\quad \text{wr } w:Y \triangleq \\
proc\text{-}body \\
\text{chg } w \\
\text{pre } pre \\
\text{post } post
\end{array}
$$

By transforming the implicit procedure specification into the explicit form that has a specification command as its body the refinement process that eventually leads to executable code has begun. We would like to specify a procedure implicitly and use this specification to decide on where to place calls to the procedure, knowing that if we transform the implicit specification into the explicit form and refine it, the calls would have the desired effect (as given by the original specification). The following theorem guarantees this is what happens:

Theorem 11.1
$$\text{def } a:A = E \text{ in } body \sqsubseteq \text{def } a:A = E \text{ in } body'$$

if and only if

$$body \sqsubseteq body'$$

Proof
For any R defined over the state

$$[\text{def } a:A = E \text{ in } body]R$$
$$\iff$$
$$\forall a:A \cdot a = E \Rightarrow [body]R$$
$$\iff$$
$$([body]R)[a\backslash E]$$

and

$$[\text{def } a:A = E \text{ in } body']R$$
$$\iff$$
$$\forall a:A \cdot a = E \Rightarrow [body']R$$

$$\Longleftrightarrow$$
$$([body]R')[a\backslash E]$$

and the theorem follows immediately.
∎

It is this theorem that allows a call to a procedure to be used, relying on the specification to define the action of the procedure. If the procedure is refined into code, the call is still valid. The following corollary confirms this:

Corollary 11.1
For two proper procedures f and g

$$f(E) \sqsubseteq g(E)$$

if and only if

$$body \sqsubseteq body'$$

Where the types, order and number of the parameters of f and g are the same and $body$ is the body of f and $body'$ is the body of g.

Proof
By Theorem 11.1 and Definition 11.1.
∎

We can also replace a specification command by a call to an appropriate proper procedure and vice-versa. If a procedure is specified as before by Theorems 11.2 and 11.3, a call to this procedure $proc(E)$ can be replaced by

$$\text{def } a : A = E \text{ in } w : [\ pre,\quad post\ ]$$

Now, assuming the type of the variable w is W:

$$\text{def } a : A = E \text{ in } w : [\ pre,\quad post\ ]$$
$$=$$
$$@a : A \bullet a = E \to w : [\ pre,\quad post\ ]$$
$$=$$
$$@a : A \bullet (a = E \to$$
$$(@w' : W \bullet post(a, w, w') \to w := w'\ \square\ \neg pre(a, w) \to \text{chaos}))$$
$$=$$
$$@a : A \bullet$$
$$(a = E \to @w' : W \bullet post(a, w, w') \to w := w'\ \square$$
$$a = E \to \neg pre(a, w) \to \text{chaos})$$
$$=$$
$$@a : A \bullet a = E \to @w' : W \bullet post(a, w, w') \to w := w'\ \square$$

$$@a : A \bullet a = E \rightarrow \neg\, pre(a, w) \rightarrow \text{chaos}$$

$=$

$$@a : A \bullet @w' : W \bullet a = E \land post(a, w, w') \rightarrow w := w' \;[\!]$$
$$@a : A \bullet a = E \land \neg\, pre(a, w) \rightarrow \text{chaos}$$

$=$

$$@w' : W \bullet \exists a : A \cdot a = E \land post(a, w, w') \rightarrow w := w' \;[\!]$$
$$\exists a : A \cdot a = E \land \neg\, pre(a, w) \rightarrow \text{chaos}$$

$=$

$$@w' : W \bullet post(E, w, w') \rightarrow w := w' \;[\!]\; \neg\, pre(E, w) \rightarrow \text{chaos}$$

$=$

$$w : \left[\; pre[a\backslash E],\; post[a\backslash \overleftarrow{E}\,] \;\right] \qquad \text{where } \overleftarrow{E} \text{ is } E[w\backslash \overleftarrow{w}]$$

The next theorem follows from this – a specification command that 'matches' a specification can be replaced by a call to the procedure:

Theorem 11.2 (introduce proper procedure call rule)
If an implicit proper procedure is defined by:

   $proc\,(a : A)$
   ext rd $d : X$
      wr $w : Y$
  pre pre
  post $post$

then

   chg w
   pre $pre[a\backslash E]$ $=$ $proc(E)$
   post $post[a\backslash \overleftarrow{E}\,]$

where $\overleftarrow{E}$ is $E[w\backslash \overleftarrow{w}]$.
$\square$

By match we mean that if we replace all occurrences of a in the procedure specification by the expression E and the result matches the specification command, the command can be replaced by a call to the procedure.

It could be that the specification command we are replacing by a call is a call to the procedure that is being refined – we have recursion. There is a problem with recursive calls – that of guaranteeing termination, for the procedure could keep calling itself (either directly or indirectly) and never terminate. A way of solving this problem is to borrow the approach used for proving termination with the iterated statement. The approach is to find an ordered set T with a well-founded subset $(C, <)$ and a variant expression that is strictly decreasing with a result in the set C. The variant expression should depend on the arguments to the procedure and have a result type of T; thus we have

$e : A \to T$

Now if on every entry to the procedure, with an argument value that can be denoted by a, we arrange that $e(a) \in C$, and on a subsequent recursive call to the procedure with an argument of E we arrange that $e(E) < e(a)$. For this recursive call, on entry to the body we would have $e(E) \in C$. Because of the condition enforced on the call and the entry to the body of the procedure, we have a series of strictly decreasing values for the expression e, all of which are in C; since C is well-founded this series of decreasing values must be finite and thus we can deduce that recursive chain of calls must terminate.

We need the result of the expression e to be in C, but this is only necessary if the call to the procedure is valid, which means that the pre-condition must be satisfies, so all that is necessary is that:

$pre \Rightarrow e \in C$

If this is all put together we get the following theorem:

Theorem 11.3 (introduce proper recursive call rule)
If an implicit proper procedure is defined by:

> $proc\ (a : A)$
> $\text{ext rd}\ d : X$
> $\quad\quad \text{wr}\ w : Y$
> $\text{pre}\ pre$
> $\text{post}\ post$

and

$\text{if}\ \left\{ \begin{array}{c} e : A \to T \\ \_ < \_ : T \times T \\ C \subseteq T \\ (C, <)\ \text{is well-founded} \\ pre \Rightarrow e \in C \\ pre \Rightarrow e[a \backslash E] < e \end{array} \right\}\ \text{then}$

> $\text{chg}\ w$
> $\text{pre}\ pre[a \backslash E]$
> $\text{post}\ post[a \backslash \overleftarrow{E}]$ $\quad\equiv\quad \overleftarrow{proc(E)}$

> where $\overleftarrow{E}$ is $E[w \backslash \overleftarrow{w}]$

□

Note that a denotes the value of the argument on entry to the procedure, and e will need to be a function of a (i.e. an expression containing a as a free variable). The last two proof obligations just state that the pre-condition ensures that the value of e is still in the well-founded set and that e evaluated on entry to the procedure is less than the value of e calculated on entry at the next call – E denotes the argument for the next call, the value of the parameter a for the next call. Thus at the start of each recursive call, the value of e is decreasing but still in C which, since it is well-founded, has a least element. Therefore the recursion must stop at some point.

For indirect recursive calls, a single variant expression e must be found, and the conditions described above must hold for each procedure involved in the chain of calls.

11.2 Function Procedures and their Calls

The same pattern of definitions can be used to introduce function procedures – procedures that return a result. First we define a function procedure definition:

Definition 11.3 (Function procedure definitions and calls)
An explicit function procedure definition takes the form:

$fun\,(a:A)\,:R$
ext wr $w:X$
 rd $d:Y\;\triangleq$
 [dcl $r:R$ in
  $commands$;
  return r]

A call to this function is defined as:

$x := fun(E) \;\triangleq\; [\![\text{dcl } r : R \text{ in def } a = E \text{ in } commands\,;\; x := r]\!]$

We can also introduce the concept of a specification for a function procedure and this can be defined as:

11.2 Function Procedures and their Calls

Definition 11.4 (Implicit function procedure definitions)

$$fun(a:A)r:R \\ \text{ext wr } w:X \\ \text{rd } d:Y \\ \text{pre } pre \\ \text{post } post$$

$\triangleq$

$$fun(a:A):R \\ \text{ext wr } w:X \\ \text{rd } d:Y \\ [\![\text{ dcl } r:R \text{ in} \\ fun\text{-}body \\ \text{chg } w,r \\ \text{pre } pre \\ \text{post } post \\ ; \\ \text{return } r]\!]$$

Refining the body of a function procedure has the required effect:

Theorem 11.4

$[\![\text{dcl } r:R \text{ in def } a = E \text{ in } body \, ; \, x := r]\!] \sqsubseteq$
$[\![\text{dcl } r:R \text{ in def } a = E \text{ in } body' \, ; \, x := r]\!]$

if and only if

$body \sqsubseteq body'$

□

A corollary is:

Corollary 11.2
For two function procedures f and g

$x := f(E) \sqsubseteq x := g(E)$

if and only if

$body \sqsubseteq body'$

where the types, order and number of the parameters f and g are the same and $body$ is the body of f and $body'$ is the body of g.
□

We can also introduce an abbreviation for cases when we assign to a variable and then return the value of that variable:

Definition 11.5 (The return command)
return $E \triangleq r := E;$ return r

Remember that the expression E cannot have any side-effects. As before we can consider replacing certain specification commands that match the definition of a function procedure by a call. With fun as a specification of a function procedure:

11. Functions and Procedures

Theorem 11.5 (introduce function procedure call rule)
If an implicit function procedure is defined by:

    fun $(a : A)\ r : R$
    ext rd $d : X$
        wr $w : Y$
    pre pre
    post $post$

A specification command that matches this can be replaced by a call to the procedure.

    chg w, x
    pre $pre[a\backslash E]$ $\equiv$ $x := fun\,(E)$
    post $post[a, r\backslash \overleftarrow{E}, x]$

    where $\overleftarrow{E}$ is $E[w, x\backslash \overleftarrow{w}, \overleftarrow{x}]$

□

Again there are problems if the call is a recursive call, the solution is identical to that of proper procedures. If is a relation $<$ defined over some set T and the refinement rule is:

Theorem 11.6 (introduce function recursive call rule)
If an implicit function procedure is defined by:

    fun $(a : A)\ r : R$
    ext rd $d : X$
        wr $w : Y$
    pre pre
    post $post$

and

if $\left\{\begin{array}{c} e : A \to T \\ \_<\_ : T \times T \\ C \subseteq T \\ (C, <) \text{ is well-founded} \\ pre \Rightarrow e \in C \\ pre \Rightarrow e[a\backslash E] < e \end{array}\right\}$ then

    chg w, x
    pre $pre[a\backslash E]$ $\equiv$ $x := fun\,(E)$
    post $post[a, r\backslash \overleftarrow{E}, x]$

where $\overleftarrow{E}$ is $E[w, x \backslash \overleftarrow{w}, \overleftarrow{x}]$

□

Note that a denotes the value of the argument on entry to the procedure.

11.3 Function Calls in Expressions

So far we have only considered function calls in the context of an assignment command of the following form:

$x := fun(E)$

The syntax in [6] defines this form as a call command. Why can we not use functions in expressions? A possible extension to a function call could be defined. Suppose F is an expression, and $E = F[t \backslash fun(expr)]$, then a possible definition to function procedure calls in an expression would be:

$x := E \triangleq [\![\mathsf{dcl}\ r : R\ \mathsf{in}\ \mathsf{def}\ a = expr\ \mathsf{in}\ command\ ;\ x := F[t \backslash r]]\!]$

The commands that make up the function body is expected to set the local state variable r to the intended result of the function call. This expansion would be correct, except that if the function has write access to a variable in the expression F, the result would not be what we would expect. For example, given:

$inc\ (n : \mathrm{N})\ r : \mathrm{N}$
ext wr $i : \mathrm{N}$
pre true
post $r = n + 1 \wedge i = \overleftarrow{i} + 1$

This is refined by

$inc\ (n : \mathrm{N})\ : \mathrm{N}$
ext wr $i : \mathrm{N} \triangleq$
$[\![\mathsf{dcl}\ r : \mathrm{N}\ \mathsf{in}\ i := i + 1\ ;\ r := n + 1\ ;\ \mathsf{return}\ r]\!]$

What would we expect the result of $m := i + inc(m)$ to be? Looking at $m := inc(i) + i$ is also quite interesting. If we use the above definition, the first example becomes:

$[\![\mathsf{dcl}\ r : R\ \mathsf{in}\ \mathsf{def}\ n = m\ \mathsf{in}\ i := i + 1\ ;\ r := n + 1\ ;\ m := i + r]\!]$

and the second is:

$[\![\mathsf{dcl}\ r : R\ \mathsf{in}\ \mathsf{def}\ n = i\ \mathsf{in}\ i := i + 1\ ;\ r := n + 1\ ;\ m := r + i]\!]$

both of which give surprising results! In each case m will be one more than we might expect it to be; in the second case we are lucky that m is not two more than expected! How can we avoid this problem? One answer is to not allow functions to be used in expressions where the identifiers occurring in the write part of the externals frame of the function also occur in the expression. A better solution is to be more drastic: only those functions that have no write access to state variables can be used in expressions, only those functions with an external frame with only read access. However this is still not enough, consider:

$pos\text{-}inc\,(n:\mathbb{N})\ r:\mathbb{N}$
post $r = n \lor r = n + 1$

and the following assignment:

$m := pos\text{-}inc(m) + pos\text{-}inc(m)$

If the initial value of m was 0, we would expect the new value of m to be 0, 1, or 2. With the definition above, the assignment is equivalent to:

$[\!\![\,\text{dcl}\ r:R\ \text{in def}\ n = m\ \text{in}\ r:[\ \text{true},\quad r = n \lor r = n + 1\ ]\ ;\ m := r + r\,]\!\!]$

which means the new value of m is either 0 or 2. Again this problem can be solved several ways, one of which is to introduce the concept of a block returning a value. We shall take a drastic solution and demand that function procedures that are to be used in expressions must not have write access the state, and therefore have no side-effects, and must be deterministic – they are only specified to produce one answer for each input. With these restrictions we have the following definition. Let f be a deterministic function procedure with no write access to the state that is defined as:

$f\,(a:A)\ r:R$
ext rd $d:X \;\triangleq\;$
$\quad [\!\![\,\text{dcl}\ r\quad :R\ \text{in}$
$\quad\quad fun\text{-}body\ ;$
$\quad\quad \text{return}\ r\,]\!\!]$

If F is an expression, and $E = F[t\backslash f(expr)]$, then:

$x := E \;\triangleq\; [\!\![\,\text{dcl}\ r:R\ \text{in def}\ a = expr\ \text{in}\ fun\text{-}body\ ;\ x := F[t\backslash r]\,]\!\!]$

There is already a mechanism for defining functions with these two restrictions, that of function definitions introduced in Chapter 8, and a way of transforming such definitions into operation definitions was also discussed in that chapter. The above discussion gives the reasons behind the transformation.

11.4 An Alternative Approach to Parameters and Arguments

The concept of a procedure has been introduced as a syntactic abbreviation. Thus a compiler for the language is at will to expand code in line or to generate a call to the subroutine that implements a procedure. Two language decisions have been made. The first is minor: the replacement text for a procedure call uses a block with a def command, rather than a block with an initialized declaration; procedure calls could have been defined as:

$$proc(a) \triangleq [\![\mathsf{dcl}\ a : A \ \mathsf{in}\ a := E\ ;\ A]\!]$$

In the approach used in this chapter, parameters to a procedure are not associated with 'storage locations' and thus cannot be assigned to. This could be changed, but the restriction means that an implementor of a procedure cannot use (the locations that might be associated with the) parameters as temporary variables – they should locally declare all temporary variables that are needed by the executable code of a procedure. It also means that if an array is passed as an argument to procedure, provided the array is not accessed as a global variable (and thus occur in the external clause as a write variable) it can be passed 'by reference' as an optimization. The second decision is related, but a large change compared with most other programming languages. The decision is that the evaluation of an expression cannot have any side-effects – the evaluation of an expression cannot change the value of a state variable. This decision has only a minor effect on the style of programming, but a major effect on the properties of the programming language. It means that it is much easier for a compiler to generate efficient code. It is much easier to reason about a program. The commands of the programming language have nice properties, and *always* have these nice properties.

11.5 Postscript

The previous chapters have all been about the following idea:

Definition 11.6
A program F is piecewise monotonic if it is constructed from operations (constructors) that are refinement monotonic.

What do we mean by the program F? Well, it means similar things to what is usually meant by a function in mathematics, but instead of using operators like + and −, we will use programming language constructs defined in this and the previous chapters. Using this definition, we can state the following theorem:

Theorem 11.7
If $A \sqsubseteq B$, $\mathcal{G}(A) = \mathcal{G}(B)$ and if F is piecewise monotonic, then $F(A) \sqsubseteq F(B)$

Proof
By Theorem 3.34 and all theorems labeled monotonicity.
∎

It is best to think of $F(A)$ as a program that contains the program fragment A, and if we replace all instances of A by another program fragment B that is a refinement of A and has the same domain, then $F(B)$ is a program that is a refinement of $F(A)$. The restriction that $\mathcal{G}(A) = \mathcal{G}(B)$ is not an onerous one. It is true if both A and B are total (a requirement if they are to be executable) or, if A and B are built from naked guards that are equivalent. Many of the theorems in this and the previous chapters have been showing that each of our language operators is monotonic and therefore any function (program) built from them is also monotonic. This theorem is about the composition, it is about re-use, it's about stepwise refinement: all of those activities that are about replacing one program fragment by another without changing the intent of the program. Most of the programming languages in use today *do not have this property*[1]!

11.6 Summary

The complete language has now been defined together with refinement rules that can be used to remove those commands that cannot be compiled. Development can start with a non-executable specification, and by a series of transformations that preserve correctness, the result will be an executable program that satisfies its specification. Common ideas can be collected into proper and function procedures to save development effort. We are now in a position to apply these ideas to real, but perhaps simple, problems.

---

[1] Could this be why there is a major problem with code reuse?

12. An Example of Refinement at Work

To illustrate the use of the rules that have been derived, we will consider a simple problem (which will be developed further in Chapter 15).

12.1 The Problem – Integer Multiplication

Consider the problem of providing an integer multiplication routine to be implemented on a microcomputer that does not have a multiply instruction. The specification for the function procedure is:

$mult\,(x, y : \mathbb{Z})\ r : \mathbb{Z}$
post $r = x \times y$

12.1.1 Getting Started

The first step is to introduce the framework for the procedure – the definition of a function procedure allow the introduction of a procedure body, so using the *introduce function procedure body* rule the first refinement step gives:

$mult\,(x, y : \mathbb{Z})\ : \mathbb{Z} \triangleq$
⟦ dcl $r : \mathbb{Z}$ in
   mult-body
   chg $r : \mathbb{Z}$
   pre true
   post $r = x \times y$
   ;
   return r ⟧

As multiplication is just repeated addition, the specification could be satisfied by a loop that does that operation. A possible strategy is to count down in a copy of the first argument until zero is reached, adding the value of the second argument into a variable that keeps track of a running total. What if the first argument is negative? Using it to count down to zero will produce an infinite loop as the value of the variable will (in theory[1]) never go through zero!

---

[1] ignoring the possibility of 'wrap-around'.

Thus, before the suggested algorithm can be used, it is necessary to guarantee that the counter is always non-negative; this suggests that the specification for *mult-body* be broken down into two sub-specifications: *makepos*, which will guarantee that the counter is non-negative, and *posmult*, which will do the multiplication of one non-negative number (to be used as the counter) by another. To accomplish this transformation, we first introduce two local variables using the *add variable* rule and re-organize using the *remove scope* rule to get:

$mult\,(x,y:\mathbb{Z})\;:\mathbb{Z}\;\triangleq$
⟦ dcl $r,s,t:\mathbb{Z}$ in
  mult-body
  chg $r,s,t:\mathbb{Z}$
  pre true
  post $r = x \times y$
  ;
  return r ⟧

and then we can decompose the specification of *mult-body* into the two sub-specifications using the *introduce command-semicolon* rule – this transformation is shown below:

mult-body ⊑ *makepos*
              chg $s,t:\mathbb{Z}$
              pre true
              post $s \times t = x \times y \wedge 0 \leq s$
              ;
              posmult
              chg $r,s,t:\mathbb{Z}$
              pre $s \times t = x \times y \wedge 0 \leq s$
              post $r = x \times y$

Two pieces of code can now be developed independently: one to satisfy the specification for *makepos* and the other to satisfy *posmult*. If the two pieces of code are combined with a 'semicolon', the resulting program fragment will satisfy the original specification *mult-body*.

12.1.2 The Refinement Strategy Continued

The next step is to refine *makepos*. If x is negative, it will be necessary to change the sign of its value when it is assigned to s. The obvious structure to introduce in this case is a alternative command – an application of the *introduce alternatives* rule gives:

makepos ⊑ if $0 \leq x \rightarrow$ *pos*
                       chg $s,t:\mathbb{Z}$

12.1 The Problem - Integer Multiplication

$$\begin{array}{l}\text{pre } 0 \leq x \\ \text{post } s \times t = x \times y \wedge 0 \leq s\end{array}$$
$$[] \; x \leq 0 \to neg$$
$$\begin{array}{l}\text{chg } s, t : \mathbb{Z} \\ \text{pre } x \leq 0 \\ \text{post } s \times t = x \times y \wedge 0 \leq s\end{array}$$
fi

Inspection suggests a simple assignment of x to s and y to t will refine *pos*:

$$pos \sqsubseteq s, t := x, y$$

the proof of the refinement is a trivial application of the *introduce assignment* rule:

$$x : \mathbb{Z} \wedge y : \mathbb{Z} \wedge 0 \leq x \;\Rightarrow\; x : \mathbb{Z} \wedge y : \mathbb{Z}$$
$$0 \leq x \wedge s = x \wedge t = y \;\Rightarrow\; s \times t = x \times y \wedge 0 \leq s$$

To refine *neg*, it is necessary to reverse the sign of x on assignment:

$$neg \sqsubseteq s, t := -x, -y$$

the proof is again trivial; it is just necessary to show:

$$x : \mathbb{Z} \wedge y : \mathbb{Z} \wedge x \leq 0 \;\Rightarrow\; x : \mathbb{Z} \wedge y : \mathbb{Z}$$
$$x \leq 0 \wedge s = -x \wedge t = -y \;\Rightarrow\; s \times t = x \times y \wedge 0 \leq s$$

which is obvious by inspection. We have now shown that

$$makepos \sqsubseteq \text{if } 0 \leq x \to s, t := x, y$$
$$[] \; x \leq 0 \to s, t := -x, -y$$
fi

12.1.3 The Next Step

The decomposition of *posmult* is a little more difficult. The algorithm that is being developed requires an iterated command. The proposed algorithm is to add the second argument to a running total and keep count in the first. To refine *posmult* it is necessary to find a guard, an invariant and a variant relation that will define the loop. The post-condition of *posmult* can be massaged using the *replace specification* rule to give:

$$posmult \sqsubseteq \text{chg } r, s, t : \mathbb{Z}$$
$$\begin{array}{l}\text{pre } s \times t = x \times y \wedge 0 \leq s \\ \text{post } r + s \times t = x \times y \wedge s = 0\end{array}$$

The post-condition suggests the following guard and invariant:

12. An Example of Refinement at Work

```
guard  s ≠ 0
inv    r + s × t = x × y ∧ 0 ≤ s
```

The first term of the conjunction is part of the post-condition; an examination of the iteration rule indicates that the invariant and the negation of the guard together must be equivalent to the post-condition. The second term of the conjunction is defining the well-ordered set that guarantees termination – in this example the natural numbers. The initialization should establish the invariant and finally the variant term should guarantee that some value defined over the termination set should be decreasing. These requirements give the following loop parameters:

```
init   r = 0
guard  s ≠ 0
inv    r + s × t = x × y ∧ 0 ≤ s
var    s < ⃖s
```

The variant is obvious from the algorithm. The exact details of where the invariant came from are explained in the next chapter. For this little example the following argument will illustrate the ideas: initially and after each iteration of the loop (since r is a running total and s is a counter) we have:

$$r + s \times t = \text{'a constant value'}$$

This is a candidate for the loop invariant, except that the constant value it is equal to is the answer, which is denoted by $x \times y$.

The loop domain proof obligation is:

$$r, s, t, x, y : \mathbb{Z} \land s \neq 0 \land$$
$$r + s \times t = x \times y \land 0 \leq s \Rightarrow s : \mathbb{N}$$

The loop parameters gives the following decomposition of the *posmult* operation using the *introduce iteration* rule:

```
posmult ⊑ r := 0;
          do s ≠ 0 → posmult-body
                    chg r, s, t : ℤ
                    pre  s ≠ 0 ∧ r + s × t = x × y ∧ 0 ≤ s
                    post r + s × t = x × y ∧ 0 ≤ s ∧ s < ⃖s
          od
```

The specification of the loop body was derived from the guard, the invariant and the variant relation. To refine the body of the loop, a good strategy would be to establish the variant and (as that would probably break the invariant) re-establish the invariant. The simplest way of decreasing the variant

12.1 The Problem – Integer Multiplication

term is to subtract 1 from it, and so using the *introduce leading assignment* rule we get:

$posmult\text{-}body \sqsubseteq s := s - 1;$
    $re\text{-}inv$
    chg $r, s, t : \mathbb{Z}$
    pre $s + 1 \neq 0 \wedge r + (s+1) \times t = x \times y \wedge 0 \leq s + 1$
    post $r + s \times t = x \times y \wedge 0 \leq s \wedge s - 1 \leq \overleftarrow{s}$

We can make s read only in *re-inv* to give:

$posmult\text{-}body \sqsubseteq s := s - 1;$
    $re\text{-}inv$
    chg $r, t : \mathbb{Z}$
    pre $s + 1 \neq 0 \wedge r + (s+1) \times t = x \times y \wedge 0 \leq s + 1$
    post $r + s \times t = x \times y \wedge 0 \leq s \wedge s - 1 \leq s$

By copying the pre-condition into the post-condition using the *assume pre-condition in post-condition* rule, it should be possible to work out what needs to be done to re-establish the invariant.

$re\text{-}inv \sqsubseteq$ chg $r : \mathbb{Z}$
    pre $r + (s+1) \times t = x \times y \wedge 0 < s + 1$
    post $\overleftarrow{r} + (s+1) \times t = x \times y \wedge 0 \leq s + 1 \wedge$
        $r + s \times t = x \times y$

From the first and third term of the post-condition we have

$\overleftarrow{r} + (s+1) \times t = r + s \times t$
$\iff$ rules of arithmetic
$\overleftarrow{r} + s \times t + 1 \times t = r + s \times t$
$\iff$ rules of arithmetic
$\overleftarrow{r} + t = r$

this suggests the following refinement using the *introduce assignment* rule:

$re\text{-}inv \sqsubseteq r := r + t$

which can easily be shown to be valid. Finally we have for the loop body:

$posmult\text{-}body \sqsubseteq s := s - 1;$
    $r := r + t$

After some practice and experience the programmer should be able to do the two steps in one. The algorithm that drove this development would suggest that *posmult-body* is satisfied by the following code:

12. An Example of Refinement at Work

$$posmult\text{-}body \sqsubseteq s, r := s - 1, r + t$$

provided

$$x : \mathbb{Z} \wedge r : \mathbb{Z} \wedge t : \mathbb{Z} \wedge$$
$$s \neq 0 \wedge r + s \times t = x \times y \Rightarrow$$
$$x - 1 : \mathbb{Z} \wedge r + t : \mathbb{Z}$$

and

$$\overleftarrow{s} \neq 0 \wedge \overleftarrow{r} + \overleftarrow{s} \times t = x \times y \wedge x = \overleftarrow{x} - 1 \wedge r = \overleftarrow{r} + t \Rightarrow$$
$$r + s \times t = x \times y \wedge 0 \leq s$$

The whole thing can now be 'back substituted' (or equivalently read backwards) to give the code for the *mult* function:

$$mult\,(x, y : \mathbb{Z}) : \mathbb{Z} \triangleq$$
$$[\![\,\mathsf{dcl}\ r, s, t : \mathbb{Z}\ \mathsf{in}$$
$$\quad \mathsf{if}\ 0 \leq x \to s, t := x, y$$
$$\quad []\ x \leq 0 \to s, t := -x, -y$$
$$\quad \mathsf{fi};$$
$$\quad r := 0;$$
$$\quad \mathsf{do}\ s \neq 0 \to s, r := s - 1, r + t\ \mathsf{od};$$
$$\quad \mathsf{return}\ r\ ]\!]$$

There are situations were the *mult* function procedure could be used to implement the multiplication operation. For example, faced with the following specification to implement:

a-multiplication
chg a : Nat
pre true
post $a = (\overleftarrow{a} + 1) \times b$

This is just the body of the specification for *mult*, but with x replaced by $\overleftarrow{a} + 1$, y replaced by b and r replaced by a; thus it can be transformed to:

chg a : Nat
pre true
post $(r = x \times y)[x, y, r \backslash \overleftarrow{a} + 1, b, a]$

which, using the *introduce function procedure call* rule, is equivalent to

$$a := mult\,(a + 1, b)$$

and all the hard work has been already done.

12.2 Logical Constants Revisited

Suppose the specification of *posmult* had been:

posmult
chg $r, s, t : \mathbb{Z}$
pre $0 \leq s$
post $r = \overleftarrow{s} \times \overleftarrow{t}$

It is difficult to transform the post-condition into the pattern $inv \land \neg guard$ and thus derive the loop parameters. For the original version of *posmult*, finding inv and var is much easier than for the specification given above. Why is this? It is because the initial values of certain variables were effectively saved – these variables were read only, and therefore unchanged by the derived code and thus could be used in the inv expression. In the above specification for *posmult*, we cannot use the answer when massaging the post-condition to derive the invariant as there is no way of referring to it. This problem occurs in any example that overwrites its input values while calculating the result – in these cases we are forced to, in some sense calculate the result using the current values (intermediate values) of some of the variables. However, there is a solution – returning to the specification of *posmult* given above, we will cheat by introducing an additional (temporary) variable c and initialize it:

$c := s \times t$

This really is cheating! Bear with this for the moment. A possible refinement of *posmult* is:

posmult $\sqsubseteq c := s \times t$;
  new-posmult
  chg $r, s, t : \mathbb{Z}$
  pre $s \times t = c \land 0 \leq s$
  post $r = c$

which can be seen to be valid. The second (specification) statement can be refined using a loop, and we can use the variable s (effectively treating it as a temporary variable) to rewrite the post-condition as

$r + s \times t = c \land s = 0$

This suggests the following guard, invariant and variant terms:

init $\quad r = 0$
guard $s \neq 0$
inv $\quad r + s \times t = c \land 0 \leq s$
var $\quad s < \overleftarrow{s}$

The loop domain proof obligation is:

$$r, s, t : \mathbb{Z} \land s \neq 0 \land r + s \times t = c \land 0 \leq s \Rightarrow s : \mathbb{N}$$

so the derivation so far looks like:

$new\text{-}posmult \sqsubseteq r := 0;$
        do $s \neq 0 \rightarrow new\text{-}posmult\text{-}body$
              pre $s \neq 0 \land r + s \times t = c \land 0 \leq s$
              post $r + s \times t = c \land 0 \leq s \land s < \overleftarrow{s}$
        od

and it is left as a simple exercise for the reader to show that the above refinement is valid. The next step is to derive the body of the loop (again an easy exercise) to get the final program:

$c := s \times t;$
$r := 0;$
do $s \neq 0 \rightarrow s, r := s - 1, r + t$ od

Notice that, having assigned a value to the variable c, it is only used in the derivation of the final code, and does not appear anywhere other than the initial assignment. Therefore that statement could be thrown away and we are left with the original solution:

$r := 0;$
do $s \neq 0 \rightarrow s, r := s - 1, r + t$ od

This trick can be used in any derivation of code from a specification that allows the initial values to be overwritten – a temporary variable is introduced and given a useful value (such as the answer), the code is derived using the techniques illustrated above, remembering not to use the temporary anywhere in the final code, and finally since the temporary is not used anywhere it can be deleted. This technique is so useful that we have already introduced a notation for it: c is just a logical constant.

12.3 Summary

This chapter has introduced the use of the transformation rules that allow specifications to be translated into programs. The application of these rules has been illustrated using some simple examples, and although the examples look complicated, with practice much of the work involved in carrying out any proofs that are necessary can be done by inspection. The next chapter will expand on these ideas.

13. On Refinement and Loops

We can gain some insight into how the guard, the invariant, and the variant relation can be discovered by looking at the fairly simple problem of calculating a factorial. The best approach to discovering these three terms is to initially ignore the variant relation and try to first find the invariant and then discover an appropriate guard. It must be remembered that the process of discovering these three terms cannot be mechanized (for if it could we might be able to automate the whole of programming) and their discovery is effectively inventing the code for a loop, as should be realized from looking at the examples given in the previous chapter.

13.1 The Factorial Problem

The specification for the factorial problem is straightforward, for $n : \mathbb{Z}$:

> *factorial*
> chg $fac : \mathbb{Z}$
> pre $0 \leq n$
> post $fac = n!$

13.1.1 The First Solution

An inspection of the proof rule for loops shows that it must be possible to derive the post-condition from the invariant and the negation of the guard, so one approach to finding these two terms would be to try to transform the post-condition into a form where the guard and invariant can be identified. In the post-condition for the factorial there is only one term, and we need to find two, but if a temporary variable is introduced the post-condition can be reorganized so that it has two terms:

> post $fac = i! \land i = n$

The new specification is now

> *factorial*
> chg $i, fac : \mathbb{Z}$

pre $0 \leq n$
post $fac = i! \wedge i = n$

with two terms in the post-condition, the first of which is a possible candidate for the invariant and the other for the guard. The invariant can be established by setting $i = 0$ and $fac = 1$, and initialization for the loop solves part of the problem:

$$1 = 0!$$

The second term is a good candidate for the guard, and the loop body will be progress i towards n, keeping $fac = i!$ The guard indicates that the iteration will stop when i is equal to n and since i is initialized to 0, it is fairly obvious what the variant should be. We also need an additional term in the invariant that guarantees the set the variant is defined over is well-ordered. Since the variant is an integer, the well-ordered set is the natural numbers bounded above by n. The parameters that give the loop can now be written down:

init $\quad i = 0 \wedge fac = 1$
guard $i \neq n$
inv $\quad fac = i! \wedge i \leq n$
var $\quad \overleftarrow{i} < i$

The first step in the refinement is thus:

$factorial \sqsubseteq i, fac := 0, 1;$
$\quad\quad\quad$ do $i \neq n \to$ loop-body
$\quad\quad\quad\quad\quad\quad$ chg $i, fac : \mathbb{Z}$
$\quad\quad\quad\quad\quad\quad$ pre $i \neq n \wedge fac = i! \wedge i \leq n$
$\quad\quad\quad\quad\quad\quad$ post $fac = i! \wedge i \leq n \wedge \overleftarrow{i} < i$
$\quad\quad\quad$ od

To derive the body of the loop we will increase i to establish the variant, however this will break the invariant. Use of the *leading assignment* rule gives:

$loop\text{-}body \sqsubseteq i := i + 1;$
$\quad\quad\quad\quad\quad$ re-inv
$\quad\quad\quad\quad\quad$ chg $i, fac : \mathbb{Z}$
$\quad\quad\quad\quad\quad$ pre $i - 1 \neq n \wedge fac = (i - 1)! \wedge i - 1 \leq n$
$\quad\quad\quad\quad\quad$ post $fac = i! \wedge i \leq n \wedge \overleftarrow{i} - 1 < i$

The remainder of the code for the body should re-establish the invariant. Copying the pre-condition to the post-condition would give (for the post-condition):

$i - 1 \neq n \wedge \overleftarrow{fac} = (i - 1)! \wedge fac = i!$

which can be re-organized as follows

$$i - 1 \neq n \wedge \overleftarrow{fac} = (i-1)! \wedge fac = i!$$
$$\Longleftrightarrow$$
$$i - 1 \neq n \wedge \overleftarrow{fac} = (i-1)! \wedge fac = i \times (i-1)!$$
$$\Longleftrightarrow$$
$$i - 1 \neq n \wedge \overleftarrow{fac} = (i-1)! \wedge fac = i \times \overleftarrow{fac}$$

giving

$$re\text{-}inv \sqsubseteq fac := i \times fac$$

Putting this all together gives the first version of the factorial program:

$i, fac := 0, 1;$
do $i \neq n \rightarrow i := i + 1;$ -- break the invariant
$ fac := fac \times i;$ -- re-establish invariant
od

The tactics used on this problem are fairly common for finding the terms from which the loop is developed:

1. Identify from the post-condition a suitable candidate for the invariant.
2. Find the guard; the guard can usually be deduced from the invariant and post-condition.
3. Find the variant; the variant can be found by finding an expression defined over the frame which evaluates to a natural number and is strictly decreasing or bounded above and strictly increasing.
4. Derive the initialization code that establishes the invariant.
5. The body of the loop can be discovered by first writing code that breaks the invariant, usually by establishing the variant, and then developing code that re-establishes the invariant.

13.1.2 A Second Solution

The first version of the factorial problem allowed the introduction of a temporary variable; in fact the specification was deliberately written to encourage this. What happens if the specification is altered to allow the value of the variable n to be changed and a temporary variable is not introduced?

factorial
chg $fac, n : \mathbb{Z}$
pre $0 \leq n$
post $fac = \overleftarrow{n}!$

Since the final value of n is not defined, there is a possibility of counting down in n and accumulating the result in *fac*. Given this, what is the invariant? This time we will not introduce a temporary variable, so there is a problem in identifying suitable terms in the post-condition to be the invariant and possibly the guard.

Suppose the values of the two variables *fac* and n are changed by the body of the loop so that

$fac \times n! =$ constant

This (invariant) expression is easily established by setting *fac* to 1, and if the body of the loop decreases n, then, when n has the value 0, *fac* has the same value as the constant. From this discussion we can deduce the value of the constant as $n!$ – the answer. The next step is to introduce a logical constant to hold this value:

⟦ con $c : \mathbb{Z}$ in
factorial
chg $fac, n : \mathbb{Z}$
pre $0 \leq n \wedge c = n!$
post $fac = c$ ⟧

The post-condition can be rewritten using the technique introduced in the previous development of *fac*:

⟦ con $c : \mathbb{Z}$ in
factorial
chg $fac, n : \mathbb{Z}$
pre $0 \leq n \wedge c = n!$
post $fac \times n! = c \wedge n = 0$ ⟧

The body of the loop will decrease n, so the variant term is obvious. The initialization, guard, invariant and variant terms are thus:

init $fac = 1$
guard $n \neq 0$
inv $fac \times n! = c \wedge 0 \leq n$
var $n < \overleftarrow{n}$

and the loop can be developed:

$factorial \sqsubseteq$ ⟦ con $c : \mathbb{Z}$ in
          $fac := 1;$
          do $n \neq 0 \rightarrow$ *loop-body*
                    chg $fac, n : \mathbb{Z}$
                    pre $n \neq 0 \wedge fac \times n! = c \wedge 0 \leq n$

$$\textsf{post } fac \times n! = c \wedge 0 \le n \wedge n < \overleftarrow{n}$$
od]

The code of the body of the loop can now be developed. A possible first step is to break the invariant by decreasing n by 1:

$$n := n - 1$$

We must now re-establish the invariant, remembering that c is a logical constant:

$$\begin{aligned}
\textit{loop-body} \sqsubseteq \ & n := n - 1; \\
& \textit{re-inv} \\
& \textsf{chg } fac, n : \mathbb{Z} \\
& \textsf{pre } n + 1 \ne 0 \wedge \\
& \qquad fac \times (n+1)! = c \wedge 0 \le n \\
& \textsf{post } fac \times n! = c \wedge 0 \le n
\end{aligned}$$

Because c is a logical constant:

$$fac \times n! = c = \overleftarrow{fac} \times (\overleftarrow{n} + 1)!$$

From the post-condition we know that n can be left unchanged, thus using the *contract frame* rule we get $n = \overleftarrow{n}$ and therefore:

$$fac = (\overleftarrow{fac} \times (n+1)!)/n! = \overleftarrow{fac} \times (n+1)$$

from which the loop body can be derived:

$$\textit{re-inv} \sqsubseteq fac := fac \times (n+1)$$

giving the final code:

$$\begin{aligned}
\textit{factorial} \sqsubseteq \ & fac := 1; \\
& \textsf{do } n \ne 0 \to n := n - 1; \\
& \qquad\qquad\ \ fac := fac \times (n+1) \\
& \textsf{od}
\end{aligned}$$

Alternatively the *introduce following assignment* rule could be used:

$$\begin{aligned}
\textit{body} \sqsubseteq \ & \textit{improve-inv} \\
& \textsf{chg } fac : \mathbb{Z} \\
& \textsf{pre } n \ne 0 \wedge fac \times n! = c \\
& \textsf{post } fac \times (n-1)! = c \\
& ; \\
& n := n - 1
\end{aligned}$$

Now using the same idea as before, we have

$$\overleftarrow{fac} \times n! = c = fac \times (n-1)!$$
$$\iff$$
$$fac = \overleftarrow{fac} \times n!/(n-1)!$$
$$\iff$$
$$fac = \overleftarrow{fac} \times n$$

An application of the assignment rule gives the following program:

$fac := 1;$
do $n \neq 0 \rightarrow fac := fac \times n;$
    $n := n - 1$
od

A final derivation can be shown that uses the fact that c is a constant. If the pre-condition is added to the post-condition, the original specification for the body of the loop can be rewritten as

loop-body
chg $fac, n : \mathbb{Z}$
pre $n \neq 0$
post $fac \times n! = \overleftarrow{fac} \times \overleftarrow{n}! \wedge 0 \leq n < \overleftarrow{n}$

and the assignment

$fac, n := fac \times n, n - 1$

will satisfy the specification for *loop-body*.

13.2 Finding Guards and Invariants

We have seen three separate solutions to the same problem. How do you choose which approach to take and thus how to find the invariant relation, the guard and the variant relation? In the problems seen so far, the guard and the invariant and variant relations are pulled out of the hat, so to speak. How were they discovered in the examples given in this and the previous chapter, and how can they be discovered for new problems? Loops are about building answers up from some initial value by repeating the execution of some operation, i.e. piece of code. Two main types of loop can be identified.

The first type of loop involves the introduction of temporary variables[1] to hold intermediate results that help with the construction of the answer.

---
[1] By a temporary variable, we mean a value that does not exist before the loop, and is not needed on completion of the loop, i.e. a variable that is not part of the original specification but is introduced as part of the loop development – typically a counter.

They contain, among other things, a record of how much work has been done. It is also probable that some part of the initial state is left undisturbed and can thus be used to check loop termination. This type of loop constructs the result with the temporaries keeping track of the work that has been done so far. We will call this type of loop an 'up' loop.

In the second type of loop, usually no new variables (temporaries) are introduced. Calculations are done *in situ* using the variables that are in the specification, i.e. that are in the state. This implies that the initial state is changed and therefore there is nothing to check completion against; therefore loop termination is checked by testing some value against some 'zero' value (0, an empty list, an empty set, etc.). The calculation is done by moving values around the variables of the state with some value decreasing; this value is the one to test for termination and measures how much work is left to do. This style of loop is called a 'down' loop.

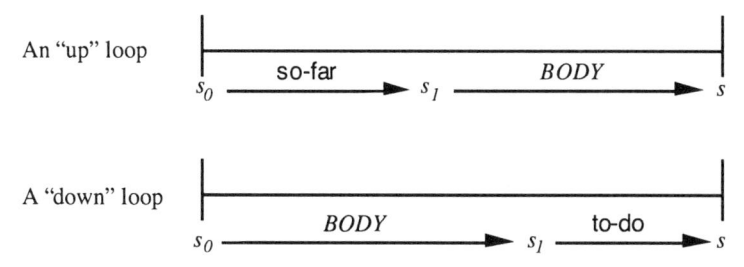

Fig. 13.1. 'Up' and 'down' loops.

The proof rule for loops is of the form:

$inv \land \neg\, guard \ldots \Rightarrow post\text{-}condition$

An approach to finding the invariant, the guard and the variant relation is to identify expressions in the post-condition that could be candidates for the three terms we are looking for. It is usually best to leave the variant relation until last and just to look for terms in the post-condition that are possible candidates for the invariant and the guard. Again, more insight can be gained from concentrating on the invariant part first and then using that to deduce the guard and finally look for some term that decreases for the variant relation.

It may be possible to rewrite the post-condition by introducing a temporary variable:

$\ldots P(n) \ldots$
is transformed to
$\ldots P(i) \ldots \land i = n$

The new term can be negated to give the guard. Alternatively, it may be possible to rewrite the post-condition by replacing a constant by a variable:

$\ldots k \ldots$
is transformed to
$\ldots i \ldots \wedge i = k$

Again the new term can be negated to provide the guard. Both of these techniques work with the 'up' loop, the variable introduced being the temporary discussed above. If, in a specification, a variable is restricted to a range, a related strategy is to enlarge the range by replacing the constants that define the range by temporary variables:

$\ldots n \in \{lb, \ldots, ub\} \ldots$
is transformed to
$\ldots n \in \{vlb, \ldots, vub\} \ldots \wedge vlb = lb \wedge vub = ub$

In this approach the body will, as part of its task, reduce the range of values defined by the temporary variables.

A version of this appears frequently when dealing with problems that include arrays. If an array is defined in the usual manner

$Array = \{1, \ldots, N\} \xrightarrow{m} Element$

and the post-condition contains a term of the form

$\ldots k \in \text{dom } x \ldots$ where $x : Array$

then this can be transformed to

$\ldots k \in \{1, \ldots, i\} \ldots \wedge i = N$

If temporaries are not to be introduced for one reason or another, we have the 'down' loop situation and it is a little trickier to find the three terms. A little insight is necessary to identify an invariant. In this case the invariant is usually some function of the variables and the result of the loop calculation. This means that some function of the (values of the) current state is equal to the result that the loop is trying to construct. The result must also be a function of the initial state. This can be expressed informally:

$f(\text{current state}) = \text{constant} = g(\text{initial state})$

where the function g calculates the answer in one go.

There are two possibilities; one is to derive an invariant expression involving decorated and undecorated terms and use this together with a transitive relation to derive the variant relation, as in the third version of the factorial problem above, or to introduce a logical constant, which reduces the problem to an 'up' loop problem. The logical constant takes the part of a state variable that is not changed by the loop; one or more of the state variables act the part of the temporaries which are introduced in the 'down' loop situation, and the sort of techniques described above for finding the three terms can now be applied. Fig. 13.2 attempts to show the difference between the two types of loop that are likely to occur.

In general, the function of 'up' loops is to build up the answer in the variables of the state. The function of any temporaries that are introduced is to measure the work that has been done so far. Each execution of the loop adds information to that already constructed. Thus the strategy of 'up' loops is:

1. build answer in steps;
2. invariant is about the steps; and
3. the variant relation is about steps being in right direction – towards the answer.

For 'up' loops the invariant can usually be found by reorganizing the postcondition and at the same time introducing temporary values. The guard can usually be deduced from any new terms introduced. The initialization can be deduced from what values must be assigned to the temporaries, and perhaps other variables to establish the invariant.

The body of a loop can be developed by writing code that initially 'breaks' the invariant and at the same time establishes the variant relation. The remainder of the loop body is about re-establishing the variant.

The other form of loop, the 'down' loop, usually occurs when the data structure already exists, but information may be hidden, in the wrong place or not yet constructed, and the purpose of the loop is to find the information, move it to the right place or construct it. This means that the result of the loop is some function of the initial values, and the purpose of the loop is to calculate this function (this is true of 'up' loops, but we are talking about reorganization versus iteration). In this case the invariant is a data type invariant about the data of the loop. A logical constant is needed to record the fact that at any iteration the current values in the state are related to previous values, via the result of the loop, and the variant relation reflects the fact that progress is being made. With the 'down' loop it is still sometimes necessary to introduce temporary values to measure the work to do. The initialization for this form of the loop is a little more difficult, but can be deduced from the result of the loop.

In either loop type, the approaches to finding invariants are:

1. Delete a conjunct and use the complement of that conjunct as a guard for the loop.
2. Replace a constant by a variable.
3. Enlarge the range of a variable.

	'up'	'down'
	Can the post-condition be weakened by introducing temporaries?	Is some function of the state constant? The function reflects functionality of loop
	Can 'next' values be based on 'current' values?	Does data-structure already exist? Loop will either 'add' structure or loop will preserve structure – we are using or establishing a data invariant
	Temporaries reflect story so far	Some state variables reflect work to do
	Each iteration contributes towards the answer	Each iteration eliminates work 'remaining'
Temporaries	Yes	No
Logical constants	No	Yes
Initialization	Results set to 'zero' Temporaries set to 'zero' (or an 'upper-bound')	Logical constants reflects whole task
Initial state	Undisturbed	Changed
Invariant	Some function of temporaries and locals	Data invariant and/or some function of variables and logical constants
Variant	Temporaries increased (or decreased)	Some state variables approaching a limit value
Loop test	Test for temporary = some initial value (or temporary = 'zero')	Test for 'zero'

Fig. 13.2. A comparison of 'up' and 'down' loops.

13.3 Identifying the Loop Type Incorrectly

Suppose we introduce a temporary variable and pretend that it is part of the state:

factorial
chg $fac, i : \mathbb{Z}$
pre $0 \leq n$
post $fac = i! \wedge i = n$

The intended algorithm will construct the answer in *fac*, so that the loop is the 'down' style. An expression that is constant across iterations needs to be found; now i is keeping track of how far we have to go, so the following would be a good guess:

$fac \times (i+1) \times (i+2) \times \ldots \times n =$ a constant $(= n!)$

This can be rewritten as

$(fac \times n!)/i! =$ a constant

The specification can be transformed to:

⟦ con $c : \mathbb{Z}$ in
factorial
chg $fac, i : \mathbb{Z}$
pre $0 \leq n \wedge c = n!$
post $c \times i! = fac \times n! \wedge i = n$ ⟧

Each iteration of the loop should increase i, and this is the variant relation. The loop is then given by

init ...
guard $i \neq n$
inv $c \times i! = fac \times n! \wedge i \leq n$
var $\overleftarrow{i} < i$

The initialization is a little tricky: if c has the value $n!$ then setting *fac* equal to 1 and i equal to 0 will do it. The loop terminates with i equal to n; thus the loop establishes $c \times n! = fac \times n!$ – it establishes $fac = c$. The program can now be derived:

$i, fac := 0, 1;$ -- establish the invariant
do $i \neq n \rightarrow i := i + 1;$
            $fac := fac \times i$
od

Thus, even if the wrong 'direction' for the loop is chosen, everything still works out in the end.

14. Functions and Procedures in Refinement

The rules for introducing procedures and procedure calls will be illustrated using some familiar examples.

14.1 Factorial

There are two possible mathematical definitions of factorial, the first involves recursion and is given by:

$$n! = \begin{cases} 0, & \text{if } 0 = n \\ n \times (n-1)!, & \text{if } 0 < n \end{cases}$$

The second uses the product operator:

$$n! = \Pi_{i=1}^{n} i$$

It is left as an exercise for the reader to show that these two definitions are equivalent. We shall use the first in the specification of a function procedure to calculate factorial:

$fac\,(n:\mathbb{N})\ r:\mathbb{N}$
post $r = n!$

The first refinement step is the usual one, introduce a procedure body:

$fac\,(n:\mathbb{N})\ :\mathbb{N} \triangleq$
⦇ dcl $r:\mathbb{N}$ in
 fac-$body$
 chg $r:\mathbb{N}$
 post $r = n!$
 ;
 return r ⦈

The mathematical definition of factorial suggests the following refinement step based on the value of the argument n.

fac-$body \sqsubseteq$ if $0 = n \rightarrow$ zero
  chg $r:\mathbb{N}$

14.1 Factorial

$$\begin{aligned}
&\text{pre } 0 = n \\
&\text{post } r = n! \\
[]\ 0 < n \to\ &\text{non-zero} \\
&\text{chg } r : \mathbb{N} \\
&\text{pre } 0 < n \\
&\text{post } r = n! \\
\text{fi}
\end{aligned}$$

When the argument is 0, the work that needs to be done is simple:

$zero \sqsubseteq r := 1$

Since from the definition of factorial we have:

$n = 0 \wedge r = 1 \Rightarrow r = n!$

The refinement of *non-zero* is a little more difficult. Again, the definition of factorial can be used to drive the derivation of the algorithm. Since n is positive, $n - 1$ is a natural number and thus the function *fac* can be used to calculate its factorial. The strategy is to apply the *introduce command-semicolon* rule to get:

$$\begin{aligned}
\textit{non-zero} \sqsubseteq\ &\text{chg } r : \mathbb{N} \\
&\text{pre } 0 < n \\
&\text{post } 0 < n \wedge r = n! \\
\sqsubseteq\ &\textit{call} \\
&\text{chg } r : \mathbb{N} \\
&\text{pre } 0 < n \\
&\text{post } r = (n-1)! \\
&; \\
&\textit{next} \\
&\text{chg } r : \mathbb{N} \\
&\text{pre } r = (n-1)! \\
&\text{post } 0 < n \wedge r = n \times (n-1)!
\end{aligned}$$

As there is a recursive call, it is necessary to prove termination. As for loops an order relation over a well-founded set is required – for this example, the order relation $<$ on the natural numbers $\mathbb{N}$ will do the job; we have:

$$\begin{aligned}
\textit{call} \sqsubseteq\ &\text{chg } r : \mathbb{N} \\
&\text{pre } 0 < n[n \backslash (n-1)] \wedge n - 1 < n \\
&\text{post } r = n![n, r \backslash (n-1), r] \\
\sqsubseteq\ &r := \textit{fac}\,(n-1)
\end{aligned}$$

The transformation that has been done is quite simple: the specification for *call* in the refinement of *non-zero* above is just the specification for *fac*, but with $n-1$ written instead of n, and the first step in the refinement of *call* above is just that written formally.

The specification for *next* can be easily refined:

next $\sqsubseteq$ chg $r : \mathbb{N}$
  pre $r = (n-1)!$
  post $0 < n \land r = n \times \overleftarrow{r}$
$\sqsubseteq r := n \times r$

The refinements can be pulled together to give the following:

$fac\,(n:\mathbb{N}) : \mathbb{N} \triangleq$
  $[\![$ dcl $r : \mathbb{N}$ in
    if $0 = n \to r := 0$
    $[\!]\ 0 < n \to\ r := fac\,(n-1);$
              $r := n \times r$
    fi;
    return $r\ ]\!]$

Since *fac* does not access the state, some (informal) transformations can be made[1] to give the final version:

$fac\,(n:\mathbb{N}) : \mathbb{N} \triangleq$
  if $0 = n \to$ return 0
  $[\!]\ 0 < n \to$ return $n \times fac\,(n-1)$
  fi

14.2 Multiply

The specification for the multiply function procedure was

$mult\,(m, n : \mathbb{Z})\ r : \mathbb{Z}$
post $r = m \times n$

We shall use recursion and the only additive operations ($+$ and $-$), and derive code that satisfies this specification. The specification can be transformed to introduce a procedure body:

$mult\,(m, n : \mathbb{Z}) : \mathbb{Z} \triangleq$
  $[\![$ dcl $r : \mathbb{Z}$ in
    mult-body
    chg $r : \mathbb{Z}$

---

[1] These transformations have, in fact, been justified in various parts of this book, but not explicitly.

post $r = m \times n$
;
return r]

The idea behind the algorithm we shall use is to count down using the value m while adding n into a running total. This algorithm is based on the following recursive definition for multiplying a positive number by another.

$$m \times n = \begin{cases} 0, & \text{if } 0 = m \\ (m-1) \times n + n, & \text{if } 0 < m \end{cases}$$

If we write × as an function rather than an infix operator, the recursive definition is easier to see:

$$multiply(m, n) = \begin{cases} 0, & \text{if } 0 = m \\ multiply(m-1, n) + n, & \text{if } 0 < m \end{cases}$$

The refinement of the function procedure body can proceed on a case basis, if m is positive then it can be used as the counter, if it is negative it will need to be made positive:

$mult\text{-}body \sqsubseteq$ if $0 \leq m \to pos$
　　　　　　　　chg $r : \mathbb{Z}$
　　　　　　　　pre $0 \leq m$
　　　　　　　　post $r = m \times n$
　　　　[] $m \leq 0 \to neg$
　　　　　　　　chg $r : \mathbb{Z}$
　　　　　　　　pre $m \leq 0$
　　　　　　　　post $r = m \times n$
　　　　fi

The next step is to introduce a new specification for multiply that assumes that the first parameter is non-negative:

$posmult\ (m, n : \mathbb{Z})\ r : \mathbb{Z}$
pre $0 \leq m$
post $r = m \times n$

Then the first specification above can be refined:

$pos \sqsubseteq r := posmult\ (m, n)$

and the second can be refined:

$neg \sqsubseteq$ chg $r : \mathbb{Z}$
　　　　pre $m \leq 0$
　　　　post $r = -m \times -n$
　　$\sqsubseteq r := posmult\ (-m, -n)$

14. Functions and Procedures in Refinement

The specification of *posmult* can be expanded by providing its body:

posmult $(m, n : \mathbb{Z}) : \mathbb{Z} \triangleq$
⟦ dcl $r : \mathbb{Z}$ in
  posmult-body
  chg $r : \mathbb{Z}$
  pre $0 \leq m$
  post $r = m \times n$
  ;
  return r ⟧

and the body refined by considering the properties of multiply. If the first operand is zero then the result is zero, otherwise recursion can be used:

posmult-body $\sqsubseteq$ if $m = 0 \rightarrow$ *zero*
                              chg $r : \mathbb{Z}$
                              pre $m = 0$
                              post $r = m \times n$
                    ▯ $m \neq 0 \rightarrow$ *posm*
                              chg $r : \mathbb{Z}$
                              pre $0 \leq m$
                              post $r = m \times n$
                    fi

Trivially we have:

zero $\sqsubseteq r := 0$

There is a need to decrease m if recursion is to be used, this suggests rewriting $m \times n$ as $n + (m-1) \times n$ and using the *introduce command-semicolon* rule to give:

posm $\sqsubseteq$ chg $q : \mathbb{Z}$
           pre $0 < m$
           post $q = (m - 1) \times n$
           ;
           chg $r : \mathbb{Z}$
           pre $q = (m - 1) \times n$
           post $r = m \times n$
    $\sqsubseteq q := posmult\,(m - 1, n);$
       chg $r : \mathbb{Z}$
       pre $q = (m - 1) \times n$
       post $r = n + q$
    $\sqsubseteq q := posmult\,(m - 1, n);$
       $r := n + q$

Finally, pulling everything together:

$mult\,(m, n : \mathbb{Z})\ : \mathbb{Z} \triangleq$
⟦ dcl $r : \mathbb{Z}$ in
  if $\ m \geq 0 \rightarrow r := posmult\,(m, n)$
  ⧠ $\ m \leq 0 \rightarrow r := posmult\,(-m, -n)$
  fi;
  return r ⟧

Since *posmult* is deterministic and does not access any variables in the state, this can be transformed to:

$mult\,(m, n : \mathbb{Z})\ : \mathbb{Z} \triangleq$
  if $\ m \geq 0 \rightarrow$ return $posmult\,(m, n)$
  ⧠ $\ m \leq 0 \rightarrow$ return $posmult\,(-m, -n)$
  fi

The code for *posmult* can be assembled from the refinement steps to give:

$posmult\,(m, n : \mathbb{Z})\ : \mathbb{Z} \triangleq$
⟦ dcl $q : \mathbb{Z}$,
     $r : \mathbb{Z}$ in
  if $\ m = 0 \rightarrow\ r := 0$
  ⧠ $\ m \neq 0 \rightarrow\ q := posmult\,(m - 1, n);$
              $r := n + q$
  fi;
  return r ⟧

This can be rewritten as:

$posmult\,(m, n : \mathbb{Z})\ : \mathbb{Z} \triangleq$
  if $\ m = 0 \rightarrow\ $ return 0
  ⧠ $\ m \neq 0 \rightarrow\ $ return $n + posmult\,(m - 1, n)$
  fi

14.3 Summary

Two simple examples have been considered, the rule looks complicated, but its application is usually straightforward. The most difficult part of a recursive refinement is finding the set and order relation over the set to guarantee termination. We will see more examples of the use of recursion in subsequent chapters.

15. Refinement and Performance

To illustrate the ideas of finding loop invariants, we can consider some simple problems. In each case the derivation occurred (more or less) as presented here, the most difficult part being the reorganization of the post-condition to try to identify a suitable invariant.

15.1 A Second Approach to Multiplication

The original algorithm depends on reducing the value of s to zero; a better solution might be obtained if we try to reduce s to zero as quickly as possible in the body of the loop. The second algorithm will use the fact that multiplication and division by 2 can be implemented on binary computers as left shift and right shift instructions respectively. We shall presume access to the shift operations are provided by multiplication by 2 and division by 2.

The main idea of the fast algorithm to be developed is based on the fact that if s is even, then it can be divided by 2 (shifted right) and t multiplied by 2 (shifted left) and these two operations used together will keep the value of $s \times t$ constant. The specification for *posmult-body* from page 204 can be written:

$\lbrack\!\lbrack$ con $c : \mathbb{Z}$ in
  posmult-body
  chg $r, s, t : \mathbb{Z}$
  pre $s \neq 0 \land r + s \times t = c \land 0 \leq s$
  post $r + s \times t = c \land 0 \leq s \land s < \overleftarrow{s}\ \rbrack\!\rbrack$

The division of s by 2 can only be done while s is even; when s is odd, the old algorithm can be used. This suggests the following refinement step using the *introduce command-semicolon* rule:

posmult-body $\sqsubseteq$ *mkodd*
            chg $s, t : \mathbb{Z}$
            pre $s \neq 0 \land r + s \times t = c \land 0 \leq s$

15.1 A Second Approach to Multiplication

post $\mathit{is\text{-}odd}(s) \wedge c = s \times t$
;
mkeven
chg $r, s, t : \mathbb{Z}$
pre $\mathit{is\text{-}odd}(s) \wedge c = s \times t$
post $r + s \times t = c \wedge 0 \leq s \wedge s < \overleftarrow{s}$

The initialization, guard, invariant and variant for a loop that satisfies mkodd is:

init true
guard $\mathit{is\text{-}even}(s)$
inv $c = s \times t \wedge 0 \leq s$
var $s < \overleftarrow{t}$

The loop developed from these terms is

$\mathit{mkodd} \sqsubseteq$ **do** $\mathit{is\text{-}even}(s) \rightarrow \mathit{mk\text{-}odd\text{-}body}$
$\qquad\qquad\qquad$ **pre** $\mathit{is\text{-}even}(s) \wedge c = s \times t \wedge 0 \leq s$
$\qquad\qquad\qquad$ **post** $c = s \times t \wedge 0 \leq s \wedge s < \overleftarrow{s}$
$\qquad$ **od**

and the body of the loop is given by:

$\mathit{mk\text{-}odd\text{-}body} \sqsubseteq s, t := s \div 2, t \times 2$

It should be noted that as s is even, division by 2 is exact. The specification for mkeven is similar to the previous specification for $\mathit{posmult\text{-}body}$ and can be satisfied by the same code (see page 204).

The various components can now be put together to give the final program:

$\mathit{mult}\,(x, y : \mathbb{Z}) : \mathbb{Z} \triangleq$
$\quad [\!\![$ **dcl** $r, s, t : \mathbb{Z}$ **in**
$\quad\quad$ **if** $x \geq 0 \rightarrow s, t := x, y$
$\quad\quad [\!] \ x \leq 0 \rightarrow s, t := -x, -y$
$\quad\quad$ **fi**;
$\quad\quad r := 0;$
$\quad\quad$ **do** $s \neq 0 \rightarrow$ **do** $\mathit{is\text{-}even}(s) \rightarrow s, t := s \div 2, t \times 2$ **od** ;
$\quad\quad\qquad\qquad\qquad s, r := s - 1, r + t$
$\quad\quad$ **od** ;
$\quad\quad$ **return** $r\ ]\!\!]$

15.2 Fast Division

We now return to the division problem that was also tackled in a previous chapter. To provide some motivation for the problem the original specification might have stated that the computer on which this algorithm was to be implemented had no multiply or divide instructions. A further (unspoken) requirement might be that the algorithm should be as fast as possible. Is there any way in which we can improve the performance of the code to do division? The approaches to solving problems suggested so far have been to look at the post-condition for a problem and, if a loop is to be used, derive the invariant, guard and variant from this post-condition.

One possibility would be to follow the example of speeding up the multiplier problem which was to preserve the invariant of the loop body, but preserve it in a different way. Another way would be to rewrite the post-condition in an equivalent way, and from this derive a new invariant. This is what we shall now do. The original specification was:

div
chg $q : \mathbb{Z}$
pre $0 \leq a \wedge 0 < b$
post $\exists r : \mathbb{N} \cdot b \times q + r = a \wedge r < b$

From the post-condition, we can deduce that

$$b \times q \leq a < b \times (q+1)$$

One possibility for a reorganization of the post-condition is to use the above equation and to replace the $q+1$ multiplier by a temporary variable u ('upper bound'). This gives the following:

$$b \times q \leq a < b \times u \wedge u = q+1$$

The guard and the invariant of loop to satisfy the specification for div are

guard $u \neq q+1$
inv $b \times q \leq a \wedge a < b \times u$

Initial values will be given to q and u so that this invariant is trivially established, and the algorithm will squeeze q and u together until they finally differ by one. To establish the invariant all that is necessary is to set q to zero and u to $a+1$. An first guess for the initial value for u might be to set it to a, but it is not always true that

$$a < b \times a$$

For example, this is certainly not true if $b = 1$ but

$$a < b \times (a+1)$$

is true provided $0 < b$, which it is. Squeezing q and u together suggests that the variant relation is

$$0 \le u - q < \overleftarrow{u} - \overleftarrow{q}$$

Putting this together suggests that the loop should be based on the following:

    init $q = 0 \wedge u = a + 1$
    guard $u \ne q + 1$
    inv $b \times q \le a < b \times u \wedge 0 \le u - q$
    var $u - q < \overleftarrow{u} - \overleftarrow{q}$

and the loop is given by:

    do $u \ne q + 1 \to$ *div-body*
                    pre $u \ne q + 1 \wedge$
                            $b \times q \le a < b \times u$
                    post $b \times q \le a < b \times u \wedge$
                            $0 \le u - q \wedge u - q < \overleftarrow{u} - \overleftarrow{q}$
    od

The body of the loop will squeeze the values of q and u together, and the quickest way of doing this will be to find the (approximate) mid-value, and set either q or u to this mid-value, depending on which of these assignments preserves the invariant. To find a value roughly halfway between q and u we can add q and u together and divide by 2 (by shifting right one place). Then we need to set q and u appropriately. An application of the *introduce leading assignment* rule and the *introduce alternatives* rule gives:

    div-body $\sqsubseteq$ $mid := (q + u) \div 2;$
                   if $b \times mid \le a \to q := mid$
                   [] $b \times mid > a \to u := mid$
                   fi

The final speeded-up code for this problem now looks like

    $q, u := 0, a + 1;$
    do $u \ne q + 1 \to mid := (q + u) \div 2;$
                             if $b \times mid \le a \to q := mid$
                             [] $b \times mid < a \to u := mid$
                             fi
    od

Can this be improved on? Yes, further optimization can be achieved by using q and a displacement d from q instead of using q and u to bracket the value. Using this we get

$$d = u - q \quad \text{i.e.} \quad u = q + d$$

and the code to calculate the mid-point becomes

$$(q + u) \div 2 = \text{floor}((q + q + d)/2) = q + d \div 2$$

With this substitution the new initialization, guard, invariant and variant relations are:

init $\quad q = 0 \wedge d = a + 1$
guard $\quad d \neq 1$
inv $\quad b \times q \leq a < b \times (q + d) \wedge 0 \leq d$
var $\quad d < \overleftarrow{d}$

The initialization code is fairly obvious, and the new body must arrange to preserve the invariant and establish the variant relation. With this change our new program is

```
q, d := 0, a + 1;
do d ≠ 1 → d := d ÷ 2;
            if  b × (q + d) ≤ a → q, d := q + d, d + 1
            ▯ b × (q + d) > a → skip
            fi
od
```

By now the observant reader should notice that the multiplication operator has been used, which is not allowed by the problem statement! Remember there is a *mult* function procedure that was derived earlier that worked using shift and addition. This procedure could be used in place of the multiplication operation in the two versions of *div* given above. However, the multiplication is used in the test operation. Can the test be rewritten in such a way that the multiplication is unnecessary? The test can be written as:

$$b \times q + b \times d \leq a$$

Two new temporary variables m and n will be introduced, defined as

$$m = b \times q$$
$$n = b \times d$$

The test is now just

$$m + n \leq a$$

and does not involve multiplication, but unfortunately all that has happened is that the multiplication has been moved to a different point in the program. Perhaps the temporary values m and n can be calculated as the algorithm proceeds, and this can be done without using any multiplication.

Since m and n are based on the current values of q and d, whenever these two variables are changed, m and n should be recalculated, this can be done by adding the definitions of m and n to the invariant:

inv $b \times q \leq a < b \times (q+d) \wedge m = b \times q \wedge n = b \times d$

The changes that are necessary to m and n can be deduced by looking at the changes that are made to q and d. This can be done by replacing q and d in the definitions of m and n by their old values. It must always be true that

$$m = b \times q$$

therefore, when a change is made to q, a corresponding change must be made to m. The latest version of q is related to the previous, or old, value by

$$q = \overleftarrow{q} + d$$

Thus

$$\begin{aligned} m &= (\overleftarrow{q} + d) \times b \\ &= \overleftarrow{q} \times b + d \times b \\ &= \overleftarrow{m} + n \end{aligned}$$

So the new value of m is related to the old value of m and the new value of n, and already we have removed the multiplication from the expression that calculates the value of m. Thus if q changes, the new value of m is given by

$$m = \overleftarrow{m} + n$$

and if q does not change, then the value of m must remain unchanged:

$$m = \overleftarrow{m}$$

This derivation can be repeated for n:

$$\begin{aligned} n &= b \times d \\ &= b \times (\overleftarrow{d} \div 2) \end{aligned}$$

In order to proceed further we must do something with the integer 'divide by 2' term. If the old value of $\overleftarrow{d}$ is even, the integer divide can be replaced by a normal divide:

$$\begin{aligned} b \times (\overleftarrow{d} \div 2) &= b \times \overleftarrow{d}/2 \\ &= (b \times \overleftarrow{d})/2 \\ &= \overleftarrow{n}/2 \\ &= \overleftarrow{n} \div 2 \end{aligned}$$

The above uses the fact that if $\overleftarrow{d}$ is even, then so is $b \times \overleftarrow{d}$, which is equal to $\overleftarrow{n}$. If $\overleftarrow{d}$ is odd

$$b \times (\overleftarrow{d} \div 2) = b \times (\overleftarrow{d} - 1)/2$$
$$= (b \times \overleftarrow{d} - b)/2$$
$$= (\overleftarrow{n} - b)/2$$

Now $\overleftarrow{n} = b \times \overleftarrow{d}$ and remembering that $\overleftarrow{d}$ is assumed to be odd, then if b is odd, then $\overleftarrow{n}$ is odd and $\overleftarrow{n} - b$ is even; and if b is even, then $\overleftarrow{n}$ is even and $\overleftarrow{n} - b$ is even. Thus:

$$(\overleftarrow{n} - b)/2 = (\overleftarrow{n} - b) \div 2$$

and we have

$$n = \begin{cases} \overleftarrow{n} \div 2, & \text{if } \overleftarrow{d} \text{ is even} \\ (\overleftarrow{n} - b) \div 2, & \text{if } \overleftarrow{d} \text{ is odd} \end{cases}$$

We have now expressed the new value of n in terms of the old value of n and the only operation used is a divide by 2, which can be implemented as a shift operation.

The original initialization to establish the invariant before the new terms were added was

$$q, d := 0, a + 1$$

So to establish the new invariant, it will be necessary to initialize m and n:

$$q, d, m, n := 0, a + 1, 0, b \times (a + 1)$$

There is still a multiplication to do but at least it is outside the loop. Can even this be replaced? The initialization is just required to set up the invariant; the multiplication is required to set up

$$\ldots \; a < b \times (q + d) \wedge \; \ldots \; \wedge n = b \times d$$

so in fact any code that establishes this can be used. Since b is positive and as we set q to zero then we just need to set d so that $b \times d$ is greater than a. The multiplication can be replaced and the initialization changed to

$$q, m := 0;$$
$$d, n := 1, b;$$
$$\mathbf{do}\; n \leq a \to d, n := d \times 2, n \times 2 \;\mathbf{od}$$

The initialization has a further advantage: the initial value of d is such that it is either 1 or it is even. Within the body of the loop d is always even, this fact can be used when calculating the new value of n. This now gives us our latest (and final) version of the program:

⟦ dcl $d, m, n : \mathbb{Z}$ in
  $q, m := 0$;
  $d, n := 1, b$;
  do $n \leq a \rightarrow d, n := d \times 2, n \times 2$ od ;
  do $d \neq 1 \rightarrow d, n := d \div 2, n \div 2$;
        if $m + n \leq a \rightarrow q, m := q + d, m + n$
        ▯ $m + n > a \rightarrow$ skip
        fi
  od ⟧

It is left for the reader to complete the derivation to obtain this result.

This problem is a subclass of the 'down' loop category, but perhaps it deserves a class of its own. If you look at the revised specification for this problem, what is happening is that a set is being searched for a value that satisfies a predicate. In the above example the set of integers is being searched for a value that is the result of dividing one number by another. The set that is to be searched is initially restricted by placing an upper and lower bound on it, and then reducing the size of the set to be searched as fast as possible, roughly halving the number of elements to be searched at each iteration. This approach can be used to solve many styles of problems, the trick being to identify the bounds and the set.

15.3 Summary

The sort of transformations that were carried out in this example are difficult to do if applied to code, but having a mathematical model available allows transformation experiments to be tried quickly and easily. It is usually much easier to reason in this way while the program is being written, rather than to try to do similar transformations on the final program.

16. Searching and Sorting

This chapter looks at the standard problems of searching an array for a particular value that may be stored in it and of sorting an array. Before tackling these, it is first necessary to consider how to model an array in the language.

16.1 A Diversion – the Array Data Type

One view of an array is that it is a mapping, with restrictions on the domain – it is restricted to be a (small) simple set, either a subrange of the integers or a set that can be put in a one-to-one correspondence with a subrange of the integers. Thus a possible candidate to simulate an array in the executable part of the language is a mapping:

  array $Index$ to $Component$

will be simulated by

  $Index \xrightarrow{m} Component$

There is a problem with simulating an array with a mapping. What does the empty map represent? It simulates an uninitialized array: if a component of an array has not been set, it is (or at least should be) forbidden to index that component. Few compilers check this, and in fact any un-initialized array can be indexed and the result is whatever value that particular location had been initialized to. Thus, there are two choices to model an uninitialized array, if m has been defined as an array:

  $m : Index \xrightarrow{m} Component$

for compilers that check for uninitialized variables, m can be set to the empty map:

  $m = \{\mapsto\}$

and for compilers that do not check for uninitialized values, an arbitrary mapping such that:

dom $m = Index$

The arbitrary mapping that is chosen is supposed to reflect the random values that will be found if the array if it is not initialized.

If the program is correct, it does not matter which model is chosen, since the program will *not* be accessing uninitialized variables. Therefore in what follows, we will assume that the programs will be translated into a language that does check for initialized variables and we will use the simple mapping model for an array.

With this model updating (equivalently setting) an array element would be written as:

$$m := m \dagger \{i \mapsto e\}$$

there is an abbreviation that can be used to make programs more readable:

$$m(i) := e$$

16.2 Linear Search

A table which can hold at most $MAXSYM$ symbols is implemented as an array with a counter that contains the current number of entries in the table – the counter is a 'high-water-mark' pointer. The state for the system is given by:

values

$\quad MAXSYM : \mathbb{N} = \ldots$

types

$\quad Symbol = \ldots;$

$\quad Sym\text{-}array = \{1, \ldots, MAXSYM\} \xrightarrow{m} Symbol;$

$\quad Irange = \{0, \ldots, MAXSYM\}$

state $Symbol\text{-}table$ **of**
$\quad items : Sym\text{-}array$
$\quad n \quad\ \, : Irange$
$\quad$**inv** $mk\text{-}Symbol\text{-}table\,(items, n) \,\triangleq\,$
$\quad\quad \{1, \ldots, n\} \subseteq$ **dom** $items \land$
$\quad\quad is\text{-}uniques\,(items, n)$
end

functions

$$\text{is-uniques} : \text{Sym-array} \times \text{Irange} \to \mathbb{B}$$
$$\text{is-uniques}\,(sa, n) \triangleq \forall i, j \in \{1, \ldots, n\} \cdot i \neq j \Rightarrow sa(i) \neq sa(j)$$

The first term of the invariant guarantees that the array is initialized correctly – that the array elements between 1 and the high-water-mark are defined. The second term requires that each symbol has only one entry in the table.

It is useful to have a function that can be used to extract all the symbols in the table – it is not part of the specification, but will be useful when expressing properties of the table. Its definition is:

$$\text{elements} : \text{Sym-array} \times \text{Irange} \to \text{Symbol-set}$$
$$\text{elements}\,(items, n) \triangleq \{items(i) \mid i \in \text{dom}\ items \cap \{1, \ldots, n\}\}$$

The problem is to develop a program that checks to see if a particular symbol sym is in the table. The easiest way to do this is to use a linear search algorithm. The idea behind the algorithm is that if the first (and only) occurrence of the symbol in the table is found, an index i will 'point' to it; if it is not present in the table then the index i will point off the end of the table. This suggests the following first sketch of the post-condition for the *find* operation:

$$sym = items(i) \vee i = n + 1$$

unfortunately this is not sufficient – a valid refinement would be just to set i equal to $n + 1$. We need to add a term to the embryo post-condition for the case when the symbol sym is not in the table. Because of the invariant property that there are no duplicate symbols in the table, we can do better than this, it can be stated that the symbol is not present in the table before entry i:

$$i \in \{1, \ldots, n+1\} \wedge$$
$$sym \notin elements(items, i - 1)$$

Putting these two ideas together suggests the following post-condition:

$$i \in \{1, \ldots, n+1\} \wedge$$
$$sym \notin elements(items, i - 1) \wedge$$
$$(sym = items(i) \vee i = n + 1)$$

and if it is established, it is easy to show that (dropping decorations for the moment) the predicate $sym \in elements(items, n)$ is equivalent to $i < n + 1$.

The above discussion suggests the following specification of an operation *find*:

16.2 Linear Search

find (*sym* : *Symbol*) *i* : $\mathbb{N}$
ext rd *items* : *Sym-array*
  rd *n* : *Irange*
post $i \in \{1, \ldots, n+1\} \land$
  $sym \notin elements(items, i-1) \land$
  $(sym = items(i) \lor i = n+1)$

The first refinement step is to introduce a function body to get the following:

find (*sym* : *Symbol*) : $\mathbb{N}$
ext rd *items* : *Sym-array*
  rd *n* : *Irange* $\triangleq$
$[\![$ **dcl** *i* : $\mathbb{N}$ **in**
find-body
  chg *i* : $\mathbb{N}$
  post $i \in \{1, \ldots, n+1\} \land$
    $sym \notin elements(items, i-1) \land$
    $(sym = items(i) \lor i = n+1)$
;
return *i* $]\!]$

The body of the function can be refined using a loop, possible candidates for the initialization, guard, invariant and variant terms are:

init $i = 1$
guard $items(i) \neq sym \land i \neq n+1$
inv $i \in \{1, \ldots, n+1\} \land sym \notin elements(items, i-1)$
var $\overleftarrow{i} < i$

The domain rule is just:

$items(i) \neq sym \land i \neq n+1 \land$
$i \in \{1, \ldots, n+1\} \land$
$sym \notin elements(items, i-1) \Rightarrow 0 \leq n - i$

which is trivial, and thus the loop body is given by

loop-body
chg *i*
pre $item(i) \neq sym \land$
  $i < n+1 \land$
  $i \in \{1, \ldots, n+1\} \land$
  $sym \notin elements(items, i-1)$

post $i \in \{1, \ldots, n+1\} \land$
  $sym \notin elements(items, i-1) \land$
  $\overleftarrow{i} < i$

and can be refined by:

$loop\text{-}body \sqsubseteq i := i+1$

Thus the executable version of *find* is:

$find\,(sym : Symbol)\, : \mathbb{N}$
ext rd $items : Sym\text{-}array$
  rd $n : Irange$ $\triangleq$
$[\!|$ dcl $i : \mathbb{N}$ in
  $i := 1;$
  do $i < n+1$ cand $items(i) \neq sym \to i := i+1$ od ;
  return $i\,]\!|$

Now the guard is $items(i) \neq sym \land i \neq n+1$ and this expression must be defined in the programming language. Notice that, as most languages are not terribly good at three-valued logic, the $\land$ operator has been replaced by cand. This is the executable version of $\land$: if the first argument evaluates to false, then the second argument is not evaluated; if the first argument is true, then the second argument must be evaluated to obtain the value of the conjunction. Remembered that the evaluation of an expression has no side-effects, thus no harm will come from not evaluating an expression.

16.3 Binary Search

The next example will add some additional structure to the table being searched that can be used to speed up the algorithm. First a slightly different model of a table:

types

  $Table = \{1, \ldots, N\} \xrightarrow{m} Data;$

  $Data :: key : Key$
  $data : \ldots$

  state *Search* of
    $table : Table$
    inv $mk\text{-}Search(t) \triangleq is\text{-}ordered\text{-}table(t, 1, N)$
  end

16.3 Binary Search

functions

    $is\text{-}ordered\text{-}table : Table \times \mathbb{N} \times \mathbb{N} \to \mathbb{B}$

    $is\text{-}ordered\text{-}table\ (t, s, f) \triangleq$
        $\forall\, i, j \in \{s, \ldots, f\} \cdot i < j \;\Rightarrow\; t(i).key < t(j).key$

The keys have an order defined on them, and the entries in the table are sorted according to this order. The specification of the problem is

$find\text{-}entry\ (target : Key)\ m : \mathbb{N}$
ext rd $table : Table$
    wr $m : \mathbb{N}$
post $m \in \{1, \ldots, N\} \wedge table(m).key = target$
      $\vee$
      $target \notin \{entry.key \mid entry \in \mathsf{elems}\ table\}$

The strategy to be used is the one outlined in the integer division problem. Since the keys are ordered, we will use a binary search algorithm to scan the table. We will also introduce a logical constant to help with the solution. (It should be noted that the approach described below was discovered after trying a development that did not use a logical constant – the logical constant was introduced to solve the problem of the last entry in the table.)

The first step is to introduce an operation with a body, and to also introduce the logical constant. This should, perhaps, be done in two steps, but with practice two or more small steps can be combined into one.

$find\text{-}entry\ (target : Key)\ : \mathbb{N}$
ext rd $table : Table \triangleq$
    $[\![$ con $t : \{0, \ldots, N+1\} \xrightarrow{m} Data\mathit{x}$ in
    dcl $m : \mathbb{N}$ in
    $find\text{-}body$
    chg $m : \mathbb{N}$
    pre $t = table \cup \{0 \mapsto mk\text{-}Data(-\infty, \ldots), N+1 \mapsto mk\text{-}Data(+\infty, \ldots)\}$
    post $m \in \{1, \ldots, N\} \wedge t(m).key = target$
          $\vee$
          $target \notin \{entry.key \mid entry \in \mathsf{elems}\ t\}$
    ;
    return $m\ ]\!]$

where the types $Data$ and Key have been extended in an obvious way.

The post-condition of $find\text{-}body$ can be rewritten:

$m, n \in \{0, \ldots, N+1\}\ \wedge$
$t(m).key \leq target \wedge target < t(n).key\ \wedge$
$m + 1 = n$

16. Searching and Sorting

The loop parameters for this example are

- init $\quad m = 0 \land n = N + 1$
- guard $m + 1 \neq n$
- inv $\quad m, n \in \{0, \ldots, N + 1\} \land$
  $\quad\quad t(m).key \leq target \land target < t(n).key \land$
  $\quad\quad 0 \leq n - m$
- var $\quad n - m < \overleftarrow{n} - \overleftarrow{m}$

and a loop can be derived from these

$m, n := 0, N + 1;$
do $m + 1 \neq n \to$ body
$\quad\quad$ chg $m, n : \mathbb{N}$
$\quad\quad$ pre $\;\; m + 1 \neq n \land$
$\quad\quad\quad\quad m, n \in \{0, \ldots, N + 1\} \land$
$\quad\quad\quad\quad t(m).key \leq target \land target < t(n).key \land$
$\quad\quad\quad\quad 0 \leq n - m$
$\quad\quad$ post $m, n \in \{0, \ldots, N + 1\} \land$
$\quad\quad\quad\quad t(m).key \leq target \land target < t(n).key \land$
$\quad\quad\quad\quad 0 \leq n - m \land$
$\quad\quad\quad\quad n - m < \overleftarrow{n} - \overleftarrow{m}$
od

In fact the answer to the worked example has established a stronger postcondition; the entry (if it is to be inserted) would go between m and n.

To refine the loop body the strategy will be to find a new value, mid, between m and n such that either

$$t(m).key \leq target \land target < t(mid).key$$

or

$$t(mid).key \leq target \land target < t(n).key$$

If the first case occurs then we will set n equal to mid, and in the second case m equal to mid – in either case the invariant will be preserved. The specification can be split using the *introduce command-semicolon* rule.

body $\sqsubseteq$ calc-mid
$\quad\quad$ chg $mid : \mathbb{N}$
$\quad\quad$ pre $\;\; m + 1 \neq n \land$
$\quad\quad\quad\quad t(m).key \leq target \land target < t(n).key \land$
$\quad\quad\quad\quad 0 \leq n - m$

post $m \leq mid \land mid \leq n \land$
$\quad t(m).key \leq target \land target < t(n).key \land$
$\quad 0 \leq n - m$
;
update-limits
chg $m, n : \mathbb{N}$
pre $m \leq mid \land mid \leq n \land$
$\quad t(m).key \leq target \land target < t(n).key \land$
$\quad 0 \leq n - m$
post $t(m).key \leq target \land target < t(n).key \land$
$\quad 0 \leq n - m \land$
$\quad n - m < \overleftarrow{n} - \overleftarrow{m}$

The second operation can be refined using the *introduce alternatives* rule:

update-limits $\sqsubseteq$
if $t(mid).key \leq target \rightarrow$ *move-up*
$\quad\quad\quad\quad\quad\quad\quad\quad\quad$ chg m, n
$\quad\quad\quad\quad\quad\quad\quad\quad\quad$ pre $t(mid).key \leq target \land$
$\quad\quad\quad\quad\quad\quad\quad\quad\quad\quad\quad m \leq mid \land mid \leq n$
$\quad\quad\quad\quad\quad\quad\quad\quad\quad$ post $t(m).key \leq target \land target < t(n).key \land$
$\quad\quad\quad\quad\quad\quad\quad\quad\quad\quad\quad 0 \leq n - m \land$
$\quad\quad\quad\quad\quad\quad\quad\quad\quad\quad\quad n - m < \overleftarrow{n} - \overleftarrow{m}$
[] $t(mid).key > target \rightarrow$ *move-down*
$\quad\quad\quad\quad\quad\quad\quad\quad\quad$ chg m, n
$\quad\quad\quad\quad\quad\quad\quad\quad\quad$ pre $t(mid).key < target \land$
$\quad\quad\quad\quad\quad\quad\quad\quad\quad\quad\quad m \leq mid \land mid \leq n$
$\quad\quad\quad\quad\quad\quad\quad\quad\quad$ post $t(m).key \leq target \land target < t(n).key \land$
$\quad\quad\quad\quad\quad\quad\quad\quad\quad\quad\quad 0 \leq n - m \land$
$\quad\quad\quad\quad\quad\quad\quad\quad\quad\quad\quad n - m < \overleftarrow{n} - \overleftarrow{m}$
fi

$\sqsubseteq$
if $t(mid).key \leq target \rightarrow m := mid$
[] $target < t(mid).key \rightarrow n := mid$
fi

A trivial check shows that these two refinement steps are correct. We now need to satisfy

calc-mid
chg $mid : \mathbb{N}$
pre $m + 1 \neq n \land t(m).key \leq target \land target < t(n).key$
post $m \leq mid \land mid \leq n \land t(m).key \leq target \land target < t(n).key$

A simple solution to this is to just choose the middle value between m and n, so

$$\text{calc-mid} \sqsubseteq mid := (m + n) \div 2$$

The final code is thus

$m, n := 0, N + 1;$
$\text{do } m + 1 \neq n \rightarrow mid := (m + n) \div 2;$
$\qquad\qquad\qquad\quad \text{if } t(mid).key \leq target \rightarrow m := mid$
$\qquad\qquad\qquad\quad [\!] \ \ t(mid).key > target \rightarrow n := mid$
$\qquad\qquad\qquad\quad \text{fi}$
od

which is correct except that it contains a logical constant! However, all is not lost. Now from the guard and the relation we can deduce that

$\quad m + 1 < n \Rightarrow m < n - 1$
$\qquad\qquad\quad \Rightarrow 2 \times m < m + n - 1$
$\qquad\qquad\quad \Rightarrow m < (m + n - 1)/2 \leq \text{floor}((m + n)/2)$
$\qquad\qquad\quad \Rightarrow m < (m + n) \div 2$
$\qquad\qquad\quad \Rightarrow m < mid$

Similarly we can show

$\quad m < n \Rightarrow m + n < 2 \times n$
$\qquad\quad \Rightarrow (m + n)/2 < n$
$\qquad\quad \Rightarrow \text{floor}((m + n)/2) \leq (m + n)/2 < n$
$\qquad\quad \Rightarrow (m + n) \div 2 < n$
$\qquad\quad \Rightarrow mid < n$

Now m is always increased and n is always decreased; thus

$$0 \leq m < mid < n \leq N + 1$$

and when the logical constant version of the table is indexed, it is always mid that is used and the extra entries on the ends of the logical constant are never accessed. Thus we can replace the logical constant by the table everywhere in the program to get the final version:

find-entry (target : Key) : $\mathbb{N}$
ext rd table : Table ≜
$\lbrack\!\lbrack$ **dcl** $m, n, mid : \mathbb{N}$ **in**
$\quad m, n := 0, N + 1;$
$\quad \text{do } m + 1 \neq n \rightarrow mid := (m + n) \div 2;$
$\qquad\qquad\qquad\quad\ \ \text{if } \ table(mid).key \leq target \rightarrow m := mid$

$$\Box\ table(mid).key > target \rightarrow n := mid$$
fi

od ;
return m]

and this completes the development and proof of *find-entry*.

16.4 A Simple Sort Algorithm

Suppose a set S has an order defined on it by the relation '<', then we can consider developing a program to sort an array of elements of type S. The state for the program is:

values

$N : \mathbb{N} = \ldots$

types

$Array\text{-}of\text{-}S = \{1, \ldots, N\} \xrightarrow{m} S$

state *State* **of**
  $t : Array\text{-}of\text{-}S$
  $\ldots : \ldots$
end

The specification for a code fragment that sorts the array is given by:

sort
chg $t : Array\text{-}of\text{-}S$
post $\forall i, j \in \text{dom } t \cdot i \leq j \Rightarrow t(i) \leq t(j) \wedge \textit{is-perm}(\overleftarrow{t}, t)$

The function *is-perm* will not be defined, except that it does have the following properties:

- interchanging the ith and jth element gives a permutation:

$\textit{is-perm}(t, \textit{swop}(t, i, j))$

- if t is a permutation of s, then s is a permutation of t:

$\textit{is-perm}(s, t) = \textit{is-perm}(t, s)$

- if t is a permutation of s, and u is a permutation of t, then u is a permutation of s:

$\textit{is-perm}(s, t) \wedge \textit{is-perm}(t, u) \Rightarrow \textit{is-perm}(s, u)$

The function *swop* needs to be specified:

swop $(a : \textit{Array-of-S}, i, j : \mathbb{N})\ r : \textit{Array-of-S}$
pre $i, j \in \text{dom } a$
post $r = a \dagger \{i \mapsto a(j), j \mapsto a(i)\}$

As the array will be sorted gradually, we are going to slowly add order to the structure. A predicate that allows a partly sorted array to be described might be useful:

is-ordered : $\textit{Array-of-S} \times \mathbb{N} \times \mathbb{N} \to \mathbb{B}$
is-ordered $(t, m, n) \triangleq \forall i, j \in \{m, \ldots, n\} \cdot i \leq j \Rightarrow t(i) \leq t(j)$
pre $m, n \in \text{dom } t$

and the specification can be rewritten in terms of this predicate, writing N for len t we get:

sort
chg $t : \textit{Array-of-S}$
pre true
post *is-ordered*$(t, 1, N) \land$ *is-perm*$(\overleftarrow{t}, t)$

16.4.1 The First Attempt

In Chapter 13 various approaches to finding the loop parameters were discussed. In this example some sort of 'structure' is to be added to the array so a 'down' loop seems to be indicated, and the recommended approach is to introduce a logical constant. There are at least two possibilities for the value of the logical constant – the initial value of the sequence to be sorted and the final value of the sequence after it has been sorted. Taking the first possibility we get:

⟦ con $c : \textit{Array-of-S}$ in
  sort
  chg $t : \textit{Array-of-S}$
  pre $c = t$
  post *is-ordered*$(t, 1, N) \land$ *is-perm*(c, t) ⟧

A temporary variable can be introduced and the post-condition rewritten:

is-ordered$(t, 1, p) \land$ *is-perm*$(c, t) \land p = N$

This is a case where, even though we have a 'down' loop, a temporary variable is needed to keep track of how much more work there is still to do – the variable p such that everything to the left of p has been sorted (see Fig. 16.1).

16.4 A Simple Sort Algorithm

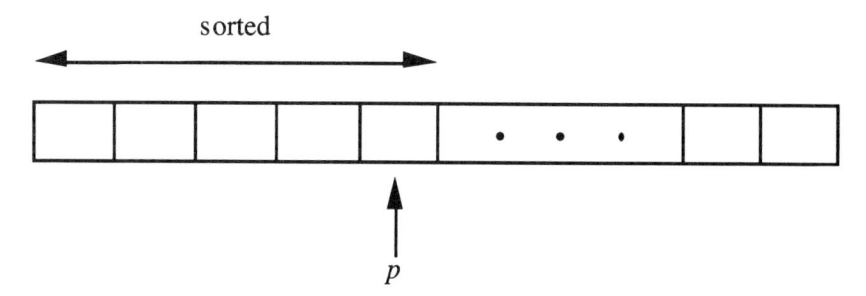

Fig. 16.1. Sorting an array.

The initialization, guard, invariant and variant for a loop that traverses the array can easily be derived:

init $p = 1$
guard $p \neq N$
inv $\textit{is-ordered}(t, 1, p) \land \textit{is-perm}(c, t) \land p \leq N$
var $\overleftarrow{p} < p$

The first step for the derivation of the loop is thus:

$p := 1;$
do $p \neq N \rightarrow$ loop-body
               chg $t : \textit{Array-of-S}$
                   $p : \mathbb{N}$
               pre $p \neq N \land$
                   $\textit{is-ordered}(t, 1, p) \land \textit{is-perm}(c, t) \land p \leq N$
               post $\textit{is-ordered}(t, 1, p) \land \textit{is-perm}(c, t) \land p \leq N \land$
                   $\overleftarrow{p} < p$
od

The loop body can be derived by first breaking the invariant to establish the variant relation; this can be done by increasing p by (at least) 1 and then re-establishing the invariant. Applying the *introduce leading assignment* rule we get

loop-body $\sqsubseteq$ $p := p + 1;$
               re-establish
               chg $t : \textit{Array-of-S}$
               pre $p - 1 \neq N \land$
                   $\textit{is-ordered}(t, 1, p - 1) \land \textit{is-perm}(c, t) \land p - 1 \leq N$
               post $\textit{is-ordered}(t, 1, p) \land \textit{is-perm}(c, t) \land p \leq N$

After increasing p by 1, one of two things could happen: the new element indexed by p is in the right place with respect to the invariant and there is nothing to do, or the new element is not in the right place and there is some work to do to insert it into the correct place – this will need a loop. As *re-establish* does not change p we can see that the last term of the post-condition is established and the post-condition can be rewritten as

post $is\text{-}ordered(t, 1, p) \land is\text{-}perm(c, t)$

The technique is as before: introduce a temporary and reorganize the post-condition to identify the invariant and guard. A first attempt at this is

$is\text{-}ordered(t, 1, q) \land is\text{-}ordered(t, q, p) \land q = 1$

For this to work it is necessary to show that

$is\text{-}ordered(t, 1, q) \land is\text{-}ordered(t, q, p) \Rightarrow is\text{-}ordered(t, 1, p)$

which is fairly straightforward and is left as an exercise. Unfortunately it is difficult to do the initialization to establish the invariant – the initialization involves placing the element at p in its correct place, which is what we are trying to do. Another possible reorganization is

$is\text{-}ordered(t, 1, q-1) \land is\text{-}ordered(t, q, p) \land (t(q-1) \leq t(q) \lor q = 1)$

This will work as the invariant if the last two terms are deleted and (their negation) used as the guard. This invariant is easily established by setting $q = p$.

The initialization, guard, invariant and variant for the inner loop can be derived:

init $q = p$
guard $t(q-1) > t(q) \land q \neq 1$
inv $is\text{-}ordered(t, 1, q-1) \land is\text{-}ordered(t, q, p) \land 0 \leq q \land is\text{-}perm(c, t)$
var $q < \overleftarrow{q}$

The code for the loop body can be derived using the usual strategy:

$q := q - 1$ -- break the invariant

The invariant can be re-establish by swopping the qth and $(q+1)$th element – *is-perm* is preserved by the swop:

$t := swop\,(t, q, q+1)$

The final code not use the logical constant and it can be removed using the *remove logical constant* rule; everything can be put together to give the final program:

```
p := 1;
do p < N → p := p + 1;
             q := p;
             do t(q − 1) > t(q) cand q ≠ 1 → q := q − 1;
                                              t := swop (t, q, q + 1)
             od
od
```

16.4.2 The Other Approach

The second refinement of *sort* is obtained by setting the logical constant to the answer:

[con c : *Array-of-S* in
  sort
  chg t : *Array-of-S*
  pre *is-ordered*$(c, 1, N)$ ∧ *is-perm*(c, t)
  post $c = t$]

This can be rewritten by introducing a temporary variable as

sort
chg t : *Array-of-S*
    i : ℕ
pre *is-ordered*$(c, 1, N)$ ∧ *is-perm*(c, t)
post $c(1, \ldots, i) = t(1, \ldots, i) \land i = N$

and using the usual strategy this can be refined to

sort ⊑ *init*
         pre $c = $ *is-ordered*$(c, 1, N)$ ∧ *is-perm*(c, t)
         post $c(1, \ldots, i) = t(1, \ldots, i)$
         ;
         do $i \neq N$ → *body*
                         pre $i \neq N$ ∧
                             $c(1, \ldots, i) = t(1, \ldots, i) \land i \leq N$
                         post $c(1, \ldots, i) = t(1, \ldots, i) \land i \leq N$ ∧
                              $\overleftarrow{i} < i$
         od

The next step is to refine the body of the loop; we will increase i by 1 to establish the variant and apply the *introduce leading assignment* rule to produce:

body ⊑ $i := i + 1$;
         mini-sort
         chg t : *Array-of-S*

pre $c(1,\ldots,i-1) = t(1,\ldots,i-1) \wedge i-1 \leq N$
post $c(1,\ldots,i) = t(1,\ldots,i) \wedge i \leq N$

The pre-condition can be assumed in the post-condition and some reorganization can be done to get

body $\sqsubseteq i := i+1$;
  mini-sort
  chg $t: Array\text{-}of\text{-}S$
  pre $c(1,\ldots,i-1) = t(1,\ldots,i-1)$
  post $c(1,\ldots,i) = t(1,\ldots,i)$

The specification for *mini-sort* assumes that the first $i-1$ elements of the array are sorted, and the operation must improve this – the first i elements should be sorted on completion of the operation. This could be achieved by finding the smallest element in the array between i and N inclusive. It should be realized that, because of the value of the logical constant c – it is sorted and a permutation of t – this is the only strategy that will work, setting $t(i)$ to any other value would make the post-condition of *mini-sort* false and thus refine it with miracle. This suggests the next step: the operation *mini-sort* can be refined first by using the *add variable* rule to introduce j and then using *introduce command-semicolon* rule to obtain:

mini-sort $\sqsubseteq$ findmin
  chg $j: \mathbb{N}$
  pre $c(1,\ldots,i-1) = t(1,\ldots,i-1)$
  post $\forall m \in \{i,\ldots,N\} \cdot t(j) \leq t(m) \wedge$
    $c(1,\ldots,i-1) = t(1,\ldots,i-1)$
;
  swopx
  chg $t: Array\text{-}of\text{-}S$
  pre $\forall m \in \{i,\ldots,N\} \cdot t(j) \leq t(m) \wedge$
    $c(1,\ldots,i-1) = t(1,\ldots,i-1)$
  post $c(1,\ldots,i) = t(1,\ldots,i)$

The post-condition of *findmin* can be rewritten as

$$\forall m \in \{i,\ldots,n\} \cdot t(j) \leq t(m) \wedge n = N \wedge c(1,\ldots,i-1) = t(1,\ldots,i-1)$$

and the operation can be refined thus:

findmin $\sqsubseteq j, n := i$;
  do $n \neq N \rightarrow$
    findmin-body
    chg $j, n: \mathbb{N}$

pre $n \neq N \land$
$\forall m \in \{i, \ldots, n\} \cdot t(j) \leq t(m) \land$
$c(1, \ldots, i-1) = t(1, \ldots, i-1)$
post $\forall m \in \{i, \ldots, n\} \cdot t(j) \leq t(m) \land$
$c(1, \ldots, i-1) = t(1, \ldots, i-1) \land$
$\overleftarrow{n} < n$

od

The next step is to refine *findmin-body* using the standard strategy of establishing the variant first and use the *introduce leading assignment* rule to see what this suggests for the remainder of the body of the loop:

findmin-body $\sqsubseteq n := n+1;$
    choice
    chg $j, n : \mathbb{N}$
    pre $\forall m \in \{i, \ldots, n-1\} \cdot t(j) \leq t(m) \land$
        $c(1, \ldots, i-1) = t(1, \ldots, i-1)$
    post $\forall m \in \{i, \ldots, n\} \cdot t(j) \leq t(m) \land$
        $c(1, \ldots, i-1) = t(1, \ldots, i-1)$

Use of the *introduce alternatives* rule solves *choice*:

choice $\sqsubseteq$ **if** $t(j) \leq t(n) \rightarrow$ *in-order*
            chg $j, n : \mathbb{N}$
            pre $\forall m \in \{i, \ldots, n-1\} \cdot t(j) \leq t(m) \land$
                $c(1, \ldots, i-1) = t(1, \ldots, i-1) \land$
                $t(j) \leq t(n)$
            post $\forall m \in \{i, \ldots, n\} \cdot t(j) \leq t(m) \land$
                $c(1, \ldots, i-1) = t(1, \ldots, i-1)$
        [] $t(j) > t(n) \rightarrow$ *out-of-order*
            chg $j, n : \mathbb{N}$
            pre $\forall m \in \{i, \ldots, n-1\} \cdot t(j) \leq t(m) \land$
                $c(1, \ldots, i-1) = t(1, \ldots, i-1) \land$
                $t(j) > t(n)$
            post $\forall m \in \{i, \ldots, n\} \cdot t(j) \leq t(m) \land$
                $c(1, \ldots, i-1) = t(1, \ldots, i-1)$
    fi

The bodies of the two legs of the conditional command are trivial:

in-order $\sqsubseteq$ **skip**
out-of-order $\sqsubseteq j := n$

It is left as an exercise to show that *swopx* can be refined by *swop*, and everything can be put together to give the final program:

⟦ dcl $j : \mathbb{N}$ in
　$i := 0$;
　do $i \neq N \to i := i + 1$;
　　　　　　$j, n := i$;
　　　　　　do $n \neq N \to n := n + 1$;
　　　　　　　　　　　if $t(j) \leq t(n) \to$ skip
　　　　　　　　　　　▯ $t(j) > t(n) \to j := n$
　　　　　　　　　　fi
　　　　　　od ;
　　　　　　$t := swop\,(t, i, j)$
　od ⟧

Note that, as before, the final code does not use the logical constant, and its declaration has been removed.

16.5 Summary

The ideas behind decomposition are twofold. The first is to allow the separate development of the various components of a computer program. The second is to develop a proof of correctness hand in hand with the development of the code. Both of these requirements have been shown to be satisfied by a single development technique.

The most difficult refinement step is the introduction of a loop, but finding the four terms for deriving a loop is usually very straightforward. The two cases to look for are an 'up' loop, or a 'down' loop. In the first case the answer is to be built up in temporaries and in the second case either a data structure either already exists or is being built up. If it is a 'down' loop, then it is usually best to introduce a logical constant that contains either the answer or some initial configuration that can be used to measure progress. In both cases the strategy is to reorganize the post-condition and then look for terms that will serve as an invariant and a guard. The invariant will either summarize the work done ('up' loop) or the work to be done ('down' loop). In the latter case the answer is needed to measure the work to be done – hence the need for a logical constant that contains the answer. The initialization is usually obvious; finally it is necessary to find some integer expression over the state that is never negative and is strictly decreasing – this will show termination.

17. Data refinement

Previous chapters have been concerned with program refinement, this chapter will illustrate solutions to the other problem associated with developing executable programs from specifications – that of implementing the abstract data structures of the specification in terms of data structures available in a favourite programming language; this process is called *data refinement*.

17.1 The Refinement Strategy

To realize a specification as an executable program, it is necessary to convert the abstract data types into data structures that can be implemented in a programming language; and the implicit specification of the operations of a system need to be converted into executable algorithms. Thus a technique is needed that will allow the representation of an abstract data-type to be derived from its specification, with a proof of correctness driving the development. The gap between a specification and its implementation will be closed by a step-wise process.

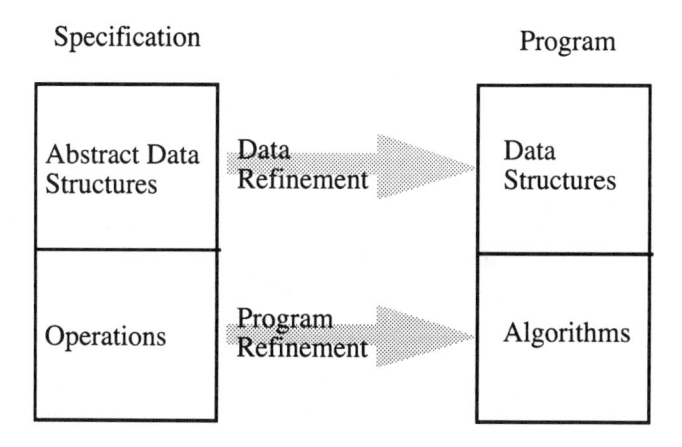

Fig. 17.1. The stepwise refinement process.

The basic abstract data types of the specification language are sets, sequences, mappings, unions and composite objects. In most programming languages, such as C, Pascal, ADA, or Modula-2, data can be represented using scalars, arrays, structures (records), and pointers. With these basic building blocks a variety of data-structures can be constructed which are implementations of the abstract data models.

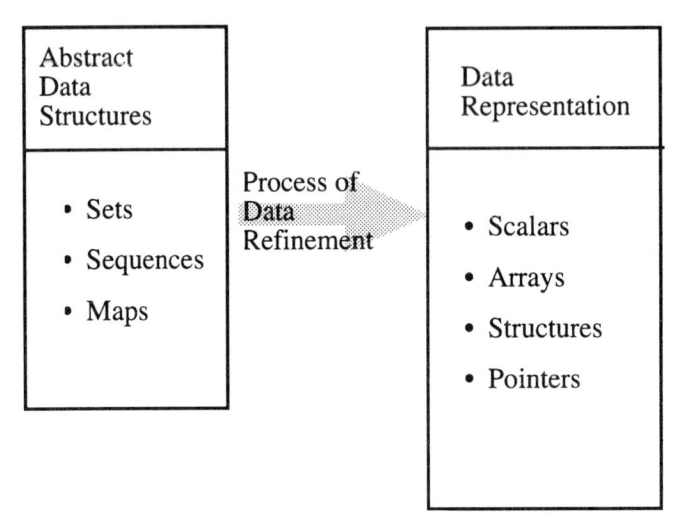

Fig. 17.2. The data refinement process.

17.1.1 The Problem

To illustrate some of the ideas we will consider a simple security system – it will show the approach in use, but will not to overwhelm the reader with too much detail. Consider the problem of the Acme Widget Company Security System described below.

> The Acme Widget Company has decided to develop a new widget. The development work for this device is to be done in a high security area. The security manager requires a program that records the names of employees who enter and leave the high security area. Each door into the security area is controlled by an electronic lock that can be opened under computer control. The doors have badge-readers connected to the computer which can read a magnetic stripe on identification badges issued to all staff that have access to the area – to open any door of the security area, either to enter or to leave, staff must use their identification badge. Thus the system can

detect and record when anyone wishes to leave or enter the security area and can open the doors as necessary.

Staff have been asked to always use their badge when entering or leaving the security area, but doors are held open out of politeness, and not everyone remembers to swipe their card through the card reader.

The room is locked-up at night, so can be guaranteed to be empty in the morning – the system will be re-initialized when security unlock the area in the morning.

The security manager will need to have an operation so that she can find out if a particular employee is in the security area.

The specification for this system is given below. The state for this system consists of a set whose elements are names that record the employees who are in the high security area.

values

$\quad MAXNAMES : \mathbb{N} = \ldots$

types

$\quad Name = \ldots;$

$\quad Names = Name\text{-set}$

state $Security$ of
$\quad area : Names$
$\quad$ inv $mk\text{-}Security(area) \triangleq $ card $area \leq MAXNAMES$
$\quad$ init $mk\text{-}Security(area) \triangleq area = \{\,\}$
end

At the start of the day the security area is known to be empty:

$start\text{-}day\,()$
ext wr $area : Names$
post $area = \{\,\}$

An employee wishing to enter the security area will register their arrival:

$enter\,(nm : Name)$
ext wr $area : Names$
pre card $area < MAXNAMES$
post $area = \overleftarrow{area} \cup \{nm\}$

An employee leaving the security area to go elsewhere will register their departure:

leave (*nm* : *Name*)
ext wr *area* : *Names*
post *area* = $\overleftarrow{area} \setminus \{nm\}$

The security manager can check if an employee is in the high security area:

check (*nm* : *Name*) *r* : $\mathbb{B}$
ext rd *area* : *Names*
post *r* ⇔ *nm* ∈ *area*

The upper limit to the number of employees (*MAXNAMES*) may seem an artificial constraint, but consider a real-life implementation. If the security file is to be held in some local store, there will be an upper limit on the number of employees that will be dictated by the size of the store, so the restriction is a realistic one. The size of the local store can be thought of as a parameter that can be changed at system generation time to fit in with the amount of storage space available on the computer.

The specification of the system uses a set to model who is working in the security area: employees in the security area are represented by a set containing their names. Thus an empty security area is represented by an empty set; the security area with JONES, THOMAS, and FOGG is represented by sets containing just those elements (see Fig. 17.3).

{ JONES, THOMAS, FOGG }

Fig. 17.3. The secure area.

An employee entering the security area is modelled by adding their name to the set that represents who is in the security area; an employee leaving a security area is modelled by removing their name from the set; and the answer to the question 'is a particular employee present in the security area' is modelled by set membership. Thus the specification is a model that agrees with our understanding of the problem.

The design will consider ways of representing sets of values: The data structures in the implementation language suggests a representation of sets in terms of ordered objects of some kind, so it should not come as too much of a surprise that the initial step for the data refinement is to respecify the problem in terms of a table. We shall implement the table as an array that will be simulated by a mapping.

17.2 The Refinement to Executable Code

The first step will be the development of a new specification in terms of a table (an array with a 'high-water-mark' pointer[1]) and will be carried out in two steps:

1. the data refinement: that of representing a set by a table; and
2. equivalent specification: the operations that have been specified in terms of sets will be converted into operations that are described in terms of operations on tables.

It will be necessary to show that the new data representation is, in some sense, 'equivalent' to the old one and to show the operations defined in terms of operations on the table are in some sense equivalent to the old ones defined in terms of operations on sets – put simply, the new representation should provide the same functionality as the original one. This will be done by showing that the new, less abstract, state contains at least as much information as the old one. The new representation may contain more information than the original one, but this additional information will probably be about implementation – it is extra information to aid performance and even to enable an implementation to be built. Also the new operations should be related to the old – the new operations should change the information content of the state in the same way as the original ones.

The implementation of the set abstract data type used in the specification of the security system will be a table using the employee name obtained from the security badge (read from the magnetic card stripe). An entry in the table would record that the owner of the card had gained entry to the security area. The new data representation is such that a set of names will be modelled by a table containing just those names; the set containing the employee names 'THOMAS', 'JONES', and 'FOGG' will be represented by a table containing those names.

[1] In future diagrams we shall just show the active part of the table

252   17. Data refinement

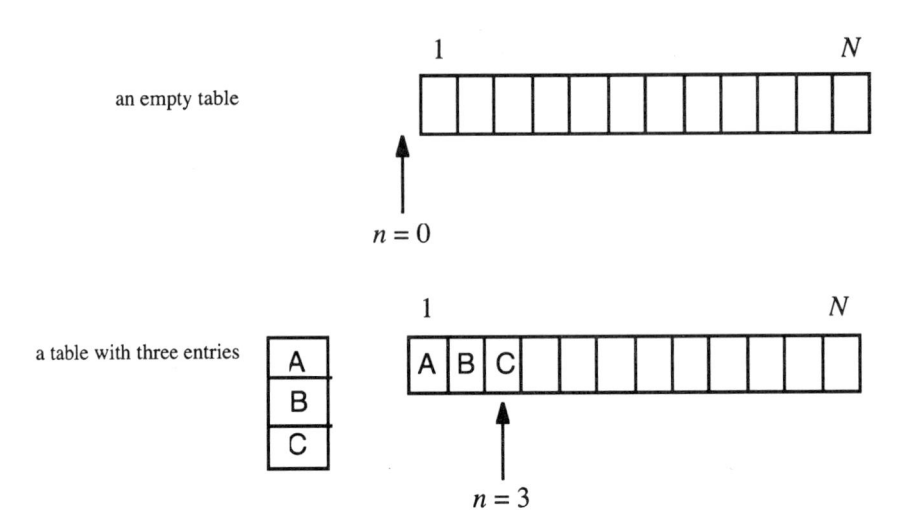

Fig. 17.4. Modelling a table by an array and a high-water-mark pointer.

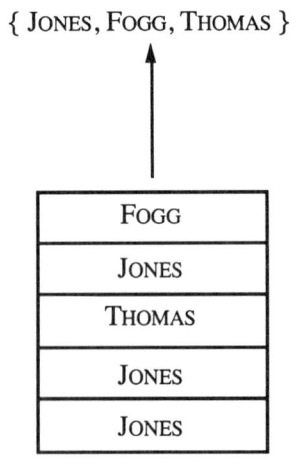

Fig. 17.5. A representation, with duplicates allowed.

However, if repetition of elements in a table are allowed, and there is no ordering to the entries in the table – an employee could occur once, twice or more times. Potentially there are an infinite number of tables whose element are 'THOMAS', 'JONES', and 'FOGG'.

An implementation based on this representation would have a particularly easy task when adding a new employee: the operation *enter* just places the new name representing the employee on the end of the table; an operation of $O(1)$ time complexity. The operation *check* would need to scan the table until it found the first entry of the name it is searching for in the table. However there is a problem with the operation *leave* – it must scan the whole table deleting all occurrences of a name, otherwise there would be the problem of introducing inconsistencies. In this case the performance of these two operations is $O(n)$. The representation could be written, using a mapping to simulate an array (see page 230), as follows:

values

$\quad MAXNAMES : \mathbb{N} = \ldots$

types

$\quad Name = \ldots;$

$\quad Name\text{-}array = \{1, \ldots, MAXNAMES\} \xrightarrow{m} Name;$

$\quad Number = \{0, \ldots, MAXNAMES\}$

state *Security-file* of
$\quad names : Name\text{-}array$
$\quad n : Number$

$\quad$ inv $mk\text{-}Security\text{-}file(names, n) \triangleq \{1, \ldots, n\} \subseteq$ dom $names$
end

The invariant demands that (at least) the first n elements in the table are defined – remember that the table is being simulated with an array which is simulated with a mapping[2].

This representation is rather generous, one entry of a particular name in the table is all that is really necessary. The first thing we could do to tighten-up things is to improve the consistency of the table by disallowing duplicates – the generosity of the representation can be restricted by adding to the data-type invariant. For our example the number of possible tables that represent a particular set of names can be restricted to a finite number by requiring that the entries in a table are unique; thus there are only six possibilities for representing the set {THOMAS, JONES, FOGG} (see Fig. 17.4).

---

[2] An array is really a mapping with a restriction on what sets can be used as the domain.

More generally, for a particular set of n employees, there would be $n!$ possible ways of storing the entries in the table. The representation in this case would be as follows:

state *Security-file* **of**
   names : *Name-array*
   n : *Number*
   inv *mk-Security-file*(*names*, n) $\triangleq$
      $\{1, \ldots, n\} \subseteq$ **dom** *names* $\wedge$
      is-uniques(*names*, n)
end

The auxiliary function *is-uniques* checks that there are no duplicate entries in the table:

is-uniques : *Name-array* $\times$ *Number* $\to \mathbb{B}$

is-uniques $(a, n) \triangleq \forall i, j \in \{1, \ldots, n\} \cdot i \neq j \Rightarrow a(i) \neq a(j)$

Now we have solved the consistency problem. The performance of the *enter* operation to add a new employee has decreased somewhat. We must check that an employee entry is not in the table before adding it, and we have made some improvements to the operation to remove an employee – it need only find the first occurrence of a employee and delete that; the implementation of the operation does not have to search the whole table to delete possible duplicate occurrences. Even in this simple example various trade-offs are appearing.

An alternative representation could require that the names in the table be both unique and in an order dictated by the employee name. In this case there is only one representative sequence of table entries for each possible set of names. This would give the following representation:

state *Security-file* **of**
   names : *Name-array*
   n : *Number*
   inv *mk-Security-file*(*names*, n) $\triangleq$
      $\{1, \ldots, n\} \subseteq$ **dom** *names* $\wedge$
      is-ordered(*names*, n)
end

is-ordered : *Name-array* $\times$ *Number* $\to \mathbb{B}$

is-ordered $(r, n) \triangleq \forall i, j \in \{1, \ldots, n\} \cdot i < j \Rightarrow s(i) < s(j)$

We have improved the performance of searching for an employee's entry – a binary search algorithm can be used so that on average it takes $N \log_2 N$ operations to look up a particular name. The operations to add a new employee and delete an employee are now more difficult: in an implementation based on this representation will involve shuffling employee entries up and down in the table; however, this may be a small price to pay if the *check* operation is the most important one.

The fourth possibility is to demand that the employee entries in the sequence are sorted, but to allow duplicate entries. This is a workable, but a rather strange implementation so it will not be discussed any further.

{ JONES, FOGG, THOMAS }

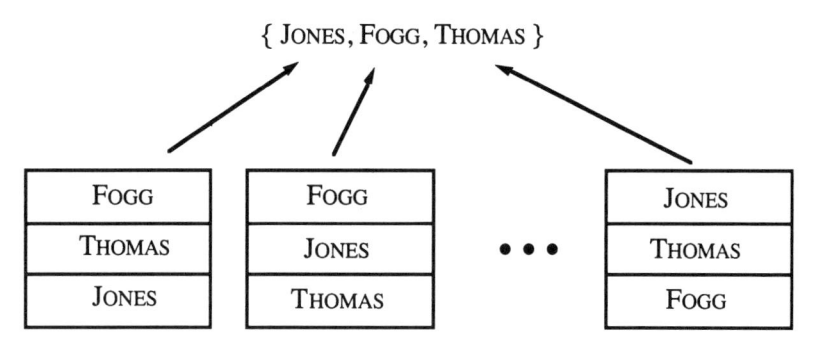

FOGG	FOGG		JONES
THOMAS	JONES	• • •	THOMAS
JONES	THOMAS		FOGG

Fig. 17.6. Modelling a set with no duplicates.

In this example the second invariant is chosen – the elements in the table must be unique, but not necessarily in some fixed order.

The design has in this example involved two things: choosing a representation and choosing an invariant for that representation. In most data refinements we will see this pattern emerging, choose a representation and choose an invariant on that representation, both together giving us the performance trade-offs we require to produce a good implementation of the original system. Implementing an abstract data representation involves adding extra information (such as order) which will aid the implementation.

17.3 The Next Step

The next step is to relate the representation to the original abstract model. We shall do this with a relation between the abstract state and the concrete state. Each element in the refined state will be related to or 'coupled' to the elements in the abstract state that it represents (typically just one, so normally our relation will really be a function – more of this later). It is unlikely (but not impossible) that a single state in the refinement represents two or more states in the specification, for if it did it means that two specification states would merge into one implementation state and it is highly probable that information would be lost. On the other hand, it is possible for two or more refinement states to represent the same specification state.

The relationship between abstract and refined state elements will be described by a relation called a coupling invariant or coupling relation. This is a

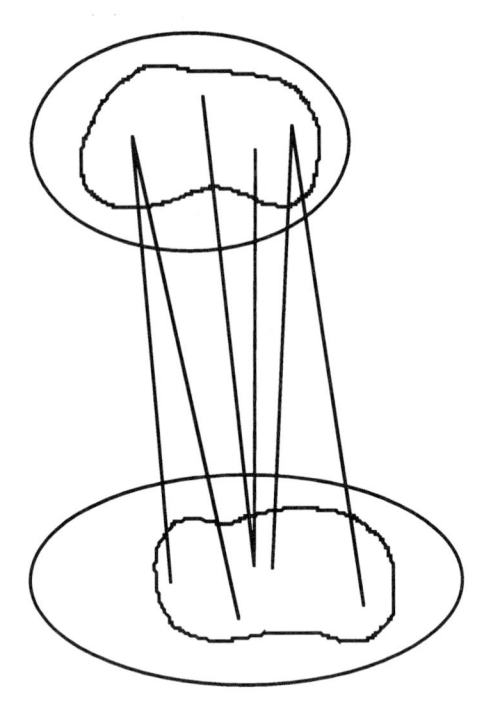

Fig. 17.7. The coupling invariant.

predicate which relates instances of an abstract data type to instances of its refinement. For example, if a set was used in a specification of a system and was refined by a table, then the coupling invariant would relate the contents of the set to be equal to the elements of the table.

$couple : Con \times Abs \to \mathbb{B}$

$couple\,(k, a) \triangleq \ldots$

An element of the data refinement is equivalent to, or is modelling, an element of the abstract representation if they both belong to the coupling invariant – the *couple* relation returns true for that pair of elements.

One obvious property that the representation must have is that of having enough elements in it – all possible abstract state values should be modelled, the representation is in some sense is 'adequate'. Adequate in the sense that any value that can occur in the original specification will have at least one representative in the refined state so that the pair of values is in the coupling invariant. To see why this is necessary, consider the situation where there is a value of the abstract state that does not have a corresponding value in the concrete state. This means that

$\exists\, a \in Abs \cdot \forall\, k \in Con \cdot \neg\, couple(k, a)$

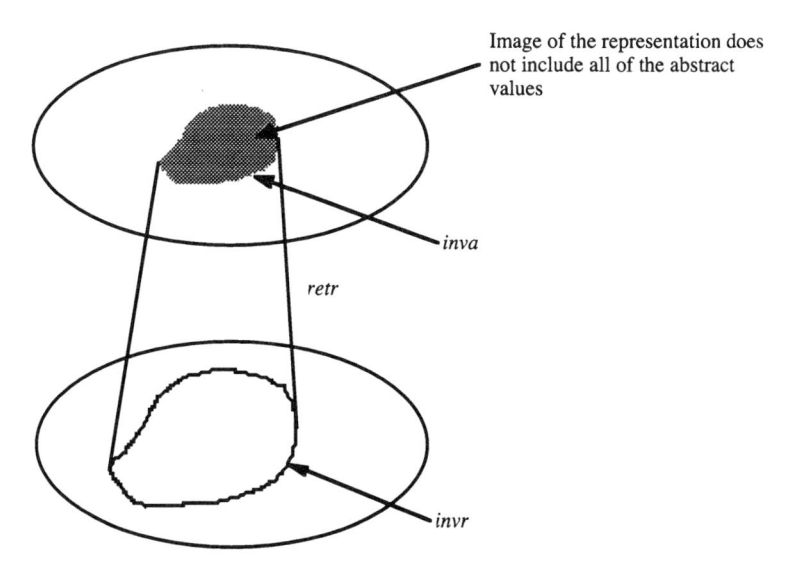

Fig. 17.8. Adequacy – a problem in the domain of the coupling invariant.

Now what happens if the value that does not have an element representing it in the refined state occurs as the result of an operation? The new data model is not adequate, it cannot model this value; something is wrong. This situation must not occur, therefore:

$$\neg \exists\, a \in Abs \cdot \forall k \in Con \cdot \neg\, couple(k, a)$$

must always be true, i.e.

$$\forall\, a \in Abs \cdot \exists k \in Con \cdot couple(k, a)$$

must always be true. This is just stating that for every value in the abstract state (in the specification) there must exist a value in the refinement state (in the data refinement), that represents it.

Having an adequate representation and a coupling invariant is still not enough. There are other problems: the representation must not be too big ('too adequate'): it should not include values that do not occur in the specification (Fig. 17.9). Suppose this was not true; this means that there is at least one value in the concrete state that does not represent a value in the abstract state:

$$\exists k \in Con \cdot \neg \exists\, a \in Abs \cdot couple(k, a)$$

There is a question to ask: what is this value doing in the concrete state? The invariant on the concrete state is not 'tight' enough – it allows values which are not modelling anything. Therefore we require

$$\neg \exists k \in Con \cdot \neg \exists\, a \in Abs \cdot couple(k, a)$$

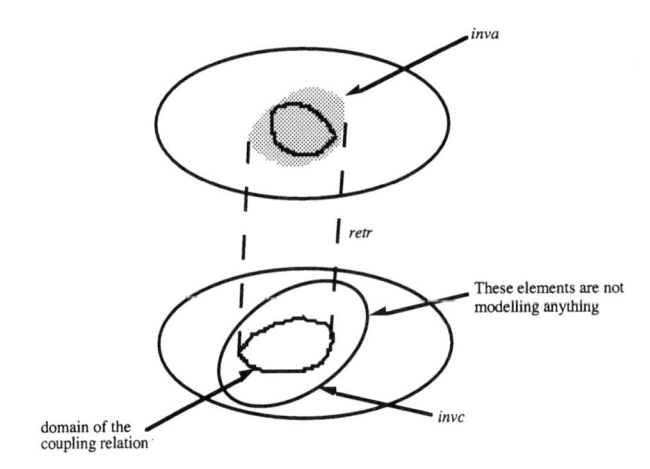

Fig. 17.9. Totality – a problem in the range of the coupling invariant.

which is

$$\forall k \in Con \cdot \exists a \in Abs \cdot couple(k, a)$$

This property is about the refinement being 'small-enough' i.e. not too adequate. If the property did not hold, there could be a state in the refinement which did not correspond to a state in the abstract syntax. This would seem to indicate that there is a missing component in the invariant of the refinement that would otherwise disallow the state.

If the coupling invariant is total and onto, we then know that all the values occurring in the refinement are modelling values that could occur in the specification, and that there are no superfluous values in the representation – all the values are modelling something. With these two conditions met, our representation can be considered valid – no element in the abstract state is 'under represented' and all elements in the refinement are modelling something. As every element of our original state modelled something in the real world, every element of the original state must be modelled by at least one element in our new state.

The coupling invariant may throw extra information away that a representation may have when it relates the representation to the abstraction – for example the names in the table have some sort of order that was not present in the original specification.

The data-type invariant for the refinement may contain two components, one is design decision – to do with this particular choice of data-refinement. The other occurs if there is an abstract data-type invariant defined in the original state, the adequacy rule checks that its equivalent is 'captured' in the concrete data-type invariant. It should be noted that sometimes the abstract invariant disappears because the choice of representation is such that it is contained as part of the data-structure.

17.3 The Next Step

Returning to our example, having chosen a way of representing set by a table, it is necessary to show that the new model is 'adequate' and 'complete': in the sense that every set that can occur in the original specification can be represented by a table that satisfies the data invariant (Fig. 17.5). The coupling invariant for this example is:

$couple : Security\text{-}file \times Security \rightarrow \mathbb{B}$

$couple\,(mk\text{-}Security\text{-}file(names, n), mk\text{-}Security(s)) \triangleq$
$\quad s = els(names, n)$

$els : Name\text{-}array \times Number \rightarrow Names$

$els\,(names, n) \triangleq \{names(i) \mid i \in \{1, \ldots, n\}\}$

The adequacy proof is fairly straightforward: it is necessary to show that for every element in the set of employee names there exists a table with unique entries that is related to the set. An informal proof follows: given a set, construct a table from the set by removing the elements one by one from the set, and placing them in a table. Hence, the elements in the table are identical to those in the set and the table does not contain any duplicates. It is easy to see that this satisfies the adequacy rule. A more rigorous proof is possible.

The original specification was a reasonable model of the real world of the Acme Widget Company; employees in the security area were modelled by a set containing their names. Any 'configuration' of the real world is matched by a value in the state. So if a new specification or model is to be developed from the original, this must also match the real world. The new specification could be based on a more concrete, less abstract, data structures using the real world as the base, but this would ignore the fact that there already exists a simple and elegant mathematical model of the Acme Widget Company.

A question that should be asked is: why not write the specification for the security system using a table rather than a set in the first place? A model using data structures that were less abstract than sets would contain some implementation details and would thus be in some sense 'biased' – the model would contain implementation detail which was not relevant to the problem, and would encourage a development strategy that produces that implementation. The implementation details would also cloud the model's accuracy and correctness.

The specification process should try an produce the 'most abstract' model that contains no implementation detail, and models the real world most accurately. Then the refinement should then be based on the abstract model. It is difficult to quantify 'most abstract', Jones in [23] provided some guidelines based on the ideas of algebraic specifications. A rule of thumb is to try and define a state which has the simplest (preferably no) invariant.

Real World

Specification

Representation

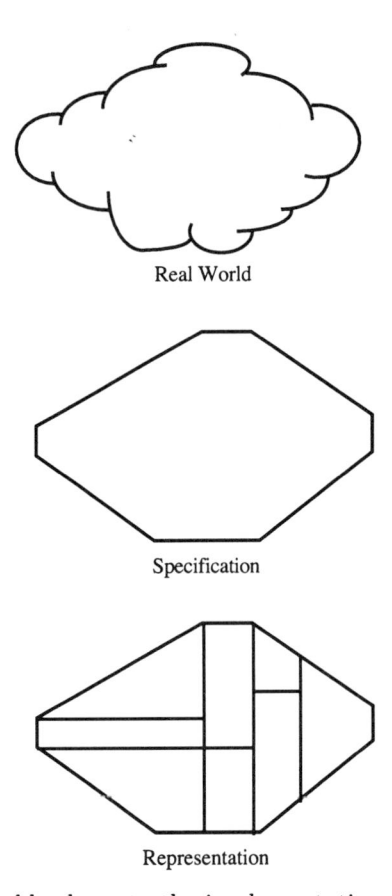

Fig. 17.10. Real-world relates to the implementation.

Another question that can be asked is: can every possible configuration of the real world be modelled? The question can be rephrased: are all possible values that can be represented by the original 'abstract' state be represented in the refinement? If this is not true some obvious problems occur; either the original specification was wrong, or the data refinement is wrong. If the abstract specification matches the real world (or rather that part of the real world we are interested in) and a more detailed (in the sense that it contains implementation detail) refinement matches the abstract one, then the more detailed specification should match the real world. All that is necessary is some reasonable definition of the concept of 'matches' for specifications.

17.4 The Refinement of the Operations

The next step is to transform the operations so that they are defined in terms of the new representation of the state – operations on sets must be replaced by operations on tables. The first step will be to produce the most general specification that can be managed; the equivalent specification rule will allow pre-conditions to be widened and post-conditions to be strengthened.

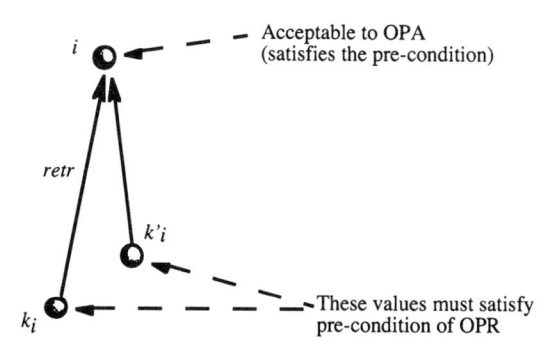

Fig. 17.11. Modelling a pre-condition.

Consider an input value i that is acceptable to an abstract operation OPA. This means that it must satisfy the pre-condition for OPA, i.e. that $pre\text{-}OPA(i)$ is true. Suppose k_i is a value in the representation that is 'coupled' to the input value i. If i is acceptable to the abstract operation, then the representative of this value should be acceptable for the new operation OPR. To see if the value k_i is acceptable to OPR, use the coupling invariant to move to the abstract definition and check that the equivalent value is acceptable – satisfies the pre-condition – in the abstract state. This suggests the following definition for $pre\text{-}OPR$:

$$pre\text{-}OPR(k_i) = \exists i \in Abs \cdot couple(k_i, i) \wedge pre\text{-}OPA(i)$$

It should be remembered that both the refinement state and the abstract state are restricted by the appropriate invariants.

This starting point for the refinement is the least general pre-condition, it defines the smallest set of values that must be acceptable. A further refinement step using the equivalent specification rule will allow us to widen this, but there does not exists a stronger, more restrictive pre-condition. For suppose there was a more restrictive pre-condition. This would mean there was a value ks such that $pre\text{-}OPR(ks)$ was false, and if as was the equivalent abstract value – $couple(ks, as)$ was true – and $pre\text{-}OPA(as)$ held. This means that the value as is acceptable to the operation OPA, a valid implementation must deliver a correct answer given this input value. But the value representing it in the refinement, ks, is such that the new version of the operation need not deliver a correct answer given this input – not a happy state of affairs!

For the actual operations themselves, things are a little bit more difficult. It is easier to consider a simpler example first, where each value in our abstract

262   17. Data refinement

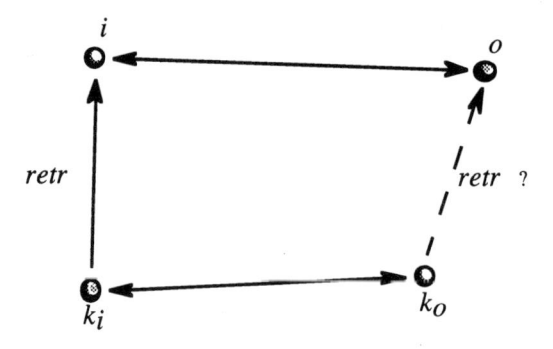

Fig. 17.12. Modelling a post-condition.

state is only represented by a single value in our representation state and there is only one answer that satisfies the post-condition for each input value in the specification (Fig. 17.12). In this case, if i is related to o through a post-condition (this implies that i satisfies a precondition) then k_i ought to be related to k_o in the representation. This can be characterized by saying, that if the operation is carried out in the concrete representation, we can calculate the answer by taking the input, going 'upstairs' to the abstract representation using the coupling invariant, 'executing' the operation there to get a result and going back 'downstairs' again using the coupling invariant.

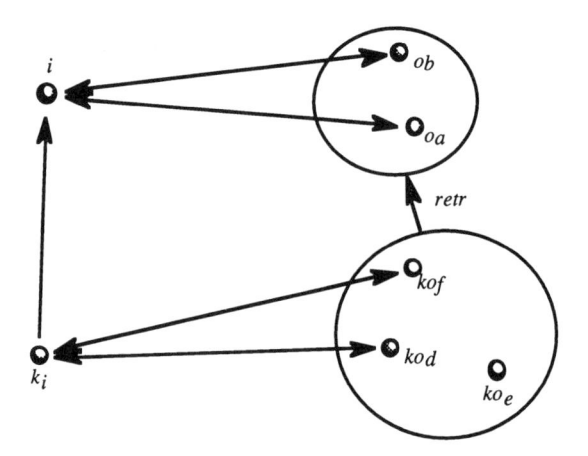

Fig. 17.13. The retrieve function and operations.

In the more general case, life is not this easy. There could be more than one representation state which is related to the specification state by the coupling invariant and more than one possible answer that satisfies the post-condition (Fig. 17.13). However, the same idea should apply – go 'upstairs',

17.4 The Refinement of the Operations

'across', and 'downstairs'. We would expect that whatever pair of values that satisfy the post-condition of an operation on the refined state, if the coupling invariant is used to relate that pair of values to a pair of values in the abstract state, that pair should satisfy the post-condition of the abstract operation.

The process can be illustrated with our little system – the argument that *enter* models $enter_1$ can be done by chasing round the diagram in Fig. 17.14. The table containing the names 'JONES' and 'THOMAS', represents the state of the area at a particular instant in time. If 'FOGG' enters the security area, the table containing the entries 'JONES', 'THOMAS', and 'FOGG' models the new situation. In terms of the abstract specification, the set containing 'THOMAS' and 'JONES' models the security area before Fogg has entered; after he has entered, the set containing 'JONES', 'THOMAS', and 'FOGG' represents the new situation. If $enter_1$ is modelling *enter*, then coupling invariant works in the obvious way. We can indicate where the rule comes from as follows: if a state is valid input to the concrete operation and satisfies the (concrete) invariant, then the result of the operation should satisfy the abstract specification.

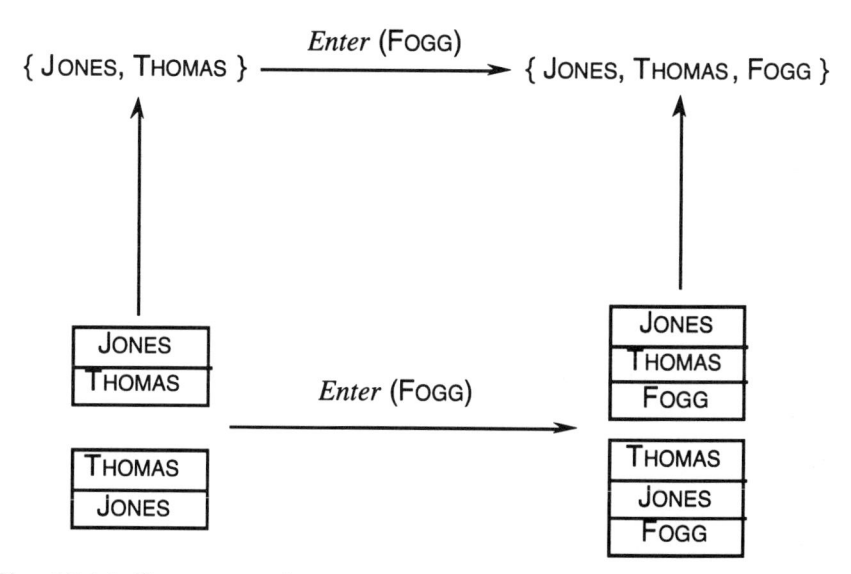

Fig. 17.14. Fogg enters the security area.

For the general case, given a pair of input-output values k_i and k_o there should be an abstract pair of input-output values that satisfy the original post-condition and are related to the refinement pair of values by the coupling invariant:

$post\text{-}OPR(k_i, k_o) =$
$\qquad \exists i, o \in Abs \cdot couple(k_i, i) \land post\text{-}OPA(i, o) \land couple(k_o, o)$

Is this a reasonable definition for *post-OPR*? Could it be weakened: made more general, allow more input-output pairs? This would mean allowing situations where a valid input-output pair in the refinement was such that it did not satisfy the right-hand side of the equation above: one of the three terms in the conjunction might be false and this, somehow, seems wrong. A pair of values that were not related via the coupling invariant, or a pair of values that did not satisfy the abstract post-condition. Could it be made stronger: made less general, allow less input-output pairs? Yes, but the equivalent specification rule could do this for us later in the development.

We can now put all of these ideas together, given a state Abs

state Abs of
  $a : A$
  inv $mk\text{-}Abs(a) \triangleq inv(a)$
  init $mk\text{-}Abs(a) \triangleq init(a)$
end

and an operation op defined on that state

op
chg $a : Abs$
pre $pre(a)$
post $post(\overleftarrow{a}, a)$

a possible data-refinement could be based on a new state Con

state Con of
  $k : K$
  inv $mk\text{-}Con(k) \triangleq inv_1(k)$
  init $mk\text{-}Con(k) \triangleq init_1(k)$
end

With a coupling invariant defined between the abstract state and the new refinement state defined as follows:

$couple : Con \times Abs \to \mathbb{B}$
$couple\,(mk\text{-}Con(k), mk\text{-}Abs(a),) \triangleq CI(k, a)$

The specification op is refined by

⟦ con $c : A$ in
  op_1
  chg $k : K$
  pre $\exists\,a : A \cdot CI(k, a) \wedge pre(a) \wedge c = a$
  post $\exists\,a : A \cdot CI(k, a) \wedge post(c, a)$ ⟧

17.4 The Refinement of the Operations

For programs A and A' then we shall write $A \preceq A'$ to mean that A is data refined by A'. Note that the invariant for the refinement state Con must hold in both the pre- and post-condition. The presence of logical constants and existential quantifiers in the post-condition can make further refinement – either data or program – awkward. However if the coupling invariant is of the form

$couple: Con \times Abs \to \mathbb{B}$

$couple\,(mk\text{-}Con(k), mk\text{-}Abs(a)) \triangleq a = f(k)$

(or a conjunction of terms of this form) then the pre-condition becomes:

$\exists\, a: A \cdot a = f(k) \wedge pre(a) \wedge c = a$

and provided f is total the calculation of the new version of the pre-condition is much simpler and it can be rewritten as

$pre(f(k)) \wedge c = f(k)$

the post-condition can also be transformed to

$\exists\, a: A \cdot a = f(k) \wedge post(c, a)$

However, the transformation of the post-condition involves other issues: the original specification is implementable if

$\forall\, \overleftarrow{a}: A \cdot pre(\overleftarrow{a}) \;\Rightarrow\; \exists\, a: A \cdot post(\overleftarrow{a}, a)$

the new version is implementable if

$\forall\, \overleftarrow{k}: K \cdot (\exists\, a: A \cdot a = f(k) \wedge pre(a) \wedge c = a \;\Rightarrow\;$
$\quad\quad \exists\, k: K \cdot \exists\, a: A \cdot a = f(k) \wedge post(c, a))$

If the original specification is implementable and f is an onto function, then it is easy to show that the new version is implementable. Further, if f is also total, the post-condition can be simplified to

$post(c, f(k))$

The logical constant can be removed to give the new version of the specification

op_1
chg $k: K$
pre $pre(f(k))$
post $post(f(\overleftarrow{k}), f(k))$

Thus if f is total and onto (i.e. a retrieve function of traditional VDM data-refinement) then the above gives the specification with respect to the new data-refinement, and if the original specification was implementable, then this one is. The new initialization is given by $init(f(k))$.

Rather than return to the retrieve function of traditional VDM refinement, this paper will continue with the coupling invariant approach, with its definition consisting of conjunctions of the form $a = f(k)$, where each of the fs in the conjunction are total and onto. Using this approach it is much easier to see the relationship between the various components of the abstract state and the refinement state.

17.5 The First Refinement Step

The specification can be refined into one which is closer to the data structures of a programming language. The data structure chosen for the purposes of this example is that of a state with two components; a an array where $MAXNAMES$ is used to give the size of the array, and a natural number which counts the actual number of names stored in the array. A design (or refinement) decision is that there will be no duplicates in the (active part of the) array. This refinement is shown below:

values

$\quad MAXNAMES : \mathbb{N} = \ldots$

types

$\quad Name = \ldots$;

$\quad Name\text{-}array = \{1, \ldots, MAXNAMES\} \xrightarrow{m} Name$;

$\quad Number = \{0, \ldots, MAXNAMES\}$

state $Security\text{-}file$ of
$\quad names : Name\text{-}array$
$\quad n : Number$

inv $mk\text{-}Security\text{-}file(names, n) \triangleq$
$\quad is\text{-}uniques(names, n) \land$
$\quad \{1, \ldots, n\} \subseteq \text{dom } names$

init $mk\text{-}Security_1(names, n) \triangleq n = 0$
end

functions

$\quad is\text{-}uniques : Name\text{-}array \times Number \to \mathbb{B}$

$\quad is\text{-}uniques\,(nms, n) \triangleq \forall i, j \in \{1, \ldots, n\} \cdot i \neq j \Rightarrow nms(i) \neq nms(j)$

17.5 The First Refinement Step

The first term of the invariant guarantees that there are no duplicate entries in the symbol table; and the second term requires that the array is initialized correctly – that the array elements between 1 and the high-water-mark n are defined.

The coupling invariant chosen for this example was:

couple : *Security-file* × *Security* → $\mathbb{B}$

couple (*mk-Security-file*(*names*, n), *mk-Security*(s)) $\triangleq$
  $s = els(names, n)$

els : *Name-array* × *Number* → *Names*

els (*names*, n) $\triangleq$ {$names(i) \mid i \in \{1, \ldots, n\}$}

By inspection, the coupling invariant is total on the representation state (the invariant guarantees this), and the adequacy proof is left as an exercise. The coupling invariant can be used to derive the new operations. The refinement of the *start-day* and *enter* operations are carried out in detail to illustrate the ideas.

The pre-condition for *start-day* is just true and this carries over to the refinement. The post-condition for this operation is:

$area = \{\,\}$

and this transforms to:

$els(names, n) = \{\,\}$

The new frame for the operation is:

  ext wr *names* : *Name-array*
    wr n : *Number*

This can be assembled to give:

start-day ()
  ext wr *names* : *Name-array*
    wr n : *Number*
  post $els(names, n) = \{\,\}$

The pre-condition of *enter* is transformed by simple substitution to

  card $els(names, n) < MAXNAMES$

Similarly, the post-condition of *enter* is transformed to

  $els(names, n) = els(\overleftarrow{names}, \overleftarrow{n}) \cup \{sym\}$

The operation $enter_1$ is thus:

$enter_1$ (nm : $Name$)
ext wr $names$: $Name$-$array$
   wr n : $Number$
pre card $els(names, n) < MAXNAMES$
post $els(names, n) = els(\overleftarrow{names}, \overleftarrow{n}) \cup \{sym\}$

The remaining operations can be calculated in a similar way; they are shown below:

$leave_1$ (nm : $Name$)
ext wr $names$: $Name$-$array$
   wr n : $Number$
post $\{names(i) \mid i \in \{1, \ldots, n\}\} = \{\overleftarrow{names}(i) \mid i \in \{1, \ldots, \overleftarrow{n}\}\} \setminus \{nm\}$

$check_1$ (nm : $Name$) r : $\mathbb{B}$
ext rd $names$: $Name$-$array$
   rd n : $Number$
post $r \Leftrightarrow nm \in \{names(i) \mid i \in \{1, \ldots, n\}\}$

So far the only commitment to an algorithm is from the data-type invariant – the new specifications are the most general possible and define what must be done with respect to the new representation as given by the state.

17.6 The Next Refinement Step

The representation and the invariant together suggest that our actions depend on whether the name of the employee entering the security area is in the table or not, and whether we are adding the name to the table or removing it. These ideas will be used to develop the code from the specifications.

The Initialization. First consider the refinement of the initialization of the set data type.

$area = \{\}$

the refinement (found by calculation) is thus

$els(names, n) = \{\}$

This can be inferred from

$n = 0$

and this, using the replace specification rule (see page 393), is the new initialization as given above.

17.6 The Next Refinement Step

We can write this derivation more formally, we have

$n = 0$
$\implies$ definition of *els*
$els(names, n) = \{\,\}$

The Operation *start-day*. The above analysis can be used to refine *start-day*:

start-day ()
  ext wr n : *Number*
  post $n = 0$

The *contract frame* rule has been used to drop *names* from the frame.

The Operation *enter*. The development can proceed by considering a possible algorithm. The specification states that the name should be added to the table – the invariant prevents a name being added to the table a second time. There are thus two possible cases that can occur, depending on whether the name is or is not in the table. Starting with the first of the two cases there is (or may be) nothing to do: we could choose to re-organize the table, but the name must not be added. In the second case the name must be added to the table, just where in the table has been left open.

Before considering the two cases derived from this analysis, the first step is the usual one to introduce a procedure body:

$enter_1$ (*nm* : *Name*)
  ext wr *names* : *Name-array*
     wr n : *Number* $\triangleq$
  enter-body
  chg *names* : *Name-array*
       n : *Number*
  pre card $els(names, n) < MAXNAMES$
  post $els(names, n) = els(\overleftarrow{names}, \overleftarrow{n}) \cup \{nm\}$

The specification of *enter-body* can be refined using the *introduce alternatives* rule to introduce the two possibilities discussed above:

enter-body $\sqsubseteq$
 if $nm \in els(names, n) \rightarrow$ *in-table*
                              chg *names* : *Name-array*
                                      n : *Number*
                                pre card $els(names, n) < MAXNAMES \wedge$
                                        $nm \in els(names, n)$
                              post $els(names, n) = els(\overleftarrow{names}, \overleftarrow{n}) \cup \{nm\}$
 $[]$ $nm \notin els(names, n) \rightarrow$ *enter-name*
                              chg *names* : *Name-array*
                                   n : *Number*

$\qquad$ pre card $els(names, n) < \mathit{MAXNAMES} \land$
$\qquad\quad\; nm \notin els(names, n)$
$\qquad$ post $els(names, n) = els(\overleftarrow{names}, \overleftarrow{n}) \cup \{nm\}$

fi

The operation *in-table* will be investigated first. If the pre-condition is assumed in the post-condition, it is easy to show the resulting post-condition is equivalent to:

$els(names, n) = els(\overleftarrow{names}, \overleftarrow{n})$

the above condition can be inferred from $names = \overleftarrow{names}$ and $n = \overleftarrow{n}$. It would be possible to reorganize the elements in *names* between the indices 1 and n, but we shall be conservative and leave the order of the elements in the table alone. The formal derivation is

$\qquad n = \overleftarrow{n} \land names = \overleftarrow{names}$
$\implies$ property of a total function
$\qquad els(names, n) = els(\overleftarrow{names}, \overleftarrow{n})$

an application of the *replace specification* rule gives

in-table $\sqsubseteq$
chg $names$: $Name\text{-}array$
$\qquad n$: $Number$
pre card $els(names, n) < \mathit{MAXNAMES} \land$
$\qquad nm \in els(names, n)$
post $names = \overleftarrow{names} \land n = \overleftarrow{n}$

and the refinement can be completed to give

in-table $\sqsubseteq$ skip

The next step is to consider the case that occurs when the name nm is not in the table, consider the refinement of *enter-name*. The pre-condition for this operation is

card $els(names, n) < \mathit{MAXNAMES} \land$
$nm \notin els(names, n)$

The approach is to realize that the following two lemmas[3] hold:

---

[3] These are two of the theorems that would be included in a theory of data types for the representation. Notice that it comes out naturally as a consequence of the initial substitution which is part of the data refinement step. In posit-and-prove this has to be developed separately.

Lemma 17.1
　card $els(names, n) = n$

Proof
　　　card $els(names, n)$
$=$　definition of els
　　　card $\{names(i) \mid i \in \{1, \ldots, n\}\}$
$=$　invariant
　　　n

■

Lemma 17.2
　$nm \in els(names, n) \Leftrightarrow \exists i \in \{1, \ldots, n\} \cdot nm = names(i)$

Proof
　　　$nm \in els(names, n)$
$\Longleftrightarrow$　definition of els
　　　$nm \in \{names(i) \mid i \in \{1, \ldots, n\}\}$
$\Longleftrightarrow$　property of set comprehension
　　　$\exists i \in \{1, \ldots, n\} \cdot nm = names(i)$

■

and use these to (trivially) transform the pre-condition. With this approach two theorems about the representation have been identified; such theorems may help provide an better understanding of the representation and convince of its correctness.

Under the assumption that nm is not in the table, we must establish

$$els(names, n) = els(\overleftarrow{names}, \overleftarrow{n}) \cup \{nm\}$$

If we can rewrite the right-hand side of this equation in the form

$$els(g(\overleftarrow{names}, nm, \overleftarrow{n}), h(\overleftarrow{names}, nm, \overleftarrow{n}))$$

for some functions g and h; then, since equal arguments for total functions imply equal function values, we can remove the els function – we would have:

　　　$names = g(\overleftarrow{names}, nm, \overleftarrow{n}) \wedge$
　　　$n = h(\overleftarrow{names}, nm, \overleftarrow{n})$
$\Longrightarrow$　property of total functions
　　　$els(names, n) = els(g(\overleftarrow{names}, nm, \overleftarrow{n}), h(\overleftarrow{names}, nm, \overleftarrow{n}))$
$\Longrightarrow$
　　　$els(names, n) = els(\overleftarrow{names}, \overleftarrow{n}) \cup \{nm\}$

and this can be used by the *replace specification* rule.

17. Data refinement

For this example, a way of finding the (two) functions is to notice that placing the new element at the end of the array and increasing the high-water-mark pointer by one has the effect of adding the name to the table; the following lemma encapsulates this:

Lemma 17.3
$$els(names, n) \cup \{nm\} = els(names \dagger \{n+1 \mapsto nm\}, n+1)$$

Proof

$\quad els(names, n) \cup \{nm\}$
$=\quad$ definition of *els*
$\quad \{names(i) \mid i \in \{1, \ldots, n\}\} \cup \{nm\}$
$=\quad$ property of maps
$\quad \{(names \dagger \{n+1 \mapsto nm\})(i) \mid i \in \{1, \ldots, n\}\} \cup$
$\quad \{(names \dagger \{n+1 \mapsto nm\})(i) \mid i = n+1\}$
$=\quad$ property of union
$\quad \{(names \dagger \{n+1 \mapsto nm\})(i) \mid i \in \{1, \ldots, n+1\}\}$
$=\quad$ definition of *els*
$\quad els(names \dagger \{n+1 \mapsto nm\}, n+1)$

■

This lemma can be used to strengthen the post-condition, the complete argument can be written out rigorously:

$\quad names = \overleftarrow{names} \dagger \{\overleftarrow{n} + 1 \mapsto nm\} \wedge$
$\quad n = \overleftarrow{n} + 1$
$\Longrightarrow$ property of total functions
$\quad els(names, n) = els(\overleftarrow{names} \dagger \{\overleftarrow{n} + 1 \mapsto nm\}, \overleftarrow{n} + 1)$
$\Longrightarrow$ Lemma 17.3
$\quad els(names, n) = els(\overleftarrow{names}, \overleftarrow{n}) \cup \{nm\}$

which is the post-condition for *in-table*. Thus using the *replace specification* rule, and with a little, trivial, work the new version of the operation *enter-name* can be written as:

$\quad$ *enter-name*
$\quad$ **chg** *names* : *Name-array*
$\qquad n$: *Number*
$\quad$ **pre** $n < MAXNAMES \wedge$
$\qquad \neg \exists i \in \{1, \ldots, n\} \cdot nm = names(i)$
$\quad$ **post** $names = \overleftarrow{names} \dagger \{\overleftarrow{n} + 1 \mapsto nm\} \wedge$
$\qquad n = \overleftarrow{n} + 1$

The result of this work is the following function procedure:

$enter_1\ (nm: Name)$
ext wr $names: Name\text{-}array$
   wr $n: Number$ ≙
if $\neg \exists i \in \{1, \ldots, n\} \cdot nm = names(i) \rightarrow enter\text{-}name$
▯ $\exists i \in \{1, \ldots, n\} \cdot nm = names(i) \rightarrow$ skip
fi

By using the property that there are no duplicate entries in the table, we have significantly simplified the problem and identified several useful lemmas about the data representation that provide insight and might also be used in later development steps.

The Operation *leave*. We proceed as in the previous case – introducing a procedure body and then consider the two possibilities: the name is in the table, or the name is not in the table. These two steps will be carried out together:

$leave_1\ (nm: Name)$
ext wr $names: Name\text{-}array$
   wr $n: Number$ ≙
if $nm \in els(names, n) \rightarrow remove\text{-}name$
                             chg $names: Name\text{-}array$
                                   $n: Number$
                             pre $nm \in els(names, n)$
                             post $els(names, n) = els(\overleftarrow{names}, \overleftarrow{n}) \setminus \{nm\}$
▯ $nm \notin els(names, n) \rightarrow no\text{-}action$
                             chg $names: Name\text{-}array$
                                   $n: Number$
                             pre $\neg nm \in els(names, n)$
                             post $els(names, n) = els(\overleftarrow{names}, \overleftarrow{n}) \setminus \{nm\}$
fi

Starting with the second of the two cases – nm is not in the table – as before the pre-condition can be assumed in the post-condition to give:

     $nm \notin els(\overleftarrow{names}, \overleftarrow{n})$
=   property of $\setminus$ operator
     $els(\overleftarrow{names}, \overleftarrow{n}) \setminus \{nm\} = els(\overleftarrow{names}, \overleftarrow{n})$

thus, in this case the post-condition can be inferred from

     $els(\overleftarrow{names}, \overleftarrow{n}) = els(names, n)$

This situation has already occurred in the development of the *enter* operations and thus we can deduce:

274   17. Data refinement

$$no\text{-}action \sqsubseteq \textsf{skip}$$

justifying the name of the operation.

The other case where nm is in the table involves a more work. The first step is the introduction of a local identifier i such that $\overleftarrow{names}(i) = nm$. The refinement step is carried out by first introducing the new variable i using the *add variable* rule, and then conjoining the additional term (justified by the *replace specification* rule).

remove-name
chg $names : Name\text{-}array$
     $n : Number$
     $i : Number$
pre $nm \in els(names, n)$
post $\overleftarrow{names}(i) = nm \land$
    $els(names, n) = els(\overleftarrow{names}, \overleftarrow{n}) \setminus \{nm\}$

We can re-organize the order of the elements in the relevant part of $names$ under the umbrella of the els function; the following lemma can be derived from the right-hand term of the post-condition:

Lemma 17.4
$els(names, n) \setminus \{names(i)\} = els(names \dagger \{i \mapsto names(n)\}, n-1)$

Proof

$\quad els(\overleftarrow{names}, \overleftarrow{n}) \setminus \{names(i)\}$
$=\quad$ definition of els
$\quad \{names(j) \mid j \in \{1, \ldots, n\}\} \setminus \{names(i)\}$
$=\quad$ invariant
$\quad \{names(j) \mid j \in \{1, \ldots, i-1\} \cup \{i+1, \ldots, n\}\}$
$=\quad$ invariant
$\quad \{names(j) \mid j \in \{1, \ldots, i-1\} \cup \{i+1, \ldots, n\}\}$
$=$
$\quad \{names(j) \mid j \in \{1, \ldots, i-1\} \cup \{n\} \cup \{i+1, \ldots, n-1\}\}$
$=$
$\quad \{names(j) \mid j \in \{1, \ldots, i-1\} \cup \{n\} \cup \{i+1, \ldots, n-1\}\}$
$=$
$\quad \{names\dagger\{i \mapsto names(n)\}(j) \mid j \in \{1, \ldots, i-1\} \cup \{i\} \cup \{i+1, \ldots, n-1\}\}$
$=$
$\quad \{names \dagger \{i \mapsto names(n)\}(j) \mid j \in \{1, \ldots, n-1\}\}$
$=$
$\quad els(names \dagger \{i \mapsto names(n)\}, n-1)$

∎

17.6 The Next Refinement Step

and this can be use to rewrite the post-condition:

$$els(names, n) = els(\overleftarrow{names} \dagger \{i \mapsto names(\overleftarrow{n})\}, n-1)$$

which suggests that the new post-condition should specify that

$$names = \overleftarrow{names} \dagger \{i \mapsto names(\overleftarrow{n})\}$$

and

$$n = n - 1$$

The formal derivation of the new post-condition is given below; because of the pre-condition, for some integer i:

$$\overleftarrow{names}(i) = nm \land$$
$$names = \overleftarrow{names} \dagger \{i \mapsto \overleftarrow{names}(\overleftarrow{n})\} \land$$
$$n = \overleftarrow{n} - 1$$

$$\Longrightarrow$$

$$els(names, n) = els(\overleftarrow{names} \dagger \{i \mapsto \overleftarrow{names}(\overleftarrow{n})\}, \overleftarrow{n} - 1)$$

$$\Longrightarrow$$

$$els(names, n) = els(\overleftarrow{names}, \overleftarrow{n}) \setminus \{names(i)\}$$

$$\Longrightarrow$$

$$els(names, n) = els(\overleftarrow{names}, \overleftarrow{n}) \setminus \{nm\}$$

The post-condition can now be completed to give the new specification for *remove-name*:

remove-name
chg $names : Name\text{-}array$
　　　$n : Number$
　　　$i : Number$
pre $nm \in els(names, n)$
post $\overleftarrow{names}(i) = nm \land$
　　　$n = \overleftarrow{n} - 1 \land$
　　　$names = \overleftarrow{names} \dagger \{i \mapsto \overleftarrow{names}(\overleftarrow{n})\}$

An alternative possibility is to just remove the name from the table by shifting array elements along one, this approach suggests the following lemma:

Lemma 17.5
$$els(names, n) \setminus \{names(i)\} =$$
$$els(names \dagger \{k \mapsto names(k+1) \mid k \in \{i, \ldots, n-1\}\}, n-1)$$
□

$start\text{-}day_1$ (nm : $Name$)
ext wr n : $Number$
post $n = 0$

$enter_1$ (nm : $Name$)
ext wr $names$: $Name\text{-}array$
  wr n : $Number$ $\triangleq$
  if $\neg \exists j \in \{1, \ldots, n\} \cdot nm = names(j) \rightarrow$
      $enter\text{-}name$
      chg $names$: $Name\text{-}array$
          n : $Number$
        pre $n < MAXNAMES \wedge$
            $\neg \exists j \in \{1, \ldots, n\} \cdot nm = names(j)$
        post $names = \overleftarrow{names} \dagger \{\overleftarrow{n} + 1 \mapsto nm\} \wedge$
            $n = \overleftarrow{n} + 1$
  $\square$ $\exists j \in \{1, \ldots, n\} \cdot nm = names(j) \rightarrow$ skip
  fi

$leave$ (nm : $Name$)
ext wr $names$: $Name\text{-}array$
  wr n : $Number$ $\triangleq$
  $[\![$ dcl $i : \mathbb{N}$ in
  if $\exists j \in \{1, \ldots, n\} \cdot nm = names(j) \rightarrow$
      $remove\text{-}name$
      chg $names$: $Name\text{-}array$
          n : $Number$
          i : $\mathbb{N}$
        pre $\exists j \in \{1, \ldots, n\} \cdot nm = names(j)$
        post $\overleftarrow{names}(i) = nm \wedge$
            $n = \overleftarrow{n} - 1 \wedge$
            $names = \overleftarrow{names} \dagger \{i \mapsto \overleftarrow{names}(\overleftarrow{n})\}$
  $\square$ $\neg \exists j \in \{1, \ldots, n\} \cdot nm = names(j) \rightarrow$ skip
  fi $]\!]$

$check_1$ (nm : $Name$) r : $\mathbb{B}$
ext rd $names$: $Name\text{-}array$
  rd n : $Number$
post $r \Leftrightarrow \exists j \in \{1, \ldots, n\} \cdot names(j) = nm$

Fig. 17.15. After the first refinement step.

17.6 The Next Refinement Step

which could lead to an inefficient implementation.

Finally, after some simple changes, and using Lemma 17.1 to adjust the pre-conditions and introducing a local variable i, we have:

leave ($nm : Name$)
ext wr *names* : *Name-array*
    wr $n : Number$ $\triangleq$
  $[\![$ dcl $i : \mathbb{N}$ in
    if $\exists j \in \{1,\ldots,n\} \cdot nm = names(j) \to$ *remove-name*
    $[\!]$ $\neg \exists j \in \{1,\ldots,n\} \cdot nm = names(j) \to$ skip
    fi$]\!]$

where

remove-name
chg *names* : *Name-array*
    $n : Number$
    $i : Number$
pre $\exists j \in \{1,\ldots,n\} \cdot nm = names(j)$
post $\overleftarrow{names}(i) = nm \wedge$
    $n = \overleftarrow{n} - 1 \wedge$
    $names = \overleftarrow{names} \dagger \{i \mapsto \overleftarrow{names}(\overleftarrow{n})\}$

17.6.1 The *check* Operation

Using Lemma 17.2 it is easy to show that a possible refinement of the operation $check_1$ becomes:

$check_1$ ($nm : Name$) $r : \mathbb{B}$
ext rd *names* : *Name-array*
    rd $n : Number$
post $r \Leftrightarrow \exists i \in \{1,\ldots,\overleftarrow{n}\} \cdot \overleftarrow{names}(i) = nm$

the development of this operation will be left to a later stage.

17.6.2 Putting it all Together

The refinement step has now been completed – the set model with operations on sets have been replaced by a table and operations on it. The final specification is given in Fig. 17.15.

The new model could be related back to the real world. The initial state, that of an empty security area, is modelled by an empty table. An employee entering the security area is modelled by adding the employee's name to the table that represents who is currently in the security area. An employee leaving the security area is modelled by deleting the employee's name from the table. This check does not always work, especially when the implementation uses a technique which does not easily relate to the original model, but the check is worth doing if it is possible.

17.6.3 Further Development

The next step in the development of this little system is to continue to develop executable code by introducing some auxiliary operations.

A Useful Function. Each of the new refinements uses a predicate of the form:

$$\exists i \in \{1, \ldots, n\} \cdot nm = names(i)$$

Then next step in the refinement will exploit this fact. The easiest way to check whether a name is in the table for this particular implementation is linear search. The idea behind linear search is that if the first (and in this case the only) occurrence of the name in the table is found an index i will 'point' to it, if the name is not present in the table then we can arrange for the index i to point off the end of the table. This problem has already been dealt with in Chapter 16. The specification for the version of *find* needed here is:

$$\begin{aligned}
&\textit{find } (nm : Name) \; i : \mathbb{N} \\
&\textsf{ext rd } names : Name\text{-}array \\
&\qquad \textsf{rd } n : Number \\
&\textsf{post } i \in \{1, \ldots, n+1\} \land \\
&\qquad nm \notin names(1, \ldots, i-1) \land \\
&\qquad (i < n+1 \land nm = names(i) \\
&\qquad \quad \lor \\
&\qquad i = n+1)
\end{aligned}$$

The refinement of this function procedure exactly mirrors that of Chapter 16 and will not be repeated. The final code for the operation is in Fig. 17.16.

17.6.4 The Final Step

The operations that use the predicate of the form $\exists i \in \{1, \ldots, n\} \cdot names(i) = nm$ can be refined by introducing a local variable i and then setting it to the result of $find(nm)$. This will establish an environment where the predicate can be replaced by $i = n+1$, or by $i < n+1$ if its negation is required. This transformation can be applied to each of the relevant operations. The result is shown in Fig. 17.16.

17.7 A Summary of the Approach

We can summarize the approach:

$find\,(nm:Name)\;:\mathbb{N}$
ext rd $names:Name\text{-}array$
  rd $n:Number\;\triangleq$
  [**dcl** $i:\mathbb{N}$ **in**
  $i:=1;$
  do $names(i)\neq nm$ **cand** $i<n+1\to i:=i+1$ **od** ;
  return i]

$start\text{-}day\,()$
ext wr $n:Number\;\triangleq$
  $n:=0$

$enter\,(nm:Name)$
ext wr $names:Name\text{-}array$
  wr $n:Number\;\triangleq$
  [**dcl** $i:\mathbb{N}$ **in**
  $i:=find(nm);$
  if $i\neq n+1\to$ **skip**
  [] $i=n+1\to n:=n+1;$
              $names(n):=nm$
  fi]

$leave\,(nm:Name)$
ext wr $names:Name\text{-}array$
  wr $n:Number\;\triangleq$
  [**dcl** $i:\mathbb{N}$ **in**
  $i:=find(nm);$
  if $i\neq n+1\to names(i):=names(n);$
                 $n:=n-1$
  [] $i=n+1\to$ **skip**
  fi]

$check\,(nm:Name)\;:\mathbb{B}$
ext rd $names:Name\text{-}array$
  rd $n:Number\;\triangleq$
  [**dcl** $i:\mathbb{N}$ **in**
  $i:=find(nm);$
  return $i<n+1$]

Fig. 17.16. The final code for the security system.

17. Data refinement

Step 1. Given a state

    state Abs **of**
        $a : A$
        inv $mk\text{-}Abs(a) \triangleq inv(a)$
        init $mk\text{-}Abs(a) \triangleq init(a)$
    end

and an operation op defined on that state

    op
    chg $a : A$
    pre $pre(a)$
    post $post(\overleftarrow{a}, a)$

discover a new state *Refinement* together with a new invariant $inv_1(c)$ which will be easier to implement than the original abstract state. The state may contain additional information that can be used in the implementation.

    state Con **of**
        $k : K$
        inv $mk\text{-}Con(k) \triangleq inv_1(k)$
        init $mk\text{-}Con(k) \triangleq \ldots$
    end

Step 2. Construct a coupling invariant based on a conjunction of terms involving total, onto functions defined between the new refinement state and the abstract state:

    $couple : Con \times Abs \to \mathbb{B}$
    $couple\,(mk\text{-}Con(k), mk\text{-}Abs(a)) \triangleq a = retr(k)$

where

    $retr : K \to A$

The new initialization is given by $init(retr(k))$.

Step 3. Transform the specification. The frame $a : A$ is replaced by $k : K$ where K is the domain of the retrieve function and A is the range of the retrieve function. The pre- and post-conditions are transformed by replacing a by $retr(k)$ and $\overleftarrow{a}$ by $retr(\overleftarrow{k})$ to give:

    op_1
    chg $k : K$
    pre $pre(retr(k))$

post $post(retr(\overleftarrow{k}), retr(k))$

Step 4. The purpose of this step is to try and eliminate *retr* from both pre- and post-conditions so that specifications of operations are in terms of the refined state and thus possible to implement. By examining the expressions occurring in pre- and post-conditions, try to identify and prove any 'interesting theorems' that relate the abstract and the refined state, typically post-conditions will be of the form:

$$retr(k) = f(retr(\overleftarrow{k}))$$

The approach is to look for theorems which will swop f and *retr*; something like:

$$f(retr(k)) = retr(g(k))$$

for some function g. In many cases such theorems will provide insight into the representation – hence the idea of 'interesting theorems'.

Step 5. Use the theorems together with the equivalent specification rule to transform the specification and remove any reference to the coupling invariant. Using the theorems, post-conditions of the form

$$retr(k) = f(retr(\overleftarrow{k}))$$

can then be written

$$retr(k) = retr(g(\overleftarrow{k}))$$

and, since *retr* is total and $k = g(k) \Rightarrow retr(k) = retr(g(k))$, this can be replaced in a post-condition (using the replace specification rule) by

$$k = g(\overleftarrow{k})$$

an expression with no retrieve functions.

Examination of pre-conditions will also suggest transformations of a similar kind, but remember the implication is the other way around.

17.8 Summary

In this chapter the concept of data refinement has been introduced. The method and rules for data refinement have been introduced informally. Both data and program refinement have been done in tandem, assuming that the two refinement techniques interact correctly. These ideas need to be put on a formal footing – the task of the next chapter.

18. A Theory of Data Refinement

Examples of both program and data refinement have been shown. We would like to be able to choose at each refinement stage whether to do algorithmic or data refinement. The rules for data refinement given so far only allow specifications to be refined; to develop executable code it is necessary to do all the data refinement first followed by the algorithmic refinement. It could be that an intermediate data representation would be just right for developing an algorithm, but this might involve data types that do not exist in the final executable language. Having carried out a program refinement it would be useful to be able to do a further data refinement; however this would need some theory to guarantee that if individual components of a program are refined, and the components are put back together, the result is still a data refinement. Roughly speaking what is required is that if $F(X)$ is a program structure with a component denoted by X and if the component S is data refined by the component S', written $S \preceq S'$, then $F(S) \preceq F(S')$. This would mean that components of a program could be data refined independently of each other and put them back together again. This is the data refinement equivalent of Theorem 11.7 on page 196, and the two ideas together will allow a developer to refine a program either by carrying out a algorithmic refinement or a data refinement. It would also encouraging the removal of the distinction between the two refinement techniques. The previous chapter only considered the refinement of implicit specifications, these ideas need to be extended to the refinement of any command or program.

18.1 An Approach to Data Refinement

Given a coupling invariant

$$CI : Con \times Abs \rightarrow \mathbb{B}$$

the coupling invariant CI can be thought of as a command that starts its execution in the concrete state, the input values to CI are in Con, and the execution terminates in the abstract state, the outcomes are in Abs. This interpretation fits with its relational definition. Now in Chapter 2 we considered an alternative interpretation of a command, that of defining it

18.1 An Approach to Data Refinement

as a predicate transformer. However there are two state spaces to deal with, how can the coupling invariant be considered as a predicate transformer? In the previous chapter we saw how a specification of the form

    op
    chg $a : A$
    pre $pre(a)$
    post $post(\overleftarrow{a}, a)$

was transformed by data refinement into

    [con $c : A$ in
    op_1
    chg $k : K$
    pre $\exists a : A \cdot CI(k, a) \wedge pre(a) \wedge c = a$
    post $\exists a : A \cdot CI(k, a) \wedge post(c, a)$]

Consider the form of the pre- and post-condition, in both instances (ignoring the logical constant for the moment) these can be written in the form:

$\exists a \in A \cdot CI(k, a) \wedge P(a)$

We could define a predicate transformer rep given by

$rep(P(a)) \triangleq \exists a \in A \cdot CI(k, a) \wedge P(a)$

Notice that if P is defined over Abs, then $rep(P)$ is defined over Con. The data refined specification can be written in terms of rep:

    [con $c : A$ in
    op_1
    chg $k : Con$
    pre $rep(pre(a) \wedge c = a)$
    post $rep(post(c, k))$]

This idea can be taken further: consider an abstract state that defines two sets of variables a and g.

    state Abs of
        $a : A$
        $g : G$
    end

Any predicate P defined on this state will therefore depend on the variables a and g. We now choose to do a data-refinement to give a new concrete state where the set of variables g are left alone, but we replace the set of variables a by a new set k.

state Con of
   $k : K$
   $g : G$
end

The data refinement is defined in terms of (rep, a, k); note that the the concrete variables denoted by k cannot be free in any abstract programs. It turns out that this data refinement need not be defined in terms of a coupling invariant, but can be defined in terms of a suitable predicate transformer rep with just two simple properties. The predicate transform will transform predicates defined over a and g into predicates defined over k and g – thus we can transform any predicate over the abstract state into a predicate over the concrete state; and since all commands can be defined in terms of predicates we can transform all commands. First a closer look at rep:

$$\text{if } P : A \times G \to \mathbb{B} \text{ then } rep \circ P : K \times G \to \mathbb{B}$$

we can write the signature of rep as follows:

$$rep : (A \times G \to \mathbb{B}) \to (K \times G \to \mathbb{B})$$

The next question is: what is a 'suitable predicate transformer' and what are the two simple properties that such a transformer should have?

Definition 18.1
A data refinement predicate transformer rep satisfies

rep is monotonic: $(\forall a : A \cdot R \Rightarrow S) \Rightarrow (\forall k : K \cdot rep(R) \Rightarrow rep(S))$
rep is $\vee$-distributive: $rep(\exists i \in I \cdot P_i) = \exists i \in I \cdot rep(P_i)$

If the reader is at all worried by the lack of hard facts about rep, only that it satisfies these two fairly simple constraints, remember that we identified more than one program refinement relation in Chapter 5 and then chose the one to use by the software engineering requirements of the problem. The same approach applies to data refinement – we can later give more substance to rep. A shorter name for data refinement predicate transformer would also be useful, from now we shall call them just refinement transformers. Now some simple properties enjoyed by refinement transformers:

Lemma 18.1
   $rep(\text{false}) = \text{false}$
   $rep(\forall i \in I \cdot P_i) \Rightarrow \forall i \in I \cdot rep(P_i)$

and if R is dependent only on g:

   $rep(R) \Rightarrow R$

□

18.1 An Approach to Data Refinement

We will need another data transformer based on *rep*, its definition takes a (by now) familiar form:

Definition 18.2
$$\overline{rep}(R) \triangleq \neg\, rep(\neg R)$$

Some useful properties of this operator that we shall need later on are:

Lemma 18.2
$\overline{rep}$ is monotonic: $(\forall\, a : A \cdot R \Rightarrow S) \Rightarrow (\forall\, k : K \cdot \overline{rep}(R) \Rightarrow \overline{rep}(S))$
$\overline{rep}$ is $\wedge$-distributive: $\overline{rep}(\forall\, i \in I \cdot P_i) = \forall\, i \in I \cdot \overline{rep}(P_i)$
$\overline{rep}(\text{true}) = \text{true}$
$\exists\, i \in I \cdot \overline{rep}(P_i) \Rightarrow \overline{rep}(\exists\, i \in I \cdot P_i)$

and if R is dependent only on g:

$$R \Rightarrow \overline{rep}(R)$$

Proof
From the definition of $\overline{rep}$ and Lemma 18.1
∎

Another useful lemma is the following:

Lemma 18.3
If R is a predicate over a and g and Q is a predicate over g, then

$$rep(R) \wedge Q \Rightarrow rep(R \wedge Q)$$

Proof
Since a is not free in Q we have

$\qquad Q \Rightarrow (\forall\, a \cdot R \Rightarrow R \wedge Q)$
$\Longleftrightarrow$ monotonicity of *rep*
$\qquad Q \Rightarrow (rep(R) \Rightarrow rep(R \wedge Q))$
$\Longleftrightarrow$ predicate calculus
$\qquad rep(R) \wedge Q \Rightarrow rep(R \wedge Q)$

∎

Since commands are also predicate transformers, a data transformer *rep* can be combined with them. We will use ∘ to denote function (in the sense of predicate transformer) composition, thus:

$\langle f \circ S \rangle R \triangleq f(\langle S \rangle R) \qquad [f \circ S]R \triangleq f([S]R)$
$\langle S \circ f \rangle R \triangleq \langle S \rangle f(R) \qquad [S \circ f]R \triangleq [S]f(R)$

Given these definitions, it is possible to interpret *rep* as a command that starts execution in the concrete state and completes in the abstract state, in fact we could almost use ';' in place of '∘'.

We can now write down what we mean by a data refinement:

Definition 18.3
If $rep \circ S \sqsubseteq S' \circ rep$ then $S \preceq S'$.

Consider what this means, interpret rep as a statement, this definition says that if the program defined by moving from *Con* to *Abs* using rep followed by executing S can be refined by executing S' followed by using rep to move from *Con* to *Abs*, then S' is a data refinement of S. Remember that S' executes in the concrete state. It should also be noted that to prove $rep \circ S \sqsubseteq S' \circ rep$ it is necessary to show that for all predicates R over the *abstract state* (this means that the R are independent of the concrete state variables) that

$$[rep \circ S]R \Rightarrow [S' \circ rep]R$$

If the variables that are data refined are inside a block, outside the block the refinement should look like algorithmic refinement:

Theorem 18.1
If, for a data refinement transformer rep, $S \preceq S'$ then

$$[\![\text{dcl } a : A \text{ be st } init \text{ in } S]\!] \sqsubseteq [\![\text{dcl } k : K \text{ be st } rep(init) \text{ in } S']\!]$$

Proof
Let R be any predicate defined over the global variables then

$\quad [\![[\![\text{dcl } a : A \text{ be st } init \text{ in } S]\!]\!] R$
$\Longleftrightarrow$ semantics
$\quad \forall a : A \cdot init \Rightarrow [S]R$
$\Longrightarrow$ monotonicity of rep
$\quad \forall k : K \cdot rep(init) \Rightarrow rep([S]R)$
$\Longrightarrow$ hypothesis
$\quad \forall k : K \cdot rep(init) \Rightarrow [S']rep(R)$
$\Longrightarrow$ Lemma 18.1 and monotonicity of S'
$\quad \forall k : K \cdot rep(init) \Rightarrow [S']R$
$=\quad$ semantics
$\quad [\![[\![\text{dcl } k : K \text{ be st } rep(init) \text{ in } S']\!]\!] R$

■

If we do an algorithmic refinement followed by a data refinement or a data refinement followed by an algorithmic refinement, then the two steps together should look like a data refinement.

Theorem 18.2
If

$$S \sqsubseteq T$$
$$T \preceq T'$$
$$T' \sqsubseteq U'$$

then

$$S \preceq U'$$

□

How does *rep* interact with domains?

Theorem 18.3
If $S \sqsubseteq S'$ then $\mathcal{G}(S') \Rightarrow \overline{rep}(\mathcal{G}(S))$

Proof
From the various definitions. ■

■

Next a lemma that show that *rep* commutes with the primitive commands.

Lemma 18.4
If *rep* is a data transformer then

$$rep \circ \text{skip} = \text{skip} \circ rep$$
$$rep \circ \text{loop} = \text{loop} \circ rep$$
$$rep \circ \text{havoc} = \text{havoc} \circ rep$$

Proof
We will just prove the identity for skip; the proof of the others follows a similar pattern.

For R defined over the abstract state:

$[rep \circ \text{skip}]\text{true}$ \qquad $\langle rep \circ \text{skip}\rangle R$

$\Longleftrightarrow$ \qquad $\Longleftrightarrow$

$rep([\text{skip}]\text{true})$ \qquad $rep(\langle \text{skip}\rangle R)$

$\Longleftrightarrow$ \qquad $\Longleftrightarrow$

$rep(\text{true})$ \qquad $rep(R)$

$\Longleftrightarrow$ \qquad $\Longleftrightarrow$

$[\text{skip}]rep(\text{true})$ \qquad $\langle \text{skip}\rangle rep(R)$

$\Longleftrightarrow$ \qquad $\Longleftrightarrow$

$[\text{skip} \circ rep]\text{true}$ \qquad $\langle \text{skip} \circ rep\rangle R$

■

288   18. A Theory of Data Refinement

The first data refinement follows trivially from the above lemma:

Theorem 18.4
skip $\preceq$ skip
loop $\preceq$ loop
havoc $\preceq$ havoc

□

The next theorem about refinement shows how things will go for the semicolon operator:

Theorem 18.5
If $S \preceq S'$ and $T \preceq T'$ then $S\ ;\ T \preceq S'\ ;\ T'$

Proof
For R defined over the abstract state:

$$[rep \circ (S\ ;\ T)]R$$
$$\Longleftrightarrow$$
$$rep([S][T]R)$$
$$\Longrightarrow$$
$$[S']rep([T]R)$$
$$\Longrightarrow$$
$$[S'][T']rep(R)$$
$$\Longleftrightarrow$$
$$[(S'\ ;\ T') \circ rep]R$$

thus $rep \circ (S\ ;\ T) \sqsubseteq (S'\ ;\ T') \circ rep$
∎

Before continuing it is worth considering a series of lemmas to show that a suitable data refinement transformer rep 'distributes' through the various operators of the basic language (note that $\sqsubseteq$ is sometimes needed for left distribution, but that $=$ can be used for right distribution). The $\circ$ operator left-distributes through unbounded choice:

Lemma 18.5
$rep \circ @i \in I \bullet S_i \sqsubseteq @i \in I \bullet rep \circ S_i$

Proof
For R defined over the abstract state:

$$[rep \circ @i \in I \bullet S_i]R$$
$$\Longleftrightarrow$$
$$rep([@i \in I \bullet S_i]R)$$
$$\Longleftrightarrow$$
$$rep(\forall\, i \in I \cdot [S_i]R)$$

$\Longrightarrow$
$$\forall i \in I \cdot rep([S_i]R)$$
$\Longrightarrow$
$$\forall i \in I \cdot [rep \circ S_i]R$$
$\Longrightarrow$
$$[@i \in I \bullet rep \circ S_i]R$$
∎

A simplified version of this theorem holds for bounded choice:

Corollary 18.1
$$rep \circ (S \mathbin{\square} T) \sqsubseteq rep \circ S \mathbin{\square} rep \circ T$$
□

The $\circ$ operator right-distributes through unbounded choice:

Lemma 18.6
$$@i \in I \bullet (S_i \circ rep) = (@i \in I \bullet S_i) \circ rep$$

Proof

For R defined over the abstract state:

$$[(@i \in I \bullet S_i) \circ rep]\text{true} \qquad \langle(@i \in I \bullet S_i) \circ rep\rangle R$$
$\Longleftrightarrow$
$$[@i \in I \bullet S_i]rep(\text{true}) \qquad \langle(@i \in I \bullet S_i)\rangle rep(R)$$
$\Longleftrightarrow$
$$\forall i \in I \cdot [S_i]rep(\text{true}) \qquad \forall i \in I \cdot \langle S_i\rangle rep(R)$$
$\Longleftrightarrow$
$$\forall i \in I \cdot [S_i \circ rep]\text{true} \qquad \forall i \in I \cdot \langle S_i \circ rep\rangle R$$
$\Longleftrightarrow$
$$[@i \in I \bullet (S_i \circ rep)]\text{true} \qquad \langle@i \in I \bullet (S_i \circ rep)\rangle R$$

∎

Again a simplified version holds for bounded choice:

Corollary 18.2
$$(S \mathbin{\square} T) \circ rep = S \circ rep \mathbin{\square} T \circ rep$$
□

With these lemmas, is it possible to derive more rules about data refinement.

Theorem 18.6
If $S_i \preceq S'_i$ then $@i \in I \bullet S_i \preceq @i \in I \bullet S'_i$

Proof
By Lemmas 18.1 and 18.2.
∎

Corollary 18.3
If $S \preceq S'$ and $T \preceq T'$ then $S \mathbin{\square} T \preceq S' \mathbin{\square} T'$
□

Lemma 18.7
$rep \circ (p \to S) = \overline{rep}(p) \to rep \circ S$

Proof

For R defined over the abstract state:

$[rep \circ (p \to S)]\text{true}$
$\iff$ semantics
$rep(p \Rightarrow [S]\text{true})$
$\iff$ predicate calculus
$rep(\neg p \lor [S]\text{true})$
$\iff$ $\lor$-distributivity
$rep(\neg p) \lor rep([S]\text{true})$
$\iff$
$\neg \overline{rep}(p) \lor [rep \circ S]\text{true}$
$\iff$ predicate calculus
$\overline{rep}(p) \Rightarrow [rep \circ S]\text{true}$
$\iff$ semantics
$[\overline{rep}(p) \to rep \circ S]\text{true}$

$\langle rep \circ (p \to S)\rangle R$
$\iff$ semantics
$rep(p \Rightarrow \langle S\rangle R)$
$\iff$ predicate calculus
$rep(\neg p \lor \langle S\rangle R)$
$\iff$ $\lor$-distributivity
$rep(\neg p) \lor rep(\langle S\rangle R)$
$\iff$
$\neg \overline{rep}(p) \lor \langle rep \circ S\rangle R$
$\iff$ predicate calculus
$\overline{rep}(p) \Rightarrow \langle rep \circ S\rangle R$
$\iff$ semantics
$\langle \overline{rep}(p) \to rep \circ S\rangle R$

∎

Lemma 18.8
$(p \to S) \circ rep = p \to S \circ rep$

Proof

For R defined over the abstract state:

$[(p \to S) \circ rep]\text{true}$
$\implies$ semantics
$[(p \to S)]rep(\text{true})$

$\langle(p \to S) \circ rep\rangle R$
$\implies$ semantics
$\langle(p \to S)\rangle rep(R)$

$$\begin{array}{ll} \implies & \text{semantics} \\ & p \implies [S]rep(\text{true}) \\ \implies & \\ & p \implies [S \circ rep]\text{true} \\ \iff & \\ & [p \to S \circ rep]\text{true} \end{array} \qquad \begin{array}{ll} \implies & \text{semantics} \\ & p \implies \langle S \rangle rep(R) \\ \implies & \\ & p \implies \langle S \circ rep \rangle R \\ \iff & \\ & \langle p \to S \circ rep \rangle R \end{array}$$

∎

Theorem 18.7
If $S \preceq S'$ then $p \to S \preceq \overline{rep}(p) \to S'$

Proof
From Lemmas 18.7 and 18.8
∎

Corollary 18.4
If $S \preceq S'$ and $q \implies p$ then $p \to S \preceq \overline{rep}(q) \to S'$

Proof
From Lemma 18.2.
∎

At this point it is worth pausing for a moment and considering using some of the properties we have proved so far. We know that for any command S that $S = \mathcal{G}(S) \to S$. Suppose that $S \preceq S'$ then there are at least two possible refinement routes. The first is

$$\begin{array}{ll} & S \\ \preceq & \text{assumption} \\ & S' \\ = & \text{semantics} \\ & \mathcal{G}(S') \to S' \end{array}$$

the other route is:

$$\begin{array}{ll} & S \\ = & \text{semantics} \\ & \mathcal{G}(S) \to S \\ \preceq & \text{Theorem 18.6} \\ & \overline{rep}(\mathcal{G}(S)) \to S' \\ = & \\ & \ldots \end{array}$$

and things look a little inconsistent, however we can proceed:

...

$$
\begin{aligned}
&= \quad \text{semantics} \\
&\quad \overline{rep}(\mathcal{G}(S)) \rightarrow \mathcal{G}(S') \rightarrow S' \\
&= \quad \text{Theorem 3.14} \\
&\quad \overline{rep}(\mathcal{G}(S)) \wedge \mathcal{G}(S') \rightarrow S' \\
&= \quad \text{Theorem 18.3} \\
&\quad \mathcal{G}(S') \rightarrow S'
\end{aligned}
$$

and all is well. Assertions can be moved through a data refinement:

Theorem 18.8
If $S \preceq S'$ then $\{p\}S \preceq \{rep(p)\}S'$.

Proof

$$
\begin{aligned}
&\quad [rep \circ \{p\}S]R \\
&= \quad \text{semantics} \\
&\quad rep(p \wedge [S]R) \\
&\Longrightarrow \quad \wedge\text{-distributivity} \\
&\quad rep(p) \wedge rep([S]R) \\
&= \\
&\quad rep(p) \wedge [rep \circ S]R \\
&\Longrightarrow \\
&\quad rep(p) \wedge [S' \circ rep]R \\
&= \quad \text{semantics} \\
&\quad [\{rep(p)\}S' \circ rep]R
\end{aligned}
$$

■

Proceeding with the constructors used to define the iteration operator, we can show the following series of properties:

Lemma 18.9
If $S \preceq S'$ then $S^n \preceq S'^n$

Proof
By induction using Theorems 18.4 and 18.5.
■

Lemma 18.10
If $S \preceq S'$ then $S^* \preceq S'^*$

Proof
By Lemma 18.9 and Theorem 18.6.
■

Given the recurrent definitions for circ S and circ S', and the definition of $\overline{rep}$, by using induction the following lemma can be proved:

Lemma 18.11
$$\text{circ } S' \Rightarrow \overline{rep}(\text{circ } S)$$
□

Using this, the following refinement rule can be proved:

Lemma 18.12
If $S \preceq S'$ then $S^\circ \preceq S'^\circ$

Proof
For R defined over the abstract state:

$$[rep \circ S^\circ]R$$
$$=$$
$$rep([S^\circ]R)$$
$$=$$
$$rep([\text{circ } S \to \text{loop}]R)$$
$$=$$
$$rep(\neg \text{circ } S)$$
$$=$$
$$\neg \overline{rep}(\text{circ } S)$$
$$\Longrightarrow$$
$$\neg (\text{circ } S')$$
$$=$$
$$\text{circ } S' \Rightarrow [\text{loop}] rep(R)$$
$$=$$
$$[(\text{circ } S' \to \text{loop}) \circ rep]R$$
$$=$$
$$[S'^\circ \circ rep]R$$
■

Theorem 18.9
If $S \preceq S'$ then $S^\star \preceq S'^\star$

Proof
$$rep \circ S^\star$$
$$=$$
$$rep \circ S^\star \sqcap rep \circ S^\circ$$
$$\sqsubseteq$$
$$S'^\star \circ rep \sqcap S'^\circ \circ rep$$
$$=$$
$$(S'^\star \sqcap S'^\circ) \circ rep$$
$$=$$
$$S'^\star \circ rep$$
■

18. A Theory of Data Refinement

Theorem 18.10
If $S \preceq S'$ and $rep(\mathcal{G}(S)) \Rightarrow \mathcal{G}(S')$ then if S fi $\preceq$ if S' fi.

Proof
Now

$$\text{if } S \text{ fi} = S \,[\!]\, \neg \mathcal{G}(S) \to \text{loop}$$

and

$$S \preceq S'$$

and by Theorem 18.4, Corollary 18.4 and the hypothesis:

$$\neg \mathcal{G}(S) \to \text{loop} \preceq \neg \mathcal{G}(S') \to \text{loop}$$

Thus by Corollary 18.3

$$S \,[\!]\, \neg \mathcal{G}(S) \to \text{loop} \preceq S \,[\!]\, \neg \mathcal{G}(S') \to \text{loop}$$

∎

Theorem 18.11
If $S \preceq S'$ and $rep(\mathcal{G}(S)) \Rightarrow \mathcal{G}(S')$ then do S od $\preceq$ do S' od

Proof
Now

$$\text{do } S \text{ od} = S^* \,;\, \neg \mathcal{G}(S) \to \text{skip}$$

by Theorem 18.9

$$S^* \preceq S'^*$$

and by Theorem 18.4, Corollary 18.4 and the hypothesis:

$$\neg \mathcal{G}(S) \to \text{skip} \preceq \neg \mathcal{G}(S') \to \text{skip}$$

Thus by Theorem 18.5

$$S^* \,;\, \neg \mathcal{G}(S) \to \text{skip} \preceq S'^* \,;\, \neg \mathcal{G}(S') \to \text{skip}$$

∎

The refinement rules for selection and iteration both rely on the fact that the improper outcome $\perp$ can be replaced by any proper outcome during refinement.

The refinement rules for selection or iteration in this form are simple, but not useful. For an executable program the body of either of these statements is a set of guarded commands combined with the choice operator. Typically we are trying to refine a command of the form (taking a simple example):

$$\text{if } p \to T \,[\!]\, q \to U \text{ fi}$$

18.1 An Approach to Data Refinement

where both T and U are total commands. The guard of the body of this command (which we shall denote by S) is easily calculated:

$$\mathcal{G}(S) = \mathcal{G}(p \to T \,\square\, q \to U) = p \vee q$$

The first step is to find a refinement S' of S that satisfies the constraints of Theorem 18.10. The easiest way to do this is to find data refinements of T and U – typically both of these will be specification statements, so their refinements T' and U' can be calculated. By Theorems 18.3 and 18.7 we have

$$p \to T \,\square\, q \to U \preceq \overline{rep}(p) \to T' \,\square\, \overline{rep}(q) \to U'$$

the guard of the refinement is again easily calculated to be $\overline{rep}(p) \vee \overline{rep}(q)$, so providing

$$rep(p \vee q) \Rightarrow \overline{rep}(p) \vee \overline{rep}(q)$$

then by Theorem 18.10

if $p \to T \,\square\, q \to U$ fi $\preceq$ if $\overline{rep}(p) \to T' \,\square\, \overline{rep}(q) \to U'$ fi

This analysis can be easily generalized to give the following theorem:

Theorem 18.12

$$\text{if } \left\{ \begin{array}{c} S_i \text{ are total} \\ S_i \preceq S'_i \\ \exists i \in I \cdot rep(p_i) \Rightarrow \exists i \in I \cdot \overline{rep}(p_i) \end{array} \right\} \text{ then}$$

if $@i \in I \bullet p_i \to S_i$ fi $\preceq$ if $@i \in I \bullet \overline{rep}(p_i) \to S'_i$ fi

□

An identical analysis gives the equivalent theorem for iteration:

Theorem 18.13

$$\text{if } \left\{ \begin{array}{c} S_i \text{ are total} \\ S_i \preceq S'_i \\ \exists i \in I \cdot rep(p_i) \Rightarrow \exists i \in I \cdot \overline{rep}(p_i) \end{array} \right\} \text{ then}$$

do $@i \in I \bullet p_i \to S_i$ od $\preceq$ do $@i \in I \bullet \overline{rep}(p_i) \to S'_i$ od

□

18.1.1 The Data Refinement of Declarations

The refinement of a block containing a local variable is very easy, by Theorem 18.1 we have if rep' relates predicates over A to predicates over K and $S \preceq S'$ using rep then

$$[\![\text{dcl } a : A \text{ be st } init \text{ in } S]\!] \sqsubseteq [\![\text{dcl } k : K \text{ be st } rep(init) \text{ in } S']\!]$$

the local variable has now been data-refined – any global variables can now be refined in the usual way. The reader should be reminded that if $rep(init)$ is not a useful initialization, the equivalent specification rule can be used to strengthen it. Without initialization we get:

$$[\![\text{dcl } a : A \text{ in } S]\!] \sqsubseteq [\![\text{dcl } k : K \text{ in } S']\!]$$

The same approach works for the definition command:

$$\text{def } a : A \text{ be st } init \text{ in } S \sqsubseteq \text{def } k : K \text{ be st } rep(init) \text{ in } S'$$

The refinement of the other variants of commands that introduce new identifiers can be easily deduced from the above. Note that in general it is not necessary to refine let commands.

18.1.2 Refinement and Specifications

In many instances a data refinement step involves a specification command, the first theorem formalizes the informal derivation in the previous chapter. The proofs are adapted from [27].

Lemma 18.13
Validity – the following refinement is always valid:

$$a, g : [\ pre,\ \ post\ ] \preceq k, g : [\ rep(pre),\ \ rep(post)\ ]$$

Proof
For R defined over the abstract state:

$\quad rep([a, g : [\ pre,\ \ post\ ]]R)$
$\iff$ semantics
$\quad rep(pre \wedge \forall a : A, g : G \cdot post \Rightarrow R)$
$\implies$ Lemma 18.2
$\quad rep(pre) \wedge rep(\forall a : A, g : G \cdot post \Rightarrow R)$
$\implies$ Lemma 18.1
$\quad rep(pre) \wedge \forall a : A, g : G \cdot post \Rightarrow R$
$\implies$ monotonicity of rep
$\quad rep(pre) \wedge \forall k : K, g : G \cdot rep(post) \Rightarrow rep(R)$

$\Longleftrightarrow$ semantics

$$[k, g : [\ rep(pre), \quad rep(post) \ ]] rep(R)$$

$\Longleftrightarrow$

$$[(k, g : [\ rep(pre), \quad rep(post) \ ]) \circ rep] R$$

∎

It is easy to show that any algorithmic refinement of a calculated data refinement is a data refinement of the abstract specification.

Corollary 18.5
If $k : [\ rep(pre), \quad rep(post) \ ] \sqsubseteq S$ then $a : [\ pre, \quad post \ ] \preceq S$.
□

The refinement that is calculated from a specification is the best one, in the sense that any data refinement that we construct by other means is a program refinement of the new specification.

Lemma 18.14
Generality – for all programs S, if

$$a, g : [\ pre, \quad post \ ] \preceq S$$

then

$$k, g : [\ rep(pre), \quad rep(post) \ ] \sqsubseteq S$$

Proof
let R be a predicate on the concrete state, and is thus a predicate on k and g, then

$$[k, g : [\ rep(pre), \quad rep(post) \ ]] R$$

$\Longleftrightarrow$ semantics

$$rep(pre) \wedge (\forall k : K, g : G \cdot rep(post) \Rightarrow R)$$

$\Longrightarrow$ property of $\vee$

$$rep(pre) \wedge (\forall a, g \cdot post \Rightarrow \bigvee_{\forall k : K, g : G \cdot rep(p) \Rightarrow R} p)$$

$\Longrightarrow$ property of rep

$$rep(pre \wedge \forall a, g \cdot post \Rightarrow \bigvee_{\forall k : K, g : G \cdot rep(p) \Rightarrow R} p)$$

$\Longrightarrow$ semantics

$$rep([a, g : [\ pre, \quad post \ ]] (\bigvee_{\forall k : K, g : G \cdot rep(p) \Rightarrow R} p))$$

$\Rightarrow$ hypothesis

$$[S]rep(\bigvee_{\forall k : K, g : G \cdot rep(p) \Rightarrow R} p)$$

$\Rightarrow$ property of rep

$$[S] \bigvee_{\forall k : K, g : G \cdot rep(p) \Rightarrow R} rep(p)$$

$\Rightarrow$ property of $\vee$, monotonicity of S

$$[S]R$$

■

These to lemmas can be put together to show that the calculated data refinement is, in some sense, always the best.

Theorem 18.14
$$a, g : [\ pre, \quad post\ ] \preceq S$$

if and only if

$$k, g : [\ rep(pre), \quad rep(post)\ ] \sqsubseteq S$$

□

If the refinement only involves those variables that are not common to both the abstract state and the concrete state, the refinement rule is slightly simpler, and familiar in its form:

Theorem 18.15
If

> S does not change any g
> $rep(pre) \Rightarrow [S]rep(post)$

then

$$a : [\ pre, \quad post\ ] \preceq S$$

□

It is now possible to give a refinement rule for assignment, later we shall provide a more useful one.

Corollary 18.6
If

> S does not change any g
> $\delta(E : X) \Rightarrow [S]rep(a = E)$

then

$$a := E \preceq S$$

□

18.2 Data Refinement in Practice

In the motivation for this chapter we used the fact that *rep* could be defined as

$$rep(P) \triangleq \exists a \cdot CI \wedge P$$

Rather than use this as the definition of *rep*, we just imposed the conditions on *rep* defined in Definition 18.1. It is easy to show that the above definition of *rep* satisfies these constraints. Thus we can use this definition of data refinement in our calculations. In addition $\overline{rep}$ has a simple form:

$$\overline{rep}(P) = \forall a \cdot CI \Rightarrow P$$

When *rep* has this relatively simple form, which agrees with the definition for data refinement given in the earlier chapter, we can consider some simple extensions to the rules. If we are refining a specification that does not change all of the (non-shared) abstract variables, it must be transformed into one that does so that the data refinement transformations can be applied – this is easy to do, but rather messy. If not all the abstract variables are changed, then we would expect that it is only necessary to deal with those abstract variables that are changed. The refinement does involve introducing some logical constants, but they are usually in a context where they are easy to remove.

Theorem 18.16
If a is partitioned into two sets of variables $b:B$ and $c:C$ where the abstract variables denoted by b are not changed by the specification, then

$$c, g : [\ pre,\quad post\ ] \sqsubseteq [\![\operatorname{con} a : A \text{ in } k, g : [\ CI \wedge pre,\quad \exists c \cdot CI \wedge post\ ]]\!]$$

Proof

$$c, g : [\ pre,\quad post\ ]$$

$$=$$

$$[\![\operatorname{con} cb : B \text{ in } b, c, g : [\ pre \wedge b = cb,\quad post \wedge b = cb\ ]]\!]$$

$$\preceq$$

$$[\![\operatorname{con} cb : B \text{ in}$$
$$k, g : [\ \exists b : B, c : C \cdot CI \wedge pre \wedge b = cb,$$
$$\exists b : B, c : C \cdot CI \wedge post \wedge b = cb\ ]]\!]$$

$$=$$

$$[\![\operatorname{con} cb : B \text{ in}$$

$$k, g : [\ (\exists c : C \cdot CI \land pre)[b\backslash cb], \quad (\exists c : C \cdot CI \land post)[b\backslash cb]\ ]$$

$$=$$

$$[\![\, \text{con } cb : B \text{ in } k, g : [\ \exists c \cdot CI \land pre, \quad \exists c : C \cdot CI \land post\ ]\,]\!]$$

$$=$$

$$[\![\, \text{con } a : A \text{ in } k, g : [\ CI \land pre, \quad \exists c : C \cdot CI \land post\ ]\,]\!]$$

■

Corollary 18.7
If a is partitioned into two sets of variables $b : B$ and $c : C$, CI is total and of the form $CJ(b, k) \land CK(c, k)$, and the b abstract variables do not occur in the specification then:

$$c, g : [\ pre, \quad post\ ] \sqsubseteq k, g : [\ \exists c : C \cdot CK \land pre, \quad \exists c : C \cdot CK \land post\ ]$$

□

The requirements of this corollary may seem rather strict, but for many data refinements they are the norm. The corollary means that when carrying out a refinement, we only need concentrate on the variables in question.

18.3 Another View of Data Refinement

Supposing that we have a data refinement *rep* between two states *Abs* and *Con* given by

$$rep(P(a)) = \exists a : A \cdot CI(k, a) \land P(a)$$

Another approach to understanding data refinement is to carry out a data refinement in three stages. The first stage is to add the concrete state to the abstract state, the second stage is to carry out some algorithmic refinement, and the final stage is to remove the abstract state. The second stage is only necessary if some adjustments need to be made and we can ignore this under certain circumstances, more of this later – for the first analysis we shall ignore the middle stage and concentrate on the first and last.

In the first stage we just introduce the concrete variables and carry out the data refinement $(AJ, , k)$, we move from

state *Abs* of
    $a : A$
end

to

state *Abs-Con* of
    $a : A$
    $k : K$
end

18.3 Another View of Data Refinement

In this refinement step, the abstract variables being left alone, they are not being refined. Using a coupling invariant AJ defined in terms of the full refinement relation:

$$AJ : (Con \times Abs) \times () \to \mathbb{B}$$
$$AJ(k, a,) \triangleq CI(k, a)$$

The refinement relation rep_c based on this first step is given by:

$$rep_c(P(a)) = CI(k, a) \land P(a)$$

As there are no abstract variables being refined in this step, the empty quantification has been dropped. Operations on the abstract state are extended to operations on the combined state using the normal data-refinement techniques. It turns out that the new operations, if viewed through glasses that only 'see' the abstract state are just algorithmic refinements of the original operations. The next step is (after some adjustments) to remove the abstract state. A data refinement is carried out to do this, we get a refinement based on (true, a,)

state Con of
   $k : K$
end

with a coupling invariant

$$JC : () \times Abs \to \mathbb{B}$$
$$JC(, a) \triangleq \text{true}$$

this just throws the abstract state components away. The refinement transformation rep_r for the second step is given by:

$$rep_r(P(a, k)) = \exists\, a : A \cdot P(a, k)$$

The following theorem shows that the two steps are equivalent to a single data refinement step using CI in the usual way:

Theorem 18.17
If S is data refined to M by rep_c and M to T by rep_r then S is data refined to T by rep.

Proof
For all R not containing k, $S \preceq M$ is defined by

$$rep_c \circ S \sqsubseteq M \circ rep_c$$

which is equivalent to

$$CI \land [S]R \Rightarrow [M](CI \land R)$$

Now $M \preceq T$ is defined by

$rep_r \circ M \sqsubseteq T \circ rep_r$

which is equivalent to, for all S:

$\exists a : A \cdot [M]S \Rightarrow [T](\exists a : A \cdot S)$

Now

$\exists a : A \cdot CI \wedge [S]R$

$\Longrightarrow$

$\exists a : A \cdot [M](CI \wedge R)$

$\Longleftrightarrow$

$[T](\exists a : A \cdot CI \wedge R)$

Thus $S \preceq T$.
∎

The first stage can be thought of as introducing the operations on the concrete state as a puppet that is linked by strings defined by the coupling invariant to the puppet master – operations on the abstract state. Thus as the puppet master 'executes' the operations of the abstract state, the puppet executes the equivalent operations of the concrete state. If we are happy with the puppets movements, the second stage is equivalent to hiding the puppet master and the strings so that we just view the puppet.

The next theorem states that if the abstract variables only are considered then M is an algorithmic refinement of S:

Theorem 18.18

if $\left\{ \begin{array}{c} R \text{ independent of } k \\ [S]R \Rightarrow [M]R \\ CI \wedge [S]\text{true} \Rightarrow [S]CI \end{array} \right\}$ then $S \preceq M$

Proof

$CI \wedge [S]R$

$\Longleftrightarrow$

$CI \wedge [S]\text{true} \wedge [S]R$

$\Longrightarrow$

$[M]R \wedge [M]CI$

$\Longrightarrow$

$[M](CI \wedge R)$

∎

The first part of the hypothesis states that R is a predicate that is independent of k (the concrete part of the state): we are just looking at the abstract state – we are looking at the puppet master. The second part of the hypothesis states that M program refines S. The third part states that when S terminates, the coupling invariant is preserved. Under these assumptions S is data refined by M by rep_c.

The next theorem formalizes the idea that if we are happy with the behaviour of the puppet, we can stop looking at the puppet master.

Theorem 18.19

$$\text{if } \left\{ \begin{array}{c} R \text{ independent of } a \\ [M]R \Rightarrow [S]R \\ [S]R \text{ is independent of } a \end{array} \right\} \text{ then } M \preceq S$$

M is data-refined by S using rep_r.

Proof
For R defined over the abstract state:

$\exists\, a : A \cdot [M]R$
$\Longrightarrow$ hypothesis
$\exists\, a : A \cdot [M](\exists\, a : A \cdot R)$
$\Longrightarrow$
$[M](\exists\, a : A \cdot R)$
$\Longrightarrow$
$[S](\exists\, a : A \cdot R)$

∎

Considering just the concrete variables, S is an algorithmic refinement of M. The second assumption states that in M the final values in the concrete state do not depend on the initial values in the abstract state.

It may be that this second condition that $[S]R$ be independent of a is not satisfied after the first stage. It may be necessary to do some algorithmic refinements that transforms M to M', so that in M' the final values do not depend on the initial values. Hence the middle step mentioned above.

18.4 Functional Refinement

We have already stated in Chapter 17 that in most cases the refinement relation can be written using a retrieve function, the refinement relation is of the form

$CI : Con \times Abs \to \mathbb{B}$
$CI(k, a) = (a = retr(k))$

where

$retr : Con \to Abs$

In this case we can easily calculate rep and $\overline{rep}$:

$rep(p) = \overline{rep}(p) = p[a\backslash retr(k)]$

The refinement rules for specifications using this form of coupling invariant have already been given in Chapter 17.

18.5 An Alternative Data Refinement of Assignments

If we use the (two/three stage) approach described in Section 18.3 then there is a way of refining assignment statements without translating them into specifications. To refine the abstract assignment $a := AE$ the first step is to guess at a refinement CE of the expression AE which is defined over the abstract variables. Next we introduce the concrete variables while maintaining the coupling invariant:

Theorem 18.20
For an abstract expression AE and a refinement of this expression CE, if

$CI \Rightarrow [a, k :- AE, CE] CI$

then

$a := AE \preceq a, k := AE, CE$

Proof
For R independent of k we have

$\quad CI \wedge [a := AE]R$
$\Longleftrightarrow$
$\quad CI \wedge R[a\backslash AE]$
$\Longrightarrow$ hypothesis
$\quad [a, k := AE, CE] CI \wedge R[a\backslash AE]$
$\Longrightarrow$
$\quad CI[a\backslash AE, k\backslash CE] \wedge R[a\backslash AE]$
$\Longleftrightarrow R$ independent of k
$\quad CI[a\backslash AE, k\backslash CE] \wedge R[a, k\backslash AE]CE$
$\Longleftrightarrow R$ independent of k
$\quad [a, k := AE, CE] CI \wedge R$

■

If the expression CE contains any abstract variables, then at this stage it is necessary to do some algorithmic refinement to remove them. If this has been done we can proceed to the next step:

Theorem 18.21
If CE is independent of the abstract variables a then

$a := AE \preceq \mathsf{skip}$

$k := CE \preceq k := CE$

Proof
$\exists a : A \cdot [a := AE]R$

$\iff$

$\delta(AE : \wedge) \exists a : A \cdot R[a \backslash AE]$

$\implies$ predicate calculus

$\delta(AE : \wedge) \exists a \cdot R$

$\iff$

$[\mathsf{skip}](\exists a \cdot R)$

$\exists a : A \cdot [k := CE]R$

$\iff$

$\delta(AE : \wedge) \exists a : A \cdot R[k \backslash CE]$

$\implies$ predicate calculus

$\delta(AE : \wedge) \exists a \cdot R[k \backslash CE]$

$\iff$

$[k := CE](\exists a : A \cdot R)$

∎

Thus the refinement of an assignment statement can be done in two or three stages, to refine $a := AE$:

1. Guess at a possible CE, and show $CI \Rightarrow [a, k := AE, CE]CI$ to get the data refinement $a, k := AE, CE$;
2. (optional) carry out some algorithmic refinement to remove any abstract variables from CE; and finally
3. throw away the abstract assignment $a := AE$, leaving just $k := CE$.

The first part of step (1) involved guessing at a possible refinement for the abstract expression AE, some insight into what would be a good guess can be obtained from looking at the refinement of a specification that is equivalent to the assignment $a := AE$.

$$a := AE$$

$$=$$

$$a : [\text{ true}, \quad a = AE[a\backslash \overleftarrow{a}]]$$

$$\preceq$$

$$k : [\text{ true}, \quad rep(a = AE[a\backslash \overleftarrow{a}])]$$

Now for functional refinement we have

$$rep(P(a)) = (a = retr(k))$$

thus the above becomes

$$k : [\text{ true}, \quad rep(a = AE[a\backslash \overleftarrow{a}])]$$

$$=$$

$$k : [\text{ true}, \quad retr(k) = AE[a\backslash \overleftarrow{a}]]$$

If we can find an CE such that

$$retr(CE) = AE[a\backslash retr(k)]$$

then

$$k : [\text{ true}, \quad retr(k) = AE[a\backslash \overleftarrow{a}]]$$

$$=$$

$$k : [\text{ true}, \quad retr(k) = retr(CE[k\backslash \overleftarrow{k}])]$$

$$\sqsubseteq$$

$$k : [\text{ true}, \quad k = CE[k\backslash \overleftarrow{k}]]$$

$$\sqsubseteq$$

$$k := CE$$

Based on this it is easy to show:

Theorem 18.22
If $retr(CE) = AE[a\backslash retr(k)]$ then

$$a := AE \preceq a, k := AE, CE$$

Proof
We need to prove:

$$CI \Rightarrow [a, k := AE, CE]CI$$

$$\Longleftrightarrow$$

$$a = retr(k) \Rightarrow AE = retr(CE)$$

$$\begin{aligned}
&\Longleftrightarrow\\
&\quad a = retr(k) \;\Rightarrow\; AE = AE[a\backslash retr(k)]\\
&\Longleftrightarrow\\
&\quad AE[a\backslash retr(k)] = AE[a\backslash retr(k)]\\
&\Longleftrightarrow\\
&\quad \text{true}
\end{aligned}$$

∎

Discovering a CE such that $retr(CE) = AE[a\backslash retr(k)]$ should be easier than trying to guess at a CE. Notice that our CE in this case does not contain any abstract variables, thus we do not need to do any algorithmic refinement to throw away the abstract assignment.

18.6 Summary

A data refinement step undertaken on a program has been shown to preserve any algorithmic structure that the program has. To do a data-refinement, it is only necessary to transform any guards, and replace any component of the program by its data refinement.

19. An Alternative Refinement of the Security System

The next example illustrates the approach applied again to produce executable code. The security system will be refined to (a simulation of) a linked list. To keep the derivation of code simple, rather than carry out the refinement in terms of pointers, the refinement will be done in terms of hd, tl and $\curvearrowright$ which are easily implemented with pointers. This will keep the mechanics of simulating pointers out of the exposition.

19.1 A Data Refinement

The intended strategy is to place a new name at the front of the sequence for the *enter* operation; search the sequence when checking for a name; and just remove the name from the sequence for the *leave* operation. The refinement of the state for this design strategy is:

    values

        $MAXNAMES : \mathbb{N} = \ldots$

    types

        $Name = \ldots;$

        $Name\text{-}seq = Name^*$

    state $Names$ of
        $l : Name\text{-}seq$
      inv $mk\text{-}Names(l) \triangleq$
        card elems $l \leq MAXNAMES \wedge$
        $is\text{-}uniques\,(l)$
      init $mk\text{-}Names \triangleq$ elems $l = \{\,\}$
    end

    functions

        $is\text{-}uniques : Name^* \to \mathbb{B}$
        $is\text{-}uniques\,(l) \triangleq \forall\, i,j \in \text{inds } l \cdot i \neq j \;\Rightarrow\; l(i) \neq l(j)$

19.1 A Data Refinement

The coupling invariant is:

$couple : Names \times Security \to \mathbb{B}$

$couple\ (mk\text{-}Names(l), mk\text{-}Security(names)) \triangleq names = \mathsf{elems}\ l$

and can be shown to be total and adequate in the standard VDM style. The operations on the new state are also easily defined:

operations

$start\text{-}day_1\ ()$
ext wr $l : Name\text{-}seq$
post $\mathsf{elems}\ l = \{\ \}$;

$enter_1\ (nm : Name)$
ext wr $l : Name\text{-}seq$
pre $\mathsf{card}\ \mathsf{elems}\ l < MAXNAMES$
post $\mathsf{elems}\ l = \mathsf{elems}\ \overleftarrow{l} \cup \{nm\}$;

$leave_1\ (nm : Name)$
ext wr $l : Name\text{-}seq$
post $\mathsf{elems}\ l = \mathsf{elems}\ \overleftarrow{l} \setminus \{nm\}$;

$check_1\ (nm : Name)\ r : \mathbb{B}$
ext rd $l : Name\text{-}seq$
post $r \Leftrightarrow nm \in \mathsf{elems}\ l$

We need to identify some theorems that allow the pre- and post-conditions to be transformed. An examination of the post-condition for *enter* suggests that we base a lemma on

$\mathsf{elems}\ l \cup \{nm\} = \mathsf{elems}\ (l \curvearrowright [nm])$

Note that the *is-uniques* invariant is not necessary for the theorem. An alternative base for a theorem could be:

$\mathsf{elems}\ l \cup \{nm\} = \mathsf{elems}\ ([nm] \curvearrowright l)$

However, we can be more general than this:

Lemma 19.1
For any $i \in \{0, \ldots, \mathsf{len}\ l\}$

$\mathsf{elems}\ l \cup \{nm\} = \mathsf{elems}\ (l(1,\ldots,i) \curvearrowright [nm] \curvearrowright l(i+1,\ldots,\mathsf{len}\ l))$

□

A lemma about removing an element from the sequence is required; an auxiliary function *del* is required, its definition is:

$del : X^* \times \mathbb{N} \to X^*$
$del\,(l, i) \triangleq l(1, \ldots, i-1) \curvearrowright l(i+1, \ldots, \text{len } l)$
pre $i \in$ inds el

the lemma is given below, note that it does rely on the invariant *is-uniques*.

Lemma 19.2
For $l : \textit{Name-seq}$ and $k \in$ inds l such that $l(k) = nm$ then

elems $l \setminus \{nm\} = del(l, k)$

Proof

$\quad\quad$ elems $l \setminus \{nm\}$
$=\quad$ definition of elems
$\quad\quad \{l(i) \mid i \in$ inds $l\} \setminus \{nm\}$
$=\quad$ hypothesis
$\quad\quad \{l(i) \mid i \in$ inds $l\} \setminus \{l(k)\}$
$=\quad$ definition of elems , invariant
$\quad\quad \{l(i) \mid i \in$ inds $l \setminus \{k\}\}$
$=\quad$ definition of *del*
$\quad\quad del(l, k)$

■

The *start-day* operation is straightforward – the details are left to the reader:

$start\text{-}day_1$ ()
ext wr $l : \textit{Name-seq} \triangleq$
$\quad l := [\,]$

The refinement strategy is similar to the previously example given in Chapter 18 so only the final stage will be shown. For the *enter* operation we obtain – after an application of the *introduce proper procedure body* rule, the *introduce alternatives* rule (to preserve the invariant), and the *replace specification* rule – the following:

$enter_1\,(nm : \textit{Name})$
ext wr $l : \textit{Name-seq} \triangleq$
$\quad$ if $nm \notin$ elems $l \to$ *enter-name*
$\quad []\;\; nm \in$ elems $l \to$ skip
$\quad$ fi

where

enter-name
chg $l : \textit{Name-seq}$
pre len $l < \textit{MAXNAMES} \land$
   $nm \notin \text{elems } l$
post $l = [nm] \frown \overleftarrow{l}$

A similar refinement, the final step uses Lemma 19.2, gives the following for the operation *remove*.

$\textit{remove}_1 \, (nm : \textit{Name})$
ext wr $l : \textit{Name-seq} \; \triangleq$
  if $nm \in \text{elems } l \rightarrow \textit{remove-name}$
  $[\!]$ $nm \notin \text{elems } l \rightarrow$ skip
  fi

where

remove-name
chg $l : \textit{Name-seq}$
pre $nm \in \text{elems } l$
post $\exists\, i \in \text{inds } \overleftarrow{l} \cdot nm = \overleftarrow{l}\,(i) \land$
  $ l = \textit{del}(\overleftarrow{l}, i)$

The operation *exists* will be left alone.

$\textit{exists}_2 \, (nm : \textit{Name}) \; r : \mathbb{B}$
ext rd $l : \textit{Name-seq}$
post $r \Leftrightarrow nm \in \text{elems } l$

Before adding a name to the sequence it is necessary to check that the name is not currently contained in the sequence; to remove a name from the sequence it must first be found. This can be done by a function that splits a sequence of names into three components, one of which is the target name:

$\textit{front} \frown [nm] \frown \textit{back}$

There is a problem when the name, denoted by nm, is not in the sequence; to solve this and to reduce the number of values that need to be returned from the function we will divide the sequence into a front component and a back component with nm at the head of the back part if it is present. This means that if it is not present, then after the division, the second component will be empty. This suggests the following definition of *find*:

$\textit{find}\, (nm : \textit{Name}) \; r : \textit{Name-seq} \times \textit{Name-seq}$
ext rd $l : \textit{Name-seq}$

post $\exists\, front, back : Name\text{-}seq \cdot front \frown back = l \wedge nm \notin \text{elems } front \wedge$
$\qquad (nm = \text{hd } back \vee back = [\,]) \wedge$
$\qquad r = mk\text{-}(front, back)$

A function procedure can be introduced, and with some re-organization the following refinement can be derived:

$find\,(nm : Name) : Name\text{-}seq \times Name\text{-}seq$
ext rd $l : Name\text{-}seq \triangleq$
⟦ dcl $front, back : Name\text{-}seq$ in
$\quad find\text{-}body$
$\quad$chg $front, back : Name\text{-}seq$
$\quad$post $front \frown back = l \wedge nm \notin \text{elems } front \wedge$
$\qquad (nm = \text{hd } back \vee back = [\,])$
;
$\quad$return $mk\text{-}(front, back)$ ⟧

The motivation behind the operation *find* together with its specification suggests that the body be refined by a loop, candidates for the loop parameters are:

init $\quad front = [\,] \wedge back = l$
guard $nm \neq \text{hd } back \wedge back \neq [\,]$
inv $\quad front \frown back = l \wedge nm \notin \text{elems } front$
var $\quad \text{len } back < \text{len } \overline{back}$

The variant domain proof obligation is trivial. An application of the *introduce iteration* rule will give the following refinement of the operation operation *find*:

$find\text{-}body \sqsubseteq front, back := [\,], l;$
$\qquad\quad$do $back \neq [\,]$ cand $nm \neq \text{hd } back \rightarrow$
$\qquad\qquad\quad front, back := front \frown [\text{hd } back], \text{tl } back$
$\qquad$od

We can put everything together to give the following code for the operation *find*:

$find\,(nm : Name) : Name\text{-}seq \times Name\text{-}seq$
ext rd $l : Name\text{-}seq \triangleq$
⟦ dcl $front, back : Name\text{-}seq$ in
$\quad front, back := [\,], l;$
$\quad$do $back \neq [\,]$ cand $nm \neq \text{hd } back \rightarrow$
$\qquad\quad front, back := front \frown [\text{hd } back], \text{tl } back$
$\quad$od ;
$\quad$return $mk\text{-}(front, back)$ ⟧

Now the other operations can be completed, the derivation is again in the same style as the example in the previous chapter. The result of this refinement step is shown in Fig. 19.1.

19.2 Another Approach to the Refinement

An alternative approach is to change the algorithm used for searching the table so that it adjusts the position of a name that has just been found. The adjustment involves the movement of the name to the front of the list. This means that, on average, frequently accessed names will be at the front of the list. This arrangement is effective in terms of lookup time when a small number of names in the table are frequently accessed, and for relatively large tables makes a linear search a feasible proposition. An example of this occurring is shown in Fig. 19.2 – the top half shows the state of the list before the operation *check* occurs, while the bottom half shows the state of the list after the *check* operation has been carried out with the name 'F' as its argument.

The new strategy, when checking the existence of a name, is to move it to the front of the sequence if the name is found; otherwise leave the sequence unchanged. The original specification for *check* is

$check\,(nm:name)\ r:\mathbb{B}$
ext rd $names:Name\text{-}set$
post $r \Leftrightarrow nm \in names$

This can be rewritten, changing *names* from a read variable to a write variable. This change is based on the intended algorithm – the order, but not content, of the sequence can change.

$check\,(nm:name)\ r:\mathbb{B}$
ext wr $names:Name\text{-}set$
post $(r \Leftrightarrow nm \in names) \wedge names = \overleftarrow{names}$

The first step is to use the coupling invariant to calculate the new pre- and post-conditions:

$check_1\,(nm:name)\ r:\mathbb{B}$
ext wr $l:Name\text{-}seq$
post $(r \Leftrightarrow nm \in \text{elems}\ l) \wedge$
  $\text{elems}\ l = \text{elems}\ \overleftarrow{l}$

The next step is to introduce a procedure:

start-day ()
ext wr l : *Name-seq* ≜
  $l := []$

enter (nm : *Name*)
ext wr l : *Name-seq* ≜
  [dcl *front, back* : *Name-seq* in
    front, back := *find*(nm);
    if *back* = [] → $l := [nm] \frown l$
    ▯ *back* ≠ [] → skip
    fi]

leave (nm : *Name*)
ext wr l : *Name-seq* ≜
  [dcl *front, back* : *Name-seq* in
    front, back := *find*(nm);
    if *back* ≠ [] → $l := front \frown tl\ back$
    ▯ *back* = [] → skip
    fi]

check (nm : *Name*) r : $\mathbb{B}$
ext rd l : *Name-seq* ≜
  [dcl *front, back* : *Name-seq* in
    front, back := *find*(nm);
    return *back* ≠ []]

Fig. 19.1. The executable code for a linked-list implementation

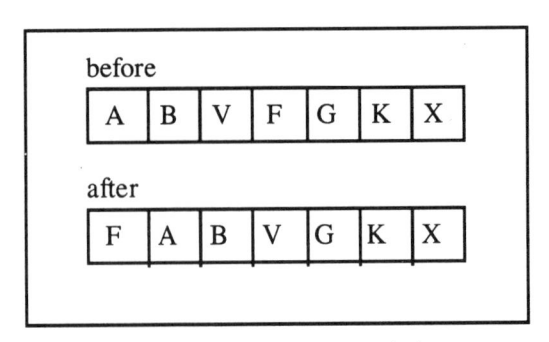

before

| A | B | V | F | G | K | X |

after

| F | A | B | V | G | K | X |

Fig. 19.2. An example table used for the *check*(F) operation.

19.2 Another Approach to the Refinement

$check_1\ (nm : name)\ :\mathbb{B}$
ext wr $l : Name\text{-}seq\ \triangleq$
$[\![$ dcl $r : \mathbb{B}$ in
  check-body
  chg $l : Name\text{-}seq$
    $r : \mathbb{B}$
  post $(r \Leftrightarrow nm \in $ elems $l) \wedge $ elems $l = $ elems $\overleftarrow{l}$
  ;
  return $r\ ]\!]$

Now the task is to refine *exists-body*; the intended algorithm will be used to derive some transformations of the post-condition. The implementation is to return true and move the name to the front of the sequence if it can be found, and return false and do nothing with the sequence if it is not present. This suggests rewriting the post-condition to handle these two cases. This approach suggests:

$(r \Leftrightarrow nm \in $ elems $l) \wedge $ elems $l = $ elems $\overleftarrow{l}$

$\Longleftrightarrow$

$r \wedge nm \in $ elems $l \wedge $ elems $l = $ elems $\overleftarrow{l}$
$\vee$
$\neg r \wedge nm \notin $ elems $l \wedge l = \overleftarrow{l}$

With the algorithm still in mind, the next step is to further transform the post-condition – the sequence needs to be split into three: a *front* part that does not contain the target name, the target name nm and (the tail of) a *back* part of the sequence. This means that if the name is to be found in the sequence the required re-organization of the sequence can be expressed as

$[nm] \frown front \frown $ tl $back$

where

$front \frown back = $ the original sequence

Continuing with the re-organization of the post-condition, the algorithm suggests:

$front \frown back = \overleftarrow{l}\ \wedge$
$r \wedge nm \notin $ elems $front \wedge nm = $ hd $back \wedge l = [nm] \frown front \frown $ tl $back$
$\vee$
$\neg r \wedge nm \notin $ elems $l \wedge l = \overleftarrow{l}$

Notice that the second part of the disjunction can be written in terms of *front* and *back* which will aid with the program development step – experience indicates that the final algorithm will consist of a loop followed by some house-keeping adjustments. The post-condition can be further transformed to give:

$$front \curvearrowright back = \overleftarrow{l} \land nm \notin \text{elems } front \land$$
$$(r \land nm = \text{hd } back \land l = [nm] \curvearrowright front \curvearrowright \text{tl } back$$
$$\lor$$
$$\neg r \land back = [\,] \land l = \overleftarrow{l}\,)$$

The data invariant is preserved by either of the disjuncts in the above version of the post-condition, so the final version of the specification is now

exists-body
chg $l : Name\text{-}seq$
   $front, back : Name\text{-}seq$
   $r : \mathbb{B}$
post $front \curvearrowright back = \overleftarrow{l} \land nm \notin \text{elems } front \land$
   $(r \land nm = \text{hd } back \land l = [nm] \curvearrowright front \curvearrowright \text{tl } back$
   $\lor$
   $\neg r \land back = [\,] \land l = \overleftarrow{l}\,)$

The post-condition now expresses the intended refinement step, there is no refinement proof to do – it was 'hidden' in the transformations – and the resulting specification is also in a suitable shape for deriving the code. An application of the *introduce command-semicolon* rule will give the specification of the *find* operation and a specification of some necessary housekeeping – note that it is unnecessary to change the sequence when we search through it.

exists-body $\sqsubseteq$ *find-op*
   chg $front, back : Name\text{-}seq$
   post $front \curvearrowright back = l \land nm \notin \text{elems } front \land$
      $(nm = \text{hd } back \lor back = [\,])$
   ;
   h-keeping
   chg $l : Name\text{-}seq$
      $r : \mathbb{B}$
   pre $front \curvearrowright back = l \land nm \notin \text{elems } front \land$
      $(nm = \text{hd } back \lor back = [\,])$
   post $front \curvearrowright back = \overleftarrow{l} \land nm \notin \text{elems } front \land$
      $(r \land nm = \text{hd } back \land l = [nm] \curvearrowright front \curvearrowright \text{tl } back$
      $\lor$
      $\neg r \land back = [\,] \land l = \overleftarrow{l}\,)$

The function procedure *find* has already been defined and developed and it satisfies *find-op*. The *h-keeping* operation can be refined using the conditional rule, and after some reorganization becomes:

h-keeping $\sqsubseteq$ if $back \neq [\,] \rightarrow l := [nm] \frown front \frown$ tl $back;$
$\phantom{h\text{-}keeping \sqsubseteq \text{if }back \neq [\,] \rightarrow{}} r := \text{true}$
$\phantom{h\text{-}keeping \sqsubseteq \text{i}}[\!]\ \ back = [\,] \rightarrow r := \text{false}$
fi

The final code, after some straight-forward substitutions and transformations, is thus:

check (*nm* : *name*) : $\mathbb{B}$
ext wr l : *Name-seq* $\triangleq$
$[\![$ dcl *front*, *back* : *Name-seq* in
front, *back* := *find*(*nm*);
if $back \neq [\,] \rightarrow l := [nm] \frown front \frown$ tl *back*; return true
$[\!]\ \ back = [\,] \rightarrow$ return false
fi$]\!]$

19.3 Summary

This chapter illustrated the use of theorem about the refinement of the state to transform the specification of the operations. Frequently such theorems can be used in more than one refinement step and they should provide insight into the chosen refinement. The approach is thus: spot and prove theorems about the data refinement and use these theorems to transform the pre- and post-condition of specifications.

20. Stacks and Queues

No collection of examples on refinement would be complete without either an example of a stack or a queue. The following four examples cover these two data structures, and the opportunity is taken to show refinement at work.

20.1 A Finite Stack

The first example is the specification and refinement of a finite stack; the specification is given below – the stack can hold at most N elements.

values

$N : \mathbb{N} = \ldots$

types

$Element = \ldots;$

$Stack = Element^*$

state $LIFO$ **of**
$\quad st : Stack$
$\quad$ **inv** $mk\text{-}LIFO(st) \triangleq \text{len } st \leq N$
end

The operations on the stack can now be defined. First, an operation to empty a stack, the empty stack is modelled by an empty sequence:

$empty\text{-}stack\,()$
ext wr $st : Stack$
post $st = [\,]$

An operation to place an element on the top of a stack that is not full:

$push\,(e : Element)$
ext wr $st : Stack$
pre $\text{len } st < N$

post $st = [e] \curvearrowright \overleftarrow{st}$

An operation to remove the element from the top of the stack – the stack must not be empty:

pop ()
ext wr $st : Stack$
pre $st \neq []$
post $st =$ tl $\overleftarrow{st}$

An operation to read the element from the top of the stack – again the stack must not be empty:

read () $r : Element$
ext rd $st : Stack$
pre $st \neq []$
post $r =$ hd st

An operation to check if the stack is empty:

is-empty () $r : \mathbb{B}$
ext rd $st : Stack$
post $r \Leftrightarrow st = []$

Finally, an operation to check if the stack is full:

is-full () $r : \mathbb{B}$
ext rd $st : Stack$
post $r \Leftrightarrow$ len $st = N$

20.1.1 The Refinement

The refinement will consist of an array that is large enough to hold N elements – the size of the largest stack – and a pointer to the array element that represents the top of the stack. The elements to the left of the pointer are the other elements already in the stack. As usual, a mapping will be used to simulate an array.

$Sarray = \{1, \ldots, N\} \xrightarrow{m} Element$

state $CLIFO$ of
  $buf : Sarray$
  $top : \{0, \ldots, N\}$
  inv $mk\text{-}CLIFO\,(buf, top) \triangleq \{1, \ldots, top\} \subseteq$ dom buf
end

The invariant guarantees that the array is initialized correctly.

The coupling invariant relates the two representations:

$couple : CLIFO \times LIFO \to \mathbb{B}$

$couple\,(mk\text{-}CLIFO(buf, top), mk\text{-}LIFO(st)) \triangleq st = to\text{-}stack(buf, top)$

$to\text{-}stack : Sarray \times \mathbb{N} \to Stack$

$to\text{-}stack\,(buf, top) \triangleq [buf(top - i + 1) \mid i \in \{1, \ldots, top\}]$

The top of the stack in the abstract specification is given by hd st, which is equal to $st(1)$; in the refinement the equivalent element on the stack is $buf(top)$, so the elements of the array need to be reversed when assembling the sequence representation.

The refinement progresses in the prescribed manner – the new versions of the operations are derived using the coupling invariant:

$empty\text{-}stack_1\,()$
ext wr $buf : Sarray$
    wr $top : \{0, \ldots, N\}$
post $to\text{-}stack(buf, top) = [\,]$

$push_1\,(e : Element)$
ext wr $buf : Sarray$
    wr $top : \{0, \ldots, N\}$
pre len $to\text{-}stack(buf, top) < N$
post $to\text{-}stack(buf, top) = [e] \frown to\text{-}stack(\overleftarrow{buf}, \overleftarrow{top})$

$pop_1\,()$
ext wr $buf : Sarray$
    wr $top : \{0, \ldots, N\}$
pre $to\text{-}stack(buf, top) \neq [\,]$
post $to\text{-}stack(buf, top) = \text{tl } to\text{-}stack(\overleftarrow{buf}, \overleftarrow{top})$

$read_1\,()\,r : Element$
ext rd $buf : Sarray$
    rd $top : \{0, \ldots, N\}$
pre $to\text{-}stack(buf, top) \neq [\,]$
post $r = \text{hd } to\text{-}stack(\overleftarrow{buf}, \overleftarrow{top})$

$is\text{-}empty_1\ ()\ r : \mathbb{B}$
ext rd $buf : Sarray$
    rd $top : \{0, \ldots, N\}$
post $r \Leftrightarrow to\text{-}stack(buf, top) = [\,]$

$is\text{-}full_1\ ()\ r : \mathbb{B}$
ext rd $buf : Sarray$
    rd $top : \{0, \ldots, N\}$
post $r \Leftrightarrow \text{len } to\text{-}stack(buf, top) = N$

20.1.2 Reorganizing the Operations

The approach that we will take is to examine the pre- and post-conditions of each of the operations to try and see what properties of the representation they could rely on. These properties can be wrapped up as general theorems and lemmas about the representation and proved correct; they then can be used to remove the *to-stack* function using the *replace specification* rule.

Some General Lemmas. The length of the stack is needed by two operations, so this suggests investigating a term of the form $\text{len } to\text{-}stack(b,t)$:

$$\text{len } to\text{-}stack(b,t)$$
$= \quad \text{definition of coupling invariant}$
$$\text{len } [b(t-i+1) \mid i \in \{1, \ldots, t\}]$$
$= \quad \text{sequence definition}$
$$t$$

giving the first lemma:

Lemma 20.1
    $\text{len } to\text{-}stack(b,t) = t$
□

This agrees with the idea behind the array pointer. There is an immediate corollary:

Corollary 20.1
    $to\text{-}stack(b,t) = [\,] \Leftrightarrow t = 0$
□

The post-condition for $push_1$ is of the form

$$[e] \frown to\text{-}stack(b,t) = to\text{-}stack(b',t')$$

this suggests trying to derive an equality of this form from the coupling invariant; now:

$$\textit{to-stack}(b,t)$$
= definition of coupling invariant
$$[b(t-i+1) \mid i \in \{1,\ldots,t\}]$$
= definition of sequence
$$[b(t-i+1) \mid i \in \{1\}] \curvearrowright [b(t-i+1) \mid i \in \{2,\ldots,t\}]$$
= simplify and re-organize
$$[b(t)] \curvearrowright [b((t-1)-i+1) \mid i \in \{1,\ldots,t-1\}]$$
= simplify and re-organize
$$[b(t)] \curvearrowright \textit{to-stack}(b, t-1)$$

giving the second lemma for the stack refinement:

Lemma 20.2
$$\textit{to-stack}(b,t) = [b(t)] \curvearrowright \textit{to-stack}(b,t-1)$$
□

Again, there is an immediate corollary to this lemma:

Corollary 20.2
hd $\textit{to-stack}(b,t) = b(t)$
tl $\textit{to-stack}(b,t) = \textit{to-stack}(b,t-1)$
□

and this corollary can be used in the refinement of pop_1 and $read_1$.

The *empty-stack* Operation. The post-condition for *empty-stack*$_1$ is

$$\textit{to-stack}(\textit{buf}, \textit{top}) = [\,]$$

which, using Lemma 20.1, can be inferred from $top = 0$, i.e. we have

$$top = 0 \Rightarrow \textit{to-stack}(\textit{buf}, \textit{top}) = [\,]$$

Notice that the value of *buf* is not used, thus we will choose to leave it unchanged. As the pre-condition of *empty* is true, and true $\Rightarrow$ true, the *replace specification* rule can be used to give a new specification for *empty-stack*$_1$:

empty-stack$_1$ ()
ext wr $top : \{0,\ldots,N\}$
post $top = 0$

and is refined by the *introduce proper procedure body* rule and *introduce assignment* rule to:

empty-stack ()
ext wr $top : \{0,\ldots,N\} \triangleq$
    $top := 0$

The *push* Operation. Now to refine the operation $push_1$, the pre-condition is

len $to\text{-}stack(buf, top) < N$

using Lemma 20.1 this is equivalent to

$top < N$

The post-condition for $push_1$ is

$to\text{-}stack(buf, top) = [e] \frown to\text{-}stack(\overleftarrow{buf}, \overleftarrow{top})$

The term to the left of the equality can be transformed using Lemma 20.2 to give:

$[buf(top)] \frown to\text{-}stack(buf, top - 1) = [e] \frown to\text{-}stack(\overleftarrow{buf}, \overleftarrow{top})$

comparing this with the post-condition suggests the following refinement step:

$e = buf(top) \land buf = \overleftarrow{buf} \land top - 1 = \overleftarrow{top}$

to give, using the *replace specification* rule:

$push_1$ (e : *Element*)
ext wr buf : *Sarray*
  wr top : $\{0, \ldots, N\}$
pre $top < N$
post $e = buf(top) \land$
  $buf = \overleftarrow{buf} \land$
  $top - 1 = \overleftarrow{top}$

However, though this is a valid refinement step, it cannot be implemented by executable code – this specification is miracle in disguise: the specification demands that the buffer is unchanged, but changed by adding the new element denoted by e. A slightly weaker, but implementable, refinement step that allows the buffer to changed is:

$e = buf(top) \land to\text{-}stack(\overleftarrow{buf}, \overleftarrow{top}) = to\text{-}stack(buf, top - 1)$

the second expression above and the invariant forces $\overleftarrow{top} = top - 1$, we also have:

$to\text{-}stack(\overleftarrow{buf}, \overleftarrow{top}) = to\text{-}stack(buf, top - 1)$

which is implied by

$\overleftarrow{buf}(1, \ldots, \overleftarrow{top}) = buf(1, \ldots, top - 1)$

So the following is a possible refinement step for the post-condition:

$$e = buf(top) \land$$
$$buf(1, \ldots, top - 1) = \overleftarrow{buf}(1, \ldots, \overleftarrow{top}) \land$$
$$top = \overleftarrow{top} + 1$$

The first two expressions in the conjunction are equivalent to:

$$buf = \overleftarrow{buf} \dagger \{top \mapsto e\}$$

The whole derivation can be written out as follows:

$$to\text{-}stack(buf, top) = [e] \frown to\text{-}stack(\overleftarrow{buf}, \overleftarrow{top})$$
$\iff$ apply Lemma 20.2 to the left-hand side
$$[buf(top)] \frown to\text{-}stack(buf, top - 1) = [e] \frown to\text{-}stack(\overleftarrow{buf}, \overleftarrow{top})$$
$\Longleftarrow$ property of equality
$$e = buf(top) \land$$
$$to\text{-}stack(buf, top - 1) = to\text{-}stack(\overleftarrow{buf}, \overleftarrow{top}) \land$$
$$top - 1 = \overleftarrow{top}$$
$\Longleftarrow$ definition of to-stack
$$e = buf(top) \land$$
$$buf(1, \ldots, top - 1) = \overleftarrow{buf}(1, \ldots, \overleftarrow{top}) \land$$
$$top - 1 = \overleftarrow{top}$$
$\Longleftarrow$ property of †; reorganize
$$buf = \overleftarrow{buf} \dagger \{top \mapsto e\} \land$$
$$top = \overleftarrow{top} + 1$$

Notice that at one point in the derivation the post-condition contained the expression:

$$buf(1, \ldots, top - 1) = \overleftarrow{buf}(1, \ldots, \overleftarrow{top})$$

and this would allow the implementation to do anything with those array elements above the high-water mark top – the refinement choses, as indicated in the last step of the derivation, to leave them unchanged.

The new specification for $push_1$ is thus:

$push_1$ (e : $Element$)
  ext wr buf : $Sarray$
    wr top : $\{0, \ldots, N\}$
  pre $top < N$
  post $buf = \overleftarrow{buf} \dagger \{top \mapsto e\} \land$
     $top = \overleftarrow{top} + 1$

20.1 A Finite Stack

and it is easy to show that this can be refined using the *introduce proper procedure body* rule and the *introduce assignment* rule to:

$\text{push}\,(e : Element)$
ext wr $buf : Sarray$
  wr $top : \{0, \ldots, N\} \;\triangleq$
$[\![top := top + 1;$
  $buf(top) := e]\!]$

The *pop* Operation. The pre-condition for pop_1 is

$\text{to-stack}(buf, top) \neq [\,]$

using Corollary 20.1 above, this is equivalent to

$top \neq 0$

The post-condition for pop_1 is

$\text{to-stack}(buf, top) = \text{tl}\ \text{to-stack}(\overleftarrow{buf}, \overleftarrow{top})$

Now, from Corollary 20.2 above

$\text{to-stack}(\overleftarrow{buf}, \overleftarrow{top}) = \text{to-stack}(\overleftarrow{buf}, \overleftarrow{top} - 1)$

this suggests trying

$buf = \overleftarrow{buf} \wedge top = \overleftarrow{top} - 1$

as the step to remove the retrieve function, and it is easy to show:

$buf = \overleftarrow{buf} \wedge top = \overleftarrow{top} - 1 \;\Rightarrow\; \text{to-stack}(buf, top) = \text{to-stack}(\overleftarrow{buf}, \overleftarrow{top} - 1)$

The *replace specification* rule can be used to give the following specification for pop_1:

$pop_1\,()$
ext wr $buf : Sarray$
  wr $top : \{0, \ldots, N\}$
pre $top \neq 0$
post $buf = \overleftarrow{buf} \wedge$
  $top = \overleftarrow{top} - 1$

which, since the buffer is not changed, can be rewritten as

$pop_1\,()$
ext wr $top : \{0, \ldots, N\}$
pre $top \neq 0$

post $top = \overleftarrow{top} - 1$

Using the *introduce proper procedure body* rule and the *introduce assignment* rule, the specification can be refined to:

pop ()
ext wr $top : \{0, \ldots, N\}$ ≙
$\quad top := top - 1$

The *read* Operation. The refinement for the *read* operation follows a similar pattern to that of *pop*. The pre-condition for $read_1$ is identical to that of *pop*, so its refinement is the same. The post-condition for $read_1$ is

$r = \text{hd } to\text{-}stack(buf, top)$

Now, from Corollary 20.2 above

$r = buf(top)$

and it follows that:

$r = buf(top) \Rightarrow r = \text{hd } to\text{-}stack(buf, top)$

The *replace specification* rule can be used to give the following specification for $read_1$:

$read_1$ () r : *Element*
ext rd buf : *Sarray*
$\quad$ rd $top : \{0, \ldots, N\}$
pre $top \neq 0$
post $r = buf(top)$

Using the *introduce function procedure body* rule, the *introduce assignment* rule and merging the assignment command and the return command, the operation $read_1$ is refined to:

read () : *Element*
ext rd buf : *Sarray*
$\quad$ rd $top : \{0, \ldots, N\}$ ≙
$\quad$ return $buf(top)$

The *is-empty* Operation. Moving on to the operation $is\text{-}empty_1$, applying Lemma 20.1 gives

$is\text{-}empty_1$ () $r : \mathbb{B}$
ext rd $top : \{0, \ldots, N\}$
post $r \Leftrightarrow top = 0$

which can be refined by:

$is\text{-}empty\ ()\ :\ \mathbb{B}$
  ext rd $top : \{0, \ldots, N\}$ $\triangleq$
    return $top = 0$

The *is-full* Operation. Similarly the specification to $is\text{-}full_1$ can be written using Lemma 20.1 as

$is\text{-}full_1\ ()\ r : \mathbb{B}$
  ext rd $top : \{0, \ldots, N\}$
  post $r \Leftrightarrow top = N$

and can be refined to

$is\text{-}full\ ()\ :\ \mathbb{B}$
  ext rd $top : \{0, \ldots, N\}$ $\triangleq$
    return $top = N$

This completes the refinement of a simple stack.

20.2 A stack of Boolean Values

The second example is an unusual refinement for a finite stack of Boolean values; the specification of a stack has already been given, but now the elements of the stack are Booleans:

values

  $N : \mathbb{N} = \ldots$

types

  $Element = \mathbb{B}$;

  $Stack = Element^*$

A refinement can be base on the natural numbers by interpreting the sequence of Booleans as a binary number. There could be a problem with adequacy with this representation. If the stack of Booleans is interpreted as a binary number, there is a problem with all stacks that contain just false, they all would be represented as zero. If however a dummy entry of one is placed on the bottom of the stack, and the stack read from bottom to top to give the binary representation of the number, then this problem does not arise. The new representation is:

types

  $Bstack = \mathbb{N}_1$

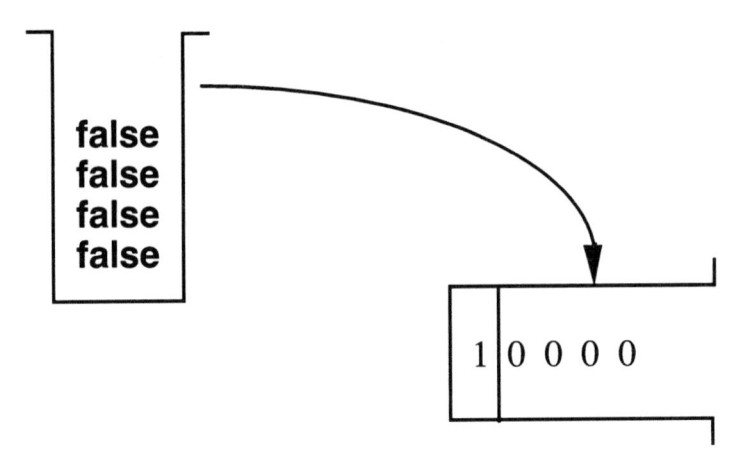

Fig. 20.1. A Boolean stack.

    state $BLIFO$ **of**
      $n : Bstack$
      inv $mk\text{-}BLIFO(n) \triangleq n < 2^{N+1}$
    end

The coupling invariant is given by:

    $couple : BLIFO \times LIFO \rightarrow \mathbb{B}$
    $couple\ (mk\text{-}BLIFO(n), mk\text{-}LIFO(st)) \triangleq st = to\text{-}stack(n)$

    $to\text{-}stack : Bstack \rightarrow Stack$
    $to\text{-}stack\ (n) \triangleq$ **if** $n = 1$ **then** $[\,]$ **else** $[is\text{-}odd(n)] \curvearrowright to\text{-}stack(n \div 2)$

The coupling invariant define above can be shown to be onto and total. The operations in terms of the new representation are given below:

$empty\text{-}stack_1\ ()$
ext wr $n : Bstack$
post $to\text{-}stack(n) = [\,]$

$push_1\ (e : Element)$
ext wr $n : Bstack$
pre **len** $to\text{-}stack(n) < N$
post $to\text{-}stack(n) = [e] \curvearrowright to\text{-}stack(\overleftarrow{n})$

$pop_1\ ()$
ext wr $n : Bstack$

pre $to\text{-}stack(n) \neq []$
post $to\text{-}stack(n) = \text{tl } to\text{-}stack(\overleftarrow{n})$

$read_1 \text{ () } r : Element$
ext rd $n : Bstack$
pre $to\text{-}stackn \neq []$
post $r = \text{hd } to\text{-}stack(n)$

$is\text{-}empty_1 \text{ () } r : \mathbb{B}$
ext rd $n : Bstack$
post $r \Leftrightarrow to\text{-}stack(n) = []$

$is\text{-}full_1 \text{ () } r : \mathbb{B}$
ext rd $n : Bstack$
post $r \Leftrightarrow \text{len } to\text{-}stack(n) = N$

20.2.1 Some Lemmas about the Representation

Now from the coupling invariant:

$$to\text{-}stack(2 \times n) = [is\text{-}odd(2 \times n)] \curvearrowright to\text{-}stack((2 \times n) \div 2)$$
$\Longleftrightarrow$ rules of arithmetic
$$to\text{-}stack(2 \times n + 0) = [\text{false}] \curvearrowright to\text{-}stack(n)$$

and

$$to\text{-}stack(2 \times n + 1) = [is\text{-}odd(2 \times n + 1)] \curvearrowright to\text{-}stack((2 \times n + 1) \div 2)$$
$\Longleftrightarrow$ rules of arithmetic
$$to\text{-}stack(2 \times n + 1) = [\text{true}] \curvearrowright to\text{-}stack(n)$$

these two can be combined for a Boolean value b to give:

Lemma 20.3
$$to\text{-}stack(2 \times n + value(b)) = [b] \curvearrowright to\text{-}stack(n)$$
□

where the function *value* is defined as follows:

$value : Element \to \{0, 1\}$
$value\ (b) \triangleq \text{if } b \text{ then } 1 \text{ else } 0$

The *value* operation just maps **true** to one and **false** to zero.

20.2.2 The *empty-stack* Operation

Starting with the post-condition for *push* and strengthening it we can carry out the following transformations:

$\quad$ *to-stack*$(n) = [\,]$
$\Longleftarrow$ definition of *to-stack*
$\quad n = 1$

The new operation to empty the stack is thus:

$\quad$ *empty-stack*$_1$ ()
$\quad$ ext wr $n : Bstack$
$\quad$ post $n = 1$

20.2.3 The *push* Operation

Starting with the post-condition for *push* and strengthening it we can carry out the following transformations:

$\quad$ *to-stack*$(n) = [e] \curvearrowright$ *to-stack*$(\overleftarrow{n})$
$\Longleftarrow$ Lemma 20.3
$\quad$ *to-stack*$(n) =$ *to-stack*$(2 \times \overleftarrow{n} +$ *value*$(e))$
$\Longleftarrow$ property of total functions
$\quad n = 2 \times \overleftarrow{n} +$ *value*(e)

The new operation is thus

$\quad$ *push*$_1$ $(e : Element)$
$\quad$ ext wr $n : Bstack$
$\quad$ pre $2^n < N$
$\quad$ post $n = 2 \times \overleftarrow{n} +$ *value*(e)

Shift the number left by one place, and add in the new element to the stack.

20.2.4 The *pop* Operation

The post-condition for *pop* can be transformed in a similar way to that of *push*:

$\quad$ *to-stack*$(n) =$ tl *to-stack*$(\overleftarrow{n})$
$\Longleftrightarrow$ arithmetic
$\quad$ *to-stack*$(n) =$ tl *to-stack*$(\overleftarrow{n} \div 2 +$ *value*$($*is-odd*$(\overleftarrow{n})))$
$\Longleftrightarrow$ Lemma 20.3
$\quad$ *to-stack*$(n) =$ tl $([$*is-odd*$(\overleftarrow{n})] \curvearrowright$ *to-stack*$(\overleftarrow{n} \div 2))$

$$\iff$$
$$\text{to-stack}(n) = \text{to-stack}(\overleftarrow{n \div 2})$$
$$\impliedby$$
$$n = \overleftarrow{n \div 2}$$

The new operation is thus

pop_1 ()
ext wr $n : Bstack$
pre $n \neq 1$
post $n = \overleftarrow{n} \div 2$

The stack is popped by shifting right by one place.

20.2.5 The *read* Operation

The post-condition for *read* can be transformed in a similar way to that of *pop*:

$r = (\text{hd } \text{to-stack}(n))$
$\iff$ arithmetic
$\quad r = (\text{hd } \text{to-stack}(n \div 2 + \text{value}(\text{is-odd}(n))))$
$\iff$ Lemma 20.3
$\quad r = \text{hd } ([\text{is-odd}(n)] \frown \text{to-stack}(n \div 2))$
$\iff$
$\quad r = \text{is-odd}(n)$

The new operation is thus

$read_1$ () $r : Element$
ext rd $n : Bstack$
pre $n \neq 1$
post $r = \text{is-odd}(n)$

The result of the $read_1$ operation depends on whether then current number representing the stack is odd or not.

20.2.6 The *is-empty* Operation

is-empty_1 () $r : \mathbb{B}$
ext wr $n : Bstack$
post $r \iff n = 1$

If the number representing the stack is one, then the stack is empty.

20.2.7 The *is-full* Operation

The post-condition of *is-full* is

$$r \Leftrightarrow \text{len } to\text{-}stack(n) = N$$

now the definition of len means that

    len $to\text{-}stack(n)$
=   definition of *to-stack*
    len (if $n = 1$ then $[\,]$ else $[is\text{-}odd(n)] \frown to\text{-}stack(n \div 2))$
=   definition of len
    if $n = 1$ then 0 else $1 +$ len $to\text{-}stack(n \div 2)$

It would be useful to have a non-recursive version of this, from our understanding of the representation we know that if the length of the stack is l, then

$$2^l \leq n \text{ and } n < 2^{l+1}$$

thus a good guess for the length of the boolean stack would be

len $to\text{-}stack(n) = $ let $l : \mathbb{N}$ be st $2^l \leq n \wedge n < 2^{l+1}$ in l

and this suggests the following function:

$nlength : \mathbb{N} \to \mathbb{N}$
$nlength\,(n) \triangleq$ let $l : \mathbb{N}$ be st $2^l \leq n \wedge n < 2^{l+1}$ in l

and then we have:

len $to\text{-}stack(n) = nlength(n)$

We can show by induction that this is correct, the base case is $n = 1$:

    len $to\text{-}stack(1)$
=   definition of *to-stack*
    0
=   by above
    $nlength(1)$

the second case is $1 < n$:

    len $to\text{-}stack(n)$
=   definition of *to-stack*
    $1 +$ len $to\text{-}stack(n \div 2)$
=   by above
    $1 +$ let $l : \mathbb{N}$ be st $2^l \leq n \div 2 \wedge n \div 2 < 2^{l+1}$ in l

= definition of let
   let $l : \mathbb{N}$ be st $2^l \leq n \div 2 \wedge n \div 2 < 2^{l+1}$ in $l + 1$
= arithmetic
   let $l : \mathbb{N}$ be st $2^{l+1} \leq n \wedge n < 2^{l+1+1}$ in $l + 1$
= property of let
   let $l : \mathbb{N}$ be st $2^l \leq n \wedge n < 2^{l+1}$ in l
= definition of *nlength*
   $nlength(n)$

thus

len *to-stack*$(n) = N \Leftrightarrow nlength(n) = N \Leftrightarrow 2^N \leq n \wedge n < 2^{N+1}$

and the new version of *is-full* is

is-full () $r : \mathbb{B}$
ext rd $n : Bstack$
post $r \Leftrightarrow 2^N \leq n \wedge n < 2^{N+1}$

20.2.8 The Code

The refinement to code is fairly straight-forward; note that it is necessary to implement the functions *value*. The result is shown in Fig. 20.2.

20.2.9 Some Lessons

The data representation used in the reification is different in style and approach from the data-type used in the original specification. The retrieve function relates the new model to the old and once again adequacy helps with the problem of an incorrect representation, it is necessary to represent the empty stack by the number one rather than by zero. As the representation is so different, it is worth doing the modelling proofs if only to convince ourselves of its correctness.

20.3 A Finite Queue

The next example of this chapter is a finite queue or circular buffer; processes working at different rate can use such a structure to interchange data.

The producer places information in the buffer at the next free slot, the consumer removes information from the buffer from the next slot to be processed. The buffer (which is really a finite queue) and its operations can be modelled as a finite sequence that can hold at most N elements; the specification follows:

$empty\text{-}stack\,()$
ext wr $n : Bstack$ ≜
$n := 1$

$pop\,()$
ext wr $n : Bstack$ ≜
$n := n \div 2$

$read\,()\ :\ Element$
ext rd $n : Bstack$ ≜
return $is\text{-}odd(n)$

$push\,(e : Element)$
ext wr $n : Bstack$ ≜
$n := 2 \times n + value(e)$

$is\text{-}empty\,()\ :\ \mathbb{B}$
ext wr $n : Bstack$ ≜
return $n = 1$

$is\text{-}full\,()\ :\ \mathbb{B}$
ext wr $n : Bstack$ ≜
return $2^N \leq n$ cand $n < 2^{N+1}$

Fig. 20.2. The refinement of a Boolean stack.

values

$N = \mathbb{N}$

types

$Element = \ldots\,;$

$Queue = Element^*$

state $FIFO$ of
queue : $Queue$
inv $mk\text{-}FIFO(queue)$ ≜ len $queue \leq N$
end

The operations are defined below. First, an operation (re-)initialize the queue; the queue can be cleared by this operation:

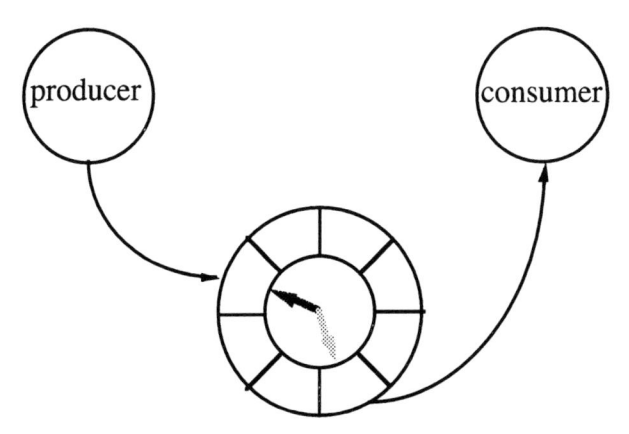

Fig. 20.3. A finite queue.

empty-queue ()
ext wr *queue* : *Queue*
post *queue* = [ ]

An operation to be used by the consumer to read the first element in the queue – the queue must not be empty:

read () *r* : *Element*
ext rd *queue* : *Queue*
pre *queue* ≠ [ ]
post *r* = hd *queue*

If the queue is not empty, the next element is removed from the front of the queue by the consumer with the *dequeue* operation:

dequeue ()
ext wr *queue* : *Queue*
pre *queue* ≠ [ ]
post *queue* = tl $\overleftarrow{queue}$

If the queue is not full, the new element is appended on the end by the producer with the *enqueue* operation:

enqueue (*e* : *Element*)
ext wr *queue* : *Queue*
pre len *queue* < *N*
post *queue* = $\overleftarrow{queue}$ ⁀ [*e*]

The next two operation can be used by the consumer to check whether the queue is empty and by the producer to check whether the queue is full:

is-empty () $r : \mathbb{B}$
ext rd *queue* : *Queue*
post $r \Leftrightarrow \text{len } queue = 0$

is-full () $r : \mathbb{B}$
ext rd *queue* : *Queue*
post $r \Leftrightarrow \text{len } queue = N$

20.3.1 A Refinement of the Queue

The first step is to choose a new representation for the data:

values

$N : \mathbb{N} = \ldots$

types

$Barray = \{0, \ldots, N-1\} \xrightarrow{m} Element$

state *Buffer* **of**
  buf : *Barray*
  reads : $\mathbb{N}$
  writes : $\mathbb{N}$
  inv *mk-Buffer*(*buf*, *reads*, *writes*) $\triangleq$
    $0 \leq writes - reads \wedge$
    $writes - reads \leq N$
end

The idea behind the refinement is that *reads* denotes the number of reads of data from the buffer and *writes* denotes the number of writes to the buffer; the buffer is large enough to hold N elements. The invariant encapsulates some properties of the representation:

- the buffer is finite, and its size is thus fixed and must be less then or equal to N;
- the number of writes can never be such as to overfill the buffer – and hence loose something; and
- the number of reads can never exceed the number of writes.

The values for *reads* and *writes* will be used to deduce where in the buffer to read the next element for a *dequeue* operation and were to writes the next element for a *enqueue* operation. The coupling relation encapsulates this:

$couple : Buffer \times FIFO \rightarrow \mathbb{B}$
$couple\ (mk\text{-}Buffer(b, r, w), mk\text{-}FIFO(q)) \triangleq q = to\text{-}q(b, r, w)$

$to\text{-}q : Barray \times \mathbb{N} \times \mathbb{N} \to Queue$

$to\text{-}q(b, r, w) \triangleq [b((r + i) \bmod N) \mid i \in \{0, \ldots, (w - r) - 1\}]$

The refinement of the operations is carried out in the normal way, using the coupling invariant to derive the new representation.

$empty\text{-}queue_1\ ()$
ext wr $buf : Barray$
    wr $reads, writes : \mathbb{N}$
post $to\text{-}q(buf, reads, writes) = [\,]$

$read_1\ ()\ r : Element$
ext rd $buf : Barray$
    rd $reads, writes : \mathbb{N}$
pre $to\text{-}q(buf, reads, writes) \neq [\,]$
post $r = \text{hd } to\text{-}q(\overleftarrow{buf}, \overleftarrow{reads}, \overleftarrow{writes})$

$dequeue_1\ ()$
ext wr $buf : Barray$
    wr $reads, writes : \mathbb{N}$
pre $to\text{-}q(buf, reads, writes) \neq [\,]$
post $to\text{-}q(buf, reads, writes) = \text{tl } to\text{-}q(\overleftarrow{buf}, \overleftarrow{reads}, \overleftarrow{writes})$

$enqueue_1\ (e : Element)$
ext wr $buf : Barray$
    wr $reads, writes : \mathbb{N}$
pre len $to\text{-}q(buf, reads, writes) < N$
post $to\text{-}q(buf, reads, writes) = to\text{-}q(\overleftarrow{buf}, \overleftarrow{reads}, \overleftarrow{writes}) \frown [e]$

$is\text{-}empty_1\ ()\ r : \mathbb{B}$
ext rd $buf : Barray$
    rd $reads, writes : \mathbb{N}$
post $r \Leftrightarrow \text{len } to\text{-}q(buf, reads, writes) = 0$

$is\text{-}full_1\ ()\ r : \mathbb{B}$
ext rd $buf : Barray$
    rd $reads, writes : \mathbb{N}$
post $r \Leftrightarrow \text{len } to\text{-}q(buf, reads, writes) = N$

20.3.2 Some Theorems

We start with the length of the buffer: from the data refinement, the number of elements currently in it is given by:

$$\mathsf{len}\ \textit{to-q}(b, r, w)$$
$$=\quad \text{definition of } \textit{to-q}$$
$$\mathsf{len}\ [b((r+i) \bmod N) \mid i \in \{0, \ldots, (w-r)-1\}]$$
$$=\quad \text{sequence definition}$$
$$w - r$$

thus

Lemma 20.4
$$\mathsf{len}\ \textit{to-q}(b, r, w) = w - r$$

□

The length of a queue is equal to the excess number of writes over reads, which is what we would expect. Since an empty sequence has a zero length, an immediate corollary is:

Corollary 20.3
$$w = r \Leftrightarrow \textit{to-q}(b, r, w) = []$$

□

The two operations *read* and *dequeue* deal with operations on the front of the queue. This suggests investigating the following term:

$$\textit{to-q}(b, r, w) = [e] \frown \ldots$$

Starting with the left-hand term:

$$\textit{to-q}(b, r, w)$$
$$=\quad \text{definition of } \textit{to-q}$$
$$[b((r+i) \bmod N) \mid i \in \{0, \ldots, (w-r)-1\}]$$
$$=\quad \text{definition of sequence}$$
$$[b((r+i) \bmod N) \mid i \in \{0\}] \frown$$
$$[b((r+i) \bmod N) \mid i \in \{1, \ldots, (w-r)-1\}]$$
$$=\quad \text{simplify and re-organize}$$
$$[b(r \bmod N)] \frown [b((r+1+i) \bmod N) \mid i \in \{0, \ldots, (w-(r+1))-1\}]$$
$$=\quad \text{simplify and re-organize}$$
$$[b(r \bmod N)] \frown \textit{to-q}(b, r+1, w)$$

Thus we have shown:

Lemma 20.5
$$\text{to-}q(b, r, w) = [b(r \bmod N)] \frown \text{to-}q(b, r+1, w)$$
□

and this states that a queue with r reads against it is like a queue with $r+1$ reads plus an additional element on the front – the element that will be read next. A corollary immediately follows:

Corollary 20.4
$$\text{hd } \text{to-}q(b, r, w) = b(r \bmod N)$$
$$\text{tl } \text{to-}q(b, r, w) = \text{to-}q(b, r+1, w)$$
□

The post-condition for *enqueue* is

$$\text{to-}q(\mathit{buf}, \mathit{reads}, \mathit{writes}) = \text{to-}q(\overleftarrow{\mathit{buf}}, \overleftarrow{\mathit{reads}}, \overleftarrow{\mathit{writes}}) \frown [e]$$

and this suggests investigating

$\quad\quad \text{to-}q(b, r, w)$
$=\quad$ definition of *to-q*
$\quad\quad [b((r+i) \bmod N) \mid i \in \{0, \ldots, (w-r)-1\}]$
$=\quad$ definition of sequence
$\quad\quad [b((r+i) \bmod N) \mid i \in \{0, \ldots, (w-r)-2\}] \frown$
$\quad\quad [b((r+i) \bmod N) \mid i \in \{(w-r)-1\}]$
$=\quad$ simplify
$\quad\quad [b((r+i) \bmod N) \mid i \in \{0, \ldots, (w-1-r)-1\}] \frown [b((w-1) \bmod N)]$
$=\quad$ simplify
$\quad\quad \text{to-}q(b, r, w-1) \frown [b((w-1) \bmod N)]$

The lemma base on the above derivation is:

Lemma 20.6
$$\text{to-}q(b, r, w) = \text{to-}q(b, r, w-1) \frown [b((w-1) \bmod N)]$$
□

and it states that a buffer with w writes against it is the same as a buffer with $w - 1$ writes against it with an additional element on the end – the element that has just been added to the queue.

20.3.3 The Operations Transformed

The *empty-queue* Operation. The *empty-queue* operation can be transformed by replacing the *to-q* function to get

$empty\text{-}queue_1$ ()
ext wr buf : $Barray$
  wr $reads, writes$: $\mathbb{N}$
post $to\text{-}q(buf, reads, writes) = [\,]$

The post-condition can be transformed thus:

$to\text{-}q(buf, reads, writes) = [\,]$
$\Longleftrightarrow$ by Corollary 20.3
  $writes = reads$
$\Longleftarrow$
  $writes = 0 \wedge reads = 0$

and the above together with the *remove variable* rule gives:

$empty\text{-}queue_1$ ()
ext wr $reads, writes$: $\mathbb{N}$
post $writes = 0 \wedge reads = 0$

The *read* Operation. Starting with the *read* operation, the pre-condition can be weakened as follows

$to\text{-}q(buf, reads, writes) \neq [\,]$
$\Longleftrightarrow$ by Corollary 20.3
  $writes \neq reads$

The post-condition can be strengthened:

$r = \text{hd } to\text{-}q(buf, reads, writes)$
$\Longleftrightarrow$ from Corollary 20.4
  $r = buf(reads \bmod N)$

This gives the new version of *read*:

$read_1$ () r : $Element$
ext rd buf : $Barray$
  rd $reads, writes$: $\mathbb{N}$
pre $writes \neq reads$
post $r = buf(reads \bmod N)$

The *dequeue* Operation. Starting with the *dequeue* operation, the pre-condition for this operation is the same as for *read*. The post-condition can be strengthened:

$$to\text{-}q(buf, reads, writes) = \mathsf{tl}\ to\text{-}q(\overleftarrow{buf}, \overleftarrow{reads}, \overleftarrow{writes})$$
$\Longleftrightarrow$ from Corollary 20.4
$$to\text{-}q(buf, reads, writes) = to\text{-}q(\overleftarrow{buf}, \overleftarrow{reads}+1, \overleftarrow{writes})$$
$\Longleftarrow$ property of total functions
$$buf = \overleftarrow{buf}\ \wedge$$
$$reads = \overleftarrow{reads} + 1\ \wedge$$
$$writes = \overleftarrow{writes}$$

This gives the new version of *dequeue*:

dequeue$_1$ ()
ext wr *buf* : *Barray*
　　wr *reads, writes* : $\mathbb{N}$
pre *writes* $\neq$ *reads*
post $buf = \overleftarrow{buf}\ \wedge$
　　$reads = \overleftarrow{reads} + 1\ \wedge$
　　$writes = \overleftarrow{writes}$

By introducing some read-only variables, and since *writes* is read-only and is not referenced, the above can be transformed to:

dequeue$_1$ ()
ext rd *buf* : *Barray*
　　wr *reads, writes* : $\mathbb{N}$
pre *writes* $\neq$ *reads*
post $reads = \overleftarrow{reads} + 1$

The number of reads is increased by one, and thus the next piece of information to be processed is read from the appropriate place in the buffer.

The *enqueue* Operation. The *enqueue* operation can be handled similarly. The pre-condition transformation is:

$$\mathsf{len}\ to\text{-}q(buf, reads, writes) < N$$
$\Longleftarrow$ by Lemma 20.4
$$writes - reads < N$$

The transformation of the post-condition is

$$to\text{-}q(buf, reads, writes) = to\text{-}q(\overleftarrow{buf}, \overleftarrow{reads}, \overleftarrow{writes}) \curvearrowright [e]$$
$\Longleftarrow$ from Lemma 20.6
$$to\text{-}q(buf, reads, writes) =$$

$to\text{-}q(buf, reads, writes - 1) \curvearrowright [buf((writes - 1) \bmod N)]$
$\Longleftarrow$ property of total functions

$to\text{-}q(buf, reads, writes - 1) = to\text{-}q(\overleftarrow{buf}, \overleftarrow{reads}, \overleftarrow{writes}) \land$
$[buf((writes - 1) \bmod N)] = [e]$
$\Longleftarrow$

$buf = \overleftarrow{buf} \land$
$reads = \overleftarrow{reads} \land$
$writes - 1 = \overleftarrow{writes} \land$
$buf((writes - 1) \bmod N) = e$

As in the stack example, this transformation will lead to miracle in disguise! Realizing that the buffer will need to be updated, an alternative approach is to consider:

$to\text{-}q(buf, reads, writes - 1) = to\text{-}q(\overleftarrow{buf}, \overleftarrow{reads}, \overleftarrow{writes}) \land$
$reads = \overleftarrow{reads} \land$
$writes - 1 = \overleftarrow{writes} \land$
$buf((writes - 1) \bmod N) = e$

With some simple re-organization, this can be written:

$buf = \overleftarrow{buf} \dagger \{(writes - 1) \bmod N \mapsto e\} \land$
$reads = \overleftarrow{reads} \land$
$writes = \overleftarrow{writes} + 1$

The new version of *enqueue* is thus:

$enqueue_1\ (e: Element)$
ext wr $buf : Barray$
　　wr $reads, writes : \mathbb{N}$
pre $writes - reads < N$
post $buf = \overleftarrow{buf} \dagger \{(writes - 1) \bmod N \mapsto e\} \land$
　　$reads = \overleftarrow{reads} \land$
　　$writes = \overleftarrow{writes} + 1$

which can be rewritten:

$enqueue_1\ (e: Element)$
ext wr $buf : Barray$
　　rd $reads : \mathbb{N}$
　　wr $writes : \mathbb{N}$
pre $writes - reads < N$

post $buf = \overleftarrow{buf} \dagger \{\overrightarrow{writes} \bmod N \mapsto e\} \land$
$writes = \overleftarrow{writes} + 1$

The number of writes has gone up by one, and the buffer is modified in the appropriate position.

The *is-empty* and *is-full* Operations. Using the first lemma the specification for *is-empty*$_1$ becomes

is-empty$_1$ () $r : \mathbb{B}$
ext rd $buf : Barray$
    rd $reads, writes : \mathbb{N}$
post $r \Leftrightarrow writes - reads = 0$

and the specification for *is-full*$_1$ is

is-full$_1$ () $r : \mathbb{B}$
ext rd $buf : Barray$
    rd $reads, writes : \mathbb{N}$
post $r \Leftrightarrow writes - reads = N$

These two operations check to see if the buffer is full or empty: if it is empty then the number of reads is equal to the number of writes, and if it is full they differ by the size of the buffer.

Using the rules to introduce function procedures or proper procedures together with the introduce assignment rule, each of the specifications can be refined to give the code shown in Fig. 20.4.

20.3.4 An Extension to the System

Each read from the buffer increases the read count and each write to the buffer increases the writes count, so there could be a problem with these two counters overflowing. Intuition indicates that the critical value in this refinement is the value *writes* − *read*, so it may be possible to change both *read* and *writes* by the same amount. This intuition turns out to be wrong, however the two values can be changed by some multiple of the size of the buffer.

$\quad to\text{-}q\,(b, r + n \times N, w + n \times N)$
$=$
$\quad [b((r+i+n \times N) \bmod N) \mid i \in \{0, \ldots, ((w+n \times N)-(r+n \times N))-1\}]$
$=$
$\quad [b((r+i) \bmod N) \mid i \in \{0, \ldots, (w-r)-1\}]$
$=$
$\quad to\text{-}q\,(b, r, w)$

20. Stacks and Queues

empty-queue ()
ext wr *reads, writes* : $\mathbb{N}$ ≙
  reads, writes := 0

read () : *Element*
ext rd *buf* : *Barray*
  rd *reads* : $\mathbb{N}$ ≙
  return *buf*(*reads* mod *N*)

dequeue ()
ext wr *reads* : $\mathbb{N}$ ≙
  reads := *reads* + 1

enqueue (*e* : *Element*)
ext rd *buf* : *Barray*
  wr *writes* : $\mathbb{N}$ ≙
  ⟦ *buf*(*writes* mod *N*) := *e*;
    writes := *writes* + 1⟧

is-empty () : $\mathbb{B}$
ext rd *reads, writes* : $\mathbb{N}$ ≙
  return *writes* = *reads*

is-full () : $\mathbb{B}$
ext rd *reads, writes* : $\mathbb{N}$ ≙
  return *writes* − *reads* = *N*

Fig. 20.4. The refinement of a finite queue.

To use this transformation, we can first introduce a new operation:

reduce-pointers ()
ext wr *queue* : *Queue*
pre '*N* ≤ number of *write* operations'
post *queue* = $\overleftarrow{queue}$

which, on refinement, becomes:

reduce-pointers ()
ext wr *buf* : *Barray*
  wr *reads, writes* : $\mathbb{N}$
pre *N* ≤ *writes*

post $to\text{-}q\,(buf, reads, writes) = to\text{-}q\,(\overleftarrow{buf}, \overleftarrow{reads}, \overleftarrow{writes})$

By using the transformation given above, we can refine this by

reduce-pointers ()
ext wr $buf : Barray$
 wr $reads, writes : \mathbb{N}$
pre $N \leq writes$
post $buf = \overleftarrow{buf} \wedge$
 $reads = \overleftarrow{reads} - N \wedge$
 $writes = \overleftarrow{writes} - N$

to give finally an operation that can be used to reduce the values of the two pointers:

reduce-pointers ()
ext wr $reads, writes : \mathbb{N}$
pre $N \leq writes$
post $reads = \overleftarrow{reads} - N \wedge$
 $writes = \overleftarrow{writes} - N$

which can be refined using the *introduce assignment* rule to give:

reduce-pointers ()
ext wr $reads, writes : \mathbb{N}$ ≙
 $reads, writes := reads - N, writes - N$

20.4 An Efficient Queue

If the specification for a queue is changed slightly by adding another operation, we can consider a different data refinement. The new operation is given by:

push ($e : Element$)
ext wr $queue : Queue$
post $queue = [e] \frown \overleftarrow{queue}$

This operation just adds an element to the front of the queue.

With the data refinement we have in mind, the operation *is-full* is not really needed (or applicable), but we shall leave it in for completeness, and to provide another operation to refine.

In this data refinement the intention is to ultimately implement the queue as a linked list, for example the queue:

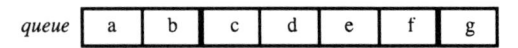

could be represented by the following linked list:

With this representation the operation *enqueue* is expensive compared with the other five operations. If the queue is stored in the reverse order:

the *enqueue* operation is now very efficient, however all but the *create-queue* operation are now inefficient.

A compromise solution would be to store the front of the queue in the correct order so that *read*, *dequeue* and *push* are efficient; and the back part is held in reverse order so that *enqueue* is efficient. With this representation, the queue given above might look as follows:

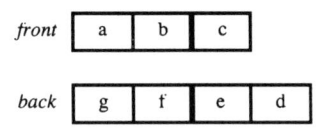

The only problem is to decide how to split the queue between the two parts. A simple solution is to only demand that, whenever the front queue is empty, the back part must be empty too. As an intermediate step towards the final linked list representation, the following state and invariant could be used:

types

$Queue = Element^*;$

$Element = \ldots$

state $EFIFO$ **of**
front : $Queue$
back : $Queue$

inv $mk\text{-}EFIFO\,(front, back) \triangleq front = [\,] \Rightarrow back = [\,]$
end

The coupling invariant can be based on

$couple : EFIFO \times FIFO \to \mathbb{B}$

$couple\,(mk\text{-}EFIFO(front, back), mk\text{-}FIFO(queue)) \triangleq$
 $queue = to\text{-}q(front, back)$

$to\text{-}q : Queue \times Queue \to Queue$

$to\text{-}q\,(f, b) \triangleq f \curvearrowright rev(b)$

Where the following function defines the reversal of a sequence:

$rev : Queue \rightarrow Queue$

$rev\,(q) \triangleq$ if $q = [\,]$ then $[\,]$ else $rev(\text{tl } q) \frown [\text{hd } q]$

and it is easy to show that:

$rev(a \frown b) = rev(b) \frown rev(a)$

The complete specification for the refinement after transforming each of the operations is given in Fig. 20.5.

20.4.1 Some Properties

The operations *is-empty* and *empty* and the pre-condition for *dequeue* suggest the following analysis:

$to\text{-}q(front, back) = [\,]$

$\Longleftrightarrow$

$front \frown rev(back) = [\,]$

$\Longleftrightarrow$

$front = [\,] \land back = [\,]$

$\Longleftrightarrow$ by the invariant

$front = [\,]$

which gives the first theorem:

Theorem 20.1
$to\text{-}q(front, back) = [\,] \Longleftrightarrow front = [\,]$

□

The operation *read* suggests that under the assumption $front \neq [\,]$, we could investigate:

$\text{hd } to\text{-}q(front, back) = \text{hd } (front \frown rev(back)) = \text{hd } front$

giving the second theorem:

Theorem 20.2
$\text{hd } to\text{-}q(front, back) = \text{hd } front$

□

The *dequeue* operation suggests, under the assumption $front \neq [\,]$, that the following transformation is carried out:

empty-queue ()
ext wr *front, back* : *Queue*
post *to-q(front, back)* = [ ]

read () *r* : *Element*
ext rd *front, back* : *Queue*
pre *to-q(front, back)* ≠ [ ]
post *r* = hd *to-q(front, back)*

dequeue ()
ext wr *front, back* : *Queue*
pre *to-q(front, back)* ≠ [ ]
post *to-q(front, back)* = tl *to-q($\overleftarrow{front}, \overleftarrow{back}$)*

enqueue (*e* : *Element*)
ext wr *front, back* : *Queue*
post *to-q(front, back)* = *to-q($\overleftarrow{front}, \overleftarrow{back}$)* ⌢ [*e*]

push (*e* : *Element*)
ext wr *front, back* : *Queue*
post *to-q(front, back)* = [*e*] ⌢ *to-q($\overleftarrow{front}, \overleftarrow{back}$)*

is-empty () *r* : $\mathbb{B}$
ext rd *front, back* : *Queue*
post *r* ⇔ *to-q(front, back)* = [ ]

is-full () *r* : $\mathbb{B}$
ext rd *front, back* : *Queue*
post *r* ⇔ len *to-q(front, back)* = *N*

Fig. 20.5. The new specification for an efficient queue

$empty\text{-}queue\,()$
ext wr $front, back : Queue$
post $front = [\,] \land back = [\,]$

$read\,()\ r : Element$
ext rd $front : Queue$
pre $front \neq [\,]$
post $r = \mathsf{hd}\ front$

$dequeue\,()$
ext wr $front, back : Queue$
pre $front \neq [\,]$
post $\mathsf{tl}\ \overleftarrow{front} \neq [\,] \land front = \mathsf{tl}\ \overleftarrow{front} \land back = \overleftarrow{back}$
$\qquad \lor$
$\qquad \mathsf{tl}\ \overleftarrow{front} = [\,] \land front = rev(\overleftarrow{back}) \land back = [\,]$

$push\,(e : Element)$
ext wr $front : Queue$
post $front = [e] \frown \overleftarrow{front}$

$enqueue\,(e : Element)$
ext wr $front, back : Queue$
post $\overleftarrow{front} = [\,] \land front = [e] \land back = \overleftarrow{back}$
$\qquad \lor$
$\qquad \overleftarrow{front} \neq [\,] \land front = \overleftarrow{front} \land back = [e] \frown \overleftarrow{back}$

$is\text{-}empty\,()\ r : \mathbb{B}$
ext rd $front : Queue$
post $r \Leftrightarrow front = [\,]$

$is\text{-}full\,()\ r : \mathbb{B}$
ext rd $front, back : Queue$
post $r \Leftrightarrow (\mathsf{len}\ front + \mathsf{len}\ back = N)$

Fig. 20.6. An efficient finite queue.

tl $to\text{-}q(front, back)$

$=$

tl $(front \frown rev(back))$

$=$

tl $(front) \frown rev(back)$

$=$

$to\text{-}q(\text{tl } front, back)$

However the last step cannot be done if tl $front = [\,]$ since the invariant will be broken. Now, if tl $front = [\,]$, the transformation could continue:

$$\text{tl } front \frown rev(back) = rev(back) = to\text{-}q(rev(back), [\,])$$

Thus we can write:

$to\text{-}q(front, back) = \text{tl } to\text{-}q(\overleftarrow{front}, \overleftarrow{back})$

$\Longleftrightarrow$

tl $\overleftarrow{front} \neq [\,] \wedge to\text{-}q(front, back) = to\text{-}q(\text{tl } \overleftarrow{front}, \overleftarrow{back})$

$\vee$

tl $\overleftarrow{front} = [\,] \wedge to\text{-}q(front, back) = to\text{-}q(rev(\overleftarrow{back}), [\,])$

$\Longleftarrow$

tl $\overleftarrow{front} \neq [\,] \wedge front = \text{tl } \overleftarrow{front} \wedge back = \overleftarrow{back}$

$\vee$

tl $\overleftarrow{front} = [\,] \wedge front = rev(\overleftarrow{back}) \wedge back = [\,]$

The *push* operation suggests:

$$[e] \frown to\text{-}q(front, back) = [e] \frown front \frown rev(back)$$
$$= to\text{-}q([e] \frown front, back)$$

giving the next theorem:

Theorem 20.3

$[e] \frown to\text{-}q(front, back) = to\text{-}q([e] \frown front, back)$

□

The operation *enqueue* suggests:

$to\text{-}q(front, back) \frown [e]$

$=$

$front \frown rev(back) \frown [e]$

$=$

$front \frown rev([e] \frown back)$

$=$

$to\text{-}q(front, [e] \frown back)$

giving another theorem:

Theorem 20.4
$$\textit{to-q}(\textit{front}, \textit{back}) \frown [e] = \textit{to-q}(\textit{front}, [e] \frown \textit{back})$$
☐

Finally, let us investigate the term found in the post-condition of *is-full*:

    len *to-q*(*front*, *back*)

=   len (*front* $\frown$ *rev*(*back*))
    property of len operator
  len *front* + len *rev*(*back*)

=   property of *rev*
  len *front* + len *back*

providing us with our last theorem:

Theorem 20.5
    len *to-q*(*front*, *back*) = len *front* + len *back*
☐

It is left as an exercise for the reader to prove the lemmas used in the proof of this theorem, namely len $(a \frown b)$ = len a + len b and len $rev(a)$ = len a.

The new specifications of the operations can now be derived using the above theorems and applying the *replace specification* rule and the results of this are shown in Fig. 20.6.

20.4.2 Lessons

Each of the theorems again adds more insight to the representation and should provide more understanding as to what is going on. We should need convincing that the queue is only empty if the front part of the queue is empty, and that adding something to the end of the queue actually does adds it to the end, and not to the middle! This is quite a difficult refinement, but the development together with the proofs should convince the reader of its correctness. The final step to produce code is left for the reader.

21. Dynamic Data Structures

Many problems need some sort of dynamic data structures. There are two approaches to adding these to a programming language. The first is to hide the pointers from the programmer, they are created and destroyed by the code generated by the compiler. C. A. R. Hoare suggested such semantics in [19] in a precursor to Pascal. The disadvantage of this approach is that data-structures that need pointers that pointed back into itself cannot be easily programmed – the advantages are numerous! The second approach is to have explicit pointers, as can be found in nearly all procedural programming languages. The difficulty with this second approach is that pointer management has to be done by the programmer, and if not done correctly the misuse of pointers can lead to dead storage (also called storage leakage, storage that cannot be accessed from the program) and dangling pointers (pointers that point to storage that, in some sense, does not exist). This chapter deals with both approaches to dynamic data structures.

21.1 Simulating a Linked List

Yet another implementation of a stack is a linked list; this version will use hidden pointers. The necessary data types and state are:

values

$N : \mathbb{N} = \ldots$

types

$Element = \ldots;$

$List\text{-}el :: data : Element$
$\qquad next : Stackl\ ;$

$Stackl = [List\text{-}el]$

state $List$ of
$\quad front : Stackl$
end

couple-st : *List* × *LIFO* → $\mathbb{B}$
couple-st (*mk-List* (*front*), *mk-LIFO* (*st*)) $\triangleq$ *st* = *to-stack*(*front*)

to-stack : *Stackl* → *Stack*
to-stack (*front*) $\triangleq$
   if *front* = nil then [ ] else [*front.data*] $\frown$ *to-stack*(*front.next*)

Because of the nature of this implementation, we will assume that there is no upper limit to the size of the stack, thus a new version of *push* will be used that has no pre-condition:

push (*e* : *Element*)
ext wr *st* : *Stack*
post *st* = [*e*] $\frown$ $\overleftarrow{st}$

and because of this, the operation *is-full* will not be needed.

The refinement step is similar to that in Chapter 21, with suitable changes to the frame and the name of the retrieve function; the results of this step is shown in Fig. 21.1.

21.1.1 Some Theorems

The usual approach of identifying useful theorems is taken, many of the easier proofs are left for the reader. By considering the form of the retrieve function and the post-conditions of the operations, the following two theorems are suggested:

Theorem 21.1
    to-stack(nil) = [ ]
□

Theorem 21.2
If *front* ≠ nil then
    to-stack(*front*) = [*front.data*] $\frown$ *to-stack*(*front.next*)
□

An immediate corollary:

Corollary 21.1
If *front* ≠ nil then
    hd *to-stack*(*front*) = *front.data*
    tl *to-stack*(*front*) = *to-stack*(*front.next*)
□

These theorems can be used to remove the retrieve function *to-stack*, for example the post-condition for *push* can be transformed as follows:

$$to\text{-}stack(front) = [e] \frown to\text{-}stack(\overleftarrow{front})$$
$$\iff$$
$$[front.data] \frown to\text{-}stack(front.next) = [e] \frown to\text{-}stack(\overleftarrow{front})$$
$$\impliedby$$
$$front.data = e \land front.next = \overleftarrow{front}$$
$$\iff$$
$$front = mk\text{-}List\text{-}el\,(e, \overleftarrow{front})$$

This gives the following that can be used to transform *push*:

$$front = mk\text{-}List\text{-}el\,(e, \overleftarrow{front}) \implies to\text{-}stack(front) = [e] \frown to\text{-}stack(\overleftarrow{front})$$

21.1.2 The Operations Transformed

The above theorems can be used to transform the operations in the usual way. Using Theorem 21.1 the *empty-stack* operation becomes:

empty-stack$_1$ ()
ext wr *front* : *Stackl*
post *front* = nil

The *push* operation has already been dealt with:

push$_1$ (*e* : *Element*)
ext wr *front* : *Stackl*
post *front* = *mk-List-el*(*e*, $\overleftarrow{front}$)

The *pop* operation can be transformed using Corollary 21.1:

pop$_1$ ()
ext wr *front* : *Stackl*
pre *front* $\neq$ nil
post *front* = $\overleftarrow{front}$.*next*

as can *read*:

read$_1$ () *r* : *Element*
ext rd *front* : *Stackl*
pre *front* $\neq$ nil
post *r* = *front.data*

$empty\text{-}stack$ ()
ext wr $front : Stackl$
post $to\text{-}stack(front) = [\,]$

$push$ ($e : Element$)
ext wr $front : Stackl$
post $to\text{-}stack(front) = [e] \curvearrowright \overleftarrow{to\text{-}stack(front)}$

pop ()
ext wr $front : Stackl$
pre $to\text{-}stack(front) \neq [\,]$
post $to\text{-}stack(front) = \mathsf{tl}\ \overleftarrow{to\text{-}stack(front)}$

$read$ () $r : Element$
ext rd $front : Stackl$
pre $to\text{-}stack(front) \neq [\,]$
post $r = \mathsf{hd}\ to\text{-}stack(front)$

$is\text{-}empty$ () $r : \mathbb{B}$
ext rd $front : Stackl$
post $r \Leftrightarrow to\text{-}stack(front) = [\,]$

Fig. 21.1. The data refinement

Theorem 21.1 allows *is-empty* to be transformed:

$is\text{-}empty_1$ () $r : \mathbb{B}$
ext rd $front : Stackl$
post $r \Leftrightarrow front = \mathsf{nil}$

The realization of the above specifications as executable code is a simple exercise left for the reader. It should be noted that any $mk\text{-}\ldots(\ldots)$ constructors would be compiled into some sort of hidden **new** operation and following a pointer may need a **dispose** operation.

21.2 Explicit Pointers

We need a way of modelling pointers and storage allocation and deallocation. In many languages storage is allocated in a heap and the values that pointers hold is a storage address in the heap. The heap can be modelled as a mapping of a set of tokens (these model the address of storage locations) to a set of elements (the piece of store that the pointer is pointing at). This suggests the following types to model a linked list:

$Addr = \text{token}$

$Heap = Addr \xrightarrow{m} Nodel$

$Nodel :: value : Element$
$\qquad\quad\; next : [Addr]$

The set token represents values that are modelling pointer values – each token is effectively an address in 'abstract storage'. The state for the representation of a linked list will be as follows:

state $Stack_1$ of
    $head : [Addr]$
    $store : Heap$
end

The set token is just an infinite set of tokens, their exact values does not matter. This refinement style happens frequently enough to be worth having its own notation. Two new type constructors will be introduced:

$C = \text{collection of } T$

This is a straightforward abbreviation for

$C = \text{compose } T \text{ of token} \xrightarrow{m} T$

this is a model of the heap, or rather a heap since it will only allow allocation for things of type T[1]. If we need to allocate storage for a different type, there are two approaches: either create another heap:

$S\text{-}or\text{-}T = \text{collection of } S \mid \text{collection of } T$

or add the new type to the existing heap:

$S\text{-}and\text{-}T = \text{collection of } (S \mid T)$

Pointers need to be defined:

$P = \text{pointer to } T$

and this is just an abbreviation for:

$P = [\text{compose } T \text{ of token}]$

---

[1] The idea of collections comes from Algol-W.

Notice that in this abstract model, pointers are tagged with the name of the type of the objects they point to.

There is an invariant:

$collection\text{-}inv$: collection of T × pointer to $T \to \mathbb{B}$

$collection\text{-}inv\,(c,p) \triangleq p \in \mathsf{dom}\,c \lor p = \mathsf{nil}$

This invariant guarantees that there are no dangling pointers. In the model, allocated storage is in the domain of the mapping – it is in the heap; unallocated (or freed) storage is not. This invariant will be referred to as the collection invariant.

A new operator for pointers and collections, if $p : P$ and $c : C$ then the operator is defined by:

$\_\!\uparrow\!\_$: pointer to T × collection of $T \to T$

$p \uparrow_c \triangleq c(p)$

pre $p \in \mathsf{dom}\,c$

The equivalent to dereferencing a pointer is to write $c(p)$. The pre-condition demands the pointer must be in the domain of the store mapping. The invariant states that if a pointer is not in the domain then it denote nil. Thus we can impose a requirement on the implementation of this operation: the implementation should diagnose an attempt to dereference nil. This could be formalized, but this informal description should suffice.

We will also provide (for readability only) a new constant, an empty heap will be denoted by empty and is defined as follows:

empty $\triangleq \{\mapsto\}$

Two additional operations are also needed:

new_ : collection of $T \to$ pointer to T

$\mathsf{new}\,c \triangleq \mathsf{let}\ p : \text{pointer to } T \text{ be st } p \notin \mathsf{dom}\,c \land p \neq \mathsf{nil}\ \mathsf{in}\ p$

This operation models the allocation of a new piece of storage to hold a value of type T. If the specification is examined carefully, it can be seen that the operation new is modelling the **new** operation found in Pascal or Modula-2. A function to de-allocate storage could be defined as follows:

$dispose$: collection of T × pointer to $T \to$ collection of T

$dispose\,(c,p) \triangleq \{p\} \mathbin{\lhd\!\!\!-} c$

pre $p \in \mathsf{dom}\,c$

The operation is intended to model the **dispose** operation of Pascal or Modula-2 and gives back a piece of storage referenced by a pointer to the system. However this definition would break the invariant – pointers must reference storage that exists. An alternative definition is to define a proper function procedure *dispose* as follows:

$dispose\,(c:\text{collection of } T, p:\text{pointer to } T)\; r:(\text{collection of } T \times \text{pointer to } T)$
pre $p \in \text{dom } c$
post $r = mk\text{-}(\{p\} \triangleleft c, \text{nil})$

and define a new statement dispose as an abbreviation for using this new function procedure:

$dispose(c, p) \;\triangleq\; mk\text{-}(c, p) := dispose(c, p)$

We will use this form in the derivations below, and talk about returning storage to the system – even though this is not really accurate.

21.3 The Stack Using Explicit Pointers

The stack example can be implemented using explicit pointers:

types

    $ListEl = \text{pointer to } Nodel;$

    $Store = \text{collection of } Nodel;$

    $Nodel :: value : Element$
                 $next : ListEl$

state $Stackh$ **of**
  $first : ListEl$
  $heap : Store$
  inv $mk\text{-}Stackh\,(first, heap) \triangleq first = \text{nil} \lor first \in \text{dom } heap$
  init $mk\text{-}Stackh\,(first, heap) \triangleq first = \text{nil} \land heap = \text{empty}$
end

What does the retrieve function look like? If *first* has the value nil then this should represent an empty stack; if *first* does not denote nil, we follow the pointer: i.e. use the storage mapping to get to the first element of our linked list, extract the element from there and follow the link using the *next* field. This gives the following retrieve function:

  $retr\text{-}pst : ListEl \times Store \to Stack$
  $retr\text{-}pst\,(first, heap) \triangleq$
    if $first = \text{nil}$ then $[\,]$
    else $[heap(first).value] \frown retr\text{-}pst(heap(first).next, heap)$

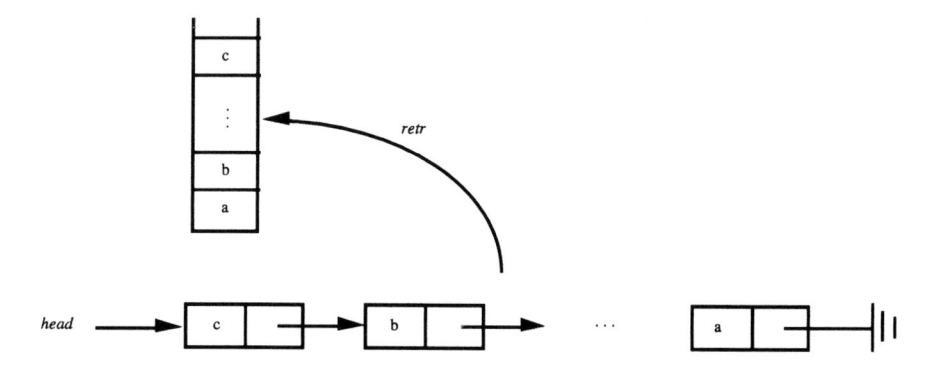

Fig. 21.2. The retrieve function for the stack.

The danger is of course to assume that everything is all right and proceed, but we still need to check that the retrieve function matches its type clause (i.e. is total) and unfortunately it does not, e.g. the following representation is of a stack

$mk\text{-}Stackh(id_1, \{id_1 \mapsto mk\text{-}Nodel(a, id_1)\})$

which corresponds to the situation shown in Fig. 21.3. This certainly is a member of the state $stack_1$, but is not actually retrieved to anything. What is needed is an invariant that says something along the line that there is always a nil to be found along a chain, or equivalently there are no cycles, and also that the *heap* contains no junk. It is a case where we need to add information – i.e. tighten up the invariant to disallow invalid stacks:

$inv\text{-}stack : Stackh \to \mathbb{B}$

$inv\text{-}stack\ (mk\text{-}Stackh(first, heap)) \triangleq$
 $\operatorname{dom} heap \cup \{\mathsf{nil}\} = collect\text{-}address(heap, first, \{\ \})$

The invariant also guarantees that there is no dead storage. The *collect-address* operation collects all the addresses in a chain; it needs to keep track of where it has been to avoid loops:

$collect\text{-}address : Store \times ListEl \times ListEl\text{-set} \to ListEl\text{-set}$

$collect\text{-}address\ (heap, first, found) \triangleq$
 $\text{if}\ first = \mathsf{nil}\ \text{then}\ \{first\} \cup found$
 $\text{elseif}\ first \in found\ \text{then}\ found$
 $\text{else let}\ mk\text{-}Nodel(\text{-}, next) = heap(first)\ \text{in}$
  $collect\text{-}address(heap, next, \{first\} \cup found)$

This function collects all the pointers together that are chained off the head of the linked list. If it finds a pointer set to nil or one that is not in the heap (not in the domain of the heap) it cannot go any further, so it returns what has been found. The operation does not follow a pointer that it has already been collected, it stops and returns what has been found so far.

The Boolean test could be *first* = nil $\vee$ *first* $\notin$ dom *heap*, but the collection invariant makes the second term unnecessary, *first* is either nil or it is in the domain of the storage map.

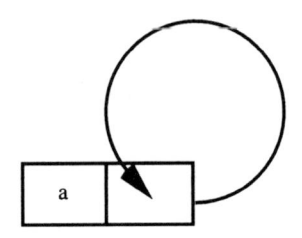

Fig. 21.3. A problem with an 'infinite' stack.

21.3.1 Standard Stack Specification to Pointers

We are now in a position to implement a stack using pointers, the new version of the operations are given below:

empty-stack ()
  ext wr *first* : *ListEl*
    wr *heap* : *Store*
  post *retr-pst*(*first*, *heap*) = []

push (*e* : *Element*)
  ext wr *first* : *ListEl*
    wr *heap* : *Store*
  post *retr-pst*(*first*, *heap*) = [*e*] $\frown$ *retr-pst*($\overleftarrow{first}$, $\overleftarrow{heap}$)

pop ()
  ext wr *first* : *ListEl*
    wr *heap* : *Store*
  pre 0 < len *first*, *heap*
  post *retr-pst*(*first*, *heap*) = tl *retr-pst*($\overleftarrow{first}$, $\overleftarrow{heap}$)

read () *r* : *Element*
  ext rd *first* : *ListEl*
    rd *heap* : *Store*

pre $0 <$ len $first, heap$
post $r =$ hd $retr\text{-}pst(first, heap)$

$is\text{-}empty\,()\ r : Bool$
ext rd $first : ListEl$
   rd $heap : Store$
post $r \Leftrightarrow retr\text{-}pst(first, heap) = [\,]$

The first obvious theorem to prove is suggested by the *empty-stack* operation and its statement is $retr\text{-}pst(\text{nil}, heap) = [\,]$. However, this is not a valid theorem for *this* state because of the collection invariant. The correct version is:

Theorem 21.3
   $retr\text{-}pst(\text{nil}, \text{empty}) = [\,]$

□

The second theorem is suggested by the forms of the post-conditions for *push* and *pop*. Again the invariant imposes a constraint that is not obvious at first sight.

Theorem 21.4
   $e = heapp(firstp).value\ \wedge$
   $firstq = heapp(firstp).next\ \wedge$
   $heapp = heapq \cup \{firstp \mapsto mk\text{-}Nodel\,(e, firstq)\}$
   $\Rightarrow$
   $retr\text{-}pst(firstp, heapp) = [e] \frown retr\text{-}pst(firstq, heapq)$

Proof
   $retr\text{-}pst(firstp, heapp) = [e] \frown retr\text{-}pst(firstq, heapq)$
   $\Longleftrightarrow$
   $[heapp(firstp).value] \frown retr\text{-}pst(heapp(firstp).next, heapp) =$
      $[e] \frown retr\text{-}pst(firstq, heapq)$
   $\Longleftarrow$
   $e = heapp(firstp).value\ \wedge$
   $firstq = heapp(firstp).next\ \wedge$
   $heapp = heapq \cup \{firstp \mapsto mk\text{-}Nodel\,(e, firstq)\}$

■

The next two theorems do not take the invariant into consideration, therefore care is needed when using them to transform operations.

Theorem 21.5
   hd $retr\text{-}pst(first, heap) = heap(first).value$

Proof

hd $retr\text{-}pst(first, heap)$

$=$

hd $[heap(first).value] \frown retr\text{-}pst(heap(first).next, heap)$

$=$

$heap(first).value$

∎

Theorem 21.6
    tl $retr\text{-}pst(first, heap) = retr\text{-}pst(heap(first).next, heap)$

Proof

tl $retr\text{-}pst(first, heap)$

$=$

tl $[heap(first).value] \frown retr\text{-}pst(heap(first).next, heap)$

$=$

$retr\text{-}pst(heap(first).next, heap)$

∎

With these theorems, the next step is to transform the operations. The *empty-stack* operation becomes:

$empty\text{-}stack_1 \,()$
ext wr $first : ListEl$
    wr $heap : Store$
post $first = $ nil $\wedge$
    $heap = $ empty

Perversely, an empty heap as far as our specification is concerned denotes an unused (full?) heap!

The specification for *empty-stack* can assume the invariant, and must preserve the invariant, therefore to see clearly what the operation must do, it is a good idea to add the invariant to the specification. This gives:

$empty\text{-}stack \,()$
ext wr $first : ListEl$
    wr $heap : Store$
post $first = $ nil $\wedge$
    $heap = $ empty $\wedge$
    dom $\overleftarrow{heap} \cup \{nil\} = collect\text{-}address(\overleftarrow{heap}, \overleftarrow{first}, \{\,\}) \wedge$
    dom $heap \cup \{$nil$\} = collect\text{-}address(heap, first, \{\,\})$

To empty the stack, all of the storage that the stack occupies must be returned to the system so that $heap = $ empty when the operation completes. This suggests that a loop is needed to free each element of the stack.

empty-stack ()
ext wr *first* : *ListEl*
  wr *heap* : *Store* ≜
  ⟦ **dcl** *temp* : *ListEl* **in**
    do *first* ≠ nil → *temp* := *first*;
                first := *first* ↑$_{heap}$.*next*;
                dispose(*heap*, *temp*)
    od ⟧

push (*e* : *Element*)
ext wr *first* : *ListEl*
  wr *heap* : *Store* ≜
  ⟦ **dcl** *temp* : *ListEl* **in**
    temp := **new** *heap*;
    temp ↑$_{heap}$:= *mk-Nodel*(*e*, *first*);
    first := *temp* ⟧

pop ()
ext wr *first* : *ListEl*
  wr *heap* : *Store* ≜
  ⟦ **dcl** *temp* : *ListEl* **in**
    temp := *first*;
    first := *first* ↑$_{heap}$.*next*;
    dispose(*heap*, *temp*) ⟧

read () : *Element*
ext rd *first* : *ListEl*
  rd *heap* : *Store* ≜
  return *first* ↑$_{heap}$.*value*

is-empty () : 𝔹
ext rd *first* : *ListEl* ≜
  return *first* = nil

Fig. 21.4. The complete refinement.

The post-condition is already in a form that is suitable for deriving the loop parameters:

> init   true
> guard $first \neq$ nil
> inv   dom $heap \cup \{nil\} = collect\text{-}address(heap, first, \{\})$
> var   dom $heap \subset$ dom $\overleftarrow{heap}$

Notice that nothing needs to be done to establish the loop-invariant: as it is also the data-invariant, it is already true. Also there is no need for a term in the invariant that guarantees that $\{\} \subseteq$ dom $heap$ since this is always true. These loop parameters give:

> do $first \neq$ nil $\rightarrow$ *loop-body*
>   chg $first : ListEl$
> $heap : Store$
>   pre $first \neq$ nil $\land$
>   dom $heap \cup \{nil\} = collect\text{-}address(heap, first, \{\})$
>   post dom $heap \cup \{nil\} = collect\text{-}address(heap, first, \{\}) \land$
>   dom $heap \subset$ dom $\overleftarrow{heap}$
> od

The usual strategy is to just establish the variant, and we would just like to do $heap = \{first\} \triangleleft \overleftarrow{heap}$ which has this effect. The definition of *dispose*, the collection invariant and the data type invariant for a stack suggest that we also do $first = \overleftarrow{first}.next$ at the same time. A little thought suggest that these two together give a possible refinement of *body*.

> *loop-body* $\sqsubseteq$ *dispose-el*
>   chg $first : ListEl$
> $heap : Store$
>   pre $first \neq$ nil $\land$
>   dom $heap \cup \{nil\} = collect\text{-}address(heap, first, \{\})$
>   post $heap = \{\overleftarrow{first}\} \triangleleft \overleftarrow{heap} \land first = \overleftarrow{heap}(\overleftarrow{first}).next$

For this to be a valid refinement, the following proof-obligation needs to be discharged:

21.3 The Stack Using Explicit Pointers

$\overleftarrow{first} \neq \mathsf{nil} \wedge$ (1)
$\mathsf{dom}\ \overleftarrow{heap} \cup \{\mathsf{nil}\} = collect\text{-}address(\overleftarrow{heap}, \overleftarrow{first}, \{\,\}) \wedge$ (2)
$heap = \{\overleftarrow{first}\} \triangleleft \overleftarrow{heap} \wedge$ (3)
$first = \overleftarrow{heap}(\overleftarrow{first}).next$ (4)
$\Rightarrow$
$\mathsf{dom}\ heap \cup \{\mathsf{nil}\} = collect\text{-}address(heap, first, \{\,\}) \wedge$
$\mathsf{dom}\ heap \subset \mathsf{dom}\ \overleftarrow{heap}$

The proof of this is non-trivial, but an outline of what needs to be done will be given. Now since $\overleftarrow{first} \neq \mathsf{nil}$ the term on the left of the implication containing *collect-address* can be expanded using the definition to give:

$\quad \mathsf{dom}\ heap \cup \{\mathsf{nil}\}$
$= \quad$ by (3)
$\quad \mathsf{dom}\ (\{\overleftarrow{first}\} \triangleleft \overleftarrow{heap}) \cup \{\mathsf{nil}\}$
$= \quad$ property of maps
$\quad (\mathsf{dom}\ (\overleftarrow{heap}) \setminus \{\overleftarrow{first}\}) \cup \{\mathsf{nil}\}$
$= \quad$ property of sets, since $\overleftarrow{first} \neq \mathsf{nil}$ by (1)
$\quad (\mathsf{dom}\ \overleftarrow{heap} \cup \{\mathsf{nil}\}) \setminus \{\overleftarrow{first}\}$
$= \quad$ by (2)
$\quad collect\text{-}address(\overleftarrow{first}, \overleftarrow{heap}, \{\,\}) \setminus \{\overleftarrow{first}\}$
$= \quad$ definition of *collect-address* with $\overleftarrow{first} \neq \mathsf{nil}$
$\quad collect\text{-}address(\overleftarrow{heap}(\overleftarrow{first}).next, \overleftarrow{heap}, \{\overleftarrow{first}\}) \setminus \{\overleftarrow{first}\}$
$= \quad$ see below
$\quad collect\text{-}address(\overleftarrow{heap}(\overleftarrow{first}).next, \{\overleftarrow{first}\} \triangleleft \overleftarrow{heap}, \{\,\})$
$= \quad$ by (4) and (3)
$\quad collect\text{-}address(first, heap, \{\,\})$

The penultimate step is very difficult to prove formally (even rigorously). Informally it can be justified: since since $\overleftarrow{first} \neq \mathsf{nil}$ and by the collection invariant $\overleftarrow{first} \in \mathsf{dom}\ \overleftarrow{heap}$, thus removing it from the heap mapping and the set of nodes that have been found is identical to removing it from the result. Finally, since $\overleftarrow{first} \in \mathsf{dom}\ \overleftarrow{heap}$ then by (3) certainly $\mathsf{dom}\ heap \subset \mathsf{dom}\ \overleftarrow{heap}$ and we have completed a sketch of the proof.

Proceeding with the refinement of *dispose-el*, the dispose command should be used to return storage to the system, the post-condition for *dispose-el* is

$heap = \{\overleftarrow{first}\} \triangleleft \overleftarrow{heap} \wedge first = \overleftarrow{first}.next$

to introduce the dispose command requires something like:

$heap = \{\overleftarrow{first}\} \triangleleft \overleftarrow{heap} \wedge first = \text{nil} \wedge$
$first = \overleftarrow{first.next}$

which is a little tricky to satisfy with any command other than miracle! If we introduce a new temporary variable *temp*, then a possible solution is to set *temp* to the value of *first* and disposing of the element using the new temporary variable.

$dispose\text{-}el \sqsubseteq copy\text{-}first$
  chg $temp : ListEl$
  pre $first \neq \text{nil} \wedge$
    $\text{dom } heap \cup \{\text{nil}\} = collect\text{-}address(first, heap, \{\,\})$
  post $temp = first$
  ;
  $dispose\text{-}of\text{-}heap$
  chg $temp : ListEl$
    $first : ListEl$
    $heap : Store$
  pre $temp = first$
  post $\overleftarrow{temp} = \overleftarrow{first} \wedge$
    $heap = \{\overleftarrow{first}\} \triangleleft \overleftarrow{heap} \wedge first = \overleftarrow{first.next}$

The refinement of the first command is trivial:

$copy\text{-}first \sqsubseteq temp := first$

The post-condition of the second command can be transformed:

$dispose\text{-}of\text{-}heap \sqsubseteq \textbf{chg } temp : ListEl$
    $first : ListEl$
    $heap : Store$
  pre $temp = first$
  post $\overleftarrow{temp} = \overleftarrow{first} \wedge temp = \text{nil} \wedge$
    $heap = \{\overleftarrow{temp}\} \triangleleft \overleftarrow{heap} \wedge first = \overleftarrow{first.next}$
  $\sqsubseteq first := first \uparrow_{heap} .next;$
    $\text{dispose}(heap, temp)$

thus

$dispose\text{-}el \sqsubseteq temp := first;$
    $first := first \uparrow_{heap} .next;$
    $\text{dispose}(heap, temp)$

which completes a sketch of the refinement of *empty-stack*.

The refinement of the other operations to executable code is left for the reader, but some indication of what needs to be done is given. The *push* operation allocates storage for the new element and adds it to the stack:

push$_1$ (*e* : *Element*)
ext wr *first* : *ListEl*
    wr *heap* : *Store*
post *first* ∈ token \ dom *heap* ∧
    heap = $\overleftarrow{heap}$ † {*first* ↦ *mk-Nodel*(*e*, $\overleftarrow{first}$)}

We need an address (token) that has not been used so far and add this to our model of store; remember that *heap* is those storage locations that have been allocated so far. Define *first* to be this new location and update our *heap* mapping accordingly.

Now the result of the *new* function is a pointer value (i.e. a token) of the right type which is unused, so the operation *push* can be rewritten using this function:

push$_1$ (*e* : *Element*)
ext wr *first* : *ListEl*
    wr *heap* : *Store*
post *first* = *new*($\overleftarrow{heap}$) ∧
    heap = $\overleftarrow{heap}$ † {*first* ↦ *mk-Nodel*(*e*, $\overleftarrow{first}$)}

The *read* operation is straightforward:

read$_1$ () *r* : *Element*
ext rd *first* : *ListEl*
    rd *heap* : *Store*
pre *first* ≠ nil
post *r* = *heap*(*first*).*value*

it reads the element on the top of the stack non-destructively. The new *pop* operation is

pop$_1$ ()
ext wr *first* : *ListEl*
    wr *heap* : *Store*
pre *first* ≠ nil
post *mk-* (*heap*,-) = *dispose*($\overleftarrow{heap}$, $\overleftarrow{first}$) ∧
    first = $\overleftarrow{heap}$($\overleftarrow{first}$).*next*

and it just pops the stack; this is achieved by disposing of the storage referenced by the old first of the list, and updating the first of the list to reference the next element of the list (stack). The storage needs to be disposed of to preserve the invariant. The existential quantifier which occurs with a straightforward operation quotation of *dispose* has been removed.

is-empty$_1$ () $r : \mathbb{B}$
ext rd *first* : *ListEl*
post $r \Leftrightarrow$ *first* = nil

This operation just checks whether the stack is empty or not; the stack is empty if the first of the list has the value nil.

The body of the refinement for the *push* operation is:

$heap := heap \dagger \{temp \mapsto mk\text{-}Nodel(e, first)\}$

using our usual short-hand, this can be written:

$heap(temp) := mk\text{-}Nodel(e, first)$

which can be further abbreviated to

$temp \uparrow_{heap} := mk\text{-}Nodel(e, first)$

Once all the proofs that involve the invariant are discharged, and the safety of the implementation proved, the refinement to code is straightforward and the result is shown in Fig. 21.4.

21.4 Summary

The refinement of the operation *empty-stack* in Section 21.3 illustrates many of the problems associated with using pointers in a refinement. Two constraints were introduced:

- pointers never point to junk, they are always either nil or denote an active 'address' in the heap; and
- every piece of 'allocated' storage in the heap has a pointer referencing it.

The first constraint means that dereferencing a pointer will be safe – either it gives a piece of data or a diagnostic. The second means that there is no dead storage: all of the storage in a heap can be accounted for. It is this second property that causes problems. For each data-structure that contains pointers it is necessary to write a blood-hound function similar to *collect-addresses* that 'sniffs-out' all heap storage and then this function should be used in an appropriate invariant to state that no storage is lost – it all can be accounted for. It is this function that makes the proofs difficult (and once they have been discharged, garbage collection easy). These two constraints impose difficult and tedious proof obligations on any refinement that involves pointers, as can be seen from the above examples. If we use the hidden pointer approach, the proofs about consistent storage can be dealt with by the compiler, it can keep track of any pointer chains and generate the appropriate code to allocate and deallocate the storage safely. The *mk-...* (...) constructor would be compiled into the **new** operation under the covers; replacing a nested component in a data structure would be a signal to the compiler to generate hidden **dispose** operations to reclaim heap storage that is no longer be accessible. Then it is just necessary to prove that the implementation satisfies the constraints. Thus it would be possible to provide some of the functions of pointers in a safe manner. However, as has already been stated, the hidden pointers approach means that 'circular' data structures cannot be built directly. It is an interesting point that both Java and Smalltalk take this approach to their pointers; any attempt to add 'real' pointers to either of these languages would break this inherent safety feature.

A further point, some safe subsets of languages such as Pascal or Ada do not allow pointers; thus if the facilities provided by pointers are required, heaps and pointers will need to be simulated using arrays and array indexes; this approach will make programs hard to read. It would be possible to introduce very safe pointers using the hidden pointer approach or almost safe pointers using the language constructs suggested in this chapter – 'sniffing' functions would need to be defined and proof obligations undertaken to make the use of pointers safe. The approach is really just arrays and array indexes in disguise, but the programming style is more familiar. A side benefit of implementing a heap for each data structure would be possibility of writing a heap to backing store; garbage collection is also a little easier – the reader is referred to Algol-W ([31]) for details.

22. Binary Trees

This chapter will consider implementing a set using one of the standard data structure, an ordered binary tree. Without any loss of generality it can be assumed that there is an order relation over the components of the set.

22.1 The Specification

The specification for a set data-type together with three simple operations is given below:

types

$Element = \ldots$ -- an order relation, $<$, is defined on this type ;

$Set = Element$-set

operations

$in\,(e : Element, s : Set)\;r : \mathbb{B}$
post $r \Leftrightarrow e \in s$;

$insert\,(e : Element, s : Set)\;r : Set$
post $r = \{e\} \cup s$;

$delete\,(e : Element, s : Set)\;r : Set$
post $r = s \setminus \{e\}$

22.2 The Refinement

The refinement is based on an ordered binary tree, however to avoid some of the complications of pointers, the data-structure will be constructed using nested composite objects. The types needed for representing a tree are:

types

$Node :: left : Tree$
$\qquad\quad data : Element$
$\qquad\quad right : Tree$

inv $n \triangleq$ ordered-node (n);

$Tree = [Node]$

The invariant is the usual one for ordered binary trees:

ordered-node : $Node \to \mathbb{B}$
ordered-node $(mk\text{-}Node(left, data, right)) \triangleq$
$\quad (\forall x \in \text{to-set}(left) \cdot x < data) \land (\forall x \in \text{to-set}(right) \cdot data < x)$

The *to-set* function extracts the data stored at each node:

to-set : $Tree \to Set$
to-set $(n) \triangleq$ if $n = $ nil then $\{\ \}$ else node-to-set (n)

node-to-set : $Node \to Set$
node-to-set $(mk\text{-}Node(left, data, right)) \triangleq$
$\quad$ to-set $(left) \cup \{data\} \cup$ to-set $(right)$

The coupling invariant can be defined in terms of the function *to-set*:

couple : $Tree \times Set \to \mathbb{B}$
couple $(s, t) \triangleq s = $ to-set (t)

22.3 The Refinement of the *in* Operation

The new version of the *in* operation is easily obtained by substitution:

in $(e : Element, t : Tree)\ r : \mathbb{B}$
post $r \Leftrightarrow e \in $ to-set (t)

The first step of the refinement is to introduce a procedure body:

in $(e : Element, t : Tree)\ : \mathbb{B} \triangleq$
$\quad \llbracket$ dcl $r : \mathbb{B}$ in
$\quad\quad$ *in-body*
$\quad\quad$ chg $r : \mathbb{B}$
$\quad\quad$ post $r \Leftrightarrow e \in $ to-set (t)
$\quad\quad$;
$\quad\quad$ return $r\ \rrbracket$

Next the two cases that occur in the coupling invariant can be used to simplify the body of the procedure: it can be seen that the tree can either be empty or non-empty. Checking whether the target element is in an empty tree is trivial. To check whether the target element is in a non-empty tree can be done by breaking the node into its three subcomponent and either the element stored at the node is the target element, or the data type invariant can be used to decide which of the two subtrees to use to continue the search. To achieve this the *introduce alternatives* rule can be used to obtain the following:

$in\text{-}body \sqsubseteq$ if $t = \text{nil} \quad \rightarrow nil\text{-}node$
$\qquad\qquad\qquad\qquad\quad\text{chg } r : \mathbb{B}$
$\qquad\qquad\qquad\qquad\quad\text{pre } t = \text{nil}$
$\qquad\qquad\qquad\qquad\quad\text{post } t = \text{nil} \land r \Leftrightarrow e \in to\text{-}set(t)$
$\qquad\quad[\!]\ is\text{-}Node(t) \rightarrow in\text{-}node$
$\qquad\qquad\qquad\qquad\quad\text{chg } r : \mathbb{B}$
$\qquad\qquad\qquad\qquad\quad\text{pre } is\text{-}Node(t)$
$\qquad\qquad\qquad\qquad\quad\text{post } is\text{-}Node(t) \land r \Leftrightarrow e \in to\text{-}set(t)$
fi

The proof obligation for this step is just

$\text{true} \Leftrightarrow t = \text{nil} \lor is\text{-}Node(t)$

which is easily discharged from the definition of the type *Tree*.

Now we can transform each of the two post-conditions, firstly that of *nil-node*:

$t = \text{nil} \land r \Leftrightarrow e \in to\text{-}set(t)$
$\Longleftrightarrow$ definition of *to-set* and assumption
$t = \text{nil} \land r \Leftrightarrow e \in \{\,\}$
$\Longleftrightarrow$
$t = \text{nil} \land r \Leftrightarrow \text{false}$

and this gives:

$nil\text{-}node \sqsubseteq r := \text{false}$

The post-condition for *in-node* can be transformed as follows:

$is\text{-}Node(t) \land r \Leftrightarrow e \in to\text{-}set(t)$
$\Longleftrightarrow$ definition of *to-set* and assumption
$is\text{-}Node(t) \land r \Leftrightarrow e \in \text{let } mk\text{-}Node(left, data, right) = t \text{ in}$
$\qquad\qquad\qquad\qquad\qquad\quad to\text{-}set(left) \cup \{data\} \cup to\text{-}set(right)$
$\Longleftrightarrow$
$is\text{-}Node(t) \land \text{let } mk\text{-}Node(left, data, right) = t \text{ in}$
$\qquad\qquad r \Leftrightarrow e \in to\text{-}set(left) \lor e = data \lor e \in to\text{-}set(right)$

In the above, the various identifiers occur in expressions; in the code that is under development, t is a state variable (or a copy of one). Thus the

22.3 The Refinement of the in Operation

convention for declarations will be used, and in the developed code let should (must) be replaced with def. This gives the following refinement step:

$in\text{-}node \sqsubseteq$ **def** $mk\text{-}Node\,(left, data, right) = t$ **in**
    $in\text{-}nodec$
    chg $r : \mathbb{B}$
    post $r \Leftrightarrow e \in to\text{-}set\,(left) \vee e = data \vee e \in to\text{-}set\,(right)$

The next step is to use the *introduce alternatives* rule again:

$in\text{-}nodec \sqsubseteq$
if $e < data \rightarrow in\text{-}left\text{-}node$
               chg $r : \mathbb{B}$
               pre $e < data$
               post $r \Leftrightarrow e \in to\text{-}set\,(left) \vee e = data \vee e \in to\text{-}set\,(right)$
[] $e = data \rightarrow equals\text{-}data$
               chg $r : \mathbb{B}$
               pre $e = data$
               post $r \Leftrightarrow e \in to\text{-}set\,(left) \vee e = data \vee e \in to\text{-}set\,(right)$
[] $data < e \rightarrow in\text{-}right\text{-}node$
               chg $r : \mathbb{B}$
               pre $data < e$
               post $r \Leftrightarrow e \in to\text{-}set\,(left) \vee e = data \vee e \in to\text{-}set\,(right)$
fi

with the following (trivial) proof obligation:

$$\text{true} \Leftrightarrow e < data \vee e = data \vee data < e$$

For the next refinement step, which will use recursion, it is necessary to define an auxiliary function *depth*:

$depth : Tree \rightarrow \mathbb{N}$
$depth\,(t\!:\!Tree) \triangleq \text{if } t = \text{nil then } 0 \text{ else } 1 + max(depth(t.left), depth(t.right))$

This function can be used to provide an order relation on trees: for two trees t_1 and t_2 we have $t_1 < t_2$ if and only if $depth(t_1) < depth(t_2)$. Now the refinement can be continued with a reorganization in preparation for the recursion step, and then the introduction of the recursion:

$in\text{-}left\text{-}node \sqsubseteq$ **chg** $r : \mathbb{B}$
                     pre $is\text{-}Node\,(t) \wedge e < data \wedge depth(t.left) < depth(t)$
                     post $r \Leftrightarrow e \in to\text{-}set\,(t)[r, t\backslash r, left]$
               $\sqsubseteq r := in\,(e, left)$

The specifications *equals-data* and *in-right-node* can be refined in a similar fashion to give executable code for *in-nodec*:

$$in\text{-}nodec \sqsubseteq \text{if } e < data \to r := in\,(e, left)$$
$$\qquad \| \ e = data \to r := true$$
$$\qquad \| \ data < e \to r := in\,(e, right)$$
$$\qquad \text{fi}$$

The refinements can be put together and some further reorganization will produce the final code:

$in\,(e: Element, t: Tree)\ :\mathbb{B} \triangleq$
  if $t = nil \quad \to$ return false
  $\| \ is\text{-}Node\,(t) \to$ def $mk\text{-}Node\,(left, data, right) = t$ in
      if $e < data \to$ return $in\,(e, left)$
      $\| \ e = data \to$ return true
      $\| \ data < e \to$ return $in\,(e, right)$
      fi
  fi

22.4 The Refinement of the *insert* Operation

The refinement of the *insert* operation is just

$insert\,(e: Element, t: Tree)\ r: Tree$
post $to\text{-}set\,(r) = \{e\} \cup to\text{-}set\,(t)$

and the first step is the introduction of a procedure body:

$insert\,(e: Element, t: Tree)\ : Tree \triangleq$
  〖 dcl $r: Tree$ in
    insert-body
    chg $r: Tree$
    post $to\text{-}set\,(r) = \{e\} \cup to\text{-}set\,(t)$
    ;
    return r 〗

A case analysis based on the coupling invariant is used as before to give the first refinement step:

$insert\text{-}body \sqsubseteq \text{if } t = nil \quad \to \ insert\text{-}in\text{-}empty$
$\qquad\qquad\qquad\qquad\qquad\quad$ chg $r: Tree$
$\qquad\qquad\qquad\qquad\qquad\quad$ pre $t = nil$
$\qquad\qquad\qquad\qquad\qquad\quad$ post $to\text{-}set\,(r) = \{e\} \cup to\text{-}set\,(t)$

22.4 The Refinement of the insert Operation

$$\Box\ \textit{is-Node}\,(t) \to \textit{insert-in-node}$$
$$\textbf{chg}\ r : \textit{Tree}$$
$$\textbf{pre}\ \textit{is-Node}\,(t)$$
$$\textbf{post}\ \textit{to-set}\,(r) = \{e\} \cup \textit{to-set}\,(t)$$

fi

The post-conditions can be simplified using the pre-conditions; consider the two cases $t = \text{nil}$ and $t \neq \text{nil}$:

case (i) $t = \text{nil}$

$\quad \textit{to-set}\,(r) = \{e\} \cup \textit{to-set}\,(t)$
$\Longleftrightarrow$ assumption and definition of *to-set*
$\quad \textit{to-set}\,(r) = \{e\} \cup \{\,\}$
$\Longleftrightarrow$ definition of *to-set*
$\quad \textit{to-set}\,(r) = \textit{to-set}\,(\textit{mk-Node}\,(\text{nil}, e, \text{nil}))$
$\Longleftarrow$ equal arguments to a function
$\quad r = \textit{mk-Node}\,(\text{nil}, e, \text{nil})$

case (ii) $t \neq \text{nil}$ and writing $t = \textit{mk-Node}\,(\textit{left}, \textit{data}, \textit{right})$

$\quad \textit{to-set}\,(r) = \{e\} \cup \textit{to-set}\,(t)$
$\Longleftrightarrow$
$\quad \textit{to-set}\,(r) = \{e\} \cup \textit{node-to-set}\,(t)$
$\Longleftrightarrow$
$\quad \textit{to-set}\,(r) = \{e\} \cup \textit{to-set}(\textit{left}) \cup \{\textit{data}\} \cup \textit{to-set}(\textit{right})$

As before, we consider three further cases: $e < \textit{data}$, $e = \textit{data}$, and $\textit{data} < e$. The first case is $e < \textit{data}$:

$\quad \textit{to-set}\,(r) = \{e\} \cup \textit{to-set}(\textit{left}) \cup \{\textit{data}\} \cup \textit{to-set}(\textit{right})$
$\Longleftrightarrow$
$\quad \textit{to-set}\,(r) = (\{e\} \cup \textit{to-set}(\textit{left})) \cup \{\textit{data}\} \cup \textit{to-set}(\textit{right})$
$\Longleftarrow$
$\quad \textit{to-set}\,(r) = (\textit{insert}\,(e, \textit{left})) \cup \{\textit{data}\} \cup \textit{to-set}(\textit{right})$
$\Longleftarrow$
$\quad \textit{to-set}\,(r) = \textit{node-to-set}\,(\textit{mk-Node}\,(\textit{insert}\,(e, \textit{left}), \textit{data}, \textit{right}))$
$\Longleftarrow$
$\quad \textit{to-set}\,(r) = \textit{to-set}\,(\textit{mk-Node}\,(\textit{insert}\,(e, \textit{left}), \textit{data}, \textit{right}))$
$\Longleftarrow$
$\quad r = \textit{mk-Node}\,(\textit{insert}\,(e, \textit{left}), \textit{data}, \textit{right})$

The second case is $e = \textit{data}$:

$$to\text{-}set\,(r) = \{e\} \cup to\text{-}set(left) \cup \{data\} \cup to\text{-}set(right)$$
$\Longleftrightarrow$
$$to\text{-}set\,(r) = to\text{-}set(left) \cup \{data\} \cup to\text{-}set(right)$$
$\Longleftarrow$
$$to\text{-}set\,(r) = node\text{-}to\text{-}set\,(mk\text{-}Node\,(left, data, right))$$
$\Longleftarrow$
$$to\text{-}set\,(r) = to\text{-}set\,(t)$$
$\Longleftarrow$
$$r = t$$

The third case $data < e$ is similar to the first case, so we shall just state the result:

$$to\text{-}set\,(r) = \{e\} \cup to\text{-}set(left) \cup \{data\} \cup to\text{-}set(right)$$
$\Longleftarrow$
$$r = mk\text{-}Node\,(left, data, insert\,(e, right))$$

Thus in a style very similar to the development of *in* we can obtain:

$insert\text{-}in\text{-}node \sqsubseteq $ if $\;e < data \rightarrow$
$\qquad\qquad\qquad\qquad insert\text{-}in\text{-}left\text{-}tree$
$\qquad\qquad\qquad\qquad $ chg $r: Tree$
$\qquad\qquad\qquad\qquad $ pre $\;is\text{-}Node\,(t)$
$\qquad\qquad\qquad\qquad $ post $r = mk\text{-}Node\,(insert\,(e, left), data, right)$
$\qquad\quad [\!]\;\;e = data \rightarrow insert\text{-}in\text{-}node$
$\qquad\qquad\qquad\qquad $ chg $r: Tree$
$\qquad\qquad\qquad\qquad $ pre $\;is\text{-}Node\,(t)$
$\qquad\qquad\qquad\qquad $ post $r = t$
$\qquad\quad [\!]\;\;data < e \rightarrow$
$\qquad\qquad\qquad\qquad insert\text{-}in\text{-}right\text{-}tree$
$\qquad\qquad\qquad\qquad $ chg $r: Tree$
$\qquad\qquad\qquad\qquad $ pre $\;is\text{-}Node\,(t)$
$\qquad\qquad\qquad\qquad $ post $r = mk\text{-}Node\,(left, data, insert\,(e, right))$
$\qquad\quad $ fi

and the various parts can be put together to get:

$insert\,(e: Element, t: Tree)\;: Tree \;\triangleq$
$\quad $ if $\;t = $ nil $\quad\rightarrow$ return $mk\text{-}Node\,($nil$, e, nil)$
$\quad [\!]\;\;is\text{-}Node\,(t) \rightarrow $ let $mk\text{-}Node\,(left, data, right) = t$ in
$\qquad\qquad\qquad\qquad $ if $\;e < data \rightarrow left\text{-}insert$
$\qquad\qquad\qquad\qquad [\!]\;\;e = data \rightarrow $ return t

$$[\!] \ data < e \rightarrow right\text{-}insert$$
           fi
    fi

where

   $left\text{-}insert \sqsubseteq$ def $nt = insert\,(e, left)$ in return $mk\text{-}Node\,(nt, data, right)$

and

   $right\text{-}insert \sqsubseteq$ def $nt = insert\,(e, right)$ in return $mk\text{-}Node\,(left, data, nt)$

The final code is:

$insert\,(e : Element, t : Tree) : Tree \triangleq$
  if $t = $ nil $\rightarrow$ return $mk\text{-}Node\,(\text{nil}, e, \text{nil})$
  $[\!]$ $is\text{-}Node\,(t) \rightarrow$ def $mk\text{-}Node\,(left, data, right) = t$ in
              if $e < data \rightarrow$ def $nt = insert\,(e, left)$ in
                             return $mk\text{-}Node\,(nt, data, right)$
              $[\!]$ $e = data \rightarrow$ return t
              $[\!]$ $data < e \rightarrow$ def $nt = insert\,(e, right)$ in
                             return $mk\text{-}Node\,(left, data, nt)$
              fi
  fi

22.5 The Refinement of the *delete* Operation

We proceed as before, the first step is to introduce the procedure body:

$delete\,(e : Element, t : Tree) : Tree \triangleq$
  $[\![$ dcl $r : Tree$ in
    $delete\text{-}body$
    chg $r : Tree$
    post $to\text{-}set\,(r) = to\text{-}set\,(t) \setminus \{e\}$
    ;
    return r $]\!]$

Then the case analysis step to give:

$delete\text{-}body \sqsubseteq$ if $t = $ nil $\rightarrow$ chg $r : Tree$
                              pre $t = $ nil
                              post $to\text{-}set\,(r) = to\text{-}set\,(t) \setminus \{e\}$
             $[\!]$ $is\text{-}Node\,(t) \rightarrow$ chg $r : Tree$
                              pre $is\text{-}Node\,(t)$
                              post $to\text{-}set\,(r) = to\text{-}set\,(t) \setminus \{e\}$
             fi

The second case can be further refined:

$$
\begin{aligned}
\textit{delete-body} \sqsubseteq\ &\textbf{if}\ t = \textsf{nil}\quad \to\ \textbf{chg}\ r: \textit{Tree}\\
&\qquad\qquad\qquad\quad \textbf{pre}\ \ t = \textsf{nil}\\
&\qquad\qquad\qquad\quad \textbf{post}\ \textit{to-set}\,(r) = \textit{to-set}\,(t) \setminus \{e\}\\
&[]\ \textit{is-Node}\,(t) \to\ \textbf{def}\ \textit{mk-Node}\,(\textit{left}, \textit{data}, \textit{right}) = t\ \textbf{in}\\
&\qquad\qquad\qquad\quad \textbf{if}\ \ e < \textit{data} \to\ \textit{left-delete}\\
&\qquad\qquad\qquad\quad []\ \ e = \textit{data} \to\ \textit{node-delete}\\
&\qquad\qquad\qquad\quad []\ \ \textit{data} < e \to\ \textit{right-delete}\\
&\qquad\qquad\qquad\quad \textbf{fi}\\
&\textbf{fi}
\end{aligned}
$$

where

left-delete
chg r : *Tree*
pre $e < \textit{data}$
post $\textit{to-set}\,(r) = (\textit{to-set}\,(\textit{left}) \cup \{\textit{data}\} \cup \textit{to-set}\,(\textit{right})) \setminus \{e\}$

node-delete
chg r : *Tree*
pre $e = \textit{data}$
post $\textit{to-set}\,(r) = (\textit{to-set}\,(\textit{left}) \cup \{\textit{data}\} \cup \textit{to-set}\,(\textit{right})) \setminus \{e\}$

right-delete
chg r : *Tree*
pre $e > \textit{data}$
post $\textit{to-set}\,(r) = (\textit{to-set}\,(\textit{left}) \cup \{\textit{data}\} \cup \textit{to-set}\,(\textit{right})) \setminus \{e\}$

This and the next refinement step are justified by again considering the cases $t = \textsf{nil}$ and $t \neq \textsf{nil}$.

case (i) $t = \textsf{nil}$

$\textit{to-set}\,(r) = \textit{to-set}\,(t) \setminus \{e\}$
$\Longleftrightarrow$ assumption and definition of *to-set*
$\textit{to-set}\,(r) = \{\,\} \setminus \{e\}$
$\Longleftrightarrow$ definition of *to-set*
$\textit{to-set}\,(r) = \{\,\}$
$\Longleftrightarrow$ definition of *to-set*
$\textit{to-set}\,(r) = \textit{to-set}\,(\textsf{nil})$
$\Longleftarrow$ equal arguments to a function
$r = \textsf{nil}$

case (ii) $t \neq \textsf{nil}$ writing $t = \textit{mk-Node}\,(\textit{left}, \textit{data}, \textit{right})$ we have

22.5 The Refinement of the delete Operation

$$to\text{-}set\,(r) = to\text{-}set\,(t) \setminus \{e\}$$
$\iff$
$$to\text{-}set\,(r) = node\text{-}to\text{-}set\,(t) \setminus \{e\}$$
$\iff$
$$to\text{-}set\,(r) = (to\text{-}set(left) \cup \{data\} \cup to\text{-}set(right)) \setminus \{e\}$$

Once more the three further cases can be considered; the first case is $e < data$:

$$to\text{-}set\,(r) = (to\text{-}set(left) \cup \{data\} \cup to\text{-}set(right)) \setminus \{e\}$$
$\iff$
$$to\text{-}set\,(r) = (to\text{-}set(left) \setminus \{e\}) \cup \{data\} \cup to\text{-}set(right)$$
$\iff$
$$to\text{-}set\,(r) = (delete\,(e, left)) \cup \{data\} \cup to\text{-}set(right)$$
$\iff$
$$to\text{-}set\,(r) = node\text{-}to\text{-}set\,(mk\text{-}Node\,(delete\,(e, left), data, right))$$
$\iff$
$$to\text{-}set\,(r) = to\text{-}set\,(mk\text{-}Node\,(delete\,(e, left), data, right))$$
$\Longleftarrow$
$$r = mk\text{-}Node\,(delete\,(e, left), data, right)$$

The second case is $e = data$:

$$to\text{-}set\,(r) = (to\text{-}set(left) \cup \{data\} \cup to\text{-}set(right)) \setminus \{e\}$$
$\iff$
$$to\text{-}set\,(r) = to\text{-}set(left) \cup to\text{-}set(right)$$

Finally for the third case $data < e$

$$to\text{-}set\,(r) = (to\text{-}set(left) \cup \{data\} \cup to\text{-}set(right)) \setminus \{e\}$$
$\Longleftarrow$
$$r = mk\text{-}Node\,(left, data, delete\,(e, right))$$

Thus we have:

$left\text{-}delete \sqsubseteq$ def $nt = delete\,(e, left)$ in
    return $mk\text{-}Node\,(nt, data, right)$

and

$right\text{-}delete \sqsubseteq$ def $nt = delete\,(e, right)$ in
    return $mk\text{-}Node\,(left, data, nt)$

The operation *node-delete* needs more work, the first step is to use the form of a *Node* to motivate an application of the *introduce alternatives* rule:

22. Binary Trees

$$node\text{-}delete \sqsubseteq \textbf{if } \begin{array}{ll} left = \text{nil} & \rightarrow \text{return } right \\ [\!]\ right = \text{nil} & \rightarrow \text{return } left \\ [\!]\ left \neq \text{nil} \land right \neq \text{nil} & \rightarrow [\![\ \textbf{dcl } res : Tree \textbf{ in} \\ & delete\text{-}data; \\ & \text{return } res\ ]\!] \end{array}$$
$$\textbf{fi}$$

There are two strategies for the implementation of *delete-data*, so we shall let its specification reflect this; the operation can be defined thus:

delete-data
chg *res* : *Tree*
pre *left* ≠ nil ∧ *right* ≠ nil
post let *mk-*(*min*, *new-right*) = *tmins* (*right*) **in**
    res = *mk-Node* (*left*, *min*, *new-right*)
    ∨
    let *mk-*(*new-left*, *max*) = *tmaxs* (*left*) **in**
    res = *mk-Node* (*new-left*, *max*, *right*)

where

tmins (*t* : *Tree*) *r* : (*Element* × *Tree*)
pre *t* ≠ nil
post let *x* = *mins* (*to-set*(*t*)) **in**
    r = *mk-*(*x*, *to-set*(*t*) \ {*x*})

and

tmaxs (*t* : *Tree*) *r* : (*Tree* × *Element*)
pre *t* ≠ nil
post def *x* = *maxs* (*to-set*(*t*)) **in**
    r = *mk-*(*to-set*(*t*) \ {*x*}, *x*)

The non-determinism can be removed, and it is easy to show that

delete-data ⊑ **def** *mk-*(*new-left*, *max*) = *tmaxs* (*left*) **in**
    res := *mk-Node* (*new-left*, *max*, *right*)

To continue, we need to refine *tmaxs*; this function is required to return the largest element of a tree, and a tree with that element removed. The invariant guarantees that largest element is always to be found in the right subtree if it exists. Thus there are two possible cases, the right subtree does not exists, in which case the largest element is the data element in the node, or the right subtree contains the largest element. We can do two steps together; introduce the procedure body and a selection statement to cover the two cases discussed:

22.5 The Refinement of the delete Operation

$tmaxs\,(t:Tree)\ :\ Tree \times Element \triangleq$
$[\![\,\mathsf{dcl}\ r:Tree \times Element\ \mathsf{in}$
  $\quad\mathsf{if}\ \ t.right = \mathsf{nil}\quad \to\ max\text{-}in\text{-}node$
  $\qquad\qquad\qquad\qquad\qquad \mathsf{chg}\ r:Tree \times Element$
  $\qquad\qquad\qquad\qquad\qquad \mathsf{pre}\ \ t.right = \mathsf{nil}$
  $\qquad\qquad\qquad\qquad\qquad \mathsf{post}\ \mathsf{let}\ x = maxs\,(to\text{-}set\,(t))\ \mathsf{in}$
  $\qquad\qquad\qquad\qquad\qquad\qquad\qquad r = mk\text{-}(to\text{-}set(t) \setminus \{x\}, x)$
  $\quad[\!]\ is\text{-}Node\,(t.right)\ \to\ max\text{-}in\text{-}right$
  $\qquad\qquad\qquad\qquad\qquad \mathsf{chg}\ r:Tree \times Element$
  $\qquad\qquad\qquad\qquad\qquad \mathsf{pre}\ \ is\text{-}Node\,(t.right)$
  $\qquad\qquad\qquad\qquad\qquad \mathsf{post}\ \mathsf{let}\ x = maxs\,(to\text{-}set\,(t))\ \mathsf{in}$
  $\qquad\qquad\qquad\qquad\qquad\qquad\qquad r = mk\text{-}(to\text{-}set(t) \setminus \{x\}, x)$
  $\quad\mathsf{fi}\ ;$
  $\quad\mathsf{return}\ r\,]\!]$

The next step is to realize that $maxs(to\text{-}set(t)) = tmax(t)$, some simple transformations will produce the final code for $tmaxs$, which can now be written down:

$tmaxs\,(t:Tree)\ :\ Tree \times Element \triangleq$
$[\![\,\mathsf{dcl}\ nt\ \ :Tree,$
  $\qquad max : Element\ \mathsf{in}$
  $\quad\mathsf{def}\ mk\text{-}Node\,(left, data, right) = t\ \mathsf{in}$
  $\quad\mathsf{if}\ \ right = \mathsf{nil}\qquad \to\ \mathsf{return}\ mk\text{-}(left, data)$
  $\quad[\!]\ is\text{-}Node\,(right)\ \to\ mk\text{-}(nt, max) := tmaxs(right);$
  $\qquad\qquad\qquad\qquad\quad\ \mathsf{return}\ mk\text{-}(mk\text{-}Node\,(left, data, nt), max)$
  $\quad\mathsf{fi}\,]\!]$

The last step is to pull everything together and with some re-organization to get the final code for $delete$:

$delete\,(e:Element, t:Tree)\ :\ Tree \triangleq$
$\quad\mathsf{if}\ \ t = \mathsf{nil}\qquad \to\ \mathsf{return}\ \mathsf{nil}$
$\quad[\!]\ is\text{-}Node\,(t) \to \mathsf{def}\ mk\text{-}Node\,(left, data, right) = t\ \mathsf{in}$
$\qquad\qquad\qquad\ \ \mathsf{if}\ \ e < data\ \to$
$\qquad\qquad\qquad\qquad\qquad \mathsf{def}\ nt = delete\,(e, left)\ \mathsf{in}$
$\qquad\qquad\qquad\qquad\qquad \mathsf{return}\ mk\text{-}Node\,(nt, data, right)$
$\qquad\qquad\qquad\ \ [\!]\ e = data\ \to$
$\qquad\qquad\qquad\qquad\ \mathsf{if}\ \ left = \mathsf{nil}\qquad\qquad\quad \to\ \mathsf{return}\ right$
$\qquad\qquad\qquad\qquad\ [\!]\ right = \mathsf{nil}\qquad\qquad\ \to\ \mathsf{return}\ left$
$\qquad\qquad\qquad\qquad\ [\!]\ left \ne \mathsf{nil} \wedge right \ne \mathsf{nil}\ \to$
$\qquad\qquad\qquad\qquad\qquad\qquad \mathsf{def}\ mk\text{-}(new\text{-}left, max) = tmaxs\,(left)\ \mathsf{in}$
$\qquad\qquad\qquad\qquad\qquad\qquad \mathsf{return}\ mk\text{-}Node\,(new\text{-}left, max, right)$
$\qquad\qquad\qquad\qquad\ \mathsf{fi}$

$[]$ $data < e \rightarrow$
  def $nt = delete\,(e, right)$ in
  return $mk\text{-}Node\,(left, data, nt)$
fi
fi

A point to notice is that it was the data type invariant that drove the development of the refinement – led to the discovery of the necessary algorithms.

22.6 An In-order Traversal

The definition of an in-order traversal of a binary tree can be given recursively as:

$inorder : Tree \rightarrow Element^*$
$inorder\,(t) \triangleq$
  if $t = $ nil then $[\,]$
  else let $mk\text{-}Node\,(left, data, right) = t$ in
    $inorder(left) \frown [data] \frown inorder(right)$

and the specification of an operation that carries out such an in-order traversal can be written thus:

$in\text{-}order\,(t : Tree)\ r : Element^*$
post $r = inorder(t)$

Using the definition of *inorder*, it is a straightforward exercise to develop a recursive procedure that traverses a tree to produce the required result. A harder problem is to develop a non-recursive procedure that satisfies this specification. The main part of the code will be a loop, and with this in mind the post-condition will be transformed to derive the loop parameters – the post-condition can be rewritten in the form:

$inorder(t) = r \frown inorder(p) \land p = $ nil

It is now in the form where an obvious guard and an invariant for a loop can be identified. With this post-condition the loop will work as follows: initially $r = [\,]$ and $p = t$ and finally $p = $ nil and $r = inorder(t)$. However, the evaluation of the *inorder* term still entails recursion. We will investigate this term to shed more light on the problem of removing the recursion; now in the case where p is not nil and thus can be written as $mk\text{-}Node\,(left, data, right)$, we have:

$$inorder(p)$$
$$= \text{ definition of } inorder$$
$$inorder(left) \frown [data] \frown inorder(right)$$

If $left = mk\text{-}Node\,(lleft, ldata, lright)$, a further application of this gives

$$inorder(p)$$
$$=$$
$$inorder(lleft) \frown [ldata] \frown inorder(lright) \frown [data] \frown inorder(right)$$

Each expansion of the first term of such a series gives rise to a new term of the form $[data] \frown inorder(right)$ to the right of it. This suggests introducing a sequence of such terms to get:

$$inorder(p) = inorder(p.left) \frown stack([p] \frown s)$$

where the *stack* function generates the required sequence:

$stack : Tree^* \to Element^*$
$stack\,(s) \triangleq$
  if $s = [\,]$ then $[\,]$
  else let $mk\text{-}Node\,(\text{-}, data, right) = \text{hd } s$ in
    $[data] \frown inorder(right) \frown stack(\text{tl } s)$

Now providing $p \neq \text{nil}$, the following holds:

$$inorder(p.left) \frown stack([p] \frown s)$$
$$=$$
$$inorder(p.left) \frown [p.data] \frown inorder(p.right) \frown stack(s)$$
$$=$$
$$inorder(p) \frown stack(s)$$

Using these properties, the post-condition of *in-order* can be written in the following equivalent form:

$$inorder(t) = r \frown inorder(p) \frown stack(s) \wedge p = \text{nil} \wedge s = [\,]$$

Now *inorder* need not be applied recursively, it can be used to add a new term on the front of the sequence defined by *stack* (hence its name). This analysis suggests the following loop parameters:

init $r = [\,] \wedge p = t \wedge s = [\,]$
guard $p \neq \text{nil} \vee s \neq [\,]$
inv $inorder(t) = r \frown inorder(p) \frown stack(s) \wedge \text{len } r \leq size(t)$
var $\text{len } \overleftarrow{r} < \text{len } r \vee size(p) < size(\overleftarrow{p})$

where the *size* function counts the number of nodes:

$size: Tree \rightarrow \mathbb{N}$

$size\,(t) \triangleq$
  if $t =$ nil then 0
  else def $mk\text{-}Node\,(left, \text{-}, right) = t$ in
    $size(left) + 1 + size(right)$

The body of the loop will be moving values from $inorder(p)$ and $stack(s)$ and adding them to r until the loop guard is no longer true. For those iterations where $p = $ nil, the guard requires that $s \neq $ nil and thus hd s is a *Node* and can be written in the from $mk\text{-}Node\,(left, data, right)$. Under these conditions, part of the invariant can be transformed as follows:

$$\begin{array}{rl} & r \frown inorder(p) \frown stack(s) \\ = & \text{assumption that } p = \text{nil} \\ & r \frown stack(s) \\ = & \\ & (r \frown [data]) \frown inorder(right) \frown stack(\text{tl } s) \end{array}$$

the data part of a node has been added to r and a new *inorder* term has been re-introduced. This suggests that the guard be rewritten in this equivalent form:

guard $p \neq $ nil $\vee$ $(p = $ nil $\wedge s \neq [\,])$

and the loop body split into two guarded statements to deal with this possibility – note that it is only necessary to process the *stack* when there are no *inorder* nodes to process.

With these investigations complete, we are in a position to develop the algorithm. The first refinement step will introduce a sufficient number of local variables and a procedure body, this step produces the following:

$in\text{-}order\,(t: Tree)\ : Element^* \triangleq$
  ⟦ dcl $r: Element^*$,
      $p: Tree$,
      $s: Tree^*$ in
  $in\text{-}order\text{-}body$
  chg $r: Element^*$
      $p: Tree$
      $s: Tree^*$
  post $inorder(t) = r \frown inorder(p) \frown stack(s) \wedge p = $ nil $\wedge s = [\,]$
  ;
  return r ⟧

and we can go on to develop an iteration using the above parameters:

$in\text{-}order\text{-}body \sqsubseteq$
$r, p, s := [\,], t, [\,];$
do $p \neq$ nil $\quad\to\quad$ $p\text{-}is\text{-}not\text{-}nil$
$\qquad\qquad\qquad\qquad$ chg $r : Element^*$
$\qquad\qquad\qquad\qquad\quad\;\;\; p : Tree$
$\qquad\qquad\qquad\qquad\quad\;\;\; s : Tree^*$
$\qquad\qquad\qquad\qquad$ pre $\;p \neq$ nil $\land$
$\qquad\qquad\qquad\qquad\qquad inorder(t) = r \frown inorder(p) \frown stack(s) \land$
$\qquad\qquad\qquad\qquad\qquad$ len $r \leq size(t)$
$\qquad\qquad\qquad\qquad$ post $inorder(t) = r \frown inorder(p) \frown stack(s) \land$
$\qquad\qquad\qquad\qquad\qquad$ len $r \leq size(t) \land$
$\qquad\qquad\qquad\qquad\qquad$ (len $\overleftarrow{r}$ < len $r \lor size(p) < size(\overleftarrow{p})$)
[ ] $p =$ nil $\land s \neq [\,] \to\;$ $p\text{-}is\text{-}nil$
$\qquad\qquad\qquad\qquad$ chg $r : Element^*$
$\qquad\qquad\qquad\qquad\quad\;\;\; p : Tree$
$\qquad\qquad\qquad\qquad\quad\;\;\; s : Tree^*$
$\qquad\qquad\qquad\qquad$ pre $\;p =$ nil $\land s \neq [\,] \land$
$\qquad\qquad\qquad\qquad\qquad inorder(t) = r \frown inorder(p) \frown stack(s) \land$
$\qquad\qquad\qquad\qquad\qquad$ len $r \leq size(t)$
$\qquad\qquad\qquad\qquad$ post $inorder(t) = r \frown inorder(p) \frown stack(s) \land$
$\qquad\qquad\qquad\qquad\qquad$ len $r \leq size(t) \land$
$\qquad\qquad\qquad\qquad\qquad$ (len $\overleftarrow{r}$ < len $r \lor size(p) < size(\overleftarrow{p})$)
od

Now the first part of the do command can be refined using the usual strategy for loop bodies: assume the pre-condition in the post-condition, the properties developed earlier can then be used to reorganize the post-conditions; this gives the following refinement steps:

$p\text{-}is\text{-}not\text{-}nil \sqsubseteq$
chg $r : Element^*$
$\quad\;\; p : Tree$
$\quad\;\; s : Tree^*$
pre $\;p \neq$ nil $\land$
$\quad\; inorder(t) = r \frown inorder(p) \frown stack(s) \land$
$\quad\;$ len $r \leq size(t)$
post $\overleftarrow{r} \frown inorder(\overleftarrow{p}) \frown stack(\overleftarrow{s}) = r \frown inorder(p) \frown stack(s) \land$
$\quad\;$ len $r \leq size(t) \land$
$\quad\;$ (len $\overleftarrow{r}$ < len $r \lor size(p) < size(\overleftarrow{p})$)
$\qquad\qquad\sqsubseteq$
pre $\;p \neq$ nil $\land$
$\quad\; inorder(t) = r \frown inorder(p) \frown stack(s) \land$
$\quad\;$ len $r \leq size(t)$

$$\text{post } \overleftarrow{r} \frown inorder(\overleftarrow{p}.left) \frown stack([\overleftarrow{p}] \frown \overleftarrow{s}) = r \frown inorder(p) \frown stack(s) \land$$
$$\text{len } r \leq size(t) \land$$
$$(\text{len } \overleftarrow{r} < \text{len } r \lor size(p) < size(\overleftarrow{p}))$$
$$\sqsubseteq$$
$$\text{pre } p \neq \text{nil} \land$$
$$inorder(t) = r \frown inorder(p) \frown stack(s) \land$$
$$\text{len } r \leq size(t)$$
$$\text{post } r = \overleftarrow{r} \land$$
$$p = \overleftarrow{p}.left \land$$
$$s = [\overleftarrow{p}] \frown \overleftarrow{s} \land$$
$$\text{len } r \leq size(t) \land$$
$$(\text{len } \overleftarrow{r} < \text{len } r \lor size(p) < size(\overleftarrow{p}))$$
$$\sqsubseteq$$
$$p, s := p.left, [p] \frown s$$

For the second component of the iterative command the same approach is used, together with the fact that $size(p) : \mathbb{N}$.

$p\text{-}is\text{-}nil \sqsubseteq \textbf{chg } r : Element^*$
$\qquad p : Tree$
$\qquad s : Tree^*$
$\quad \textbf{pre } p = \text{nil} \land s \neq [\,] \land$
$\qquad inorder(t) = r \frown stack(s) \land$
$\qquad \text{len } r \leq N$
$\quad \textbf{post } inorder(t) = r \frown inorder(p) \frown stack(s) \land$
$\qquad \text{len } r \leq size(t) \land$
$\qquad (\text{len } \overleftarrow{r} < \text{len } r \lor size(p) < 0)$
$\sqsubseteq \textbf{chg } r : Element^*$
$\qquad p : Tree$
$\qquad s : Tree^*$
$\quad \textbf{pre } p = \text{nil} \land s \neq [\,] \land$
$\qquad inorder(t) = r \frown stack(s)$
$\quad \textbf{post } \overleftarrow{r} \frown stack(\overleftarrow{s}) = r \frown inorder(p) \frown stack(s) \land$
$\qquad \text{len } \overleftarrow{r} < \text{len } r \land \text{len } r \leq size(t)$
$\sqsubseteq \textbf{pre } p = \text{nil} \land s \neq [\,] \land$
$\qquad inorder(t) = r \frown stack(s)$
$\quad \textbf{post } \overleftarrow{r} \frown [(\text{hd } \overleftarrow{s}).data] \frown inorder((\text{hd } \overleftarrow{s}).right) \frown stack(\text{tl } \overleftarrow{s}) =$
$\qquad r \frown inorder(p) \frown stack(s) \land$
$\qquad \text{len } \overleftarrow{r} < \text{len } r \land \text{len } r \leq size(t)$
$\sqsubseteq \textbf{pre } p = \text{nil} \land s \neq [\,] \land$
$\qquad inorder(t) = r \frown stack(s)$

$$\text{post } r = \overleftarrow{r} \curvearrowright [(\text{hd } \overleftarrow{s}).data] \land$$
$$p = (\text{hd } \overleftarrow{s}).right \land$$
$$s = \text{tl } \overleftarrow{s} \land$$
$$\text{len } \overleftarrow{r} < \text{len } r \land \text{len } r \leq size(t)$$
$$\sqsubseteq r, p, s := r \curvearrowright [(\text{hd } s).data], (\text{hd } s).right, \text{tl } s$$

The proof obligations are straight-forward and are left for the reader.

Substituting the refinements produces the final code for our *in-order* traversal of a tree:

$$in\text{-}order\,(t:Tree)\,:Element^*\,\triangleq$$
$$[\![\,\text{dcl } r:Element^*,$$
$$\quad p:Tree,$$
$$\quad s:Tree^*\text{ in}$$
$$r, p, s := [\,], t, [\,];$$
$$\text{do } p \neq \text{nil} \qquad \to p, s := p.left, [p] \curvearrowright s$$
$$[\!]\;p = \text{nil} \land s \neq [\,] \to r, p, s := r \curvearrowright [(\text{hd } s).data], (\text{hd } s).right, \text{tl } s$$
$$\text{od};$$
$$\text{return } r\,]\!]$$

22.7 Summary

A further refinement step could be taken to replace nested types by pointers, and sequences by arrays and pointers; this is relatively easy[1] and is thus once again left for the reader.

---

[1] Well, the sequence-to-array part is – proving the safety properties of the pointers that are used to implement the tree data type is more difficult.

23. Epilogue

The semantics using weakest pre-conditions have been given for an updated version of Meta-IV (the if statement and while statement of Meta-IV have been replaced by Dijkstra's guarded command equivalents). Using these semantics it was shown that it is easy to derive properties of commands and refinement proof rules. There are three advantages to this approach:

1. because all of the commands and constructs of the language are defined in terms of only four basic commands and three operators, many properties can be proved for these constructs only, they automatically extend to the full language;
2. because any command can be written in a normal form, many properties can be proved using just the normal form; and
3. transformation rules that can be used for both algorithmic refinement and for data refinement are easily derived and proved correct.

A further advantage of this approach appears to be the ease in which many of the properties of the basic commands and operators can be proved – this book has not supplied many proofs as they are all very straightforward and can be left as a simple exercise for the reader.

The transformation rules for both data and program refinement derived from this work are such that data and program refinement can be carried out in any order, it is sometimes easier to perform program refinement before data-refinement. Examples of this approach can be found in [9] and [10].

This book defines the major components of a specification language that is a close relative of VDM-SL. It would be relatively straight-forward to use this work as the basis of a full formal definition of VDM-SL. The form of such a formal definition would follow the style of the formal definition of VDM-SL found in the ISO Standard. A function would be defined to translate the full language into the kernel language described in Chapter 2 and the weakest pre-condition semantics given with respect to the kernel language. The tixe/exit mechanism could be handled in the style of the Meta-IV definition. ([16]).

Another step would be to show that this approach defines the same language as the relational approach taken in the VDM-SL Standard. An easy first step is to show that the specification statement of this language is equivalent to the equivalent construct in the Standard language. Since the definitions of refinement are identical in both languages, they are equivalent (in some sense) up to refinement. The proof of semantic equivalence would involve showing that the kernel language has identical semantics in both styles of definition, and that the construction techniques for new commands in this language have the same meaning in the Standard language.

23.1 An Approach to Loose Patterns and Functions

The semantics for pattern matching given in Chapter 7 can be extended to provide semantics for loose patterns matching; the only complication is the possible presence of universal quantification in some proofs. Loose functions are more difficult, but a way forward can be found using the method of defining constant values also given in Chapter 7. The definition of constant values can be extended to loose functions: it would be possible to declare (the graph of a) function f in a values definition as follows:

$f : D \to R$ be st $p(f)$

Implicitly defined local function could be introduced by the let be such that construct in a similar style.

Some simplification can be obtained by restricting the form of the predicate p. If predicates are restricted to the form:

$pre(d) \Rightarrow post(d, f(d))$

where

$pre : D \to \mathbb{B}$
$post : D \times R \to \mathbb{B}$

then some simplification is achieved without loosing too much functionality – looseness in the sense of underdetermined functions can be introduced. The definition of an underdetermined function would now look like:

$f : D \to R$ be st $\forall d : D \cdot pre(d) \Rightarrow post(d, f(d))$

The syntactic sugar for this can be written[1]:

$f : D \to R$
$f(d)$
pre $pre(d)$
post $post(d, f)$

---
[1] The syntax deviates slightly from Standard VDM-SL which only distinguishes between underdetermined functions and nondeterministic operations that do not access the state by context

Note that the occurence of the name of the function f in the post-condition denotes the result. This defines a set of deterministic functions, and should be compared with the following function procedure definition:

$f\,(a:D)\ r:R$
pre *pre*
post *post*

which defines a single non-deterministic function. Thus

$f:\mathbb{N}\to\mathbb{N}$
$f\,(a)$
pre true
post let $n \in \{-1, 0, +1\}$ in $f = a + n$

defines the following set of three functions:

$f(x) = x - 1$
$f(x) = x$
$f(x) = x + 1$

one of which could be chosen in a refinement; while

$f\,(a:\mathbb{N})\ r:\mathbb{N}$
pre true
post let $n \in \{-1, 0, +1\}$ in $r = a + n$

defines a single non-deterministic function procedure f where the only claim that can be made is that

$f(x) \in \{x - 1, x, x + 1\}$

and in a program it is not necessarily true that $f(0) = f(0)$ – which is why non-deterministic functions are not allowed in expressions; the problem was discussed in Chapter 11.

One of the purpose of function definitions is to make a specification more readable, and because the functions do not depend on the state, a function (after some work) can be replaced by its definition. It may simplify a development if the function was refined to executable code. However to refine implicit functions would need a new set of refinement rules. An alternative approach is to find a deterministic function f' that satisfies the specification. This suggests the following refinement rule:

if $\left\{ \begin{array}{c} f':D \to R \\ \forall d:D \cdot pre(d) \Rightarrow post(d, f'(d)) \end{array} \right\}$ then

$$\begin{array}{l} f:D \to R \\ f(d) \\ \textsf{pre } \textit{pre} \\ \textsf{post } \textit{post} \end{array} \quad \sqsubseteq \quad \begin{array}{l} f(d:D)r:R \\ \textsf{pre } \textit{pre} \\ \textsf{post } r = f'(d) \end{array}$$

The first proof obligation requires that f' is a deterministic function. The function procedure that is the result of the refinement step can then be refined using the rules given in the appendix. Proving a function is deterministic can be difficult; a simple approach would be to identify a subset of the expression language so that any function defined using the subset would automatically be deterministic.

A. Program Refinement Rules

In the following:

- identifiers occurring in a frame stand for a list of zero or more identifiers;
- $A \equiv B$ is equivalent to $A \sqsubseteq B$ and $B \sqsubseteq A$;
- it may be necessary to use type information to discharge some of the proof obligation;
- $\delta(E : W)$ is a predicate over the identifiers of the expression E that is true if the expression E is defined and of type W (i.e. is not $\bot$); otherwise it is false; and
- $E[x \backslash e]$ denotes the expression E with all free instances of the identifier x syntactically replaced by the expression e.

A.1 Replace Specification

if $\left\{ \begin{array}{c} pre \Rightarrow pre' \\ pre[w \backslash \overleftarrow{w}] \wedge post' \Rightarrow post \end{array} \right\}$ then

chg $w : W$ chg $w : W$
pre pre $\sqsubseteq$ pre pre'
post $post$ post $post'$

A.2 Assume Pre-condition in Post-condition

chg $w : W$ chg $w : W$
pre pre $\equiv$ pre pre
post $post$ post $pre[w \backslash \overleftarrow{w}] \wedge post$

A.3 Introduce Assignment

if $\left\{ \begin{array}{c} pre \Rightarrow \delta(E : W) \\ pre[w \backslash \overleftarrow{w}] \wedge w = E[w \backslash \overleftarrow{w}] \Rightarrow post \end{array} \right\}$ then

$$
\begin{array}{l}
\text{chg } w : W \\
\text{pre } pre \\
\text{post } post
\end{array}
\quad \sqsubseteq \quad w := E
$$

Note: w could denote a list of write variables and E a list of expressions.

A.4 Introduce Command-semicolon

For any M that does not contain hooked identifiers other than $\overleftarrow{x}$, then

$$
\begin{array}{l}
\text{chg } x : X \\
\quad\quad y : Y \\
\text{pre } pre \\
\text{post } post
\end{array}
\quad \sqsubseteq \quad
\begin{array}{l}
\text{chg } x : X \\
\text{pre } pre \\
\text{post } M \\
; \\
[\![\ \text{con } c : X \text{ in} \\
\quad \text{chg } x : X \\
\quad\quad\quad y : Y \\
\quad \text{pre } M[\overleftarrow{x} \backslash c] \\
\quad \text{post } post[\overleftarrow{x} \backslash c]\ ]\!]
\end{array}
$$

Note: If M does not contain any hooked variables, then the introduction of the logical constant is unnecessary.

A.5 Introduce Semicolon-command

$$
\begin{array}{l}
\text{chg } w : W \\
\text{pre } pre \\
\text{post } post
\end{array}
\quad \sqsubseteq \quad
\begin{array}{l}
\text{chg } w : W \\
\text{pre } pre \\
\text{post } [B]post \\
; \\
B
\end{array}
$$

A.6 Introduce Leading Assignment

if $\{\ pre[x \backslash E] \Rightarrow \delta(E : X)\ \}$ then

$$
\begin{array}{l}
\text{chg } x : X \\
\quad\quad y : Y \\
\text{pre } pre[x \backslash E] \\
\text{post } post[\overleftarrow{x} \backslash \overleftarrow{E}]
\end{array}
\quad \sqsubseteq \quad
\begin{array}{l}
x := E \\
; \\
\text{chg } x : X \\
\quad\quad y : Y \\
\text{pre } pre \\
\text{post } post
\end{array}
$$

where $\overleftarrow{E}$ is equivalent to $E[x, y \backslash \overleftarrow{x}, \overleftarrow{y}]$

if $\left\{\begin{array}{l} pre \Rightarrow \delta(f(x):X) \\ f^{-1} \text{ is defined} \end{array}\right\}$ then

$$\begin{array}{ll} & x := f(x) \\ \text{chg } x:X & ; \\ \quad y:Y & \text{chg } x:X \\ \text{pre } pre & \sqsubseteq \quad y:Y \\ \text{post } post & \text{pre } pre[x\backslash f^{-1}(x)] \\ & \text{post } post[\overleftarrow{x}\backslash f^{-1}(\overleftarrow{x})] \end{array}$$

A.7 Introduce Following Assignment

$$\begin{array}{ll} & \text{chg } x:X \\ \text{chg } x:X & \quad y:Y \\ \quad y:Y & \text{pre } pre \\ \text{pre } pre & \sqsubseteq \quad \text{post } post[x\backslash E] \wedge \delta(E:X) \\ \text{post } post & ; \\ & x := E \end{array}$$

A.8 Introduce Alternatives

if $\left\{\begin{array}{l} \forall i \in \{1,\ldots,n\} \cdot pre \Rightarrow \delta(guard_i:\mathbb{B}) \\ pre \Rightarrow \exists i \in \{1,\ldots,n\} \cdot guard_i \end{array}\right\}$ then

$$\begin{array}{ll} op & \text{if } guard_1 \rightarrow op_1 \\ \text{chg } w:W & \quad \square \quad \ldots \\ \text{pre } pre & \sqsubseteq \quad \square \, guard_n \rightarrow op_n \\ \text{post } post & \text{fi} \end{array}$$

where

op_i
chg $w:W$
pre $guard_i \wedge pre$
post $post$

A.9 Introduce Iteration

if $\left\{\begin{array}{c} var : State \rightarrow T \\ \_ < \_ : T \times T \\ (C,<) \text{ is well-founded subset of } T \\ guard \wedge inv \Rightarrow var \in C \\ inv \Rightarrow \delta(guard:\mathbb{B}) \end{array}\right\}$ then

chg $w : W$
pre pre
post $inv \wedge \neg guard$

$\sqsubseteq$

chg $w : W$
pre pre
post inv
;
do $guard \rightarrow$ chg $w : W$
pre $guard \wedge inv$
post $inv \wedge var < var[w\backslash \overleftarrow{w}]$
od

A.10 Introduce Proper Procedure Body

$proc(x : X)$
ext wr $w : W$
rd $d : D$
pre pre
post $post$

$\sqsubseteq$

$proc(x : X)$
ext wr $w : W$
rd $d : D$ $\triangleq$
[chg $w : W$
pre pre
post $post$]

A.11 Introduce Proper Procedure Call

If an implicit proper procedure is defined by:

$proc\,(a : A)$
ext wr $w : W$
rd $d : D$
pre $\;pre$
post $post$

then

chg w
pre $pre[a\backslash E]$
post $post[a\backslash \overleftarrow{E}]$ $\quad = \quad proc(E)$

where $\overleftarrow{E}$ is equivalent to $E[w\backslash \overleftarrow{w}]$

A.12 Introduce Function Procedure Body

$fun(x:X)r:R$
ext wr $w:W$
    rd $d:D$
pre pre
post $post$

$\sqsubseteq$

$fun(x:X):R$
ext wr $w:W$
    rd $d:D$ ≜
[dcl $r:R$ in
    chg $w:W$
        $r:R$
    pre pre
    post $post$
    ;
    return r]

A.13 Introduce Function Procedure Call

If an implicit function procedure is defined by:

$fun\ (x:X)\ r:R$
ext wr $w:W$
    rd $d:D$
pre pre
post $post$

then

chg w,r
pre $pre[x\backslash E]$
post $post[x, r\backslash \overleftarrow{E}, a]$ ≡ $a := fun\,(E)$

Where $\overleftarrow{E}$ is $E[w,\backslash \overleftarrow{w}]$.

A.14 Add Variable

chg $w:W$
pre pre
post $post$

$\sqsubseteq$

[dcl $x:X$ in
    chg $w:W$
        $x:X$
    pre pre
    post $post$]

A.15 Realize Quantifier

chg $w : W$ ⟦ dcl $x : X$ in
pre pre ⊑ chg $w : W$
post $\exists x : X \cdot post$ $x : X$
                        pre pre
                        post $post$⟧

A.16 Remove Scope

If A and C do not contain any free instances of y then

⟦ dcl $x : X$ in A ; ⟦ dcl $y : Y$ in B ⟧ ; C ⟧ ⊑ ⟦ dcl $x : X, \; y : Y$ in A ; B ; C ⟧

A.17 Expand Frame

If x is a state or local variable then:

                  chg $w : W$
chg $w : W$ $x : X$
pre pre ⊑ pre pre
post $post$ post $post \wedge x = \overleftarrow{x}$

A.18 Contract Frame

chg $x : X$
     $y : Y$ chg $y : Y$
pre pre ⊑ pre pre
post $post$ post $post[\overleftarrow{x}\backslash x]$

A.19 Introduce Logical Constant

if $\left\{ \begin{array}{c} c \text{ does not occur free in } w, \; pre, \text{ or } post \\ pre \Rightarrow \exists c \in C \cdot pre' \end{array} \right\}$ then

              ⟦ con $c : C$ in
chg $w : W$ chg $w : W$
pre pre ⊑ pre pre'
post $post$ post $post$ ⟧

A.20 Remove Logical Constant

If A is independent of c then

$$[\![\, \mathsf{con}\ c : C\ \mathsf{in}\ A\,]\!] \equiv A$$

A.21 Refine Block

if $\left\{ \begin{array}{c} init' \Rightarrow init \\ A \sqsubseteq A' \end{array} \right\}$ then

$[\![\, \mathsf{dcl}\ x : X\ \mathsf{be\ st}\ init\ \mathsf{in}\ A\,]\!] \sqsubseteq [\![\, \mathsf{dcl}\ x : X\ \mathsf{be\ st}\ init'\ \mathsf{in}\ A'\,]\!]$

A.22 Introduce Skip

if $\left\{ pre[w \backslash \overleftarrow{w}] \wedge w = \overleftarrow{w} \Rightarrow post \right\}$ then

chg $w : W$
pre pre $\sqsubseteq$ skip
post $post$

Bibliography

1. J. R. Abrial. Abstract machines — parts 1, 2 and 3. BCS FACS course notes — B Tutorial, University of Manchester, April 1991.
2. J. R. Abrial. B reference manual. BCS FACS course notes — B Tutorial, University of Manchester, April 1991.
3. J. R. Abrial. B tutorial. BCS FACS course notes, University of Manchester, April 1991.
4. J. R. Abrial. Introduction to set notations — parts 1 and 2. BCS FACS course notes — B Tutorial, University of Manchester, April 1991.
5. J. R. Abrial. A refinement case study. BCS FACS course notes — B Tutorial, University of Manchester, April 1991.
6. D. J. Andrews. VDM-WSL — a wide spectrum language based on Meta-IV. Technical report, The University of Leicester, Department of Mathematics and Computer Science, 1997.
7. D. J. Andrews, R. Henry (ed), D. Ward, et al. *Information technology — Programming languages — Part 1: Modula-2, Base Language*. ISO/IEC, DIS 10514-1, 1996.
8. D. J. Andrews and W. Henhapl. Pascal. In D. Bjørner and C. B. Jones, editors, *Formal Specifications and Software Development*, pages 175–251. Prentice-Hall, 1982.
9. D. J. Andrews and D. Ince. A case study of a difficult refinement: A fast dictionary for a spell checking program. *Information and Software Technology*, 37:671–680, 1995.
10. D. J. Andrews and D. Ince. Transformational data refinement and VDM. *Information and Software Technology*, 37:637–651, 1995.
11. D. J. Andrews and D. C. Ince. The development of a piece-chain editor using coupling invariants. Technical Report 33, Open University, 1992.
12. R.-J. Back. Correctness preserving program refinements: Proof theory and applications. Technical Report Tract 131, Mathematisch Centrum, Amsterdam, 1980.
13. R.-J. Back. A calculus of refinement for program derivations. Technical Report Report Ser.A 54, Swedish University of Åbo, Åbo, Finland, 1987.
14. R.-J. Back. Procedural abstraction in the refinement calculus. Technical Report Report Ser.A 55, Swedish University of Åbo, Åbo, Finland, 1987.
15. R.-J. Back. A caclulus of refinements for program derivation. *Acta Informatica*, 25:593–624, 1988.
16. D. Bjørner and C. B. Jones. *The Vienna Development Method: The Meta-Language*, volume 61 of *Lecture Notes in Computer Science*. Springer-Verlag, 1974.
17. D. Bjørner and O. N. Oest. *Towards a Formal Definition of Ada*, volume 98 of *Lecture Notes in Computer Science*. Springer-Verlag, 1980.

18. H. Bruun, B. S. Hansen, P. G. Larsen, N. Platt, D. J. Andrews, et al. *Information Technology — Programming Languages, their environments and system software interfaces — Vienna Development Method-Specification Language Part 1: Base language*. ISO, 1996.
19. O.-J. Dahl, E. W. Dijkstra, and C. A. R. Hoare. *Notes on data structuring*. A.P.I.C. Studies in Data Processing. Academic Press, 1972.
20. Edsger W. Dijkstra. *A discipline of programming*. Prentice-Hall, 1976.
21. A. J. M. van Gasteren. On the formal derivation of a proof of invariance. In E. W. Dijkstra, editor, *Formal Development of Programs and Proofs*. Addison-Wesley, 1990.
22. ISO. *The Programming Language PL/I*, 1976.
23. C. B. Jones. *Software Development: a Rigorous Approach*. Prentice-Hall, 1980.
24. C. B. Jones. *Development Methods for Computer Programs Including a Notion of Interference*. PhD thesis, Oxford University Computing Laboratory, 1981.
25. Peter Gorm Larsen. *Towards Proof Rules for the Full Standard VDM Specification Language*. PhD thesis, IFAD, 1995.
26. C. C. Morgan. *Programming from Specifications (Second Edition)*. Prentice-Hall International Series in Computer Science. Prentice-Hall, 1994.
27. Carrol Morgan and Trevor Vickers, editors. *On the Refinement Calculus*. Formal Approaches to Computing and Information Technology. Springer-Verlag, 1994.
28. J. M. Morris. Piecewise data refinement. In E. W. Dijkstra, editor, *Formal Development of Programs and Proofs*. Addison-Wesley, 1990.
29. J. M. Morris. Programs from specifications. In E. W. Dijkstra, editor, *Formal Development of Programs and Proofs*. Addison-Wesley, 1990.
30. G. Nelson. A generalization of Dijkstra's calculus. Technical report no. 16, Digital Systems Research Center, 1987.
31. N. Wirth and C. A. R. Hoare. A contribution to the development of ALGOL. *Communications of the ACM*, 9(6):413–432, 1966.

Index

abstract state, 255, 264, 280
add variable rule, 126, 198, 244, 274, 384, 397
adequacy, 256
algorithmic refinement, *see* program refinement
angelic non-determinism, 18–21, 23, 43, 118
array, 230, 231
assert command, 39
assertion, 109–112, 147, 149, 151
assignment command, 16, 21, 29, 84, 112, 113
assume pre-condition in post-condition rule, 95, 201, 218, 244, 393

binary tree, 370
- code, 374, 376, 377, 381, 387
- coupling invariant, 371
- refinement, 370
- specification, 370, 382
binds, 15
Boolean stack, 327
- code, 334
- coupling invariant, 328
- refinement, 328

chaos, 23, 38, 61, 105
code generation, 195
collection invariant, 357
collections, 356
command domain, *see* domain of a command
concrete state, 255, 264, 280
conditional command, *see* alternative command
constants, 127
contract frame rule, 127, 209, 269, 398
coupling invariant, 255, 264, 280, 309, 320, 328, 336, 346, 371, 374

- total and onto, 258
coupling relation, *see* coupling invariant

data refinement, 247, 251, 264, 278, 320, 328, 337
declaration, 117, 122
def command, 123
development method, 3, 7
dispose, 357, 363, 367
division, 1, 4, 224
- code, 2, 6, 229
domain of a command, 40, 44
down loop, 211, 212, 229, 240, 246

equivalent specifications, 95, 113
expand frame rule, 126, 398

factorial, 205, 215, 216
- code, 207, 209, 210, 215
feasibility, 40, 42
finite iteration, 37
frame, 2, 88
full refinement, *see* refinement
function procedure, 197
function procedure body, 371
function procedure call, 190, 202
function procedure definition, 190
function procedure refinement, 191

guarded command, 84
guarding, 21, 30, 147, 149, 151

havoc, 23, 61, 106
heap, 356
hooked identifiers, *see* initial values

if command, *see* alternative command
improper outcome, 13, 15, 16, 22, 29, 33
initial values, 63, 130, 132, 137, 139

introduce alternatives rule, 157, 198, 216, 219, 220, 225, 237, 245, 269, 310, 372–374, 376, 377, 379, 395
introduce assignment rule, 6, 115, 199, 201, 210, 217, 218, 220, 223, 234, 237, 245, 322, 325–327, 330, 331, 345, 372, 393
introduce command-semicolon rule, 139, 198, 217, 220, 222, 236, 244, 316, 394
introduce following assignment rule, 142, 209, 395
introduce function procedure body rule, 197, 216, 220, 233, 326, 374, 377, 384, 397
introduce function procedure call rule, 192, 202, 397
introduce function recursive call rule, 192, 217, 221
introduce iteration rule, 5, 178, 200, 223, 225, 226, 233, 236, 241, 243, 312, 384, 395
introduce leading assignment rule, 140, 201, 225, 241, 243, 245, 394
introduce logical constant rule, 132, 398
introduce proper procedure body rule, 310, 322, 325, 326, 396
introduce proper procedure call rule, 188, 396
introduce proper recursive call rule, 189
introduce semicolon rule, 143
introduce semicolon-command rule, 141, 394
introduce skip rule, 107, 399

leading assignment rule, 5, 206
let command, 122
linear search, 231
logical constant, 129, 139, 204
loop, 23, 61, 67, 78, 80, 81, 83, 105
loop guard, 210
loop invariant, 3, 200, 205, 206, 208, 210, 213
loop parameters, 5, 200, 203, 206, 208, 215, 223, 225, 226, 233, 236, 241, 242, 312, 364, 383
loop tactics, 200, 203, 207, 210, 213, 222, 225, 226, 246
loop termination, 3, 168, 171, 172, 176–178, 180, 182
loop variant, 168, 200
looping outcome, *see* improper outcome

minimal element, 168

miracle, 15, 19, 21, 22, 38, 42, 61, 87, 106
monotonic, 73, 74, 78, 79, 82
– credulously, 74, 161
– skeptically, 73
monotonicity, 136, 195
multiply, 197, 203
– code, 202, 223
multiply problem, 222

new, 355, 357, 363, 367
non-deterministic choice operator, 19, 29, 31, 84
non-executable program, 87
normal form, 50

outcome, 8

pairing condition, 26, 41, 55, 63
partial refinement, *see* refinement
pointers, 308, 356
– dereference operator, 357
– undefined, 357
procedure call, 185
procedure refinement, 186
program correctness, 1, 36
program execution, 9
program language definitions, 9
program proof, 2, 3
program refinement, 84, 88, 247
program termination, 87
program testing, 1, 9
programs as specifications, 11, 36, 50, 113
proper outcome, 13, 16, 18, 33, 41
proper procedure, 185
proper procedure call, 185
proper procedure definition, 185

queue, 333
– code, 344
– coupling invariant, 336
– refinement, 337, 348, 349
– specification, 333

realize quantifier rule, 4, 126, 398
recursion, 188, 189, 192, 217, 220
refine block rule, 125, 399
refined by, 264
refined state, *see* concrete state
refinement, 4, 115, 247, 260
– full refinement, 102
– partial refinement, 102
– simulation refinement, 103

- strong refinement, 102
- weak refinement, 101

refinement by assignment, 112, 113
refinement by iteration, 199
refinement by semicolon, 135–144, 198
refinement by the alternative command, 145
refinement rule
- add variable, 126, 397
- assume pre-condition in post-condition, 95, 393
- contract frame, 127, 398
- expand frame, 126, 398
- introduce alternatives, 157, 395
- introduce assignment, 115, 393
- introduce command-semicolon, 139, 394
- introduce following assignment, 142, 395
- introduce function procedure body, 397
- introduce function procedure call, 192, 397
- introduce function recursive call, 192
- introduce iteration, 178, 395
- introduce leading assignment, 140, 394
- introduce logical constant, 132, 398
- introduce proper procedure body, 396
- introduce proper procedure call, 188, 396
- introduce proper recursive call, 189
- introduce semicolon, 143
- introduce semicolon-command, 141, 394
- introduce skip, 107, 399
- realize quantifier, 126, 398
- refine block, 125, 399
- remove assertion, 109
- remove logical constant, 133, 399
- remove scope, 126, 398
- replace specification, 93, 393
refinement strategy, 247, 278
refining operations, 260
remove assertion rule, 109
remove logical constant rule, 133, 238, 242, 246, 399
remove scope rule, 126, 198, 398
remove variable rule, 340
replace specification rule, 93, 114, 199, 244, 270–272, 274, 310, 321–323, 325, 326, 341–343, 351, 373, 393

replacement specifications, 86
retrieve function, 262, 265, 280
- removal of, 281
return command, 218, 221, 223

satisfying a specification, 1, 8, 9, 25, 87, 88
scope, 198
searching, 231, 234
- code, 234, 238
- specification, 232, 235
semicolon operator, 17, 18, 29, 84, 135, 137
setting a variable, 56, 58, 118
side-effects, 16, 21, 118, 129, 185, 191, 193
simple security system, 248, 308
- data refinement, 266, 308
- final code, 279, 313, 317
- specification, 249
simulation refinement, *see* refinement
skip, 61, 107
slip, 38, 61, 76, 81
sorting, 239
- code, 242, 245
- specification, 239
specification command, 8, 23–25, 39, 40
stack
- code, 322, 325–327, 363
- coupling invariant, 320, 352, 358
- refinement, 320, 322, 324–327, 354, 360
- specification, 318, 352
stepwise development, *see* stepwise refinement
stepwise refinement, 4, 6, 84, 135, 137, 145, 176, 195, 247
strong refinement, *see* refinement

temporary variables, 210
termination, 41, 188
testing a variable, 56, 58, 118
transitive relation, 168
type, 15

unbounded iteration, 37
undefined, 15
up loop, 211–213, 246

variables
- setting and testing, 56, 58, 118–121

weak refinement, *see* refinement
well-founded set, 168, 188